JAVASCRIPT
INTERACTIVE
COURSE

ARMAN DANESH

WAITE GROUP PRESS™

A Division of

Sams Publishing

Corte Madera, CA

PUBLISHER • Mitchell Waite
ASSOCIATE PUBLISHER • Charles Drucker

ACQUISITIONS MANAGER • Jill Pisoni

EDITORIAL DIRECTOR • John Crudo
PROJECT EDITOR • Lisa Goldstein

PRODUCTION DIRECTOR • Julianne Ososke
PRODUCTION MANAGER • Cecile Kaufman
SENIOR DESIGNER • Sestina Quarequio
DESIGNERS • Karen Johnston, Jil Weil
INDEXERS • Christine Nelsen, Greg Pearson
PRODUCTION TEAM SUPERVISOR • Brad Chinn, Charlotte Clapp
PRODUCTION • Mona Brown, Elizabeth Deeter, Polly Lavrick, Lisa Pletka, Mark Walchle
COVER ILLUSTRATION • © Steven Hunt/Image Bank

© 1997 by The Waite Group, Inc.
Published by Waite Group Press™,
200 Tamal Plaza, Corte Madera, CA 94925

Waite Group Press is a division of Sams Publishing.

Printed in the United States of America
98 99 • 10 9 8 7 6 5 4

Library of Congress Cataloging-in-Publication Data
Danesh, Arman.
    JavaScript Interactive course / Arman Danesh.
       p.   cm.
    Includes index.
    ISBN 1-57169-084-0
    1. JavaScript (Computer program language) I. Title.
    QA76.73.J39D35   1997
    005.2'762--dc21

96-49086
CIP

www.waite.com/ezone
eZone Guided Tour

The Interactive Course title in your hands provides you with an unprecedented training system. The book itself is everything you're used to from Waite Group Press: thorough, hands-on coverage of an important cutting-edge product. There is far more, however, to the Interactive Course than the pages you are now holding. Using your Internet connection, you also get access to the eZone, where you'll find dedicated services designed to assist you through the book and make sure you really understand the subject.

FREE TUTORS, TESTING, CERTIFICATION, AND RESOURCES

The eZone provides a host of online services and resources designed to help you work through this book. If you get hung up with a particular lesson, all you have to do is ask an online mentor, a live expert in the subject you're studying. A mailing list lets you exchange ideas and hints with others taking the same course. A resource page links you to the hottest related Web sites, and a monthly newsletter keeps you up to date with eZone enhancements and industry developments.

You'll also be able to work toward a certificate of completion. You can take lesson quizzes online, receive an immediate grade, and track your progress through the course. The chapters are available online, too, so that you can refer to them when you need to. Once you've finished the course with a passing grade, you can print a personalized certificate of completion, suitable for framing.

Best of all, there's no additional cost for all of these services. They are included in the price of the book. Once you journey into the eZone, you'll never want to go back to traditional book learning.

EXPLORING THE EZONE

You'll find the eZone on the World Wide Web. Fire up your Web browser and enter the following site:

`http://www.waite.com/ezone`

From there, click the eZone icon and you're on your way.

> **NOTE**
>
> If your browser does not support frames, or if you prefer frameless pages, click the *No Frames* link. Your browser must also support "cookies." Interactive Course titles that come with a CD include a copy of Microsoft's Internet Explorer browser (version 3.01), which supports frames and cookie technology. These books include an appendix to help you with browser installation, setup, and operation.

Navigating the eZone

When you enter the eZone, the eZone home page, shown in Figure 1, appears.

As you can see in Figure 1, the screen is divided into three frames. The eZone icon in the top left frame is always visible. This icon is a link back to the eZone home page. No matter where you are, you can always find your way home by clicking this icon. Beneath the eZone icon is a navigation frame containing several icons. Each of these icons links to an area of the eZone. You'll learn about each of these areas as you read through this guide.

The largest frame on the page is the main frame. This is where you'll find the information. Scroll down this frame and you'll see text-based links to the eZone areas. Keep going and you'll find the latest eZone news and information, updated regularly. Be sure to check out this information each time you enter the eZone.

Start Here

Click the *Start Here* icon in the navigation frame. This takes you to the Getting Started page where you'll find different sets of instructions. Your options are:

```
I am a GUEST and visiting the EZONE.
I HAVE the EZONE BOOK and I am ready to start the course.
I want to BUY an EZONE COURSE and get my Book.
```

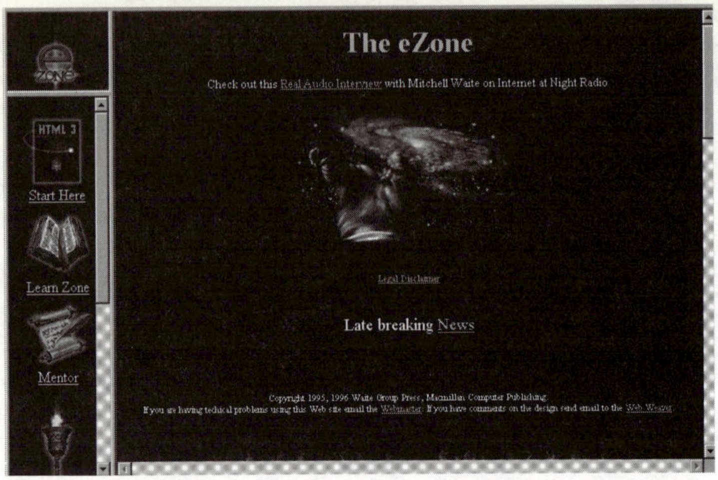

eZone main frame

eZone home page link

The eZone

Check out this Real Audio Interview with Mitchell Waite on Internet at Night Radio

HTML 3

Start Here

Learn Zone

eZone navigation frame

Mentor

Legal Disclaimer

Late breaking News

Copyright 1995, 1996 Waite Group Press, Macmillan Computer Publishing.
If you are having technical problems using this Web site email the Webmaster. If you have comments on the design send email to the Web Weaver.

Figure 1
The eZone home
page...a whole
new way to learn

Clicking these options provides instructions for how to sign on as a guest, register for a course for which you have a book, or sign up for a course and order the corresponding book.

In the next couple of pages, you'll see how to explore the eZone as a guest, register yourself, enroll in a course, and take advantage of the many service areas provided at no additional charge.

Signing on as a Guest

On your first visit to the eZone, consider signing on as a guest, even if you have a book and are anxious to get started. Signing on as guest lets you roam the eZone and familiarize yourself with its various areas and features before setting any options. You can view the first chapter of any available course and take the quizzes for that chapter (although Guests' scores aren't saved).

You can ask support questions, view the latest news, and even view the FAQs for a course. Until you register, you can't ask the mentors any questions, sign up for the eZone newsletter, or access the resource links page, but there's still plenty of stuff to check out as a Guest.

To explore the eZone as a Guest, click the *Learn* icon in the navigation frame or on the word 'Learn' at the bottom of the main frame. The first time you do this, the registration form appears. As a guest, you can ignore this form.

Just click the *Guest* link, and the Course Matrix appears. From here, you can navigate the eZone in the same manner as registered course members. Remember, however, that access for Guests is limited.

THE INITIATION ZONE

Once you're comfortable navigating the eZone, we know you'll be anxious to start learning and taking advantage of this cutting edge training system.

The first thing you have to do is create an entry for yourself in the eZone records by registering. Click the *Initiation* icon in the navigation frame or on the *Initiate* link at the bottom of the main frame, and you move into the Initiate zone, shown in Figure 2.

Initiate (Register)

You want the *Initiate (Register)* option to start the registration process. Click the *Register* link and a registration form appears.

NOTE

You don't need a book to register in the eZone. In fact, by registering before you get your hands on an Interactive Course book, you can enroll in the course as soon as you possess the book. You can save a little time by skipping the steps of creating your eZone password and ID.

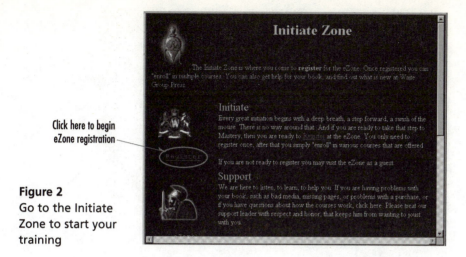

Click here to begin
eZone registration

Figure 2
Go to the Initiate
Zone to start your
training

You need to fill out the registration form completely. Click inside each text box, then type in the appropriate information; pressing the ⌜TAB⌝ key cycles you through these text fields. In addition to a little information about yourself, you'll need to enter:

`Requested User ID` — Type the name you'd like to use online.
`Password (5-8 Characters)` — Type the password you'd like to use online.
`Password (Verify)` — Retype your selected password, to be sure it's properly recorded.

Once you've supplied all the information, click the *Register* button to submit the form to the eZone's data banks. A confirming message lets you know that you've successfully registered. Registration is important. If you don't register, you can't take advantage of the full power of the eZone.

Entering the eZone as a Registered User

Once you've registered, you'll use your unique ID and password to enter the eZone. Next time you enter the eZone, you need only click the *Learn Zone* icon in the navigation frame or the *Learn* link in the main frame. A simple two-line form pops up, allowing you to type in the user ID and password you created when you registered.

THE LEARN ZONE

Now that you're registered, it's time to get down to business. Much of the course work is done in the Learn Zone, shown in Figure 3. To get here, click the *Learn* icon in the navigation frame.

The Course Matrix

When you enter the Learn Zone, you'll see lists of courses and certification programs. This is called the Course Matrix, and it provides a way to select the various eZone courses. Under each discipline—such as Web Designer, Business, or Code Master—is a list of core courses. To select a course using the Course Matrix, click the desired course (titles in underlined white letters are currently available). In a moment, a three-columned Chapters Grid appears.

Verification

The first time you select a specific course, you must enroll. You'll need a copy of the book to do so. You will be asked to provide a specific word from the book. This verifies that you have the proper book for the selected course. The verification process uses the familiar page-line-word formula; in other words, you'll need to locate and enter a word from a specified line of text on a specified page of your book. Click your mouse in the text box and type the specified word to verify that you have the course book.

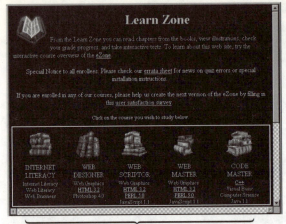

Figure 3
Use the Course
Matrix in the Learn
Zone to select
courses

Passing Percentage

You can also set a minimum passing percentage for your course. This determines what percentage of test questions you need to answer correctly in order to pass the course. The percentage is preset at 70%, but you can select 50%, 60%, 70%, 80%, 90%, or 100%.

To set a minimum passing percentage, click the text box for this option to see a list of choices, then click the option you prefer. Once you've typed in the correct word and set the desired passing percentage, click the *Verify* button to enroll in the course. The Chapters Grid appears.

The Chapters Grid

The Chapters Grid, like the one featured in Figure 4, lets you select topics and quizzes for your course, while keeping track of your progress.

The Chapters column lists the chapters of the book; clicking a chapter lets you view and select its lessons. The middle column, Score, shows your current grade for the chapter (as a percentage). The Status column uses a colored indicator to let you know with a glance whether you've passed (green), failed (red), are still working through (yellow), or have not yet started (gray) a particular chapter.

Click a chapter, and the Lessons Grid appears for that chapter. (Remember, only Chapter 1 is enabled for Guests.)

Click here to go back to the
Course Matrix

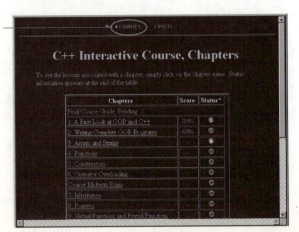

Figure 4
Work through the
course using the
Chapters Grid

The Lessons Grid

As you take the course, the Lessons Grid (Figure 5) tracks your performance within each chapter. You can use it to read a chapter lesson or take a lesson quiz.

To read a lesson, click the *Read* link in the Select column. To take a quiz, click the *Quiz* link in the Select column. The LEDs in the status column show whether you've passed (green), failed (red), or not yet started (gray) each quiz. A percentage grade appears for each completed quiz in the Score column.

Most likely, you'll achieve the best results if you read through the lessons, then take the quiz. If you prefer, however, you can jump directly to the corresponding quiz without reading through the lesson.

Click here to go back to the Chapter Grid

Click here to go back to the Course Matrix

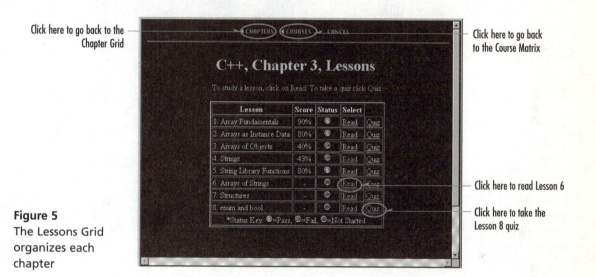

Click here to read Lesson 6

Click here to take the Lesson 8 quiz

Figure 5
The Lessons Grid organizes each chapter

Testing

Each quiz is a multiple-choice questionnaire. In some courses, there is only one answer to each question, but other courses allow more than one answer. Read the instructions for your course so you know how the quizzes work.

Taking Quizzes

To answer a quiz question, click the check box next to the answer you want to choose. When you've answered all the questions, click the *Grade My Choices* button. Your quiz is corrected and your score shown. To record your score, click either the *Lessons* or *Chapters* link at the top of the main frame.

CAUTION

Do not use your browser's Back button after taking a quiz. If you use the Back button instead of the Lessons or Chapters link, your score will not be recorded.

Midterm and Final Exams

The Interactive Course includes midterm and final examinations. The midterm covers the first half of the book, while the final is comprehensive. These exams follow the same multiple-choice format as the quizzes. Because they cover more, however, they're somewhat longer. Once you have successfully passed all the quizzes, as well as the midterm and final exams, you'll be eligible to download a certificate of completion from Waite Group Press.

MENTOR ZONE

In the Mentor Zone, shown in Figure 6, you can review FAQs (Frequently Asked Questions) for each chapter. You can also ask a question of a live expert, called a mentor, who is standing by to assist you. The mentor is familiar with the book, an expert in the subject, and can provide you with a specific answer to your content-related question, usually within one business day. You can get to this area by clicking on the *Mentor* icon in the navigation frame.

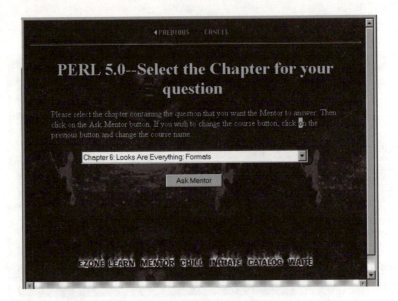

Figure 6
Get personalized
help in the
Mentor Zone

Just the FAQs

When you ask a mentor a question, you're first shown a set of FAQs. Be sure to read through the list. Since you have a limited number of questions you may ask, you'll want to use your questions carefully. Chances are that an answer to your question has already been posted, in which case you can get an answer without having to ask the question. In any event, you may learn about an issue you hadn't even considered.

If the FAQ list does not contain the answer you need, you'll want to submit your own question to the mentor.

Ask Your Mentor

eZone students may ask ten questions of their course mentor. This limit ensures that mentors will have the opportunity to answer all readers' questions. Questions must be directly related to chapter material. If you ask unrelated or inappropriate questions, you won't get an answer; however, the question will still be deducted from your allotment.

If the FAQ doesn't provide you with an answer to your question, click the button labeled *Ask Mentor*. Whenever you contact the mentor, the rules and conditions for the mentor questions are provided. After reading these, click the *Accept* button to continue. In a moment, a form like the one shown in Figure 7 appears.

This form specifies the course, the chapter, and other information pertinent to your question. The mentor emails the answer to your question directly to you, but keep in mind that Mentor Zone questions must be *directly* related to the chapter subject matter.

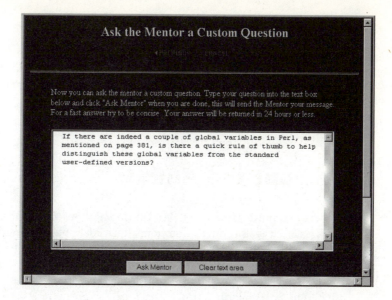

Figure 7
Use this form to
send your question
to your mentor

More Assistance

Keep in mind that there are other sources of assistance in the eZone, too. If you are experiencing technical problems with the book or CD, you'll want to contact the Webmaster; you'll find a link on the eZone's main page. If you want to discuss related issues, such as developments and applications, check out the newsgroups available in the Chill Zone. There are other ways to discuss issues with real people, as you'll discover, when you visit the eZone.

CHILL ZONE

Think of the Chill Zone as your student lounge, a place where students hang out and discuss their classes. But the Chill Zone does a student lounge one better—it's also a library chock full of information. It's a place where you can interact with others reading the same book and find expert resources to assist you as you develop and use your new skills. Perhaps the coolest thing about the Chill Zone is that its options are all included with the cost of your book.

To get into the Chill Zone, click the *Chill Zone* icon in the navigation frame. Once there, you can click three Chill Zone options:

Discussion List—You can subscribe (or unsubscribe) to a dedicated newsgroup centered on your book.

Newsletter—Select this option to subscribe (or unsubscribe) to the monthly eZone newsletter.

Resources—These are links to Web sites, tools, and other useful materials related to the course subject.

To select a Chill Zone option, click the link and follow the on-screen instructions.

THE EZONE AWAITS

As you have seen from this tour, this Interactive Course book is a lot more than the pages before you. It's a full-blown, personalized training system—including textbook, testing, guidance, certification, and support—that you can pick up and work through at your own pace and at your own convenience.

Don't settle for just a book when you can get a whole education. Thanks to this comprehensive package, you're ready to log on and learn in the eZone.

Dedication

To my parents—Michele and Hossain—for instilling in me a thirst for knowledge, and to my wife—Tahirih—who inspires me to press forward.

About the Author

Arman Danesh works as the Web Development Specialist at the Bahá'í World Centre in Haifa. He is also Editorial Director of Juxta Publishing Limited, based in Hong Kong. He received his Masters of Science in Mass Communication from Boston University in 1990. He has also worked as a technology journalist and is a regular contributor and Internet columnist for the *South China Morning Post* and *The Dataphile*. Arman lives with his wife, Tahirih, in Haifa, Israel.

Acknowledgments

Writing this book has been a process that has involved many people. I particularly would like to thank the staff at Sams.net who worked with me in developing the manuscript: Kelly Murdock, Marla Reece, Mark Taber, and many others I am sure were involved.

I would also like to thank Gautam Das at the Bahá'í World Centre in Haifa, Israel, for reading sections of the book as I was writing it.

Contents

Chapter 10　Strings, Math, and the History List 299

Chapter 11　Having Fun with JavaScript 335

Chapter 12　Creating a Spreadsheet in JavaScript 351

Introduction

The World Wide Web has come a long way since its days as a modest hypertext system used by a few scientists to share information on the Internet.

Today the World Wide Web is the medium of information exchange for millions of people. They are sharing text, video, sound, and data, and increasingly, they are trying to make their Web pages interactive. Businesses are trying to sell their products, artists are producing new forms of interactive art, and programmers are producing program development aids—all delivered via the World Wide Web and accessed from inside everyday Web browser applications.

In many ways, we are in the midst of an information revolution with a move away from document-centric computing to a network-centric paradigm. Right at the center of this shift is Netscape Communications and its immensely popular Web browser, Netscape Navigator.

By incorporating Java from Sun Microsystems and its own JavaScript scripting language into the current version of the Netscape Navigator browser, Netscape has helped generate a flurry of movement on the World Wide Web aimed at creating interactive documents and information.

Java is a platform-independent programming language designed for distributed applications on the Internet. JavaScript presently enhances the functionality of the immensely popular Netscape Navigator Web browser, enabling Web authors and developers to produce content that changes in response to user actions—dynamic data that makes information more accessible and easier to organize and digest.

In this book we are going to take a look at JavaScript—the internal scripting language Netscape has developed and included in the Navigator browser.

JavaScript is an evolving tool, like so many tools associated with the Internet and the World Wide Web. Still, the future of JavaScript is sufficiently clear since many people have already developed sophisticated Web-based applications using the language.

Goal of This Book

As I mentioned, this book is designed to teach the JavaScript scripting language.

We start by taking a broad look at Netscape Navigator 3.0, the current version of the popular Web browser, which some estimates say commands more than 80 percent of the Web browser market. Following this, we take an introductory look at JavaScript and its relationship with Java and its place in the Netscape suite of Web development tools.

Once this is done, we will be ready to look at the nuts and bolts of the JavaScript language and learn how to apply them to real-world scenarios on the Web. JavaScript can be used to add a wide range of interactivity and functionality to Web pages including the following:

- Dynamic forms that include built-in error checking
- Spread sheets and calculators

- User interaction in the form of warning messages and confirmation messages
- Dynamic changes to text and background colors
- The ability to analyze URLs and access URLs in a user's history list
- The capability to open, name, clear, and close new windows and direct output to specific frames

These types of functions already appear in numerous Web sites on the World Wide Web, and it is expected that the number will grow rapidly as JavaScript develops maturity as a programming language.

Throughout the book, you will have the opportunity to develop several small scripts that you can immediately use in your own Web pages.

Finally, we close with a review of the future of JavaScript and where it seems to be heading. We will consider Netscape's plans as well as announcements from other companies to include JavaScript in their products.

The Waite Group Interactive Series

This book differs from other JavaScript books in that it's a Waite Group Interactive book. This isn't just publisher's hype: By connecting you to the Waite Group via the World Wide Web, this new approach can actually play a significant role in helping you to learn JavaScript. There are many aspects to the Interactive Series. We won't dwell on them here, since the details are presented elsewhere. We should note, however, that this book was written from the ground up to work as part of the Interactive Series.

Who Should Read This Book?

The JavaScript scripting language naturally interests a diverse group of people, including Web designers and authors, programmers, and application developers.

Web Authors and Designers

This book is clearly of interest to Web developers and authors with experience using HTML and designing Web sites, including using Netscape extensions. Although basic knowledge of HTML is assumed throughout the book, any advanced or complicated HTML tags being used are introduced and described as needed.

Naturally, programming knowledge and an understanding of the Common Gateway Interface (CGI)—used for adding interactivity at the server end—are helpful in any discussion of Web development. However, it is not essential for learning JavaScript, and readers with a sound knowledge of HTML tags can follow the lessons in this book. By the end of the book, not only will you be able to write simple (and complex) JavaScript programs, but you also will have learned to use some of the newer Netscape extensions to HTML.

Others

Naturally, discussion of a programming language like JavaScript is not solely of interest to Web authors and designers.

Programmers looking to add the latest technology to their list of credits are increasingly interested in learning JavaScript. In addition, applications developers looking at Navigator 2.0 as an engine for deploying platform independent graphical user interface applications will quickly find that JavaScript is going to play a critical role in implementing their applications.

Preparing to Begin

In order to take full advantage of this book, you will need several tools. A copy of the latest version of Netscape 2.0 or 3.0 is essential to develop and test program code. In addition, a good editing program that you will feel comfortable using will make the program development process easier.

Where to Obtain Navigator 3.0

In order to take full advantage of the lessons in this book, it is necessary to have access to a copy of Navigator 3.0 to try the examples and exercises for yourself. Navigator 3.0 is available for most computer platforms, including all versions of Windows, Mac OS, and a wide range of UNIX variants including Sun OS, Solaris, and Linux. At the present time, there is no native OS/2 version of Netscape Navigator available.

If you need to download a copy of the current version of Navigator 3.0, you can get it from Netscape's home page at `http://home.netscape.com/` or from Netscape's numerous FTP servers or their many mirrors:

```
ftp://ftp.netscape.com/
ftp://ftp2.netscape.com/
ftp://ftp3.netscape.com/
ftp://ftp4.netscape.com/
ftp://ftp5.netscape.com/
ftp://ftp6.netscape.com/
ftp://ftp7.netscape.com/
ftp://ftp.leo.chubu.ac.jp/pub/WWW/netscape/ (Japan)
ftp://sunsite.ust.hk/pub/WWW/netscape/ (Hong Kong)
ftp://sunsite.huji.ac.il/Netscape/ (Israel)
ftp://ftp.adelaide.edu.au/pub/WWW/Netscape/ (Australia)
ftp://sunsite.doc.ic.ac.uk/computing/information-
systems/www/Netscape/ (United Kingdom)
ftp://ftp.informatik.rwth-aachen.de/pub/mirror/ftp.netscape.com/
(Germany)
ftp://wuarchive.wustl.edu/packages/www/Netscape/ (U.S.A.)
ftp://sunsite.unc.edu/pub/packages/infosystems/WWW/clients/Netscape
(U.S.A.)
```

Editing and Development Tools

In addition to a copy of Navigator 3.0, a strong editor or development tool will make the task of entering, developing, and debugging JavaScript much easier.

If you already do a lot of HTML authoring or programming, you probably have your own favorite tools that will be well-suited to JavaScript development. As long as your editing software produces plain ASCII text files, you should be just fine.

However, several tools may make it easier to develop, edit, and trouble-shoot your JavaScript programs.

In considering editors, it would be worth looking at tools that can help you identify the current line number for debugging scripts. In addition, the ability to launch Netscape Navigator from an editor is a useful feature already found in many HTML editors. Most HTML editors are suitable to JavaScript development, although a few—including leading products such as HoTMetaL—are designed to perform validation of HTML and can't be used to develop JavaScript scripts easily.

Conventions in This Book

This book uses certain conventions to aid you, the reader, in your learning process.

 A *new term* is highlighted in italics or with this icon to clarify its meaning.

 Note boxes highlight important or explanatory information in the surrounding text.

 These helpful nuggets offer insights or short cuts to programming puzzles.

 Pay special attention to warnings. They may just save your system!

 This icon appears next to a listing that you should enter to follow along with the author's lesson. A listing without an Input icon is for illustration or explanation only.

 This arrow at the end of a line of code means that a single line of code requires multiple lines on the page. Many lines of code contain a large number of characters, which might normally wrap on your screen. However, printing limitations require a break when lines reach a maximum number of characters. Continue typing all characters after the ⇐ as though they are part of the previous line.

 Besides on-screen output, this icon is often used, in this book, to point to a figure that results from the preceding code listing.

The author offers detailed explanations regarding the parts and purposes of the code. (**Hint:** If you think you might not understand what the code is meant to perform, skip to this section before you input the listings!)

This book also uses `monospaced` fonts to denote terms, functions, keywords, variables, and so on, that are taken from or are part of the code. Typically, HTML code terms are in ALL CAPS, while JavaScript terms are in the case required by this case-sensitive language.

CHAPTER 1

WHERE DOES JAVASCRIPT FIT IN?

avigator 3.0 is the most powerful version of Netscape's Web browser. Besides bringing together a collection of useful Internet-access tools, such as a mail client, a news reader, and improved support for the developing HTML 3 standard, Navigator 3.0 adds several features that enhance the ability of Web authors to develop complete, platform-independent applications deployed and executed in the Netscape browser. Going beyond the Web browser, Navigator Gold adds editing and development tools to the package.

These capabilities include an application program interface (API) for plug-ins.

New Term

Plug-ins are program modules that dynamically extend the capability of Navigator to handle new types of data and information, along with JavaScript and Java, which allow the addition of flexible programmability to Web pages.

JavaScript is also incorporated into Netscape's servers, such as LiveWire, which allows it to be used to develop server-end programs instead of the traditional CGI-BIN interface used in today's Web servers. In addition, Microsoft Internet Explorer 3.0, the latest Web browser for Windows 95 and NT from Microsoft incorporates numerous features found in Navigator 3, including JavaScript.

In this chapter we take a detailed look at the main features and aspects of JavaScript, as well as review the major strengths and weaknesses of the JavaScript language and its suitability to particular tasks.

We then dive deeper into objects and how they work, and take a look at properties and methods—the building blocks of objects. We also look at the built-in objects in JavaScript and what they offer the programmer.

In this chapter we take a broad look at Navigator and consider how JavaScript fits into the puzzle. You'll learn about the following topics:

- Frames: The ability to divide a window into multiple, independent sections

- Plug-ins: Third-party add-ons for Navigator that extend the browser's ability to handle new data and information

- Java: An object-oriented programming language for distributed applications

- JavaScript: A simple, object-based programming language incorporated into Navigator 3.0 (and the subject of this book)

- The similarities and differences between Java and JavaScript

- JavaScript as a scripting language

- Objects, properties, and methods

- The Navigator Object Hierarchy and other built-in objects

- Strengths and weaknesses of JavaScript

 **JavaScript and Netscape Navigator**

NAVIGATOR IS MORE THAN A WEB BROWSER

Although Netscape Navigator started out its life as a basic Web browser, as it has grown increasingly popular, it has become much more.

Unlike earlier browsers and today's basic Web applications, Navigator now provides authors with numerous tools to step beyond the traditional constraints of HTML. Instead of simply combining text, pictures, sound and video, authors now have finer control over document layout, fonts, and color; they are able to extend the functionality of the browser using plug-ins and Java; and they can produce interactive applications using JavaScript.

A quick look at the Netscape Web site shows that today's Navigator can do so much more than previous versions—even without special programming by Web developers. With freely available plug-ins from leading software companies, Web authors can include native CorelDRAW! graphics or Microsoft Word files in their documents, as well as view VRML (Virtual Reality Modeling Language) worlds, and view documents formatted in Adobe's device-independent Acrobat format.

On top of all this, Navigator provides several tools that Web page developers and authors can take advantage of to enhance their documents and add dynamic interaction with the information they are providing on the Internet.

Frames

Frames are the most visually noticeable extension of HTML in Navigator 2.0 and 3.0. Using frames, authors are able to partition the screen into multiple rectangular sections. Each section is independent of all the others, and a different URL is loaded into each frame. In addition, links in one frame can be used to update another frame, without disturbing any others.

Frames are being used today to produce fixed, bannerlike mastheads for Web pages, for menus that always stay on the screen and don't need to be reloaded or redrawn, and for forms-based searches where the form is always available.

In addition to the obvious visual appeal of frames technology, this extension to HTML may have an added benefit in that it reduces the amount of data that may need to be requested from the server and sent to clients. On the increasingly congested World Wide Web, this may prove to make Web browsing slightly more efficient and reduce some of the load on overburdened Web servers.

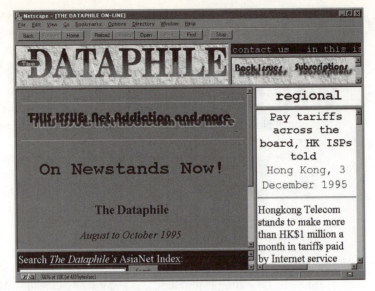

Figure 1-1
Using frames provides fixed and dynamic elements.

Technology

By providing an open application program interface for plug-ins, Netscape has made it possible for third-party software vendors to provide the ability to view a wide range of data and documents in the Navigator browser window. Netscape refers to objects displayed by plug-ins as *live objects*.

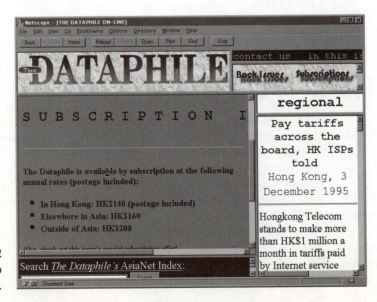

Figure 1-2
Using a menu to update one frame.

Netscape integrates plug-ins—and Java applets—into the browser environment using LiveConnect. LiveConnect provides mechanisms for plug-ins, Java applets, and JavaScript scripts to communicate with each other and to share information with each other.

To date, a significant number of vendors including Corel, Paper Software, and Adobe have produced plug-ins for their own formats. (Figure 1-3 shows one such company.) Many of these will likely be extended to support JavaScript, enabling JavaScript programs to interact with plug-ins directly and further enhancing the power of JavaScript in future versions of Netscape Navigator. At the present time there are no tools for doing this.

The number of available plug-ins is constantly changing. Netscape provides an up-to-date list of available plug-ins at this site:

`http://home.netscape.com/comprod/products/navigator/version_2.0/plugins/index.html`

Interactivity with Java and JavaScript

Using JavaScript and Java, Web developers have come up with further enhancements to Web pages beyond the ability to load multiple documents in separate frames and view new file formats.

Some of the common Java applets available today include the following:

The term *applet* has come into common use since Sun Microsystems introduced Java to the Web community in 1995. Applets are small applications that are included in Web pages and downloaded on demand to be executed by the client browser. Although the

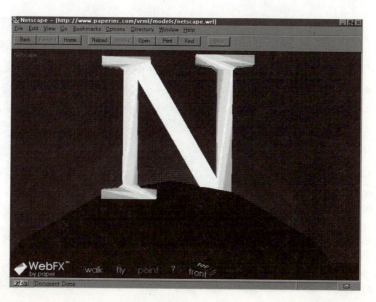

Figure 1-3
Paper Software's WebFX plug-in enables Navigator 2.0 to browse VRML worlds.

term technically only refers to the type of Java programs described above, with the introduction of JavaScript, the term is now being used by some people on the Web to describe the type of integrated scripts developed with JavaScript.

- Scrolling text applets: Java is being used to add marquees to Web pages.

- Live data feeds: Current examples include a live stock ticker, such as the financial portfolio demonstration by Sun Microsystems' Jim Graham, shown in Figure 1-4.

- Search engines: Java applets can be used to build database queries, which are then sent to remote databases.

- Adding protocols to Web browsers: One of the potential possibilities offered by Java is that, as protocols are developed on the Internet, Java can be used to add functionality to Web browsers on demand.

- New file formats: Java allows Web browsers to display new file formats by downloading applets to display the files as needed.

The widespread popularity of Java means that the range of uses will increase in the future, but today Java is being used primarily for cosmetic enhancements to Web pages.

By comparison, JavaScript is used to produce scripts designed to react to user and environment events—as well as in the future being the glue to hook Java applets more seamlessly into Web pages. The following are some examples:

- An interactive color picker for Web developers to test different background and text colors in their documents.

Figure 1-4
This Web page demo by Sun Microsystems' Jim Graham uses Java to include live data feeds.

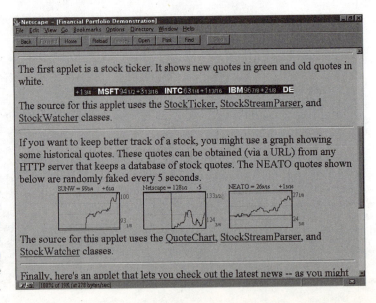

- Calculators: Examples on the Web include a unit conversion calculator and loan interest calculators.

- Dynamic output based on the current environment and the user's previous surfing history.

- Forms verification: JavaScript can be used to ensure that form data is entered properly before sending it to the server, rather than relying on the server to verify form content after it is submitted.

- Building URLs: JavaScript is used to build custom URLs based on user choices in forms.

- JavaScript can be used to replace many CGI scripts for client-side processing, easing bandwidth demands, and decreasing server load for busy Web servers.

- Newsgroup-like discussion groups can incorporate sophisticated features such as threading.

JAVASCRIPT'S PLACE IN NAVIGATOR

JavaScript is one of the least-used components of Netscape's suite of interactivity tools (although that is quickly changing), but it could be the most significant. Not only does it bring interactive programming within the reach of the average Web author with no formal programming experience, it can also be used to move much of the processing away from over-burdened servers to increasingly powerful client workstations.

JavaScript Programs Are Built into Web Pages

As opposed to the independent application files used to deliver Java applets to Web browsers, the actual source code for JavaScript scripts can be included directly in Web pages. This is distinct from Java applets, which exist independently of the HTML Web pages.

JavaScript Gives Programmers Access to Browser Properties

JavaScript is integrated tightly into HTML and the Navigator browser. Developers have available to them a wide range of tools and information to interact with the currently loaded HTML document, as well as the current browser session.

JavaScript exposes properties related to the document windows, the history list, the loaded documents, frames, forms, and links to the programmer. In addition, JavaScript can be used to trap user events, such as changing form values or pointing at links, so that appropriate programs can be developed for each event.

QUIZ 1

1. What is Netscape Navigator?
   a. A text editor.
   b. A Web-based strategy game.
   c. A Web browser with extended functionality.
   d. A Java development environment.

2. Complete the following sentence. JavaScript is used
   a. as a scripting environment for Java.
   b. to produce interactive scripts for Navigator.
   c. as a replacement for HTML.
   d. to write Java applets.

3. What is a Navigator Plug-in?
   a. A hardware peripheral specifically manufactured for Netscape.
   b. A JavaScript program.
   c. Third-party software used to view a wide range of document types from within Netscape.
   d. A Netscape function used to support plug-and-play.

4. Which of the following is not a good use for frames?
   a. As a method for breaking up the window into lots of little partitions.
   b. Partition the browser window in multiple regions for displaying different text and graphics at the same time.
   c. Display both fixed and dynamic information to the user at the same time.
   d. Reduce the amount of redrawing by placing mastheads in their own frames.

5. What is an applet?
   a. An application written in JavaScript.
   b. It is the same as a plug-in.
   c. A small Apple computer loaded with a Web browser.
   d. A small application intended for inclusion into a Web page and downloaded on demand to be executed by the client browser.

LESSON 2 Java and JavaScript

JAVA AND JAVASCRIPT: COMPARE AND CONTRAST

Given the tremendous popularity of Java since its introduction in 1995, it is important to take a look at the differences between Java and JavaScript. Although they are related—JavaScript borrows most of Java's syntax, for instance—they are fundamentally different and serve different purposes. They are complementary rather than competing with each other.

Using Java: A Complex, Complete Object-Oriented Programming Language

Java is much more than a language for developing Web-based applications. It is designed to compete in a market of full-fledged, general-purpose programming languages such as C, C++, Pascal, and FORTRAN. Unlike its predecessors, Java's claims to fame include the fact that it is platform-independent and that it can be used for both applications development and the development of in-line applets, or small applications, for Web pages.

Like C++ and SmallTalk, Java is object-oriented and relies heavily on the syntax and style of C++. With this comes the steep learning curve of a high-end object-oriented programming language.

A Compiled Language

Unlike most other general-purpose programming languages, Java is not compiled in the traditional sense. Instead of compiling to native machine code, the Java compiler converts source code into Java byte codes (known as architecture-neutral bytecodes)—a platform-independent representation of the Java program code—which are then run on a machine-dependent runtime interpreter. In this way, developers only need to develop and maintain one set of source code and compile it once, and the code can then be run using the runtime interpreters for any machine.

Like all compiled languages, though, this adds the complexity of a compilation cycle to development and especially to debugging. However, to a certain degree like other compiled languages, an efficient runtime engine means that Java should offer better performance than general-purpose, interpreted scripting languages.

Fully Extensible

A fundamental feature of true object-oriented languages is that they are extensible. That is, programmers can create their own classes—or groupings of objects and data structures—to extend the basic classes that are part of the programming languages.

New Term *Class* is a term used in object-oriented programming to refer to a set of related objects that share common characteristics. Classes, and the ability to create new classes, are what make object-oriented programming a powerful and flexible programming model.

Java is no exception to this rule. Java programmers routinely create their own extensions to the base set of tools or classes.

Steep Learning Curve

As mentioned before, object-oriented programming languages tend to have steep learning curves, especially for nonprogrammers. Java is not exempt from this difficulty.

The general consensus among beginning programmers is that learning Java is a formidable task, especially considering the complexity of the available on-line documentation on the Internet.

Enables Client-Server Interaction

The base set of classes that comes with the Java distribution make it ideally suited to client-server interactions. The ability to work with URLs and talk to HTTP servers already exists. The support for applets adds the ability to interact with user events in the client Web browser.

In addition, HotJava, the demonstration browser from Sun Microsystems, demonstrates how Java can become the means by which browsers dynamically learn to handle new protocols as that ability is needed.

 Sun developed HotJava when Java was still in alpha development to demonstrate the potential of Java for distributed applications on the World Wide Web and to show how browsers could dynamically learn to handle new protocols and file types. HotJava is available for Solaris and 32-bit Windows (Windows NT and Windows 95) from the Java home page at `http://www.javasoft.com/`.

Developing Stand-Alone Applications and Applets

Java is famous because it can be used to develop applets that are delivered on the World Wide Web and executed in client Web browsers. However, Java can also be used to develop complete, platform-independent GUI applications using the Java runtime interpreter.

Offers Sophisticated Security

Because of the extremely open and public nature of the World Wide Web, security is a major issue for Java and Java applets. After all, allowing application code from unknown remote machines to be downloaded and executed on your computer system is potentially dangerous. Not only is there potential for applets to contain viruses, but they could simply be malicious applications intent on destroying your data and rendering your computer inoperable.

To address this, Sun implemented tight security features from the earliest stages of Java development. These features include verification of bytecodes (to ensure they don't violate access restrictions and more), as well as configurable network security that ranges from disabling network access to limiting access by an applet only to the host where the code originated, all the way to completely free network access.

There have been reports of security holes in the Java environment, but both Sun and Netscape have been responsive to these reports and concerns. With each release of Java, security should be improved.

Distinct from HTML

Even though applets are a feature of the World Wide Web and are included as in-line applets in HTML files, they are distinct and separate from HTML and HTML files. New HTML tags force a Web browser to initiate a new connection to the server and tell the browser where to display the applet's output on the Web page, but beyond that, applets are separate and distinct from HTML.

Using JavaScript, a Simple, Object-Based Scripting Language

In contrast to Java, JavaScript joins the ranks of simple, easy-to-use scripting languages. JavaScript promises an easier learning curve than Java along with powerful tools to add interactivity to Web pages with little effort.

Derived from Java

JavaScript owes a lot to Java. Its syntax and basic structure are similar to Java, even if the range of functions and the style of programming can differ greatly. JavaScript started life as Netscape's own scripting language with the name LiveScript, but in late 1995, Sun endorsed the language, and it became JavaScript.

JavaScript keeps more than just the basic syntax and structure of Java—it also borrows most of Java's flow constructs and implements some of the same security precautions, such as preventing applets from writing to the local disk.

An Interpreted Language

Unlike Java, JavaScript is an interpreted language. Whereas in Java, source code is compiled prior to runtime, in an interpreted language, source code files are executed directly at runtime in JavaScript.

Interpreted languages offer several advantages—as well as several drawbacks. Interpreted languages such as JavaScript are generally simpler than compiled languages and are easy to learn. It is often easier to develop, change, and troubleshoot programs because the need to recompile with each change is removed.

On the negative side, the need to interpret commands as the program is run can produce a performance hit with some interpreted languages. In the case of JavaScript, this doesn't seem to be a problem.

JavaScript scripts are compiled to byte codes (similar to Java) as the script is downloaded and evaluated, and for most scripts, performance feels quite snappy.

Not Fully Extensible

Unlike Java, JavaScript is not fully extensible. The JavaScript model is one of a limited set of base objects, properties, methods, and data types, which provide enough capabilities to create client-side or server-side applications.

While users can create their own objects and write functions, this is not the same as the classes and inheritance offered in Java and other object-oriented programming languages.

Since JavaScript is an object-based scripting language, this book will be devoted to learning about the objects, properties, methods, and data types available in JavaScript.

Limited Client-Server Interaction

JavaScript in its current form is not designed for complete client-server interaction. Beyond analyzing, building, and invoking URLs, JavaScript can't talk directly to servers or talk different protocols. In essence, JavaScript is well suited to handling client-end activity.

Still, there are indications that future versions of JavaScript will support protocols such as HTTP and ftp, but several security issues surrounding client-server interaction through JavaScript need to be addressed by Netscape before it implements these features.

In addition, JavaScript is part of the LiveWire Web server offered by Netscape. LiveWire is aimed at groups and organizations developing interactive Web applications. In this role, JavaScript provides an alternative to traditional CGI scripting for server-end programming. In this sense, JavaScript can be used for client-server interaction.

Integrated into HTML

Where Java is only loosely tied to HTML, JavaScript is tightly integrated into HTML files. Typically, entire scripts are in the same files as the HTML that defines a page, and these scripts are downloaded at the same time as the HTML files.

QUIZ 2

1. What is Java?
   a. A cup of coffee.
   b. An object-oriented language used for programming Web-based applications.
   c. A compiled version of JavaScript.
   d. A short name for JavaScript.

2. A fundamental feature of true object-oriented languages is that they are
   a. hard to use.
   b. extensible.
   c. compiled.
   d. interpreted.

3. Which of the following statements about Java is false?
   a. Each platform has its own runtime interpreter for Java programs.
   b. Java is compiled into bytecodes that are interpreted by the Java runtime engine.
   c. Java programs need to be recompiled for each platform.
   d. Java bytecodes are a platform-independent representation of the Java program.

4. Which of the following is not a feature of Java programs?
   a. In-line applets are included as source code in the HTML document.
   b. Java security constraints prevent Java applets from accessing the local hard disk.
   c. Java applications can run outside of the browser by using the Java runtime interpreter.
   d. The source for the Java applet is hidden from the user.

5. Which of the following is not a feature of JavaScript?
   a. JavaScript is an interpreted language.
   b. JavaScript exposes properties related to the document and the browser to enable the programmer to provide interactive Web pages.
   c. JavaScript can access Java applet properties in order to assemble Web-based applications.
   d. JavaScript uses the same runtime engine as Java.

LESSON 3 JavaScript Overview

THE CURRENT STATE OF JAVASCRIPT

In undertaking the task of learning JavaScript, it is important to keep in mind the current status of the language and where its development appears to be headed.

Under Development

Both Navigator 3.0 and JavaScript are under intense development and are constantly evolving. So, JavaScript is, by definition, a language under development (as are most programming languages). In practical terms, that means that the complete language specification is not implemented yet.

In a very real way, JavaScript is a moving target. From Navigator 2.0 to Navigator 3.0, the feature set has been expanded greatly and changed noticeably. In addition, some existing methods and properties have been altered. There is no reason to believe that this development and change won't extend into future versions of Navigator.

On top of this, Microsoft's implementation of JavaScript differs subtly from Netscape's, and there is no guarantee that these differences won't persist or change over time.

Supported by Sun

In late November 1995, LiveScript became JavaScript in a joint announcement by Netscape and Sun that Sun would be supporting JavaScript as the Java-based open scripting standard for the Internet.

Given this support, there is little doubt that JavaScript will continue to resemble Java and that it will become the choice tool for gluing Java applets into Web pages, at least in the Netscape environment.

Essentially, this endorsement from Sun breathed life into a scripting language that very few people were paying attention to, but which is now the hot topic on the World Wide Web.

Endorsed by Many Companies

Sun Microsystems isn't the only company to support JavaScript. At the same time that Netscape and Sun made their announcement, more than 28 companies including America Online, Apple Computers, Oracle, Silicon Graphics, Architext, and SCO announced that they would also be endorsing JavaScript as the open scripting standard for the Internet, and many indicated they were considering licensing the technology to include in their own products.

Potential Use in Different Products

In addition to including JavaScript in its Navigator Web browser, Netscape is including JavaScript in its server-end application development environment called LiveWire.

This makes it possible that the momentum for CGI programming using Perl and Bourne or C shell may shift toward JavaScript, which would provide a consistent development environment at both the client and server ends.

In addition, the endorsements from numerous companies mean that JavaScript will start to appear in products from companies other than Netscape and in products other than Web browsers and servers. As mentioned earlier, JavaScript is already supported in Microsoft's Internet Explorer.

In addition, Netscape has proposed JavaScript as a scripting standard for the World Wide Web.

JavaScript Today—Scripting for the Netscape Web Browser

In this book, we are focusing on using JavaScript in the Navigator Web browser because this is where most JavaScript development is taking place and because this is the easiest environment in which to learn and practice JavaScript. JavaScript is also available in Microsoft's new Internet Explorer version 3. Internet Explorer also includes another scripting language, VBScript, based on the company's Visual Basic programming language. VBScript is not covered in this book.

WHAT IS JAVASCRIPT?

By now, you probably have some idea of what JavaScript is and what it isn't, but let's look more closely at the features you'll be learning and using throughout the course of this book.

JavaScript Is a Scripting Language

Scripting languages were in use long before the Web came around. In the UNIX environment, scripts have been used to perform repetitive system administration tasks and to automate many tasks for less computer-literate users. In addition, scripting languages are the basis of much of the CGI-BIN programming that is currently used to add a limited form of interactivity to Web pages..

Examples of scripting languages include Perl, well known in CGI programming, Awk and SED (designed for intensive text processing), and even HyperTalk which, like JavaScript, is an object-oriented scripting language.

Of course, this still doesn't tell you what the main advantages of scripting languages are. Like all scripting languages, JavaScript is interpreted, which provides an easy development process; it contains a limited and easy-to-learn command set and syntax; and it is designed for performing a well-defined set of tasks.

Designed for Simple, Small Programs

Because JavaScript is a scripting language, it is well suited to implementing simple, small programs. For instance, JavaScript would ideally be suited to developing a unit conversion calculator between miles and kilometers or pounds and kilograms. These tasks can be easily written and performed at acceptable speeds with JavaScript and would be easily integrated into a Web page. A more robust language such as Java would be far less suitable for the quick development and easy maintenance of these types of applications.

By contrast, JavaScript would not be well suited to implementing a distributed CAD document display and manipulation environment. While JavaScript eventually will be a tool for integrating this type of Java applet or plug-in into a Web page, to attempt to develop the actual applet in JavaScript would be at best, difficult and inefficient, and more likely, impossible.

Of course, this doesn't mean that sophisticated applications can't be—and aren't being—developed with JavaScript. Nonetheless, scripting languages are generally used for smaller tasks rather than for full, compiled programs.

Performs Repetitive Tasks

Just as JavaScript is suited to producing small programs, it is especially well designed for repetitive, event-invoked tasks. For example, JavaScript is ideal for calculating the content of one field in a form based on changes to the data in another field. Each time the data changes, the JavaScript program to handle the event is invoked, and the new data for the other field is calculated and displayed.

Designed for Programming User Events

Because of the way in which JavaScript is integrated into the browser and can interact directly with HTML pages, JavaScript makes it possible to program responses to user events such as mouse clicks and data entry in forms.

For instance, a JavaScript script could be used to implement a simple help system. Whenever the user points at a button or a link on the page, a helpful and informative message can be displayed in the status bar at the bottom of the browser window.

This adds interactivity to Web pages, makes forms dynamic, and can decrease the bandwidth requirements and server load incurred by using forms and CGI programming.

Easy Debugging and Testing

Like other scripting languages, JavaScript eases development and troubleshooting because it is not compiled. It is easy to test program code, look at the results, make changes, and test it again without the overhead and delay of compiling.

The Java Glue

When Netscape announced JavaScript, it referred to the language as the tool to "glue Java applets into Web pages." With Navigator 3.0 this has become possible. JavaScript can trigger events in Java applets, and Java applets can call JavaScript methods and functions.

1. Which of the following is false?
   a. JavaScript will become the choice tool for gluing Java applets into Web pages in the Netscape environment.
   b. JavaScript started out named LiveScript.
   c. JavaScript is endorsed by more than 28 companies as the open scripting language for the Internet.
   d. JavaScript is restricted for use by Netscape browsers only.

2. JavaScript is a scripting language. Which of the following is not a scripting language?
   a. Awk
   b. Perl
   c. HyperTalk
   d. Java

3. Since JavaScript is a scripting language, it is
   a. unsuitable for anything.
   b. naturally object-oriented.
   c. oriented towards writing applets.
   d. well suited to implementing simple, small programs.

4. Which of the following is not a good use for JavaScript?
   a. Implementing small, simple programs.
   b. Large application development.
   c. Providing limited user interaction.
   d. Quick development of programs.

5. What is JavaScript's current stage of development?
   a. It is still under active development.
   b. It is a mature language with full-featured environments.
   c. It is the primary language for enhancing Web pages.
   d. It is under review for becoming an Internet standard.

 **Scripting with Objects**

JAVASCRIPT IS OBJECT-BASED

Object-oriented is a term that has been overused by the media and marketing arm of the computer and software industries. Nonetheless, the fact that JavaScript has a limited object-oriented model is an important distinction.

JavaScript's Object Model

In order to understand what it means for JavaScript to be *object-based*, we need to look at objects and how they work.

Fundamentally, *objects* are a way of organizing information, along with the methods for manipulating and using that information.

Objects provide a way to define specific pieces of data related to the item in question; these pieces are known as *properties*. In addition, these are supplemented by *tasks* that can be performed on or with that information, known as *methods*. Together, properties and methods make up objects.

Because of the general nature of objects, specific instances can be created for each case where they are needed. For instance, a car object could then have several instances for Toyotas, Fords, and Volkswagens.

A Comparison with Procedural Languages

Defining objects in this way differs greatly from the way in which information is handled in traditional procedural programming languages such as FORTRAN and C.

In these languages, information and procedures (similar to methods) are kept separate and distinct and are not linked in the way that objects are. Also, the concept of creating instances isn't as well developed in procedural languages.

WORKING WITH OBJECTS IN JAVASCRIPT

JavaScript includes built-in objects to work with elements of the currently loaded HTML document, as well as performing other useful tasks, such as mathematical calculations. It also offers the programmer the chance to create her own objects.

Built-In Objects

JavaScript offers a set of built-in objects that provide information about the currently loaded Web page and its contents, as well as the current session of Navigator. In addition, these objects provide methods for working with their properties.

The Navigator Object Hierarchy

Most of the built-in objects in JavaScript are part of the Navigator Object Hierarchy. The Navigator Object Hierarchy is built from a single base object called the `window` object, as illustrated in the following outline.

Navigator

Window

   Location

   History

   Document

     Forms

     Anchors

Table 1-1 highlights the major JavaScript objects.

Object	Description
`navigator`	The `navigator` object provides properties that expose information about the current browser to JavaScript scripts.
`window`	The `window` object provides methods and properties for dealing with the actual Navigator window, including objects for each frame.
`location`	The `location` object provides properties and methods for working with the currently open URL.
`history`	The `history` object provides information about the history list and enables limited interaction with the list.
`document`	The `document` object is one of the most heavily used objects in the hierarchy. It contains objects, properties, and methods for working with document elements including forms, links, and anchors, and with applets.

Table 1-1 *Overview of the Navigator Object Hierarchy.*

Other Built-In Objects

In addition to the objects in the Navigator Object Hierarchy, JavaScript provides several objects that are not related to the current windows or loaded documents. Table 1-2 outlines the major features of these objects.

Object	Description
string	The string object enables programs to work with and manipulate strings of text, including extracting substrings and converting text to upper- or lowercase characters.
Math	The Math object provides methods to perform trigonometric functions, such as sine and tangent, as well as general mathematical functions, such as square roots.
Date	With the Date object, programs can work with the current date or create instances for specific dates. The object includes methods for calculating the difference between two dates and working with times.

Table 1-2 *Other built-in objects.*

Extending JavaScript by Creating Your Own Objects

In addition to a wide range of built-in objects, as a JavaScript programmer, you can create your own objects to use in your scripts.

Properties

For example, if you need to build an object in JavaScript to represent the different types of airplanes sold by an aircraft manufacturer, you would have several pieces of information related to the airplane that you would want included in the object, including the following:

● Model

● Price

● Normal seating capacity

● Normal cargo capacity

● Maximum speed

● Fuel capacity

Properties are like variables in traditional languages, such as C and Pascal. Variables are named containers which are used to hold pieces of data, such as numbers or text. Variables are discussed in more detail in Chapter 3, "Working with Data and Information."

So, in JavaScript, if you call your object **airplane**, these properties might be referred to as:

```
airplane.model
airplane.price
airplane.seating
airplane.cargo
airplane.maxspeed
airplane.fuel
```

> As you will learn later, in JavaScript, the properties of objects are referred to by the structure `object-name.property-name`.

Methods

Of course, having this information isn't worth much without ways to use the information. For instance, in this example, you want to be able to print out a nicely formatted description of the aircraft or be able to calculate the maximum distance the plane can travel based on the fuel capacity.

In object-oriented terminology, these tasks are known as methods. Like properties, your methods might be referred to as:

```
airplane.description()
airplane.distance()
```

Objects Within Objects

Objects can also include other objects in much the same way as properties and methods. For instance, the airplane manufacturer may want to include an object inside his object definition to handle information about the number of planes in use worldwide, who is using them, and their safety records. This information, along with methods for working with the information, could be combined into an object called `airplane.record`. This object could then include properties and methods such as:

```
airplane.record.number_in_use
airplane.record.crashes
airplane.record.newscale()
```

Instances

What you have created is a general description of an object that defines the information you want to work with and the ways you want to work with it. These general descriptions of objects are known as classes. In object-oriented programming, then, you can create specific instances of the class as needed.

> In object-oriented programming, creating specific copies of classes is known as creating instances. JavaScript itself is classless, but provides mechanisms to create instances of objects (thus providing the same basic functionality). We cover the details of creating objects and instances in Chapter 4, "Functions and Objects—The Building Blocks of Programs."

For instance, in this example, the airplane manufacturer might want to create an instance of the `airplane` object for its newest aircraft, the SuperPlane. If this instance were created, then a program could assign specific values to the properties of the new instance by referring to `superplane.price`, `superplane.model`, and so on. Likewise, a description of the new plane could be printed out using `superplane.description()`.

1. What is the root object in the Navigator Object Hierarchy?
   a. `Window`
   b. `Document`
   c. `Form`
   d. `System`

2. JavaScript has a set of built-in objects
   a. because it is object-based.
   b. to provide information on the currently loaded HTML document as well as perform useful tasks.
   c. to provide procedural interface for BASIC programmers.
   d. to access machine-specific system parameters.

3. Which of the following is not a JavaScript built-in object?
   a. `string`
   c. `Date`
   d. `Math`
   d. `Form`

4. An object instance is
   a. a specific copy of a class.
   b. a code segment that references a class.
   c. a reference to any class.
   d. a reference to any object.

5. What is a restriction of the JavaScript object model?
   a. You can only have one instance of a particular object at one time.
   b. There is no inheritance like in a fully object-oriented language.
   c. You cannot create your own object definitions.
   d. You cannot nest objects.

The Pros and Cons

STRENGTHS OF JAVASCRIPT

JavaScript offers several strengths to the programmer including a short development cycle, ease of learning, and small size scripts. These strengths mean that JavaScript can be easily and quickly used to extend HTML pages already on the Web.

Quick Development

Because JavaScript does not require time-consuming compilation, scripts can be developed in a relatively short period of time. This is enhanced by the fact that most of the interface features, such as dialog boxes, forms, and other GUI elements, are handled by the browser and HTML code. JavaScript programmers don't have to worry about creating or handling these elements of their applications.

Easy to Learn

While JavaScript may share many similarities with Java, it doesn't include Java's complex syntax and rules. By learning just a few commands and simple rules of syntax, along with understanding the way objects are used in JavaScript, it is possible to begin creating fairly sophisticated programs.

Platform Independence

Because the World Wide Web, by its very nature, is platform independent, JavaScript programs created for Netscape Navigator are not tied to any specific hardware platform or operating system. The same program code can be used on any platform for which Navigator 2.0 is available.

Small Overhead

JavaScript programs tend to be fairly compact and are quite small, compared to the binary applets produced by Java. This minimizes storage requirements on the server and download times for the user. In addition, because JavaScript programs usually are included in the same file as the HTML code for a page, they require fewer separate network accesses.

WEAKNESSES OF JAVASCRIPT

As would be expected, JavaScript also has its own unique weaknesses. These include a limited set of built-in methods, the inability to protect source code from prying eyes, and the fact that JavaScript still doesn't have a mature development and debugging environment.

Limited Range of Built-In Methods

Early versions of the Navigator 2.0 beta included a version of JavaScript that was rather limited. In the final release of Navigator 2.0, the number of built-in methods had significantly increased, but still didn't include a complete set of methods to work with documents and the client windows. With the release of Navigator 3.0, things have taken a further step forward with the addition of numerous methods, properties, and event handlers.

No Code Hiding

Because the source code of JavaScript script presently must be included as part of the HTML source code for a document, there is no way to protect code from being copied and reused by people who view your Web pages.

This raises concerns in the software industry about protection of intellectual property. The consensus is that JavaScript scripts are basically freeware at this point in time.

Lack of Debugging and Development Tools

Most well-developed programming environments include a suite of tools that make development easier and simplify and speed up the debugging process.

Currently, there are some HTML editors and programming editors that provide JavaScript support. In addition, there are some on-line tools for debugging and testing JavaScript scripts. However, there are really no integrated development environments such as those available for Java, C, or C++. LiveWire from Netscape provides some development features but is not a complete development environment for client-side JavaScript.

1. Which of the following is not a strength of JavaScript?
    a. Hard to learn.
    b. Platform independent.
    c. Has small overhead.
    d. Quick to develop with.

2. Which of the following is a weakness of JavaScript?
    a. Provides for source code protection.
    b. Has a poor debugger.
    c. Has no debugger.
    d. Has low overhead.

3. Why is there no code hiding in JavaScript?
   a. Because all JavaScript code should be free for use.
   b. Because JavaScript is interpreted.
   c. Because the JavaScript source code must, at present, be included as part of the HTML document source.
   d. Because the JavaScript debugger requires source code to be present.

4. What is a benefit of adding user interactivity to a Web page?
   a. Provides a more responsive interface that keeps a higher level of interest.
   b. Keeps the user from having to make any choices.
   c. Lets the user debug your code.
   d. None of the above.

5. Which of the following is a drawback of using JavaScript?
   a. JavaScript will not work with CGI scripts.
   b. Web pages using JavaScript will only work with Netscape's server.
   c. Forms will not work with JavaScript.
   d. JavaScript code cannot be copy-protected.

SUMMARY

JavaScript is one of several key components in Netscape Navigator designed to help Web developers produce interactive applications on the Internet. Other features include support for plug-ins, frames, and of course, Java.

Where Java is compiled, object-oriented, complex, and distinct from HTML, JavaScript is interpreted, object-based, simple to use and learn, and tightly integrated with HTML.

JavaScript exposes properties of the current browser session to the programmer, including elements of the currently loaded HTML pages, such as forms, frames, and links.

In this chapter we also took a look at the implications of the fact that JavaScript is a scripting language, took a close look at what objects are and how they are used in JavaScript, and took a broad look at the built-in objects in JavaScript.

You learned that, while JavaScript offers many benefits including a quick development cycle and platform independence, it still has drawbacks.

In the next chapter, you will begin taking a look at the specifics of developing JavaScript scripts and will work on your first script.

CHAPTER 2

YOUR FIRST SCRIPT

n this chapter, you finally get down to the details of producing a JavaScript script.

You learn about the following topics, which will lead to your first complete JavaScript script:

- How to incorporate JavaScript into HTML
- Command and command block structure in JavaScript
- Output functions

You then learn how to use JavaScript scripts to create text output that is directed to the client window, in sequence with an HTML file, and then is interpreted just like regular HTML.

Of course, this doesn't really allow you to do anything with JavaScript that you can't already do with HTML. So, as the chapter continues, you will take the next step: generating output in dialog boxes, as opposed to putting it on the Web page itself, and generating dynamic output that can change each time the page is loaded.

We cover the following topics:

● Creating output in a dialog box using the `alert()` method

● Prompting users for input in a dialog box using the `prompt()` method

● Displaying dynamic output by combining the prompt method with `document.write()` and `document.writeln()`

 **Using the** SCRIPT **Tag**

INCORPORATING JAVASCRIPT INTO HTML

At the present time, all JavaScript scripts need to be included as an integral part of an HTML document. To do this, Netscape has implemented an extension to standard HTML: the **SCRIPT** tag.

The SCRIPT **Tag**

Including scripts in HTML is simple. Every script must be contained inside a **SCRIPT** container tag. In other words, an opening **<SCRIPT>** tag starts the script and a closing **</SCRIPT>** tag ends it:

```
<SCRIPT>

JavaScript program

</SCRIPT>
```

The **SCRIPT** tag takes two optional attributes which determine how the JavaScript script in question is incorporated into the HTML file. These attributes are outlined in Table 2-1.

Attribute	Description
SRC	URL for a file containing the JavaScript source code. The file should have the extension `.js`. This attribute is not implemented in the final release version of Navigator 2.0 but is expected to make it into the next version of Navigator.

Attribute	Description
LANGUAGE	Indicates the language used in the script. In the current version of Navigator 2.0 this attribute can take only two values: JavaScript and LiveScript. LiveScript is provided for backward compatibility with early scripts developed when the language was called LiveScript. You should use JavaScript in your scripts.

Table 2-1 *Attributes for the SCRIPT tag.*

Using the **SCRIPT** tag and its attributes allows you to use two techniques to integrate a JavaScript program into an HTML file. In Navigator 2, however, programmers have only one choice: to include their JavaScript programs in their HTML files.

Although the final release of Navigator 2 supports the use of **LANGUAGE="LiveScript"** for backward compatibility, this will be dropped in future versions of the browser. It is best to use **LANGUAGE="JavaScript"**. In addition, **LANGUAGE="LiveScript"** is not compatible with Microsoft's Internet Explorer 3.0.

Including JavaScript in an HTML File

The first, and easiest, way is to include the actual source code in the HTML file, using the following syntax:

```
<SCRIPT LANGUAGE="JavaScript">

JavaScript program

</SCRIPT>
```

Hiding Scripts from Other Browsers

Of course, an immediate problem crops up with this type of **SCRIPT** container: Browsers that don't support JavaScript will happily attempt to display or parse the content of the script. In order to avoid this, Netscape recommends the following approach using HTML comments:

```
<SCRIPT LANGUAGE="JavaScript">
<!-- HIDE THE SCRIPT FROM OTHER BROWSERS

JavaScript program

// STOP HIDING FROM OTHER BROWSERS -->
</SCRIPT>
```

These comments (`<!-- HIDE THE SCRIPT FROM OTHER BROWSERS` and `// STOP HIDING FROM OTHER BROWSERS -->`) ensure that other Web browsers will ignore the entire script and not display it because everything between `<!--` and `-->` should be ignored by a standard Web browser. Of course, if users were to view the source code of the document, they would still see the script.

Problems with the SCRIPT Tag

This technique of combining the **SCRIPT** container tag with comments isn't foolproof, however. Right now, the **SCRIPT** tag is not an accepted part of the HTML 2.0 standard and the HTML 3.0 specification is incomplete. For the time being, competing browser makers could use the **SCRIPT** tag for another purpose.

At press time, it looked as though the **SCRIPT** tag, and possibly JavaScript itself, would become part of the HTML 3.0 specification because it is backed by Netscape and Sun, among others.

In fact, with Netscape Navigator 2.0, the latter problem has already occurred with the implementation of frames. Among several tags used to produce frames, Netscape uses a **FRAME** tag that is used by IBM's Web Explorer for another purpose.

In addition, by hiding the script from other browsers, users of these other browsers will be unaware of the script's existence. One solution to this problem could be to use the following approach:

```
<SCRIPT LANGUAGE="JavaScript">

// JavaScript Script Appears Here<BR>
// Download Netscape Navigator 2.0 to use it.

<!-- HIDING FROM OTHER BROWSERS

JavaScript Program

// STOP HIDING FROM OTHER BROWSERS -->
</SCRIPT>
```

Unlike HTML, which creates comments with the structure `<!-- Comments Here -->`, JavaScript comments start with a double-slash (`//`) anywhere on the line and continue to the end of the line. If not contained within an HTML comment structure, a JavaScript comment will be displayed by non-Netscape browsers. As you learn later in this chapter, JavaScript also includes multiline comments.

Starting with Navigator 3, Netscape has introduced the **NOSCRIPT** which provides a way for alternative text to be specified for non-JavaScript browsers. Any text between **NOSCRIPT** tags will be displayed by other browsers, but Navigator 3 will ignore it. The previous example could be implemented using the **NOSCRIPT** tag:

```
<SCRIPT LANGUAGE="JavaScript">
<!-- HIDING FROM OTHER BROWSERS
```

```
JavaScript Program

// STOP HIDING FROM OTHER BROWSERS -->
</SCRIPT>

<NOSCRIPT>

JavaScript Script Appears Here<BR>
Download Netscape Navigator 2.0 to use it.

</NOSCRIPT>
```

Where to Put Your JavaScript Code

JavaScript scripts and programs can be included anywhere in the header or body of an HTML file. Many of the examples on Netscape's Web site, as well as elsewhere, make it a habit to include the SCRIPT container in the header of the HTML file, and this is the preferred format.

Still, other developers prefer to include the JavaScript program next to the element or section of the HTML it refers to, such as a form. Because an HTML file can contain more than one SCRIPT tag, it is possible to place JavaScript functions in logical places in a file for ease of coding and debugging.

As you will see in Chapter 4, "Functions and Objects—The Building Blocks of Programs," where we discuss functions, there are compelling reasons to put certain segments of your JavaScript code in the header of the HTML file to ensure they are evaluated before users can initiate events.

Using External Files for JavaScript Programs

While including JavaScript programs directly in HTML files can be convenient for small scripts and basic HTML pages, it can quickly get out of hand when pages require long and complex scripts.

To make development and maintenance of HTML files and JavaScript scripts easier, the JavaScript specification includes the option of keeping your JavaScript scripts in separate files and using the SRC attribute of the SCRIPT tag to include the JavaScript program in an HTML file.

In its simplest form, the SRC construct can be used like this:

```
<SCRIPT LANGUAGE="JavaScript" SRC="http://www.you.com/JavaScript.js">
</SCRIPT>
```

For the SRC attribute to work, the name of the JavaScript source files should include the extension .js. In addition, your Web server needs to be configured with the correct file type for JavaScript files. Information about this is available on Netscape's Web site.

One of the benefits of this approach is that your scripts are automatically hidden from other browsers that don't support JavaScript. At the same time, though, this technique requires an additional server request and server access, which may be problematic on a slow server or across a slow connection to the Internet.

In addition, both techniques (JavaScript code in an HTML file and JavaScript code in an external file) can be used at the same time. You can do this with a single **SCRIPT** container or more than one:

```
<SCRIPT LANGAUGE="JavaScript" SRC="http://www.you.com/JavaScript.js">
<!-- HIDE FROM OTHER BROWSERS

More JavaScript code

// STOP HIDING FROM OTHER BROWSERS -->
</SCRIPT>
```

or

```
<SCRIPT LANGUAGE="JavaScript" SRC="http://www.you.com/JavaScript.js">
</SCRIPT>

<SCRIPT LANGUAGE="JavaScript">
<!-- HIDE FROM OTHER BROWSERS

More JavaScript code

// STOP HIDING FROM OTHER BROWSERS -->
</SCRIPT>
```

Listing 2-1 demonstrates a simple JavaScript script inside an HTML file.

Input   **Listing 2-1** Including a program in an HTML file.

```
<HTML>

<HEAD>
<TITLE>Listing 2-1</TITLE>
</HEAD>

<BODY>
Here's the result:

<SCRIPT LANGUAGE="JavaScript">
<!-- HIDE FROM OTHER BROWSERS

// Output "It Works!"
document.writeln("It works!<BR>");

// STOP HIDING FROM OTHER BROWSERS -->
</SCRIPT>

</BODY>

</HTML>
```

Output

This HTML file produces results similar to those in Figure 2-1. By comparison, using a browser that doesn't support JavaScript (such as NCSA Mosaic), the results look like those in Figure 2-2.

Analysis

The script in Listing 2-1 demonstrates several important points which will become clear in later chapters.

First, it is possible to generate dynamic HTML output at the time of document loading using JavaScript scripts. Second, nothing in the script is displayed on other browsers even though the rest of the HTML file loads and displays without any difficulty. To compare, delete the HTML comment lines, and the output looks like Figure 2-3. You can see that the entire JavaScript command `document.writeln("It Works!<BR>");` has been displayed, and the `<BR>` tag has been interpreted by the non-JavaScript browser.

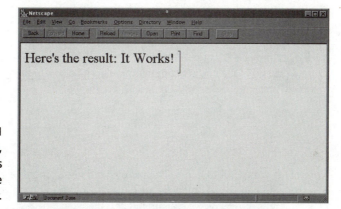

Figure 2-1
In Navigator 2.0, the output displays in source code order.

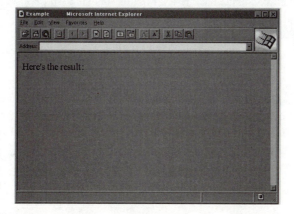

Figure 2-2
Part of the script is hidden when JavaScript is unsupported.

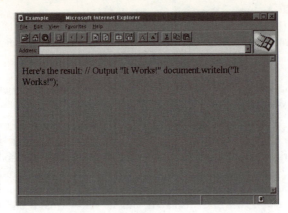

Figure 2-3
Without the
HTML comments,
the JavaScript
code displays.

In this example, you also see how JavaScript comments work. The line that begins with two slashes,

```
// Output "It Works!"
```

is a single-line JavaScript comment similar to those used in C++. Everything after the `//` until the end of the line is a comment. JavaScript also supports C-style multiline comments, which start with `/*` and end with `*/`:

```
/* This
   is
   a
   comment */
```

Comments are useful to help other people read your programs and understand what different commands and functions are doing. In addition, when you write long or complex programs, liberal use of meaningful comments will help you understand your own program if you come back to alter it after an extended period of time.

1. What are the optional attributes of the SCRIPT tag?
   a. LANGUAGE and VERSION
   b. SRC and LANGUAGE
   c. JavaScript and LiveScript
   d. LANGUAGE="JavaScript"

2. How does the method described for hiding your JavaScript code from other browsers work?
   a. By surrounding your script with JavaScript comments.
   b. Other browsers ignore everything between `<SCRIPT>` and `</SCRIPT>`.
   c. By placing HTML comments inside of JavaScript comments.
   d. By making everything between `<SCRIPT>` and `</SCRIPT>` appear as an HTML comment to other browsers.

3. How is an external file containing JavaScript code included in an HTML document?
   a. `<SCRIPT SRC="http://www.your.com/javascript.js">`
   b. `<SRC="http://www.your.com/javascript.js">`
   c. `<SCRIPT HREF="http://www.your.com/javascript.js">`
   d. `<SCRIPT> <LANGUAGE="JavaScript">`
      `<SRC="http://www.your.com/javascript.js"> </SCRIPT>`

4. Where in an HTML document can JavaScript code be placed?
   a. In the script section before the document body.
   b. Anywhere in the header or body of an HTML document.
   c. In the header of an HTML document.
   d. In the document body.

5. What types of comments are available in JavaScript?
   a. Multiline comments (between `<!--` and `-->`).
   b. Single-line comments (from `/*` to the end of line).
   c. Multiline comments (between `/*` and `*/`).
   d. Single-line comments (from `//` to the end of line).

LESSON 2 Syntax and Command Blocks

BASIC COMMAND SYNTAX

The basic syntax and structure of JavaScript looks familiar to anyone who has used C, C++, or Java. A JavaScript program is built with functions (covered in Chapter 4) and statements, operators, and expressions. The basic command unit is a one-line command or expression followed by an optional semicolon; for example:

```
document.writeln("It Works!<BR>");
```

This command invokes the `writeln()` method, which is part of the `document` object. The semicolon indicates the end of the command.

JavaScript commands can span multiple lines. Multiple commands can also appear on a single line, as long as the semicolon is there to mark the end of each command. In fact, except where it is essential to distinguish between commands, the semicolon is optional. I use it throughout this book to make source code clearer and easier to read.

COMMAND BLOCKS

Multiple commands can be combined into command blocks using curly braces ({ and }). Command blocks are used to group together sets of JavaScript commands into a single unit, which can then be used for a variety of purposes, including loops and defining functions. (These subjects will be discussed in later chapters.) A simple command block looks like this:

```
{
   document.writeln("Does it work? ");
   document.writeln("It works!<BR>");
}
```

Command blocks can be embedded, as the following lines illustrate:

```
{
JavaScript code

   {

   More JavaScript code

   }

}
```

When you embed command blocks like this, it is important to remember that all open curly braces must be closed and that the first closing brace closes the last opened curly brace. In the following example, the first } closes the second { as shown by the | markers:

```
{
| JavaScript code
|
| {
| |
| | More JavaScript code
| |
| }
|
}
```

Tip When embedding command blocks inside each other, it is common practice to indent each successive command block so that it's easy to identify where blocks start and end when reading program code. Extra spaces and tabs don't have any effect on JavaScript programs.

In JavaScript, object, property, and method names are case sensitive, as are all keywords, operators, and variable names. You learn about operators and variables in Chapter 3, "Working with Data and Information." In this way, all the following commands are different (and some are illegal):

```
document.writeln("Test");
Document.Writeln("Test");
document.WriteLN("Test");
```

1. What is the semicolon used for?
   a. Indicating the end of a comment.
   b. Terminating a JavaScript command.
   c. Indicating the end of a command block.
   d. Separating comments.

2. When is a semicolon required?
   a. It is always required to terminate a command.
   b. To terminate commands inside of command blocks.
   c. When it is essential to distinguish between commands.
   d. Only to make source code easier to read.

3. What is a command block?
   a. A set of JavaScript commands enclosed within curly braces.
   b. A set of JavaScript commands indented to the same level.
   c. Multiple JavaScript commands on one line separated by semicolons.
   d. Any sequence of JavaScript commands.

4. Indenting of nested command blocks is
   a. used to indicate to the JavaScript interpreter where the blocks begin and end.
   b. used because commands must start behind the curly braces.
   c. not used with multiline commands.
   d. used to enhance readability.

5. Which of the following are not case-sensitive?
   a. Object and property names
   b. HTML tags
   c. Keywords and variable names
   d. Method names

LESSON 3 Output

OUTPUTTING TEXT

In most programming languages, one of the basic capabilities is to output—or display—text. In JavaScript, output can be directed to several places including the current document window and pop-up dialog boxes.

Output in the Client Window

In JavaScript, programmers can direct output to the client window in sequence with the HTML file. As discussed in the previous section, JavaScript that produces output is evaluated where it occurs in the HTML file, and the resulting text is interpreted as HTML for the purpose of displaying the page.

In addition to this, JavaScript allows programmers to generate alert and confirm boxes that include text and one or two buttons. Text and numbers can also be displayed in TEXT and TEXTAREA fields in a form.

In the following sections, you look at outputting text to the document window.

The `document.write()` *and* `document.writeln()` *Methods*

The `document` object in JavaScript includes two methods designed for outputting text to the client window: `write()` and `writeln()`. In JavaScript, methods are called by combining the object name with the method name:

```
object-name.property-name
```

Data that the method needs to perform its job is provided as an argument in the parentheses; for example:

```
document.write("Test");
document.writeln('Test');
```

Arguments are data provided to a function or a method for use in its calculations and processing. They are provided (or *passed*) to the function or method by listing them in the parentheses following the function or method name. Multiple arguments are separated by commas.

A quick look at these examples shows you that strings of text are surrounded by double (or single) quotes and that the two methods (`document.write()` and `document.writeln()`) are invoked in the same manner. Open and close quotes must be of the same type—you cannot open with double quotes and close with single quotes or vice versa.

The `write()` method outputs text and HTML as a string of text to the current window in sequence with the current HTML file. Because the SCRIPT container does not affect the HTML structures where it occurs, any format tags or other elements in the

HTML file will affect the text and HTML produced by the `write()` method. For example, Listing 2-2 produces output like Figure 2-4.

Input   ## Listing 2-2 Outputting HTML tags from JavaScript.

```
<HTML>

<HEAD>
<TITLE>Ouputting Text</TITLE>
</HEAD>

<BODY>
This text is plain.<BR>
<B>
<SCRIPT LANGUAGE="JavaScript">
<!-- HIDE FROM OTHER BROWSERS

document.write("This text is bold.</B>");

// STOP HIDING FROM OTHER BROWSERS -->
</SCRIPT>

</BODY>

</HTML>
```

Output   Figure 2-4 shows the resulting effect.

Analysis   Listing 2-2 also demonstrates that HTML tags, as well as regular text, can be output by the `write()` method. You will notice that the `<B>` and `</B>` tags can either be output as part of the `write()` method or left outside the script. In either case, the text and HTML is evaluated in the order it appears in the complete HTML and JavaScript source code.

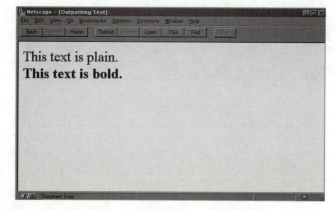

Figure 2-4
HTML tags affect
output from
JavaScript scripts.

The `writeln()` method is the same as the `write()` method except that it adds a carriage return at the end of the string that is being output. This is really only relevant inside of PRE and XMP containers where carriage returns are interpreted in displaying the text. Listing 2-3 shows an example of the `writeln()` method.

Input   **Listing 2-3** Using the `writeln()` method with the PRE tag.

```
<PRE>
<SCRIPT LANGUAGE="JavaScript">
<!-- HIDE FROM OTHER BROWSERS

document.writeln("One,");
document.writeln("Two,");
document.write("Three ");
document.write("...");

// STOP HIDING FROM OTHER BROWSERS -->
</SCRIPT>
</PRE>
```

This example produces results like those in Figure 2-5.

In JavaScript, strings of text, such as those used to produce output with the `write()` and `writeln()` methods, can include special keystrokes to represent characters that can't be typed, such as new lines, tabs, and carriage returns. The special characters are reviewed in Table 2-2.

Character	Description
\n	new line
\t	tab
\r	carriage return
\f	form feed
\b	backspace

Table 2-2 *Special characters in strings.*

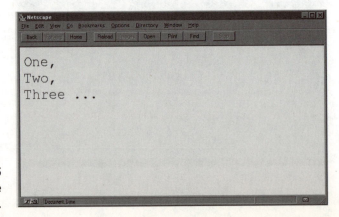

Figure 2-5
Output using the
`writeln()` method.

For example, the following command displays the text "It Works!" followed by a new line:

```
document.write("It Works!\n");
```

All special characters start with a backslash (\). This is called *escaping* characters. Escaping a character is used in many scripting and programming languages to represent a character that cannot be typed or that has special meaning in the language and would be interpreted incorrectly if left unescaped.

A perfect example of this is the backslash itself. In order to output a backslash in JavaScript, it is necessary to escape the backslash:

```
document.write("A backslash: \\");
```

In this example, the first backslash tells JavaScript that the next character is a special character and not to treat it normally. In this case it outputs a backslash rather than treating the second backslash in the normal way (as the escape character).

Listing 2-4 is a variation on the traditional Hello World program that most students learn as their first program in a new programming language. Instead of simply outputting "Hello World!" to the display window, you are going to produce the entire output using JavaScript and include a GIF image along with the phrase "Welcome to Netscape Navigator 2!" The GIF is included with the source code on the enclosed CD-ROM.

Input

Listing 2-4 Welcome to Netscape Navigator 2!

```
<HTML>

<HEAD>
<TITLE>Example 2.4</TITLE>
</HEAD>

<BODY>
<SCRIPT LANGUAGE="JavaScript">
<!-- HIDE FROM OTHER BROWSERS

document.write('<IMG SRC="welcome.gif">');
document.write("<BR><H1>Welcome to Netscape Navigator 2!</H1>");

// STOP HIDING FROM OTHER BROWSERS -->
</SCRIPT>
</BODY>

</HTML>
```

Output

This script produces output like that in Figure 2-6.

In this example, you can see how both text and HTML tags can be output to the current HTML windows using the `write()` method. Notice the use of both single quotes and double quotes to delimit the start and end of the text strings. In the first call to the `write()` method, you use the single quotes so that the text string can contain the double quotes required by the `IMG` tag.

Figure 2-6
JavaScript can be
used to generate
complete HTML
output.

STEPPING BEYOND THE DOCUMENT WINDOW

One of the restrictions of HTML has always been that Web site developers have been limited to a single client window. Even with the appearance of frames and the **TARGET** tag in Navigator 2.0, authors are still constrained to displaying HTML files in complete browser windows and are unable to direct small messages to the user through another window without having the message become part of an HTML page.

1. Where does JavaScript that produces output go?
   a. To the current target frame.
   b. To the **SCRIPT** container window.
   c. To the display window of the object specified in the output command.
   d. To the document window.

2. How are function arguments separated?
   a. By single or double quotes.
   b. By commas.
   c. By spaces.
   d. By semicolons.

3. The command `document.write('This text \\n is output\n')` is the same as
   a. `document.write('This text \n'); document.write(' is output\n')`.
   b. `document.writeln('This text is output')`.
   c. `document.writeln('this text is output")`.
   d. `document.writeln("This text n is output")`.

4. Which of the following would produce HTML output that displays an inline image.

   a. `document.write('<IMG SRC="welcome.gif">');`

   b. `document.write("<IMG SRC="welcome.gif">");`

   c. `document.write("<IMG SRC='welcome.gif'>");`

   d. none of the above

5. Which of the following would produce the following output?

```
One,
Two. . .
```

   a. `document.writeln('One,'); document.writeln('Two ');`

   b. `<PRE> document.writeln('One,'); document.write('Two '); </PRE>`

   c. `document.write('<PRE>One,\nTwo. . . \n</PRE>');`

   d. none of the above

 **Dialogs and Prompts**

WORKING WITH DIALOG BOXES

JavaScript provides the ability for programmers to generate output in small dialog boxes—the content of the dialog box is independent of the HTML page containing the JavaScript script and doesn't affect the appearance or content of the page.

The simplest way to direct output to a dialog box is to use the `alert()` method. To use the `alert()` method, you just need to provide a single string of text as you did with `document.write()` and `document.writeln()` in the previous section:

```
alert("Click OK to continue.");
```

 You will notice that the `alert()` method doesn't have an object name in front of it. This is because the `alert()` method is part of the `window` object. As the top-level object in the Navigator Object Hierarchy, the `window` object is assumed when it isn't specified.

The preceding command generates output similar to Figure 2-7. The alert dialog box displays the message passed to it in parentheses, as well as an OK button. The script and HTML holding the script will not continue evaluating or executing until the user clicks the OK button.

Generally, the `alert()` method is used for exactly that—to warn the user or alert him or her to something. Examples of this type of use include:

● Incorrect information in a form

● An invalid result from a calculation

● A warning that a service is not available on a given date

Nonetheless, the `alert()` method can still be used for friendlier messages.

Figure 2-7
Alert dialog boxes
display a message
along with an OK
button to continue.

Notice that JavaScript alert boxes include the phrase "JavaScript Alert" at the start of the message. All dialog boxes generated by scripts have similar headings in order to distinguish them from those generated by the operating system or the browser. This is done for security reasons so that malicious programs cannot trick users into doing things they don't want to do. Netscape designers have indicated that they may make dialog boxes generated by scripts visually different in future versions.

Next, take the preceding example, Listing 2-4, the "Welcome to Netscape Navigator 2!" example, and have the message display in an alert box.

To do this, you need to make only a small change in your original script, as shown in Listing 2-5:

Input

Listing 2-5 Displaying a message in an alert box.

```
<HTML>

<HEAD>
<TITLE>Example 2.5</TITLE>
</HEAD>

<BODY>
<SCRIPT LANGUAGE="JavaScript">
<!-- HIDE FROM OTHER BROWSERS

alert("Welcome to Netscape Navigator 2!");
document.write('<IMG SRC="welcome.gif">');

// STOP HIDING FROM OTHER BROWSERS -->
</SCRIPT>
</BODY>

</HTML>
```

Output   Figures 2-8 and 2-9 show the progression of events with this script.

Analysis   Notice in this example that you have reversed the order of the message and the graphic. This way, the user will see the message in a dialog box and the graphic will not load until OK has been clicked.

Figure 2-8
The alert dialog
box is displayed
first.

Figure 2-9
After OK is clicked,
the rest of the
script executes.

The `alert()` method produces different results on different platforms. On Windows versions of Netscape Navigator, script processing and parsing of HTML files waits until the user clicks on the OK button. On UNIX versions of Navigator, the alert box will be displayed and the script will continue processing and the rest of the HTML will be interpreted regardless of when the user clicks on OK.

As with `document.write()`, you can use special characters, such as \n, in the alert message to control the formatting of the text displayed in the dialog box. The following command would generate an alert box similar to the one in Figure 2-10:

```
alert("Welcome!\n\n\tYou are using Netscape Navigator 2!");
```

Figure 2-10
By using special
characters, you
can format text
in dialog boxes.

INTERACTING WITH THE USER

The `alert()` method still doesn't enable you to interact with the user. The addition of the OK button provides you with some control over the timing of events, but it still cannot be used to generate any dynamic output or customize output based on user input.

The simplest way to interact with the user is with the `prompt()` method. Like `alert()`, `prompt()` creates a dialog box with the message you specify, but it also provides a single entry field with a default entry. The user needs to fill in the field and then click OK. An example of the `prompt()` method is the following line, which generates a dialog box like the one in Figure 2-11:

```
prompt("Enter Your favourite color:","Blue");
```

You will immediately notice a difference with the way you used the `alert()` method: You are providing two strings to the method in the parentheses. The `prompt()` method requires two pieces of information: The first is text to be displayed, and the second is the default data in the entry field.

The pieces of information provided in parentheses to a method or function are known as *arguments*. In JavaScript, when a method requires more than one argument, they are separated by commas.

You might have noticed that if used by itself, the `prompt()` method accepts input from the user, but the information is essentially lost. This is solved by realizing that methods and functions can return results, as mentioned in the previous chapter. That means that the `prompt()` method will return the user's input as its result.

The result returned by a method can be stored in a variable (which you will learn about in the next chapter) or can be used as an argument to another method:

```
document.write("Your favorite color is: ");
document.writeln(prompt("Enter your favorite color:","Blue"));
```

In the second line of this code segment, the `document.writeln()` method displays the results returned by the `prompt()` method as illustrated by Figures 2-12 and 2-13.

Using the `prompt()` method, you are now in a position to generate a personalized version of the "Welcome to Netscape Navigator 2!" example you have been working with. Listing 2-6 shows the new program.

Figure 2-11
The prompt dialog box includes a message and an entry field along with an OK button and a Cancel button.

Netscape User Prompt	✕
JavaScript Prompt: Enter your favorite color:	OK
Blue	Cancel

Figure 2-12
The prompt()
method can be
used to ask the
user questions.

Figure 2-13
Based on the
answers, dynamic
content can be
created.

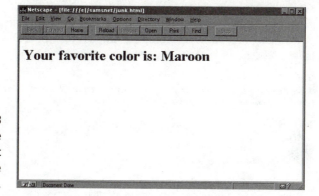

Input   **Listing 2-6** The revised welcome program.

```
<HTML>

<HEAD>
<TITLE>Example 2.6</TITLE>
</HEAD>

<BODY>
<SCRIPT LANGUAGE="JavaScript">
<!-- HIDE FROM OTHER BROWSERS

document.write('<IMG SRC="welcome.gif">');
document.write("<H1>Greetings, ");
document.write(prompt("Enter Your Name:","Name"));
document.write(". Welcome to Netscape Navigator!</H1>");

// STOP HIDING FROM OTHER BROWSERS -->
</SCRIPT>
</BODY>

</HTML>
```

Output   This script first displays the welcome graphic and the word "Greetings" in the Navigator
window. Then, a prompt dialog box asks for the user's name and once this is entered
the sentence is completed and displayed with the user's name following "Greetings."

Analysis

In this example, you have used the `prompt()` method to construct a personalized welcome greeting. However, notice that the process was somewhat cumbersome, requiring four `document.write()` commands to display what could easily be two short lines in HTML.

This can be made a little easier by combining multiple strings of text into a single string of text using what is known as concatenation.

Concatenation is discussed in more depth in Chapter 3. Using concatenation, multiple strings are combined into a single string and are treated as a single string by JavaScript. In order to do this, you can combine the various pieces of your welcome message into a single `document.write()` command using a simple plus sign (**+**):

```
document.write('<IMG SRC="welcome.gif">');
document.write("<H1>Greetings, " + prompt("<BR>Enter Your Name:","Name") +
    ". Welcome to Netscape Navigator!</H1>");
```

1. Which of the following displays an alert dialog box?
   a. `document.alert('Click OK to continue.'');`
   b. `alert('Click OK to continue.');`
   c. `window.alert('Click OK to continue.');`
   d. `JavaScript.alert('Click OK to continue.');`

2. How would you display an alert dialog with a multiline message?
   a. `alert("Line one'\n'line two")`
   b. `alert('Line one \n line two')`
   c. This cannot be done.
   d. `alert('Line one', 'line two')`

3. What does clicking on the Cancel button in the prompt dialog box do?
   a. It returns a null value.
   b. It returns the default response.
   c. It aborts the JavaScript command.
   d. It is the same as clicking OK.

4. What is the second parameter in the prompt method?
   a. It is the timeout parameter for the prompt dialog box.
   b. It is the dialog title.
   c. It specifies the default user input.
   d. It tells the user what to enter.

5. What does the **+** operator do when applied to strings?
   a. It modifies and extends the first string to include the second string.
   b. It adds the lengths of the two strings.
   c. It produces an error because this is an invalid operator for strings.
   d. It combines the contents of the two strings into a single string.

SUMMARY

In this chapter you learned how to combine JavaScript scripts into HTML files using the **SCRIPT** tag. The **SCRIPT** tag can also be used to include JavaScript code kept in separate external files. Multiple **SCRIPT** containers can be used in a single HTML file. You also learned the basic structure of JavaScript commands and how to use curly braces to build blocks of multiple commands.

We also took a look at how to use the **write()** and **writeln()** methods which are part of the **document** object, as well as reviewed the special characters which can be used when outputting text. In addition, you learned the syntax of JavaScript comments.

In this chapter you also moved beyond static output limited to the current client window.

Using the **alert()** method, it is possible to direct output from a JavaScript script to a dialog box. This can be taken a step further with the **prompt()** method.

The **prompt()** method enables you to ask the user to enter a single item of data in an entry field in a dialog box. The data the user enters is returned by the **prompt()** method and can be output using **document.write()** or **document.writeln()**. This is one way you can generate dynamic, custom output in a Web page.

COMMANDS AND EXTENSIONS REVIEW

Command/Extension	Type	Description
SCRIPT	HTML tag	Container for JavaScript scripts.
SRC	SCRIPT attribute	Holds the URL of an external JavaScript file. External files must have the extension .js. (Not yet implemented; optional.)
LANGUAGE	SCRIPT attribute	Specifies the language of the script. Currently, the only valid values for this attribute are LiveScript and JavaScript; (optional).

continued on next page

continued from previous page

Command/Extension	Type	Description
`//`	JavaScript comment	Start of a single-line comment. Comment starts with `//` and ends at the end of the line.
`/* ... */`	JavaScript comment	JavaScript multiline comments start with `/*` and end with `*/`.
`document.write()`	JavaScript method	Outputs string to the current window in sequence with HTML file containing the script.
`document.writeln()`	JavaScript method	Outputs string to current document followed by a carriage return.
`alert()`	JavaScript method	Displays a message in a dialog box.
`prompt()`	JavaScript method	Displays a message in a dialog box and provides a single input field for the user to enter a response to the message.

CHAPTER EXERCISE

1. Change Listing 2-4 so that it produces output in preformatted text (using HTML's PRE tag) with "Welcome to" and "Netscape Navigator!" on separate lines.

2. How would you rewrite the example from exercise question 1 using only one `write()` or `writeln()` command?

3. How would you customize the output in Listing 2-5 to include the user's name?

4. Try entering the following in the prompt dialog box generated by the script from Listing 2-6 and see what happens:

- Press Cancel instead of OK.

- Enter text that includes some simple HTML tags, such as John
Doe.

- Enter text that contains special characters such as John\nDoe.

What do you learn from the results?

CHAPTER 3

WORKING WITH DATA AND INFORMATION

In order to move beyond outputting text and very basic user interaction, it is necessary to work with data and information—both when it is generated by the user and by calculations in a script.

JavaScript provides four basic data types that can be used to work with numbers and text. Variables offer containers to hold information and work with it in useful and sophisticated ways by using expressions.

To help you master variables and expressions, this chapter covers the following topics:

- Data types in JavaScript
- Using and declaring variables
- Assignment expressions
- Operators
- Comparison with `if-else`
- Extending user interaction with the `confirm()` method

 **Data Types**

DATA TYPES IN JAVASCRIPT

JavaScript uses four data types—numbers, strings, boolean values, and a null value—to represent all the information the language can handle. Compared with most languages, this is a small number of data types, but it is sufficient to intelligently handle most data used in everything except the most complex programs.

The four data types in JavaScript are outlined in Table 3-1.

Type	Example
Numbers	Any number, such as 17, 21.5, or 54e7
Strings	"Greetings!" or 'Fun!'
Boolean	Either `true` or `false`
Null	A special keyword for exactly that—the `null` value (that is, nothing)

Table 3-1 *JavaScript's data types.*

LITERALS

The term *literals* refers to the way in which each of the four data types are represented. Literals are fixed values which literally provide a value in a program. For example, `11` is a literal number, `"hello"` is a string literal, and `true` is a boolean literal.

You have already seen literals in use in the previous chapters when you gave arguments to different methods in the form of text strings such as `"Welcome to Netscape Navigator 2.0!"` and `"Enter Your Name:"`.

For each data type, there are different ways of specifying literals.

Numbers

The JavaScript numbers type encompasses what would be several types in languages such as Java. Using the numbers, it is possible to express both integers and floating point values.

Integers

Integers are numbers without any portion following the decimal point; that is, they are whole numbers—no fractions. Integers can be either positive or negative numbers. The maximum integer size is dependent on the platform running the JavaScript application.

In JavaScript, you can express integers in three different bases: base 10 (*decimal*—what you normally use in everyday situations), base 8 (*octal*), and base 16 (*hexadecimal*).

Base 8 numbers can have digits only up to 7 so that a decimal value of 18 would be an octal value of 22. Similarly, hexadecimal allows digits up to F, where A is equivalent to decimal 10 and F is 15. So, a decimal value of 18 would be 12 in hexadecimal notation.

In order to distinguish between these three bases, JavaScript uses the notations outlined in Table 3-2 to specify the different bases.

Number System	Notation
Decimal (base 10)	A normal integer without a leading 0 (zero) (for example, 752)
Octal (base 8)	An integer with a leading 0 (zero) (for example, 056)
Hexadecimal (base 16)	An integer with a leading 0x or 0X (for example, 0x5F or 0XC72)

Table 3-2 *Specifying bases in JavaScript.*

Floating Point Values

Floating point values can include a fractional component. A floating point literal includes a decimal integer plus either a decimal point and a fraction expressed as another decimal number or an exponent indicator and a type suffix, as shown in the following examples:

- 7.2945

- −34.2

- 2E3

Floating point literals must, at a minimum, include a decimal integer and either the decimal point or the exponent indicator (e or E). As with integers, floating point values can be positive or negative.

It should be noted that JavaScript's handling of floating point numbers can introduce inaccuracy into some calculations. You should keep this in mind for your programs.

Strings

You have already encountered string literals in Chapter 2, "Your First Script," where you used them as arguments for several methods.

Technically, a string literal contains zero or more characters enclosed, as you know, in single or double quotes:

- `"Hello!"`

- `'245'`

- `""`

New Term

The last example is called the *empty string*. It is important to note that the empty string is distinct from the `null` value in JavaScript.

Strings are different from other data types in JavaScript. Strings are actually objects (objects are introduced in Chapter 4, "Functions and Objects—The Building Blocks of Programs").

Boolean

A boolean literal can take two values: `true` or `false`. This type of literal comes in handy when comparing data and making decisions, as you will see later in this chapter.

Unlike Java, C, and other languages, in JavaScript boolean values can only be represented with `true` and `false`. Values of **1** and **0** are not considered boolean values in JavaScript.

The `null` Value

The `null` value is a special value in JavaScript. The `null` value represents just that—nothing. If you try to reference a variable that isn't defined and therefore has no value, the value returned is the `null` value. Likewise, in a prompt dialog box, if the user selects the Cancel button, a `null` value is returned. This is distinct from a value of zero or an empty string where this is an actual value.

The `null` value is indicated in JavaScript by the term `null`.

NaN

In addition to these values, some functions return a special value called **NaN**—which means that the value is not a number. **parseInt()** and **parseFloat()** on UNIX systems are examples of functions which return **NaN** when the argument passed to them cannot be evaluated to a number.

Values can be tested to see if they are **NaN** by using the **isNaN()** function which returns **true** or **false** based on the nature of the argument passed to the function.

CASTING

JavaScript is what is called a *loosely typed* programming language. In loosely typed languages, the type of a literal or variable (which we discuss in the next section) is not defined when a variable is created and can, at times, change based on the context. By comparison, Java and C are not loosely typed.

In its earliest forms, LiveScript and JavaScript allowed programmers to combine two literals of different types, with the result being a literal value of the same type as the first literal in the expression. For instance, combining the string **"Count to "** with the integer literal **"10"** results in a string with the value **"Count to 10"**.

By contrast, adding together the numeric literal **3.5** and the string **"10"** results in the floating point numeric literal **13.5**.

| New Term |

This process is known as *casting*. The first example casts the number **10** into a string, and the second casts the string **"10"** into a number.

However, as JavaScript and Java have been brought closer together, this has begun to change. In the version of JavaScript currently available, it is no longer possible to cast a string into a number by using a form such as **0 + "1"**. JavaScript has added the **parseInt()** and **parseFloat()** functions, which convert strings into integers or floating point numbers. For instance, **parseInt("13")** returns the integer **13** and **parseFloat("45.2")** returns the floating point number **45.2**.

It is still possible to cast a number into a string as in **"Count to " + 10** evaluating to a string with the value **"Count to 10"**.

QUIZ 1

1. Which of the following is not a JavaScript data type?
   a. Number.
   b. Date.
   c. String.
   d. Boolean.

2. Which of the following literals is not a numbers data type.
   a. `'12'`
   b. `12`
   c. `2E4`
   d. `0X5F`

3. The `null` value represents
   a. zero.
   b. an out-of-bounds condition.
   c. nothing.
   d. an empty string.

4. The boolean data type can have only two values, and they are
   a. 0 or 1.
   b. `true` or `false`.
   c. `null` or `not-null`.
   d. `'true'` or `'false'`.

5. What is `NaN`?
   a. The value returned by the `isNaN()` function.
   b. A logical operator.
   c. The return value of special functions such as `parseInt()`.
   d. A special value representing "Not a Number".

 **Variables**

CREATING VARIABLES

In order to make working with data types useful, you need ways to store values for later use. This is where variables come in.

In JavaScript you can create variables that can contain any type of data. Variables have names, and after assigning values to a variable, you can refer to the value by name. If you subsequently assign a new value to the variable, you can continue referring to that new value by the name of the variable.

Declaring Variables

In order to use a variable, it is good programming style to declare it. Declaring a variable tells JavaScript that a variable of a given name exists so that the JavaScript interpreter can understand references to that variable name throughout the rest of the script.

Although it is possible to declare variables by simply using them, declaring variables helps to ensure that programs are well organized and helps keep track of the scope of variables (discussed in Chapter 4, "Functions and Objects—The Building Blocks of Programs").

You can declare a variable using the `var` command:

```
var example;
```

In this line, you have defined a variable named `example`, which currently has no value. It is also possible to assign a value to a variable when you declare it:

```
var example = "An Example";
```

Here you have declared the variable named `example` and assigned a string value of `"An Example"` to it. Because JavaScript allows variables to also be declared on first use, the command `example = "An Example"` would achieve the same result.

New Term The equal sign (=) used in assigning a value to a variable is known as an *assignment operator*. Assignment operators are discussed later in this chapter.

To better understand how to declare, assign, and use variables, the following code segment produces output similar to Figure 3-1.

```
var example="An Example";
document.write(example);
```

Valid Variable Names

Like property and method names in JavaScript, variable names are case sensitive. In addition, variable names must start with a letter or an underscore (_). After that, the remaining characters can also include numbers.

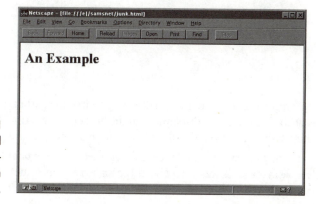

Figure 3-1
Variables can hold string literals, numbers, or boolean values.

INCORPORATING VARIABLES IN A SCRIPT

Using variables, you can simplify the personalized "Welcome to Netscape Navigator 2!" script from the previous chapters. In Listing 3-1, you want to ask for the user's name prior to using `document.write()` and store the value in a variable.

Input

Listing 3-1 Using variables in the welcome program.

```
<HTML>

<HEAD>

<TITLE>Example 3.1</TITLE>

<SCRIPT LANGUAGE="JavaScript">
<!--HIDE FROM OTHER BROWSERS

var name=prompt("Enter Your Name:","Name");

// STOP HIDING FROM OTHER BROWSERS -->
</SCRIPT>

</HEAD>

<BODY>
<SCRIPT LANGUAGE="JavaScript">
<!-- HIDE FROM OTHER BROWSERS

document.write('<IMG SRC="welcome.gif">');
document.write("<H1>Greetings, " + name + ". Welcome to Netscape Navigator!</H1>");

// STOP HIDING FROM OTHER BROWSERS -->
</SCRIPT>
</BODY>

</HTML>
```

Analysis

There are several things to note in this script. First, the part of the script that needs to execute before things are displayed is in the header of the script. This helps ensure that nothing else can be loaded and evaluated until after the user provides a name.

Second, you have assigned the result returned by the **prompt()** method to the variable **name** in the same way you previously assigned a literal value to a variable. This works because the **prompt()** method is returning a string value, which can be assigned to a variable.

This script also demonstrates how using variables can make scripts easier to read because the names of variables can be carefully selected to impart meaning to someone reading the source code of a script.

You can now take using variables a step further and look at how you can assign values to them in succession. In Listing 3-2, you ask for two names in a row.

  Listing 3-2 Assigning a new value to the variable.

```html
<HTML>

<HEAD>

<TITLE>Example 3.2</TITLE>

<SCRIPT LANGUAGE="JavaScript">
<!--HIDE FROM OTHER BROWSERS

var name=prompt("Enter Your Name:","Name");
alert("Greetings " + name + ".");
name=prompt("Enter Your Friend's Name:","Friend's Name");

// STOP HIDING FROM OTHER BROWSERS -->
</SCRIPT>

</HEAD>

<BODY>
<SCRIPT LANGUAGE="JavaScript">
<!-- HIDE FROM OTHER BROWSERS

document.write('<IMG SRC="welcome.gif">');
document.write("<H1>Greetings, " + name + ". Welcome to Netscape Navigator!</H1>");

// STOP HIDING FROM OTHER BROWSERS -->

</SCRIPT>
</BODY>

</HTML>
```

Output   This script produces a sequence of results similar to Figures 3-2, 3-3, and 3-4.

Figure 3-2 Store the first name in name.

Figure 3-3 The second name can then also be assigned to name.

Figure 3-4
The final value of
name is the second
name.

In this example, you see how assigning a new value to a variable completely replaces the previous value. Rather than combining the user's name with the friend's name, the final value of **name** is just the friend's name.

In addition, assigning subsequent values to variables works much the same way as assigning values when declaring a variable, except that the **var** command is not used.

By using two variables you can provide a final greeting to both users.

You will notice that the alert dialog box with the first name seems small. If you use a longer name, the size of the box is adjusted to accommodate the longer name.

QUIZ 2

1. JavaScript is loosely typed which means
   a. the data type of a variable changes based on what its value is.
   b. the variable type defaults to a string.
   c. the variable type must be declared.
   d. the value of a variable is always converted to string.

2. Which of the following statements does not declare a variable named `example`?
   a. `var example;`
   b. `document.write(example);`
   c. `example = 10;`
   d. `var example = 10;`

3. Which of the following two statements would result in a variable named `length` with a data type of number?
   a. `var length = parseInt('8');`
   b. `var length = '8';`
   c. `length = 1 + '8';`
   d. `length = 8;`

4. How could you ensure that a script gets executed before the document is displayed?
    a. By using the `prompt()` method which gets displayed first.
    b. By using `document.write()`.
    c. By placing the script in the header of the HTML document.
    d. By using an alert dialog.

5. Assigning a value to a variable
    a. concatenates the value to the variable.
    b. changes the name of the variable.
    c. replaces the previous value that the variable held.
    d. None of the above.

LESSON 3 Expressions

WORKING WITH VARIABLES— EXPRESSIONS

In order to make variables useful, you need to be able to manipulate variables and evaluate them in different contexts.

This ability is provided by expressions. At its most basic, an expression is nothing more than a collection of variables, operators, and other expressions—all of which evaluate to a single value.

In practical terms, that means there are two types of expressions: those that simply have a value and those that assign a value to a variable. You have seen simple examples of both: `example = "An Example"` is an expression that assigns a value to the variable `example`, while `"The Number is " + "10"` is an example of an expression that simply has value.

As with data types, JavaScript has several kinds of expressions:

● Assignment: Assigns a value to a variable

● Arithmetic: Evaluates to a number

● String: Evaluates to a string

● Logical: Evaluates to a boolean value

Assignment Expressions

Assignment expressions use assignment operators to assign value to a variable. The typical structure of an assignment expression is

```
variable operator expression
```

In other words, the operator assigns a value to the variable by performing some type of operation on the expression. Table 3-3 outlines the assignment operators in JavaScript.

New Term Technically, the element to the left of the operator is called the *left operand* and the element to the right is called the *right operand*.

Operator	Description
=	Assigns the value of the right operand to the left operand
+=	Adds the left and right operands and assigns the result to the left operand
-=	Subtracts the right operand from the left operand and assigns the result to the left operand
*=	Multiplies the two operands and assigns the result to the left operand
/=	Divides the left operand by the right operand and assigns the value to the left operand
%=	Divides the left operand by the right operand and assigns the remainder to the left operand

Table 3-3 *Assignment operators in JavaScript.*

Note The %= operand assigns the modulus to the left operand. That is, x %= y is the same as x = x % y. The modulus is the remainder when two numbers are divided.

For example, if x = 10 and y = 5, then x += y sets x to 15, x *= y sets x to 50, x /= y sets x to 2, and x %= y sets x to 0 because the remainder of 10 divided by 5 is 0.

Note There are other assignment operators known as *bitwise assignment operators*, such as <<=, >>=, and ^=, but these are advanced and require an understanding of binary (base 2) numbers.

Other Operators

Besides the assignment operators we have already discussed, JavaScript also has operators for expressions that simply evaluate to a value. These are the arithmetic operators, string operators, and logical operators, as well as the bitwise operators, which are beyond the scope of this book.

As you will see in the following examples, these operators include both operators that require two operands and those that require a single operand.

| New Term | An operator requiring a single operand is referred to as a *unary* operator, and one that requires two operands is a *binary* operator. |

In addition, all the operators under discussion here can take expressions as their operands. In these cases, the expressions that act as operands are evaluated before evaluating the final expression. For example, in the next section, you will learn about simple arithmetic expressions such as **15 + 3**. Because operators can take other expressions as their operands, you could write an expression such as **x += 15 + 3**. This adds **15** and **3**, then adds the result (**18**) to the value of **x**, and assigns the final result to **x**.

Arithmetic Operators

The standard binary arithmetic operators are the same as those on a basic calculator: addition (**+**), subtraction (**-**), multiplication (*****), and division (**/**). In addition to these basic operators is the modulus (**%**) operator, which, as mentioned before, calculates the remainder of dividing its operands. The following are examples of valid expressions using these:

```
8 + 5
```

```
32.5 - 72.3
```

```
12 % 5
```

In addition to these binary operators, there are three unary arithmetic operators that are quite useful: increment (**++**), decrement (**--**), and unary negation (**-**).

Both the increment and decrement operators can be used in two different ways: before the operand or after. For example, **++x** increments **x** by one and returns the result, while **x++** returns **x** and then increments the value of **x**. Similarly, **--x** decreases the value of **x** by one before returning a result, while **x--** returns the value of **x** before decreasing its value by one.

For example:

```
x = 5;
y = ++x;
z = x++;
```

In these lines of code, **x** is first assigned the value of **5**; then it is increased to **6** and assigned to **y**. Then, the new value of **6** is assigned to **z**, and the value of **x** is increased to **7**. So, at the end, **x** is **7**, **y** is **6**, and **z** is **6**.

Unary negation works a little differently. The operator must precede its single operand, and the result is the negation of the operand. Typically, the usage of this operand looks like this:

```
x = -x;
```

Here, if the value of **x** is **5**, then it becomes **-5**. Likewise, if **x** were **-4**, it would become **4**.

Logical Operators

Logical operators include both binary and unary operators. They take boolean values as operands and return boolean values, as outlined in Table 3-4.

Operator	Description
&&	Logical "and"—returns `true` when both operands are true; otherwise it returns `false`.
||	Logical "or"—returns `true` if either operand is true. It only returns `false` when both operands are false.
!	Logical "not"—returns `true` if the operand is false and `false` if the operand is true. This is a unary operator and precedes the operand.

Table 3-4   *Logical operators in JavaScript.*

In discussing logical operators and expressions, it is necessary to discuss *short-circuit evaluation*. With short-circuit evaluation, JavaScript will finish evaluating an expression after evaluating the first (left) operand, if the first operand provides sufficient information to evaluate the expression. Short-circuit evaluation uses the following rules:

● `false &&` anything is always `false`.

● `true ||` anything is always `true`.

For example, if x equals **10** and y equals **20**, then the expression `(x > y) && (x < y)` would immediately evaluate to **false** once the first part of the expression `(x > y)` is evaluated to **false**. Likewise, `(y > x) || (x > y)` is evaluated to **true** simply because the first part of the expression `(y > x)` is **true**. These examples use comparison operators, which are discussed in the next section.

Because the logical "not" operator (`!`) takes a single operator, there is no short-circuit evaluation for it.

Comparison Operators

Comparison operators are similar to logical operators in that they return boolean values. Unlike logical operators, they don't require that their operands be boolean values. Comparison operators are used to compare the value of the operands for equality as well as for a number of other conditions. Table 3-5 lists the comparison operators available in JavaScript.

Operator	Description
==	Returns `true` if the operands are equal
!=	Returns `true` if the operands are not equal

Operator	Description
>	Returns `true` if the left operand is greater than the right operand
<	Returns `true` if the left operand is less than the right operand
>=	Returns `true` if the left operand is greater than or equal to the right operand
<=	Returns `true` if the left operand is less than or equal to the right operand

Table 3-5 *Comparison operators in JavaScript.*

In JavaScript, all comparison operators are binary operators. Comparison operators can be used to compare numbers as well as strings; for instance:

`1 == 1` returns `true`.

`3 < 1` returns `false`.

`5 >= 4` returns `true`.

`"the" != "he"` returns `true`.

`4 == "4"` returns `true`.

When comparing string and numeric values, if the string value begins with non-numeric characters, JavaScript will generate an error.

Conditional Operators

Conditional expressions are a little different than the others you have seen so far because a conditional expression can evaluate to one of two different values based on a condition. The structure of a conditional expression is:

`(condition) ? val1 : val2`

The way a conditional expression works is that the `condition`, which is any expression that can be evaluated to a boolean value, is evaluated; based on the result, the whole expression evaluates to either `val1` (true condition) or `val2` (false condition).

The expression

`(day == "Saturday") ? "Weekend!" : "Not Saturday!"`

evaluates to `"Weekend!"` when `day` is `"Saturday"`. Otherwise, the expression evaluates to `"Not Saturday!"`.

String Operators

In Chapter 2, you learned to use the concatenation operator (**+**). Concatenation returns the union of two strings so that

`"Welcome to " + "Netscape Navigator!"`

evaluates to a single string with the value `"Welcome to Netscape Navigator !"` As with numbers, this can be done with a short cut concatenation operator. For example, if the variable `welcome` has the value `"Welcome to "`, then

```
welcome += "Netscape Navigator!";
```

would assign the string `"Welcome to Netscape Navigator !"` to the variable `welcome`.

1. Which of the following is an incorrect definition?
   a. An assignment expression assigns a value to a variable.
   b. An arithmetic expression evaluates to a number.
   c. A string expression evaluates to a string.
   d. A literal expression evaluates to either `true` or `false`.

2. The conditional operator
   a. is the conditional part of a loop.
   b. can return one of two different values based on a condition.
   c. always returns a boolean.
   d. is none of the above.

3. A short-circuit evaluation of a logical expression means
   a. that the program aborts due to a logic error.
   b. that the expression is not fully evaluated because JavaScript determined that it was not necessary.
   c. that the expression was incomplete and thus not fully evaluated.
   d. none of the above.

4. Which of the following is false?
   a. Logical "not", `!`, always returns `false`.
   b. Logical "or", `||`, returns `true` if either operand is true.
   c. Logical "and", `&&`, returns `true` when both operands are true.
   d. Logical "not", `!`, is a unary operator and precedes the operand.

5. Which of the following is not an assignment operator?
   a. `!=`
   b. `-=`
   c. `+=`
   d. `*=`

 **Operators and Comparison Expressions**

OPERATOR PRECEDENCE

Because expressions can be the operands for other expressions, it is necessary to understand operator precedence. *Operator precedence* is the set of rules that determines the order in which these compound expressions are evaluated.

The operators that you have learned are evaluated in the following order (from lowest precedence to highest):

Assignment operators (= += -= *= /= %=)

Conditional (?:)

Logical or (||)

Logical and (&&)

Equality (== !=)

Relational (< <= > >=)

Addition/subtraction (+ -)

Multiply/divide/modulus (* / %)

Parentheses (())

Based on these rules, the expression

```
5 + 3 * 2
```

evaluates to

```
5 + 6
```

which evaluates to **11**. Without these rules, the addition operator would be evaluated before the multiplication operator and the result would be **16**. Likewise, the expression

```
false || true && false
```

evaluates to

```
false
```

because the **&&** expression is evaluated to **false** first, and then the **||** expression (which becomes **false || false**) evaluates to **false**.

The rules of operator precedence can be overridden by the use of parentheses. Expressions in parentheses evaluate before those outside the parentheses, so that the expression

```
(5 + 3) * 2
```

would evaluate to **16**, instead of **11** without the parentheses.

TESTING A USER'S RESPONSE

In this example, you go beyond the "Welcome to Netscape Navigator 2!" scripts you have been working on to something a little different. In Listing 3-3, you will pose a test question to the user and based on the answer, display a different result for the user in the form of one of two different GIF images.

The question will be presented in a prompt dialog box, and the result displayed by outputting to the client window.

Input   **Listing 3-3** Using conditional operators to test input.

```html
<HTML>

<HEAD>
<TITLE>Example 3.3</TITLE>

<SCRIPT LANGUAGE="JavaScript">
<!-- HIDE FROM OTHER BROWSERS

// DEFINE VARIABLES FOR REST OF SCRIPT
var question="What is 10+10?";
var answer=20;
var correct='<IMG SRC="correct.gif">';
var incorrect='<IMG SRC="incorrect.gif">';

// ASK THE QUESTION
var response = prompt(question,"0");

// CHECK THE ANSWER
var output = (response == answer) ? correct : incorrect;

// STOP HIDING FROM OTHER BROWSERS -->
</SCRIPT>

</HEAD>

<BODY>

<SCRIPT LANGUAGE="JavaScript">
<!-- HIDE FROM OTHER BROWSERS

// OUTPUT RESULT
document.write(output);

// STOP HIDING FROM OTHER BROWSERS -->
</SCRIPT>

</BODY>

</HTML>
```

Output

The results of this script would look like Figures 3-5 and 3-6.

Analysis

In this example, you can see the use of several of the concepts learned earlier in this chapter and in earlier sections.

The first part of the script appears in the header because this is the advisable style, except where the script must generate output in sequence with the HTML file. For this reason, all the variable declarations—asking the question and checking the answer—take place in the header. The script in the body of the HTML document outputs only the final results.

Notice the extensive use of variables, both strings and numbers, all declared with the `var` command. Every important item in the script is assigned to a variable. This makes the script easier to read and easier to change. By changing the `question` and `answer` variables, you can change the test, and by changing the `correct` and `incorrect` variables, you can change the response given to the user.

In addition, you see a practical example of conditional expressions (`(response == answer) ? correct : incorrect`) and how the value of a conditional expression can be assigned to a variable.

Figure 3-5
The prompt dialog box is used to test the user.

Figure 3-6
Conditional operators determine the final Web page.

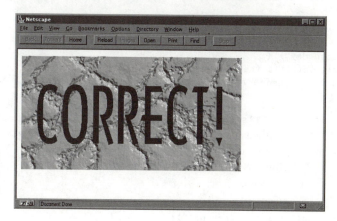

APPLYING COMPARISON
if-else CONSTRUCTS

Now that you know how to create expressions and, more importantly, how to create comparison expressions and logical expressions, you are ready to apply them.

In the preceding section you saw how an expression, such as a comparison, could be the condition in a conditional expression. The conditional operator gives you a simple way to make a decision: evaluate to one value when the condition is true and to another when the condition is false.

Still, by using conditional expressions, you cannot break beyond the bounds of a linear program flow. That is, every line of the script is evaluated and executed in order—you still can't alter the order.

Using the **if-else** construct, combined with expressions, you can alter the flow of a program—to determine which sections of program code run based on a condition. At its most simple structure, the **if** statement is used as follows:

```
if condition
  command;
```

That is, if the **condition** is true, execute the **command**. Otherwise, don't execute it and skip to the next command or condition which follows. As you learned in Chapter 2, however, commands can be grouped together in command blocks using curly braces. The **if** statement can be used with command blocks as well:

```
if condition {
  several lines of JavaScript code
}
```

For example, these lines

```
if (day == "Saturday") {
  document.writeln("It's the weekend!");
  alert("It's the weekend!");
}
```

will write **"It's the weekend!"** to both the document window and an alert dialog box only if the variable **day** has the value **"Saturday"**. If **day** has any other value, neither line is executed.

By using this you can have a different message for both Saturday and every other day of the week:

```
if (day == "Saturday") {
  document.writeln("It's the weekend!");
}
if (day != "Saturday") {
  document.writeln("It's not Saturday.");
}
```

The **if-else** construct provides an easier way to do this by using **else**:

```
if (day == "Saturday") {
  document.writeln("It's the weekend!");
} else {
  document.writeln("It's not Saturday.");
}
```

The `else` construct allows the creation of a command block to execute when the condition in the associated `if` statement is false.

Also, note that `if-else` constructs can be embedded:

```
if condition1 {
  JavaScript commands
  if condition2 {
    JavaScript commands
  } else {
    Other commands
  }
  More JavaScript commands
} else {
  Other commands
}
```

USING if FOR REPETITION

Using the `if` statement, you are going to extend Listing 3-3 one step further—you are going to enable the user to indicate if he or she wants a second chance to answer the question correctly, as shown in Listing 3-4.

What you want to do is ask the question and check the result. If the result is incorrect, you will ask the user if he or she wishes to try again. If he or she does, you ask one more time.

In order to make this easier, use the `confirm()` method, which is similar to the `alert()` and `prompt()` methods that you already know how to use. The `confirm()` method takes a single string as an argument. It displays the string in a dialog box with OK and Cancel buttons and returns a value of `true` if the user selects OK or `false` if Cancel is selected.

Input   **Listing 3-4** The `confirm()` method with the `if` statement.

```
<HTML>

<HEAD>
<TITLE>Example 3.4</TITLE>

<SCRIPT LANGUAGE="JavaScript">
<!-- HIDE FROM OTHER BROWSERS

// DEFINE VARIABLES FOR REST OF SCRIPT
var question="What is 10+10?";
var answer=20;
var correct='<IMG SRC="correct.gif">';
```

continued on next page

continued from previous page

```
var incorrect='<IMG SRC="incorrect.gif">';

// ASK THE QUESTION
var response = prompt(question,"0");

// CHECK THE ANSWER THE FIRST TIME
if (response != answer) {
  // THE ANSWER WAS WRONG: OFFER A SECOND CHANCE
  if (confirm("Wrong! Press OK for a second chance."))
    response = prompt(question,"0");
}

// CHECK THE ANSWER
var output = (response == answer) ? correct : incorrect;

// STOP HIDING FROM OTHER BROWSERS -->
</SCRIPT>

</HEAD>

<BODY>

<SCRIPT LANGUAGE="JavaScript">
<!-- HIDE FROM OTHER BROWSERS

// OUTPUT RESULT
document.write(output);

// STOP HIDING FROM OTHER BROWSERS -->
</SCRIPT>

</BODY>

</HTML>
```

Analysis　In order to add the second chance, you have to add only two embedded **if** statements. In order to grasp how this works, let's look at the program line by line starting with the first **prompt()** method.

```
var response = prompt(question,"0");
```

In this line, you declare the variable **response**, ask the user to answer the question and assign the user's answer to **response**.

```
if (response != answer)
```

Here, you compare the user's response to the correct answer. If the answer is incorrect, then the next line is executed. If the answer is correct, the program skips down to output the result.

```
if (confirm("Wrong! Press OK for a second chance."))
```

The user has made an incorrect response. Now you check whether the user wants a second chance with the `confirm()` method, which returns a boolean value, which is evaluated by the `if` statement.

```
response = prompt(question,"0");
```

If the user selects OK in the confirm dialog box, the `confirm()` method returns `true`, and this line executes. With this command, the user is again asked the question, and the second response is stored in the `response` variable, replacing the previous answer.

QUIZ 4

1. The `if-else` construct is useful for
   a. providing alternate paths of execution based on certain conditions.
   b. hiding code.
   c. creating loop structures.
   d. repetitive coding.

2. Which of the following comparisons will generate an error?
   a. `'4' == 'four'`
   b. `4 == parseInt( '5' )`
   c. `4 == 'four'`
   d. none of the above

3. In which of the following examples can you be sure that none of the statements will be executed?
   a. `if( a > b && false ) { alert('this always gets executed'); }`
   b. `if( a > b ) { a = 0; } else { a = 1;}`
   c. `if( confirm('do you want to continue?') ) { a = 0; }`
   d. `if( false ) { a = 0; } else if( a > 0 ) { a = 1; }`

4. How can the rules for operator precedence be overridden?
   a. By reordering the sequence of the expression.
   b. By using `if-else` blocks.
   c. This cannot be done.
   d. By using parenthesis to change to order of evaluation.

5. Which of the following is not a comparison operator?
   a. `==`
   b. `!=`
   c. `<<=`
   d. `<=`

SUMMARY

JavaScript has four basic data types: numeric (both integer and floating point), string, boolean, and the `null` value. Literals, which literally express a value, can be of either numeric, string, or boolean type, and specific rules govern the format of these literals. Variables, which are named containers to hold data and information in a program, are declared using the `var` statement. Because JavaScript is a loosely typed language, the type of literals and variables change dynamically depending on what actions are performed on them or with them.

Expressions provide a means to analyze and work with variables and literals. There are several types of expressions, including assignment expressions, arithmetic expressions, logical expressions, comparison expressions, string expressions, and conditional expressions. Expressions are made up of a series of operands and operators that evaluate to a single value.

The rules of operator precedence tell you the order in which compound expressions will be evaluated. Parentheses can be used to override operator precedence. The `if-else` construct enables you to decide which program code will be executed based on the value of variables, literals, or expressions.

In Chapter 4, we will look at functions and objects as the building blocks for most programs.

COMMANDS AND EXTENSIONS REVIEW

Command/Extension	Type	Description
Var	JavaScript command	Declares a variable
=	Assignment operator	Assigns the value of the right operand to the left operand
+=	Assignment operator	Adds together the operands and assigns the result to the left operand
-=	Assignment operator	Subtracts the right from the left operand and assigns the result to the left operand
*=	Assignment operator	Multiplies the operands and assigns the result to the left operand
/=	Assignment operator	Divides the left by the right operand and assigns the result to the left operand

Command/Extension	Type	Description
%=	Assignment operator	Divides the left by the right operand and assigns the remainder to the left operand
+	Arithmetic operator	Adds the operands
–	Arithmetic operator	Subtracts the right from the left operand
*	Arithmetic operator	Multiplies the operands
/	Arithmetic operator	Divides the left by the right operand
%	Arithmetic operator	Divides the left by the right operand and calculates the remainder
&&	Logical operator	Evaluates to true when both operands are true
||	Logical operator	Evaluates to true when either operand is true
!	Logical operator	Evaluates to true if the operand is false and to false if the operand is true
==	Comparison operator	Evaluates to true if the operands are equal
!=	Comparison operator	Evaluates to true if the operands are not equal
>	Comparison operator	Evaluates to true if the left operand is greater than the right operand
<	Comparison operator	Evaluates to true if the left operand is less than the right operand
>=	Comparison operator	Evaluates to true if the left operand is greater than or equal to the right operand

continued on next page

continued from previous page

Command/Extension	Type	Description
`<=`	Comparison operator	Evaluates to `true` if the left operand is less than or equal to the right operand
`+`	String operator	Combines the operands into a single string
`if`	JavaScript command	Executes a command or command block if a condition is true
`else`	JavaScript command	Executes a command or command block if the condition of an associated `if` statement is false
`parseInt()`	JavaScript function	Converts a string to an integer number
`parseFloat()`	JavaScript function	Converts a string to a floating point number
`isNaN()`	JavaScript function	Returns `true` if it's argument evaluation is `NaN`—a special value representing something that is "Not a Number"—returns false otherwise
`confirm()`	JavaScript method	Displays a message in a dialog box with OK and Cancel buttons

CHAPTER EXERCISE

1. Evaluate each of the following expressions:

   a.   7 + 5

   b.   "7" + "5"

   c.   7 == 7

   d.   7 >= 5

   e.   7 <= 7

   f.   (7 < 5) ? 7 : 5

   g.   (7 >= 5) && (5 > 5)

   h.   (7 >= 5) || (5 > 5)

2. Write the segment of a script that would ask if the user wants a greeting message and, if so, display a GIF file called `welcome.gif` and display `"Welcome to Netscape Navigator!"` in the document window following the GIF.

3. Extend Listing 3-4 so that if users answer correctly, they have the choice to answer a second question, but they get only one chance to answer the second question.

CHAPTER 4

FUNCTIONS AND OBJECTS—THE BUILDING BLOCKS OF PROGRAMS

Once you start to write more complex programs, you will quickly find the need to perform some tasks more than once during the course of a program.

This need is addressed by functions, which are similar to methods but are not attached to any particular object. As a programmer, you can create numerous functions in your programs—this helps organize the structure of your applications and makes maintaining and changing your program code easier.

In addition, functions are particularly useful in working with events and event handlers as you will learn in Chapter 5, "Events in JavaScript."

You can also use functions as the basis for creating your own objects to supplement those available to you in JavaScript.

In this chapter we will cover these topics:

- The nature of functions
- Built-in functions versus programmer-created functions
- How to define and use functions
- How to create new objects, properties, and methods
- How to use associative arrays

 **Functions**

WHAT ARE FUNCTIONS?

Functions offer the ability for programmers to group together program code that performs a specific task—or function—into a single unit that can be used repeatedly throughout a program.

Like the methods you have seen in earlier chapters, a function is defined by name and is invoked by using its name.

Also, like some of the methods you have seen before (such as `prompt()` and `confirm()`), functions can accept information in the form of arguments and can return results. JavaScript includes several built-in functions as well as methods of base objects. You have already seen these when you used `alert()`, `document.write()`, `parseInt()`, or any of the other methods and functions you have been working with. The flexibility of JavaScript, though, lies in the ability for programmers to create their own functions to supplement those available in the JavaScript specification.

USING FUNCTIONS

In order to make use of functions, you need to know how to define them, pass arguments to them, and return the results of their calculations. It is also important to understand the concept of variable scope, which governs whether a variable is available in an entire script or just within a specific function.

Defining Functions

Functions are defined using the `function` statement. The `function` statement requires a name for the function, a list of parameters—or arguments—that will be passed to the function, and a command block that defines what the function does:

```
function function_name(parameters, arguments) {
   command block
}
```

As you will notice, the naming of functions follows basically the same rules as variables: They are case sensitive, can include underscores (_), and start with a letter. The list of arguments passed to the function appears in parentheses and is separated by commas.

It is important to realize that defining a function does not execute the commands that make up the function. It is only when the function is called by name somewhere else in the script that the function is executed.

Passing Parameters

In the following function, you can see that `printName()` accepts one argument called `name`:

```
function printName(name) {
   document.write("<HR>Your Name is <B><I>");
   document.write(name);
   document.write("</B></I><HR>");
}
```

Within the function, references to `name` refer to the value passed to the function. There are several points here to note:

● Both variables and literals can be passed as arguments when calling a function.

● If a variable is passed to the function, changing the value of the parameter within the function does not change the value of the variable passed to the function.

● Parameters exist only for the life of the function—if you call the function several times, the parameters are created afresh each time you call the function, and values they held when the function last ended are not retained.

For example, if you call `printName()` with the command:

```
printName("Bob");
```

then, when `printName()` executes, the value of `name` is `"Bob"`. If you call `printName()` by using a variable for an argument:

```
var user = "John";
printName(user);
```

then `name` has the value `"John"`. If you were to add a line to `printName()` changing the value of `name`:

```
name = "Mr. " + name;
```

`name` would change, but the variable `user`, which was sent as an argument, would not change.

Note

When passing arguments to a function, two properties that can be useful in working with the arguments are created: `functionname.arguments` and `function.arguments.length`. `functionname.arguments` is an array with an entry for each argument and `functionname.argument.length` is an integer variable indicating the number of variables passed to the function. You can use these properties to produce functions that accept a variable number of arguments.

Variable Scope

This leads to a discussion of variable scope. Variable scope refers to where a variable exists.

For instance, in the example `printName()`, `name` exists only within the function `printName()`—it cannot be referred to or manipulated outside the function. It comes into existence when the function is called and ceases to exist when the function ends. If the function is called again, a new instance of `name` is created.

In addition, any variable declared using the `var` command within the function will have a scope limited to the function.

If a variable is declared outside the body of a function, it is available throughout a script—inside all functions and elsewhere.

Variables declared within a function are known as *local variables*. Variables declared outside functions and available throughout the script are known as *global variables*.

If you declare a local variable inside a function that has the same name as an existing global variable, then *inside* the function, that variable name refers to the new local variable and *not* the global variable. If you change the value of the variable inside the function, it does not affect the value of the global variable.

Returning Results

As mentioned in the previous section, functions can return results. Results are returned using the `return` statement. The `return` statement can be used to return any valid expression that evaluates to a single value. For example, in the function `cube()`,

```
function cube(number) {
   var cube = number * number * number;
   return cube;
}
```

the `return` statement will return the value of the variable `cube`. This function could just as easily have been written like this:

```
function cube(number) {
   return number * number * number;
}
```

This works because the expression `number * number * number` evaluates to a single value.

Functions in the File Header

As was mentioned in Chapter 3, "Working with Data and Information," there are compelling reasons to include function definitions inside the **HEAD** tags of the HTML file. This ensures that all functions have been *parsed* before it is possible for user events to invoke a function. This is especially relevant once you begin working with event handlers where incorrect placement of a function definition can mean an event can lead to a function call when the function has not been evaluated and Navigator doesn't know it exists. When this happens, it causes an error message to be displayed.

The term ***parsed*** refers to the process by which the JavaScript interpreter evaluates each line of script code and converts it into a pseudo-compiled bytecode (much like Java), before attempting to execute it. At this time, syntax errors and other programming mistakes that would prevent the script from running may be caught and reported to the user or programmer.

The typeof Operator

JavaScript offers an operator that we didn't discuss in the last chapter when we looked at variables, expressions, and operators. The **typeof** operator is used to identify the type of an element in JavaScript. Given an unevaluated operand (such as a variable name or a function name), the **typeof** operator returns a string identifying the type of the operand.

For instance, suppose you have the following JavaScript code:

```
var question="What is 10 x 10?";
var answer=10;
var correct=false;
function showResult(results) {
    document.write(results);
}
```

Then, **typeof question** returns **string**; **typeof answer** returns **number**; **typeof correct** returns **boolean**; and **typeof showResult** returns **function**. Other possible results returned by the **typeof** operator include **undefined** and **object**.

The **typeof** operator can be useful in determining if a function has been loaded and is ready to be called. This is especially useful in multi-frame pages where a script loaded in one frame my be trying to call a function located in another frame which hasn't completed loading.

Frames are covered in more detail in Chapter 8, "Frames, Documents, and Windows."

PUTTING FUNCTIONS TO WORK

To demonstrate the use of functions, you are going to rewrite the simple test question example you used in Listing 3.3. In order to do this, you are going to create a function that receives a question as an argument, poses the question, checks the answer, and returns an output string based on the accuracy of the user's response.

In order to do this, you need to learn the **eval()** method, which evaluates a string to a numeric value; for instance,

```
eval("10*10")
```

returns a numeric value of **100**.

Input   **Listing 4-1** Evaluating an expression with the eval() function.

```
<HTML>

<HEAD>
<TITLE>Example 4.1</TITLE>

<SCRIPT LANGUAGE="JavaScript">
<!-- HIDE FROM OTHER BROWSERS

//DEFINE FUNCTION testQuestion()
function testQuestion(question) {
  //DEFINE LOCAL VARIABLES FOR THE FUNCTION
  var answer=eval(question);
  var output="What is " + question + "?";
  var correct='<IMG SRC="correct.gif">';
  var incorrect='<IMG SRC="incorrect.gif">';

  //ASK THE QUESTION
  var response=prompt(output,"0");

  //CHECK THE RESULT
  return (response == answer) ? correct : incorrect;
}

// STOP HIDING FROM OTHER BROWSERS -->
</SCRIPT>

</HEAD<

<BODY>

<SCRIPT LANGUAGE="JavaScript">
<!-- HIDE FROM OTHER BROWSERS

//ASK QUESTION AND OUTPUT RESULTS
var result=testQuestion("10 + 10");
document.write(result);

//STOP HIDING FROM OTHER BROWSERS -->
</SCRIPT>

</BODY>

</HTML>
```

At first glance, this script may seem a little more complicated than the version used in Listing 3-3. In reality, though, it simply separates the work into logical blocks and moves most of the work into the function `testQuestion()`.

To understand the function, let's analyze the key lines.

```
function testQuestion(question) {
```

In this line, you define the function `testQuestion()` and indicate that it receives one argument, which is referred to as `question` within the function. In the case of this function, it is expected that `question` will be a string containing an arithmetic expression.

```
var answer=eval(question);
```

The first thing you do after entering the function is to declare the variable `answer` and assign to it the numeric value of the arithmetic expression contained in the string `question`. This is achieved using the `eval()` function.

```
var output="What is " + question + "?";
var correct='<IMG SRC="correct.gif">';
var incorrect='<IMG SRC="incorrect.gif">';
```

In these lines you declare several more variables. The variable `output` contains the actual question to display, which is created using the concatenation operator.

```
var response=prompt(output,"0");
```

Here you ask the question and assign the user's response to the variable `response`.

```
return (response == answer) ? correct : incorrect;
```

In this line you use the conditional operator to check the user's response. The resulting value is returned by the `return` command.

Now that you understand the function, it should be clear how you are invoking it later in the body of the HTML file. The line

```
var result=testQuestion("10 + 10");
```

calls `testQuestion()` and passes a string to it containing an arithmetic expression. The function returns a result, which is stored in the variable `result`. Then you are able to output the result using `document.write()`.

These two lines could be condensed into a single line:

```
document.write(testQuestion("10 + 10"));
```

RECURSIVE FUNCTIONS

Now that you have seen an example of how functions work, let's take a look at an application of functions called recursion.

 Recursion refers to situations in which functions call themselves. These types of functions are known as *recursive functions*.

For instance, the following is an example of a recursive function that calculates a factorial:

A factorial is a mathematical function. For example, factorial 5 (written 5!) is equal to 5×4×3×2×1 and 7! = 7×6×5×4×3×2×1.

```
function factorial(number) {
  if (number > 1) {
    return number * factorial(number - 1);
  } else {
    return number;
  }
}
```

At first glance, this function may seem strange. This function relies on the fact that the factorial of a number is equal to the number multiplied by the factorial of one less than the number. Expressed mathematically, this could be written:

```
x! = x * (x-1)!
```

In order to apply this formula, you have created a recursive function called `factorial()`. The function receives a number as an argument. Using the following `if-else` construct:

```
if (number > 1) {
  return number * factorial(number - 1);
} else {
  return number;
}
```

the function either returns a value of **1** if the argument is equal to **1**, or applies the formula and returns the number multiplied by the factorial of one less than the number.

In order to do this, it must call the function `factorial()` from within the function `factorial()`. This is where the concept of variable scope becomes extremely important. It is important to realize that when the function calls `factorial()`, a new instance of the function is being invoked, which means that a new instance of **number** is created. This continues to occur until the expression **number-1** has a value of **1**.

Recursive functions are powerful, but they can be dangerous if you don't watch out for infinite recursion. *Infinite recursion* occurs when the function is designed in such a way as to call itself forever without stopping.

At a practical level, in JavaScript, infinite recursion isn't likely to happen because of the way in which JavaScript handles some of its memory allocation. This means that deep recursions, even if they aren't infinite, may cause Navigator to crash.

It is important to note that the function `factorial()` prevents infinite recursion because the `if-else` construct ensures that eventually the function will stop calling itself once the number passed to it is equal to one. In addition, if the function is initially called with a value less than two, the function will immediately return without any recursion.

Using recursive functions, it is possible to extend the program used in Listing 4-1 so that it continues to ask the question until the user provides the correct answer, as shown in Listing 4-2.

Input   **Listing 4-2**   Using a recursive function to repeat input.

```
<HTML>

<HEAD>
<TITLE>Example 4.2</TITLE>

<SCRIPT LANGUAGE="JavaScript">
<!-- HIDE FROM OTHER BROWSERS

//DEFINE FUNCTION testQuestion()
function testQuestion(question) {
  //DEFINE LOCAL VARIABLES FOR THE FUNCTION
  var answer=eval(question);
  var output="What is " + question + "?";
  var correct='<IMG SRC="correct.gif">';
  var incorrect='<IMG SRC="incorrect.gif">';

  //ASK THE QUESTION
  var response=prompt(output,"0");

  //CHECK THE RESULT
  return (response == answer) ? correct : testQuestion(question);
}

// STOP HIDING FROM OTHER BROWSERS -->
</SCRIPT>

</HEAD<

<BODY>

<SCRIPT LANGUAGE="JavaScript">
<!-- HIDE FROM OTHER BROWSERS

//ASK QUESTION AND OUTPUT RESULTS
var result=testQuestion("10 + 10");
document.write(result);

//STOP HIDING FROM OTHER BROWSERS -->
</SCRIPT>

</BODY>

</HTML>
```

Notice that you have made only a single change to the conditional expression:

```
return (response == answer) ? correct : testQuestion(question);
```

Where you originally returned the value of the variable **incorrect** when the user provided an incorrect response, you are now returning the result of asking the question again (by calling **testQuestion()** again).

It is important to realize that this example could cause JavaScript to crash because of its memory handling problems if the user never provides the correct answer. This can be remedied by adding a counter to keep track of the number of chances the user has to provide a correct answer:

```
<HTML>

<HEAD>
<TITLE>Example 4.2</TITLE>

<SCRIPT LANGUAGE="JavaScript">
<!-- HIDE FROM OTHER BROWSERS

//DEFINE FUNCTION testQuestion()
function testQuestion(question,chances) {
  //DEFINE LOCAL VARIABLES FOR THE FUNCTION
  var answer=eval(question);
  var output="What is " + question + "?";
  var correct='<IMG SRC="correct.gif">';
  var incorrect='<IMG SRC="incorrect.gif">';

  //ASK THE QUESTION
  var response=prompt(output,"0");

  //CHECK THE RESULT
  if (chances > 1) {
    return (response == answer) ? correct : testQuestion(question,chances-1);
  } else {
    return (response == answer) ? correct : incorrect;
  }
}

// STOP HIDING FROM OTHER BROWSERS -->
</SCRIPT>

</HEAD<

<BODY>

<SCRIPT LANGUAGE="JavaScript">
<!-- HIDE FROM OTHER BROWSERS

//ASK QUESTION AND OUTPUT RESULTS
var result=testQuestion("10 + 10",3);
document.write(result);

//STOP HIDING FROM OTHER BROWSERS -->
</SCRIPT>
```

```
</BODY>

</HTML>
```

By adding the `if-else` construct when you check the user's answer, you are ensuring that you cannot enter an infinite recursion. The `if-else` construct could be replaced by a conditional expression:

```
return (response == answer) ? correct : ((chances > 1) ?
_testQuestion(question,chances-1) : incorrect);
```

What this expression says is if the user's response is correct (`response==answer` evaluates to `true`), then return the value of `correct`. Otherwise, if there are chances left (`chances > 1` evaluates to `true`), ask the question again and return the result. If there are no chances left and the answer is incorrect, return the value of the variable `incorrect`.

QUIZ 1

1. Which of the following statements is invalid for a function?
   a. Using JavaScript, you can write your own functions.
   b. Functions offer the ability for programmers to group together program code that performs a specific task.
   c. Functions only respond to events.
   d. The `function` statement is used to define a function.

2. What is a function parameter?
   a. A variable or literal argument passed to a function when it is called.
   b. A variable defined inside the function body for use inside the function.
   c. A literal used inside the function.
   d. None of the above.

3. Which of the following statements about function parameters is false?
   a. Both literals and variables can be passed as arguments when calling a function.
   b. Output parameters can be used to pass back values to the calling script.
   c. Changing the value of a parameter in a function does not change the value of the variable passed to the function.
   d. Parameters exist only for the life of the function execution.

4. Which of the following statements only apply to local variables?
   a. They go out of scope outside of the function they are defined in.
   b. They are accessible throughout the JavaScript code.
   c. If a variable is declared outside of the function, then it is not accessible inside of the function.
   d. If it is declared using the `var` command, then it is a local variable.

5. Given the following script segment, what would the two alert boxes display?

```
alert("typeof tfunc = " + typeof tfunc);
function tfunc( I ) {   };
alert("typeof tfunc = " + typeof tfunc);
```

    a. They would both display **"typeof tfunc = function"**.
    b. They would both display **"typeof tfunc = undefined"**.
    c. The first would display **"typeof tfunc = undefined function"** and the second would display **"typeof tfunc = function tfunc"**;
    d. The first would display **"typeof tfunc = undefined"** and the second would display **"typeof tfunc = function"**.

LESSON 2 Objects

BUILDING OBJECTS IN JAVASCRIPT

As you learned earlier, it is possible to use functions to build custom objects in JavaScript. In order to do this, you must be able to define an object's properties, to create new instances of objects, and to add methods to objects.

Defining an Object's Properties

Before creating a new object, it is necessary to define that object by outlining its properties. This is done by using a function that defines the name and properties of the function.

New Term   This type of function is known as a *constructor function*.

If you want to create an object type for students in a class, you could create an object named **student** with properties for **name**, **age**, and **grade**. This could be done with the function:

```
function student(name,age, grade) {
  this.name = name;
  this.age = age;
  this.grade = grade;
}
```

Notice the use of the special keyword **this**. **this** plays a special role in JavaScript and refers to the current object. You will learn more about **this** in Chapter 5, when we begin discussing event handlers.

Using this function, it is now possible to create an object using the **new** statement:

```
student1 = new student("Bob",10,75);
```

This line of JavaScript code creates an object called `student1` with three properties: `student1.name`, `student1.age`, and `student1.grade`. This is known as an *instance* of the object `student`. By creating a new object `student2` using the `new` statement,

```
student2 = new student("Jane",9,82);
```

you would be creating a new instance of the object that is independent from `student1`.

It is also possible to add properties to objects once they are created simply by assigning values to a new property. For instance, if you want to add a property containing Bob's mother's name, you could use the structure

```
student1.mother = "Susan";
```

This would add the property to `student1` but would have no effect on `student2` or future instances of the `student` object. To add the property `mother` to all instances of `student`, it would be necessary to add the property to the object definition before creating instances of the object:

```
function student(name, age, grade, mother) {
  this.name = name;
  this.age = age;
  this.grade = grade;
  this.mother = mother;
}
```

Objects as Properties of Objects

You can also use objects as properties of other objects. For instance, if you were to create an object called `grade`

```
function grade (math, english, science) {
  this.math = math;
  this.english = english;
  this.science = science;
}
```

you could then create two instances of the `grade` object for the two students:

```
bobGrade = new grade(75,80,77);
janeGrade = new grade(82,88,75);
```

 The order of arguments is important in JavaScript. In the preceding example, if Jane hasn't taken English, you would need to pass a placeholder to the function, such as zero or a string value, such as "N/A" or the empty string. The function would then need to be written to handle this eventuality.

Using these objects, you could then create the `student` objects like this:

```
student1 = new student("Bob",10,bobGrade);
student2 = new student("Jane",9,janeGrade);
```

You could then refer to Bob's Math grade as `student1.grade.math` or Jane's Science grade as `student2.grade.science`.

Adding Methods to Objects

In addition to adding properties to object definitions, you can also add a method to an object definition. Because methods are essentially functions associated with an object, first you need to create a function that defines the method you want to add to your object definition.

For instance, if you want to add a method to the **student** object to print the student's name, age, and grades to the document window, you could create a function called `displayProfile()`:

```
function displayProfile() {
   document.write("Name: " + this.name + "<BR>");
   document.write("Age: " + this.age + "<BR>");
   document.write("Mother's Name: " + this.mother + "<BR>");
   document.write("Math Grade: " + this.grade.math + "<BR>");
   document.write("English Grade: " + this.grade.english + "<BR>");
   document.write("Science Grade: " + this.grade.science + "<BR>");
}
```

 Note

Here again, you use `this` to refer to the object that is invoking the method. If you call a method as `object1.method`, then `this` refers to `object1`.

Having defined the method, you now need to change the object definition to include the method:

```
function student(name,age, grade) {
   this.name = name;
   this.age = age;
   this.grade = grade;
   this.mother = mother;
   this.displayProfile = displayProfile;
}
```

Then, you could output Bob's student profile by using the command:

```
student1.displayProfile();
```

This would produce results similar to those in Figure 4-1.

Extending Objects Dynamically

Starting with Navigator 3.0, it is possible to extend objects after they have been created with a **new** statement.

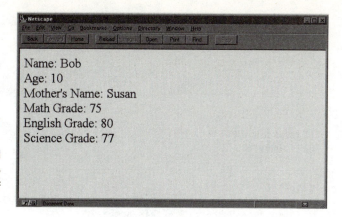

Figure 4-1
The display-
Profile() method
displays the profile
for any instance of
the student object.

Properties can be added to object definitions by setting the value of `objectName.pro-totype.propertyName`. `objectName` refers to the name of the constructor function, and `propertyName` is the name of the property or method being added to the function. For instance, if you want to add an additional method called `updateProfile()` to the `student` object definition you created earlier, you could use the command:

```
student.prototype.updateProfile = updateInfo;
```

where you have already created a function called `updateInfo()`:

```
function updateInfo() {
    this.age = prompt("Enter the correct age for " + this.name,this.age);
    this.mother = prompt("Enter the mother's name for " + this.name,this.mother);
}
```

Then, all instances of **student** that had previously been created using the **new** statement would be able to use the new method.

In the example we used above you could update the age and mother's name for Bob by using this command:

```
student1.updateProfile();
```

DEFINING YOUR OWN OBJECTS

To further demonstrate the application of objects and defining your own objects, Listing 4-3 is a program that asks the user for personnel information of an employee and then formats it for display on the screen.

In order to do this, you need to define an **employee** object, as well as a method for displaying the employee information.

Input   **Listing 4-3** Creating an employee profile.

```html
<HTML>

<HEAD>
<TITLE>Example 4.3</TITLE>

<SCRIPT LANGUAGE="JavaScript">
<!-- HIDE FROM OTHER BROWSERS

//DEFINE METHOD
function displayInfo() {
   document.write("<H1>Employee Profile: " + this.name + "</H1><HR><PRE>");
   document.writeln("Employee Number: " + this.number);
   document.writeln("Social Security Number: " + this.socsec);
   document.writeln("Annual Salary: " + this.salary);
   document.write("</PRE>");
}

//DEFINE OBJECT
function employee() {
   this.name=prompt("Enter Employee's Name","Name");
   this.number=prompt("Enter Employee Number for " + this.name,"000-000");
   this.socsec=prompt("Enter Social Security Number for " + ⇐
this.name,"000-00-0000");
   this.salary=prompt("Enter Annual Salary for " + this.name,"$00,000");
   this.displayInfo=displayInfo;
}

newEmployee=new employee();

// STOP HIDING  FROM OTHER BROWSERS -->
</SCRIPT>

</HEAD>

<BODY>
<SCRIPT LANGUAGE="JavaScript">
<!-- HIDE FROM OTHER BROWSERS

newEmployee.displayInfo();

// STOP HIDING FROM OTHER BROWSERS -->
</SCRIPT>

</BODY>

</HTML>
```

Figure 4-2
The program
prompts the user
for the employee
information.

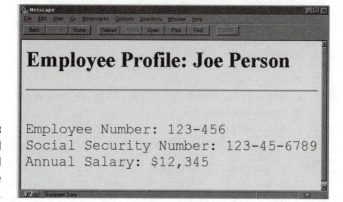

Figure 4-3
The method
you defined
displays the
formatted data.

Output

This script produces results similar to those in Figure 4-2 and 4-3.

In this example, the most noticeable variation on what you have learned is that you don't pass any arguments to the object definition function, `employee()`.

Instead, this object definition is more of a dynamic object definition in that when a new instance of the object is created, the user is prompted for all the relevant data for the properties.

Properties as Indexes

In Navigator 2.0, it was possible to refer to object properties numerically in two ways other than `objectName.propertyName`. That is, in the previous example of the **student** object, the properties of **student2** could have been referred to as:

```
student2["name"]
student2["age"]
```

and so on, or by numbers starting at zero, where

```
student2[0] == "Jane"
student2[1] == 9
```

New Term

This use of the names and numbers is known as *indexes*.

In Navigator 3.0, it is no longer possible to refer to a property both by numeric index and by name. Instead, properties can either be created as numeric indexes or names but then all subsequent references have to be the same. Numbers and names cannot be used interchangeably.

QUIZ 2

1. What two methods can be used to add a property to an object?
   a. By directly assigning a value to that object property.
   b. By using the **var** statement.
   c. By assigning a value to that object property in the constructor function for the object.
   d. By referencing the object property.

2. What is an object instance?
   a. A specific copy of an object created by the new statement.
   b. Any object reference.
   c. An object property.
   d. An object referred to by 'this'.

3. How is a method added to an object?
   a. Define the method using the keyword this in front of all variables.
   b. First define the method then set this.methodname = methodname.
   c. Just assign the method to the object.
   d. First define the method then assign the method to the object in the object's constructor function.

4. In an object constructor function, what does the this keyword refer to?
   a. All objects of the type being constructed.
   b. The instance of the object that is being constructed.
   c. It is just a placeholder used inside constructor functions.
   d. None of the above.

5. How can an object be a property of another object.
   a. This cannot be done.
   b. This can only be done with container objects.
   c. Only predefined JavaScript objects can contain other objects.
   d. Set the object property to reference another object, this will make the property be an object reference.

LESSON 3 Arrays

ARRAYS

Anyone who has programmed in other structured languages has probably encountered arrays of one sort or another and will be wondering where JavaScript's arrays are. Arrays are ordered collections of values referred to by a single variable name. For instance, if you have an array named **student**, you might have the following ordered values:

```
student[0] = "Bob"
student[1] = 10
student[2] = 75
```

Array elements are referred to by their indexes—the numbers in brackets. In JavaScript, arrays start with index zero.

Arrays in JavaScript are created using the `Array()` constructor object. You can create an array of undefined length by using the `new` keyword:

```
arrayName = new Array();
```

The length of the array changes dynamically as you assign values to the array. The length of the array is defined by the largest index number used.

For instance

```
var sampleArray = new Array();
sampleArray[49] = "50th Element";
```

creates an array with 50 elements. (Remember, indexes start at zero.)

It is also possible to define an initial length of an array by passing the length to the `Array()` object as an argument:

```
var sampleArray = new Array(100);
```

In addition, you can create an array and assign values to all its elements at the time it is defined. This is done by passing the value for all elements as arguments to the `Array()` object. For instance,

```
var sampleArray = new Array("1st Element", 2, "3rd Element);
```

creates a three-element array with the values

```
sampleArray[0] == "1st Element"
sampleArray[1] == 2
sampleArray[2] == "3rd Element"
```

As objects, arrays have several methods:

- `join()` returns all elements of the array joined together as a single string. This takes one argument: a string used as the separator between each element of the array in the final string. If the argument is omitted, `join()` uses a comma-space as the separator.

- `reverse()` reverses the order of elements in the array.

To demonstrate how arrays can be useful, Listing 4-4 builds on the personnel information example in the Listing 4-3.

In this example, you do not have the user enter the personnel information for the new employee in the same way. You present a list of information you want. The users select a number for the information they want to enter. When they are done, they select "0."

After a user finishes entering the information, the script displays the formatted employee profile.

Input   **Listing 4-4**   Creating a user menu.

```html
<HTML>

<HEAD>
<TITLE>Listing 4-4</TITLE>

<SCRIPT LANGUAGE="JavaScript">
<!-- HIDE FROM OTHER BROWSERS

//DEFINE METHOD
function displayInfo() {
  document.write("<H1>Employee Profile: " + this.data[0] + "</H1><HR><PRE>");
  document.writeln("Employee Number: " + this.data[1]);
  document.writeln("Social Security Number: " + this.data[2]);
  document.writeln("Annual Salary: " + this.data[3]);
  document.write("</PRE>");
}

//DEFINE METHOD TO GET EMPLOYEE INFORMATION
function getInfo() {
  var menu="0-Exit/1-Name/2-Emp. #/3-Soc. Sec. #/4-Salary";
  var choice=prompt(menu,"0");
  if (choice != null) {
    if ((choice < 0) || (choice > 4)) {
      alert ("Invalid choice");
      this.getInfo();
    } else {
      if (choice != "0") {
        this.data[choice-1]=prompt("Enter information","");
        this.getInfo();
      }
    }
  }
}

//DEFINE OBJECT
function employee() {
  this.data = new Array(4);
  this.displayInfo=displayInfo;
  this.getInfo=getInfo;
}

newEmployee=new employee();

// STOP HIDING FROM OTHER BROWSERS -->
</SCRIPT>

</HEAD>

<BODY>
```

```
<SCRIPT LANGUAGE="JavaScript">
<!-- HIDE FROM OTHER BROWSERS

newEmployee.getInfo();
newEmployee.displayInfo();

// STOP HIDING FROM OTHER BROWSERS -->
</SCRIPT>

</BODY>

</HTML>
```

Output This script produces a series of results similar to those in Figures 4-4, 4-5, and 4-6.

Figure 4-4
A menu in a
prompt box.

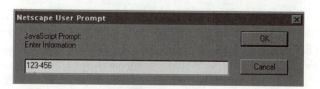

Figure 4-5
Prompting for
input.

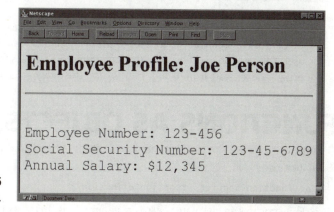

Figure 4-6
The final result.

Analysis   In this example, you can see several of the concepts you have learned in action here, including recursion and arrays.

The method `getInfo()` needs some explanation:

```
var menu="0-Exit/1-Name/2-Emp. #/3-Soc. Sec. #/4-Salary";
```

The `menu` variable contains the string that presents the choices to the user. Notice the use of the `\n` special character to create a multiline menu in a single text string.

```
var choice = prompt(menu,"0");
```

Here you present the menu to the user and ask for a choice, which is stored in the variable `choice`.

```
if (choice != null) {
    if ((choice < 0) || (choice > 4)) {
      alert ("Invalid choice");
      this.getInfo();
    } else {
      if (choice != "0") {
        this.data.[choice-1]=prompt("Enter information","");
        this.getInfo();
      }
    }
  }
```

This set of `if` statements is where the real work of the `getInfo()` method is done. The first `if` statement checks whether the user has selected Cancel. If not, then the user's choice is checked to make sure it is in range (from zero to four). If the choice is out of range, then the user is alerted, and the `getInfo()` method is called again. If the user's choice is in range, it is checked to see if the user has chosen **0** for exit. If the user doesn't select **0**, the user is prompted to enter the data he has indicated. Then the `getInfo()` method is called again to present the menu again.

You will notice the use of the `this` keyword to refer to the current object and the use of `this data [choice-1]` to refer to the array element (or property) selected by the user. You use `choice-1` because the menu presents choices from **1** to **4** to the user, but array indexes start from **0** and, in this case, the index goes up to **3**.

FUNCTIONS AS OBJECTS

Functions in JavaScript can be created as instances of the special `Function` object using the `new` keyword:

```
functionName = new Function(arglist, functionDefinition);
```

This provides an alternate way to create functions. In the example above, `arglist` is a comma-separated list of argument names, and `functionDefinition` is the JavaScript code to be executed each time the function is called. Each item in the argument list should be a string literal.

Functions defined using the `Function` object can be used in the same way as functions defined using the `function` keyword (including in event handlers) and can be called directly in expressions.

Instances of the `Function` object have two properties:

● `arguments`   An array corresponding to the arguments of the function in the order they are defined.

● `prototype`   As you learned earlier in this chapter, `prototype` can be used to add properties and methods to objects.

According to the Netscape documentation, creating functions using the `Function` object is the less efficient of the two methods of creating objects.

QUIZ 3

1. Which of the following is an invalid use of an array variable named `student`?
   a. `student["name"] = "Jerry"`
   b. `student["Jerry"] = 1`
   c. `student[1] = 9`
   d. None of the above.

2. What is an associative array?
   a. An array in which each element is associated with a string value that can also be used to reference the array element.
   b. An array that is associated with an event.
   c. An array that has object associated with it.
   d. An array that has a property name associated with it.

3. If an object is referenced as an array, what would object[0] be?
   a. The name of the object.
   b. The value of the name of the object.
   c. The first array element of the object which it the same as the first object property defined when the object was created.
   d. None of the above.

4. Given the following array element definitions:
   ```
   test["red"] = 0;
   test["green"] = 90;
   test["blue"] = 12;
   ```

   what is the value of `test["black"]`?
   a. null
   b. 0
   c. 102
   d. None of the above.

5. Given the following object definition

```
student.name = "Henry";
student.age = 112;
student.id = 1336;
```

how many array elements are there and what are they?

a. There are an unlimited number of array elements.

b. There are 6 array elements, one for each property and its value.

c. There are 3 elements, `student[0]` is `student.name`, `student[1]` is `student.age`, and `student[2]` is `student.id`.

d. There are 3 elements, one for each property, they can be in any order.

SUMMARY

Functions provide a means to define segments of code that can be used more than once in a program. Like methods, which are part of objects, functions are defined by names, can be passed arguments, and can return results.

Variable scope, whether a variable exists locally to a function or globally for the entire program, is an important concept in dealing with functions.

Recursive functions are functions that call themselves one or more times. Recursion is a powerful tool, but it needs to be used carefully to avoid infinite recursion, which occurs when a function repeatedly calls itself without ever ending. With the current implementation of JavaScript, infinite recursion can't really happen because memory handling shortcomings mean that Navigator will crash when recursion gets too deep.

Functions are also used to define the properties and objects that make up user-defined methods. Using the `new` keyword, it is possible to create multiple instances of an object that all exist independently.

Arrays provide a mechanism to group together data into ordered collections. Index numbers provide a means to access individual elements in an array.

If you have made it to the end of this chapter, you are making progress because both recursion and functions and objects are advanced topics.

To see expressions, variables, functions, and objects in action, jump to Appendix C, Lab 1, Dave Eisenberg's Calendar.

In Chapter 5, you begin to work with events and event handlers which will allow you to design programs that interact with the user in a sophisticated way.

COMMANDS AND EXTENSIONS REVIEW

Command/Extension	Type	Description
function	JavaScript keyword	Declares a function
new	JavaScript keyword	Creates a new instance of an object
eval()	JavaScript method	Evaluates a string to a numeric value
this	JavaScript keyword	Refers to the current object
type of	JavaScript operator	Returns a string indicating the type of the operand

CHAPTER EXERCISE

1. Write the object definition for an object called car with four properties: model, make, year, and price.

2. If you have an object defined as follows

```
function house(address,rooms,owner) {
    this.address = address;
    this.rooms = rooms;
    this.owner = owner;
}
```

and you create two instances of the house object

```
house1 = new house("10 Maple St.",10,"John");
house2 = new house("15 Sugar Rd.",12,"Mary");
```

then, what would be the value of the following:

a.   house1.rooms

b.   house2.owner

c.   house1["address"]

3. Create a function that calculates the value of x to the power of y. For
   instance, if you have a function called `power()` and you issue the command

   ```
   value = power(10,4);
   ```

   then `power()` should return the value of 10 to the power of 4, or 10 * 10
   * 10 * 10.

Note

If the notation **x^y** refers to **x** to the power of **y**, then it will be helpful in writing this
function to realize that **x^y = x * x^(y–1)**.

CHAPTER 5

EVENTS IN JAVASCRIPT

Now that you know how to organize programs using functions and build your own objects, you are ready to take a look at events.

Events provide the basis of interacting with the Navigator window and the currently loaded document. Events are triggered in the browser primarily by user actions, including finishing loading a page, entering data in a form, and clicking on form buttons.

Using event handlers built into JavaScript, you can write functions to perform specific actions based on the occurrence of selected events.

In this chapter, we will cover:

- What events are

- What event handlers are

- How to use event handlers

● How to emulate events

● The load and unload events and the onLoad and onUnload event handlers

● The basics of using events to interact with forms

 Events

WHAT ARE EVENTS?

Events are signals generated when specific actions occur. JavaScript is aware of these signals, and scripts can be built to react to these events.

Examples of events include when a user clicks on a hypertext link, changes data in a form entry field, or when a page finishes loading. A complete list of the events available in JavaScript appears in Table 5-1.

Event	Description
abort	Occurs when the user cancels loading of an image
blur	Occurs when input focus is removed from a form element (when the user clicks outside a field) or focus is removed from a window
click	Occurs when the user clicks on a link or form element
change	Occurs when the value of a form field is changed by the user
error	Occurs when an error happens during loading of a document or image
focus	Occurs when input focus is given to a form element or a window
load	Occurs when a page is loaded into Navigator
mouseout	Occurs when the user moves the pointer off of a link or clickable area of an imagemap
mouseover	Occurs when the user moves the pointer over a hypertext link
reset	Occurs when the user clears a form using the reset button
select	Occurs when the user selects a form element's field
submit	Occurs when a form is submitted (i.e., when the user clicks on a submit button)
unload	Occurs when the user leaves a page

Table 5-1 *Events in JavaScript.*

Input focus refers to the act of clicking on or in a form element or field. This can be done by clicking in a text field or by tabbing between text fields.

WHAT ARE EVENT HANDLERS?

In order to take advantage of events in JavaScript, it is necessary to use event handlers. Event handlers are scripts, in the form of attributes of specific HTML tags, which you as the programmer can write.

The event handlers you write are executed when the specified events occur. The basic format of an event handler is

```
<HTML_TAG OTHER_ATTRIBUTES eventHandler="JavaScript Program">
```

While any JavaScript statements, methods, or functions can appear inside the quotation marks of an event handler, typically, the JavaScript script that makes up the event handler is actually a call to a function defined in the header of the document or a single JavaScript command. Essentially, though, anything that appears inside a command block (inside curly braces {}) can appear between the quotation marks.

For instance, if you have a form with a text field and want to call the function `checkField()` whenever the value of the text field changes, you could define your text field as follows:

```
<INPUT TYPE="text" onChange="checkField(this)">
```

 The **onChange** event handler is one of many event handlers available in JavaScript. **onChange** and other event handlers are discussed in more depth later in this chapter.

Nonetheless, the entire code for the function could appear in quotation marks rather than a function call:

```
<INPUT TYPE="text" onChange="
  if (parseInt(this.value) <= 5) {
    alert('Please enter a number greater than 5.');
  }
">
```

To separate multiple commands in an event handler, use semicolons, as shown in the following lines:

```
<INPUT TYPE="text" onChange="
  alert('Thanks for the entry.');
  confirm('Do you want to continue?');
">
```

The advantage of using functions as event handlers, however, is that you can use the same event handler code for multiple items in your document and (as you saw earlier in Chapter 4, "Functions and Objects—The Building Blocks of Programs") functions make your code easier to read and understand.

For instance, you may have a form with several text entry fields and in each, the user can only enter numbers. You could use an event handler to check the value of any field if the content changes. By having a single function to check the value of a field, you don't have to write the complete code in the event handler for each text field.

`this` Keyword

Notice in the examples in the preceding section that you used the `this` keyword, which you first encountered when you learned to build your own objects in Chapter 4. The `this` keyword refers to the current object. In the case of

```
<INPUT TYPE="text" onChange="checkField(this)">
```

this refers to the current field object. In JavaScript, forms are objects and, as you'll learn in Chapter 6, "Creating Interactive Forms," they have objects for each element as properties. These form elements include text fields, checkboxes, radio buttons, buttons, and selection lists.

Which Event Handlers Can Be Used?

The names of event handlers are directly connected to the events introduced earlier in the chapter. For instance, the `click` event is associated with the `onClick` event handler, and the `load` event with the `onLoad` event handler.

Table 5-2 outlines which window and form elements have event handlers available to them. All of these elements are dealt with later in this book when we cover forms, the `document` object, and the `window` object (see Chapter 8, "Frames, Documents, and Windows").

Object	Event Handlers Available
Selection list	onBlur, onChange, onFocus
Text element	onBlur, onChange, onFocus, onSelect
Textarea element	onBlur, onChange, onFocus, onSelect
Button element	onClick
Checkbox	onClick
Radio button	onClick
Hypertext link	onClick, onMouseOver, onMouseOut
Clickable imagemap area	onMouseOver, onMouseOut
Reset button	onClick
Submit button	onClick
Document	onLoad, onUnload, onError

Object	Event Handlers Available
Window	onLoad, onUnload, onBlur, onFocus
Framesets	onBlur, onFocus
Form	onSubmit, onReset
Image	onLoad, onError, onAbort

Table 5-2 *Event handlers in JavaScript.*

EMULATING EVENTS

In addition to event handlers, it is possible to emulate events. This can prove particularly useful to submit a form without requiring the user to click on a submit button or to force the input focus into a particular form field based on user actions.

For instance, if a clothing company has on its Web site an on-line order form for ordering designer clothes and it wants to ensure that the users provide a name, address, phone number, and fax number before sending the order to the company's server for processing, then using event emulation could be useful.

When a user fills in the form and clicks on the Order button, a JavaScript script could then check whether the form is correctly filled out. If it is, then it could emulate a **submit** event to cause the content of the form to be sent to the company's server.

On the other hand, if there is a missing piece of information, the script could alert the user and then emulate a **focus** event to put input focus into the text field in question.

The following list outlines the event methods available in JavaScript.

- `blur()`
- `click()`
- `focus()`
- `reset()`
- `select()`
- `submit()`

The `select()`, `focus()`, and `blur()` methods display inconsistent behavior on different platforms—especially in Navigator 2. For instance, on Windows 95, `blur()` removes focus from a field but will leave the cursor displayed in the field even though users won't be able to enter information into the text field.

It is important to note that events generated with these methods do invoke their corresponding event handlers. This can lead to infinite loops, as illustrated in the following script:

Don't try to run this code! It is for illustration purposes *only*.

```
<HTML>

<HEAD>
<TITLE>Events</TITLE>

<SCRIPT>
<!-- HIDE FROM OTHER BROWSERS

function react(field) {

  alert("Please Enter a Value");
  field.focus();

}

// STOP HIDING FROM OTHER BROWSERS -->
</SCRIPT>

</HEAD>

<BODY>

<FORM METHOD=POST>
<INPUT TYPE=text NAME=stuff onFocus="react(this);">

</FORM>

</BODY>

</HTML>
```

You can see that because **field.focus()** invokes the **onFocus** event handler, you face a situation of infinite recursion with **react()** being continually called until it caused Navigator 2 to crash.

1. What is an event in JavaScript?
    a. The execution of a JavaScript statement
    b. A user-generated action
    c. A signal generated when an action occurs
    d. A system-generated signal

2. In JavaScript, what is an event handler?
    a. A script that is executed when an event is signaled
    b. A function that generates events

    c. A function that traps all events

    d. A statement that assigns a function to an event

3. What does the `this` keyword refer to?

    a. It refers to the current document.

    b. It refers to the current object in a script.

    c. It refers to the Navigator object.

    d. None of the above.

4. Which of the following event handlers are not valid for a selection list?

    a. `onBlur`

    b. `onChange`

    c. `onFocus`

    d. `onClick`

5. How can an event be emulated in a script?

    a. By asking the user to click on a button.

    b. By calling an event method such as `click()`.

    c. By resetting the event handler.

    d. This cannot be done.

LESSON 2 Event Handlers and Forms

USING THE onLoad AND onUnload EVENT HANDLERS

The first events you will learn to work with are `load` and `unload`. The `load` event is generated when a page has completed loading. Likewise, the `unload` event occurs when the user exits a page.

The `onLoad` and `onUnload` event handlers enable you to script JavaScript program code to execute at these times. The `onLoad` event handler, for instance, enables you to be sure a page, including associated graphics, has loaded completely before executing the event handler.

This ability to control the timing of certain actions is important. For instance, if you want an alert message to appear after a page has loaded, it would be simple to place a script at the end of the HTML file. However, it is still possible for the alert box to appear before the page, particularly in-line graphics, has completely loaded and been displayed on the screen.

The `onLoad` event solves that problem. Similarly, `onUnload` enables a script to be executed before a new page loads.

The `onLoad` and `onUnload` events are used as an attribute of the `BODY` HTML tag. For instance, in this line

```
<BODY onLoad="hello()" onUnload="goodbye()">
```

the function `hello()` is executed after the page is loaded and `goodbye()` is called when the page is exited.

In Listing 5-1, you simply generate a welcome message after a page has loaded and generate a farewell message when the user decides to move on to another page.

 Listing 5-1 Using the `onLoad` and `onUnload` event handlers.

```
<HTML>

<HEAD>
<TITLE>Example 5.1</TITLE>
</HEAD>

<BODY onLoad="alert('Welcome to my page!');"
  onUnload="alert('Goodbye! Sorry to see you go!');">


<IMG SRC="title.gif">

</BODY>

</HTML>
```

Output This script produces results similar to Figure 5-1.

This script provides a simple example of how event handlers are used.

Analysis Once the page has completed loading, the `onLoad` event handler causes the welcome alert dialog box to be displayed. Then, when the user leaves the page, such as by opening another URL, the good-bye dialog box is displayed by the `onUnload` event handler.

You could expand and personalize this script as you did in using the `prompt()` method in the "Welcome to Netscape Navigator 2!" examples earlier:

```
<HTML>

<HEAD>
<TITLE>Example 5.1</TITLE>

<SCRIPT LANGUAGE="JavaScript">
<!-- HIDE FROM OTHER BROWSERS

var name = "";

// STOP HIDING FROM OTHER BROWSERS -->
</SCRIPT>
```

Figure 5-1
The `onLoad` event
handler generates
this alert box.

```
</HEAD>

<BODY onLoad="
          name = prompt('Enter Your Name:','Name');
          alert('Greetings ' + name + ', welcome to my page!');"
      onUnload=" alert('Goodbye  ' + name + ', sorry to see you go!');">

<IMG SRC="title.gif">

</BODY>

</HTML>
```

Likewise, you could use functions for this script to make it easier to read:

```
<HTML>

<HEAD>
<TITLE>Example 5.1</TITLE>

<SCRIPT LANGUAGE="JavaScript">
<!-- HIDE FROM OTHER BROWSERS

// DEFINE GLOBAL VARIABLE
var name = "";

function hello() {
  name = prompt('Enter Your Name:','Name');
  alert('Greetings ' + name + ', welcome to my page!');
}

function goodbye() {
  alert('Goodbye ' + name + ', sorry to see you go!');

}

// STOP HIDING FROM OTHER BROWSERS -->
</SCRIPT>

</HEAD>

<BODY onLoad="hello();"  onUnload="goodbye();">


<IMG SRC="title.gif">

</BODY>

</HTML>
```

WEB-HOPPING WITH
`window.open()`

In this example, you take a closer look at using the `onLoad` event handler for a more complex task. You are going to produce a random page. That is, when the user comes to the page, a `Please Wait...Selecting Page` message is displayed and shortly after that, a randomly selected site from the Internet is loaded in a new window. In Listing 5-2, the program chooses from a list of five possible sites to jump to.

In order to achieve this, you need to use a new method: `window.open()`. The `window.open()` method takes two required arguments:

```
window.open("URL","window name")
```

The `window.open()` method is covered in more detail in Chapter 8, where we also discuss a third argument available for the `window.open()` method. For this example, you need to ensure that the window you open the URL in is the same one your message appeared in. Because you don't know how many windows are currently open when the user opens your Web page, you will open both the message and the subsequent URL in a new window by using `window.open("URL","new_window_name")`.

| Input | **Listing 5-2** A random page selector. |

```html
<HTML>

<HEAD>
<TITLE>Example 5.2</TITLE>

<SCRIPT LANGUAGE="JavaScript">
<!-- HIDE FROM OTHER BROWSERS

function urlList(a,b,c,d,e) {
   // DEFINE FIVE-ELEMENT OBJECT
   this[0] = a;
   this[1] = b;
   this[2] = c;
   this[3] = d;
   this[4] = e;
}

function selectPage(list) {
   // SELECT RANDOM PAGE
   var today = new Date();
   var page = today.getSeconds() % 5;


   // OPEN PAGE
   window.open(list[page],"Random_Page");

}
```

```
// DEFINE SELECTION LIST
choices = new urlList("http://www.yahoo.com",
                      "http://www.cnn.com",
                      "http://www.dataphile.com.hk",
                      "http://home.netscape.com",
                      "http://www.landegg.org/landegg");

// STOP HIDING FROM OTHER BROWSERS -->
</SCRIPT>

</HEAD>

<BODY onLoad = "selectPage(choices);">
<H1>
<HR>
Please Wait ... Selecting Page.
<HR>
</H1>
</BODY>

</HTML>
```

Analysis In this example you learn several useful techniques. The script is built out of two functions and a main body of JavaScript code. The function `urlList()` is an object constructor used to build an array of five URL strings. It takes five arguments and builds a five-element array.

You will notice that you don't use any property names in defining the object, but instead use numeric indexes to reference each of the five properties. This is done because you will only be using numeric references throughout the script to access the URLs in the array.

The `selectPage()` function is a little more complex. The function generates a pseudo-random number by calculating the number of seconds modulo five. This produces an integer in the range of zero to four:

```
var today = new Date();
var page = today.getSeconds() % 5;
```

Note In Navigator 3.0, JavaScript includes a built-in method to create a random number. `Math.random()` returns a number between zero and one. In this way, the random number from zero to four could be selected with `var page = Math.floor(Math.random() * 5)`. The `Math.floor()` method rounds down to the closest integer. This method is discussed in more detail in Chapter 10.

This number is then used in the command `window.open(list[page],"Random_Page")` to open the selected page in a new window called `Random_Page`.

Following the two functions, you define the five sites you have to choose from and store them in an array called `choices`. You use the constructor function `urlList()` to create the array.

Finally, the script contains a good example of using the **onLoad** event handler. The message **Please Wait... Selecting Page.** is displayed in the original browser window and then **selectPage()** is called from the event handler. For users on slower dial-up connections, the message may display for a few seconds, and users on fast direct connections may barely have time to see the message.

RESETTING EVENT HANDLERS

Starting with Navigator 3.0, it is possible to explicitly reset event handlers in a script. That is, it is possible to change the expression to be evaluated when an event occurs. This is possible when the new expression to be evaluated takes the form of a function call. For instance, if the **onClick** event handler in the **<INPUT>** tag of the form **thisForm** is defined as

```
<INPUT TYPE=button NAME="thisButton" onClick="firstFunction()">
```

then a script could subsequently change the event handler to call **secondFunction()** by assigning the function name to **document.thisForm.thisButton.onclick**:

```
document.thisForm.thisButton.onclick = secondFunction;
```

Subsequent clicks on the button would launch **secondFunction()** instead of **firstFunction()**.

Note that the event handlers are referred to entirely in lowercase within a JavaScript script (for example, **document.thisForm.thisButton.onclick**). They can still be referred to in upper-lowercase combinations inside HTML tags: **<INPUT TYPE=button NAME="this.button" onClick="firstFunction()">**.

EVENTS AND FORMS

Now that you understand the basics of events, let's take a look at working with forms. Today, most JavaScript programmers are using forms and event handlers to produce complex applications. The events generated by forms provide a fairly complete set of tools for reacting to user actions in forms.

Common Form Events

The most common events used for processing forms are the **focus**, **blur**, and **change** events with their corresponding event handlers **onFocus**, **onBlur**, and **onChange**. Using these events, it is possible for a program to keep track of when a user moves between fields in a form and when he or she changes the value of an input field.

Other Form Events

There are other events available in forms, which we will cover in Chapter 6 when we take a detailed look at working with forms. These include `click` and `submit` with their corresponding `onClick` and `onSubmit` event handlers.

Using Event Handlers with Form Tags

Event handlers are included as attributes of form and field tags. For instance, the following tag defines a text input field with three event handlers.

```
<INPUT TYPE=text NAME="test" VALUE="test"
       onBlur="alert('Thank You!');"
       onChange="check(this);">
```

When the user moves the focus out of the field by clicking anywhere outside the field (or using the tab button where there are multiple text fields in a form), an alert dialog box with the message `Thank You!` is displayed.

When the value of the field is changed, the function `check()` is called. This function would be defined elsewhere in the HTML page—probably in the header. Note the use of the `this` keyword to pass the current field object to the function.

You first saw the `this` keyword in Chapter 4, when you learned to build constructor functions. The `this` keyword refers to the current object. In the case of an event handler, `this` refers to the object the event handler applies to. For instance, in a form field definition, `this` refers to the object for the form element (which we discuss in Chapter 6 in detail). You can then refer to properties and methods for the current object as `this.methodName()` or `this.propertyName`.

AN INTERACTIVE CALCULATOR

In this example, you will use event handlers and text input fields to produce a simple calculator. You will use a form that consists of two fields: one for the user to enter a mathematical expression and another for the results to be displayed.

If the user moves the focus into the results field, a prompt dialog box is displayed asking the user for a mathematical expression which is then displayed in the entry field with the evaluated result in the results field.

You already have learned all the methods, properties, and event handlers necessary to produce the script in Listing 5-3.

Input

Listing 5-3 Using event handlers to create a JavaScript calculator.

```
<HTML>

<HEAD>
<TITLE>Example 5.3</TITLE>
```

continued on next page

continued from previous page

```
<SCRIPT LANGUAGE="JavaScript">
<!-- HIDE FROM OTHER BROWSERS

function calculate(form) {

   form.results.value = eval(form.entry.value);

}

function getExpression(form) {

   form.entry.blur();
   form.entry.value = prompt("Please enter a JavaScript mathematical ⇐
expression","");
   calculate(form);

}


// STOP HIDING FROM OTHER BROWSERS -->
</SCRIPT>

</HEAD>

<BODY>

<FORM METHOD=POST>
Enter a JavaScript mathematical expression:
<INPUT TYPE=text NAME="entry" VALUE=""
        onFocus="getExpression(this.form);">
<BR>
The result of this expression is:
<INPUT TYPE=text NAME="results" VALUE=""
        onFocus="this.blur();">

</FORM>

</BODY>

</HTML>
```

Analysis   There are several techniques employed in this script that are worth noting. In the HTML form, you have two fields, each with a single event handler. The entry field has an `onFocus` event handler which calls the function `getExpression()`, which handles the input of the expression. Notice that the function is passed `this.form` as an argument. Where this refers to the object for the current field in the HTML form, `this.form` refers to the object for the form containing the current field.

The second field's `onFocus` event handler calls `this.blur()`, which immediately removes focus so that the user cannot alter the contents of the field. Remember that on some platforms, the cursor will actually appear in the field, but the user will be unable to enter information.

The `getExpression()` function takes a single form object as an argument. The first thing it does is remove focus from the entry field. You do this so you don't get into an infinite loop with the prompt dialog box. If you don't, then focus is removed from the field when the dialog box appears and returns to the field when the dialog box closes. This triggers another `focus` event and would invoke the event handler again.

After you remove focus from the entry field, you prompt the user for an expression and store the results in the entry field to display them. Then you call the function `calculate()` and pass it the `form` object.

The `calculate()` function uses the `eval()` function to calculate the result of the expression in the entry field and displays the result in the appropriate field in the form. Throughout both functions, you will notice that you can refer to particular fields in a form as properties of the `form` object:

`formObjectName.fieldname`

Likewise, you can directly address, and change, the value of a field by using its value property (remember that while fields are properties of the `form` object, they are objects in their own right with properties of their own):

`formObjectName.fieldname.value`

It is also important to realize that with JavaScript, authors often want to create forms that actually do not submit any data back to the server with the `ACTION` attribute of the `FORM` tag. For instance, a JavaScript application may implement a simple currency calculator that uses HTML forms for its interface. All calculations and displaying of the results are done by a JavaScript script, and the contents of the forms never need to be sent to the server.

To accommodate this use of forms, it is sufficient to have no attributes in the `FORM` tag or to simply have the `METHOD=POST` attribute without an `ACTION` attribute in the `FORM` tag.

1. What is the `onLoad` event handler used for?
   a. It is used to load an HTML page.
   b. It is used to perform actions before a page is loaded.
   c. It is used to perform actions after a page is loaded.
   d. It is to load and unload HTML pages.

2. What is the `onUnload` event handler used for?
   a. It is used to unload an HTML page.
   b. It is used to prevent a page from being unloaded.
   c. It is used to perform actions after a page is unloaded.
   d. It is used to perform actions before a page is unloaded.

3. Which of the following is not a JavaScript method to emulate an event?
   a. `submit()`
   b. `focus()`
   c. `load()`
   d. `click()`

4. Which event handler(s) would you use to keep track of when a user moves between fields in a form?
   a. `onLoad()` and `onUnload()`
   b. `onFocus()` and `onBlur()`
   c. `onChange()`
   d. `focus` and `blur`

5. Which of the following would assign a blur event handler named `notice` to a field in a form?
   a. `form.fieldname.blur = notice;`
   b. `form.fieldname.notice = notice;`
   c. `<INPUT TYPE=text onBlur="notice(this)";>`
   d. `<INPUT TYPE=text onNotice="notice(this)";>`

SUMMARY

In this chapter, you have made a big step toward being able to write the type of interactive Web pages and scripts that JavaScript is widely used for today.

You learned about events and event handlers. Event handlers react to actions by the user or events generated by the browser. Scripts can also emulate many events such as the `click()` method and `submit()` method.

In particular, you used the `onLoad` and `onUnload` event handlers to react to the loading of the page and the user's opening another URL. You also began to look at events in relationship to HTML forms and learned to use `onFocus`, `onBlur`, and `onChange`.

In Chapter 6, you look at the `form` object in more detail and work more with the events and event handlers in relationship to forms.

COMMANDS AND EXTENSIONS REVIEW

Command/ Extension	Type	Description
`blur()`	JavaScript method	Removes focus from a specified object

Command/ Extension	Type	Description
click()	JavaScript method	Emulates a mouse click on an object
focus()	JavaScript method	Emulates the user focusing on a particular form field
reset()	JavaScript method	Emulates the user clicking on the Reset button of a form
submit()	JavaScript method	Emulates a click on the Submit button of a form
select()	JavaScript method	Selects the input area of a particular form field
onAbort	Event handler	Specifies JavaScript code to execute when the user cancels the loading of an image
onLoad	Event handler	Specifies JavaScript code to execute when a page finishes loading
onUnload	Event handler	Specifies JavaScript code to execute when the user opens a new URL
Math.random()	JavaScript method	Generates a random number between 0 and 1
Math.sqrt()	JavaScript method	Calculates the square root of a number
window.open()	JavaScript method	Opens a URL in a named window or frame
Math.round()	JavaScript method	Rounds a floating-point value to the closest integer
onFocus	Event handler	Specifies JavaScript code to execute when the user gives focus to a form field or a window
onBlur	Event handler	Specifies JavaScript code to execute when the user removes focus from a form field or a window

continued on next page

continued from previous page

Command/ Extension	Type	Description
onMouseOut	Event handler	Specifies JavaScript code to execute when the user moves the mouse off a link or click-able area of an imagemap
onMouseOver	Event handler	Specifies JavaScript code to execute when the user moves the mouse over a link or click-able area of an imagemap
onError	Event handler	Specifies JavaScript code to execute when the loading of a document or image gener-ates an error
onChange	Event handler	Specifies JavaScript code to execute when the user changes the value of a form field

CHAPTER EXERCISE

1. Which of the following are legitimate uses of event handlers?

   a. `<BODY onClick="doSomething();">`

   b. `<INPUT TYPE=text onFocus="doSomething();">`

   c. `<INPUT TYPE=textarea onLoad="doSomething();">`

   d. `<BODY onUnload="doSomething();">`

   e. `<FORM onLoad="doSomething();">`

   f. `<FORM onSubmit="doSomething();">`

2. What happens with the following script?

```
<HTML>

<HEAD>
<TITLE>Exercise 5.2</TITLE>
```

```
<SCRIPT LANGUAGE="JavaScript">
<!-- HIDE FROM OTHER BROWSERS

var name = "";

function welcome() {

  name = prompt("Welcome to my page! What's Your Name?","name");

}

function farewell() {

  alert("Goodbye " + name + ". Thanks for visiting my page.");

}

// STOP HIDING FROM OTHER BROWSERS -->
</SCRIPT>

</HEAD>

<BODY onLoad="welcome();" onUnload="farewell();";>

<IMG SRC="welcome.gif">

</BODY>

</HTML>
```

3. Create an HTML page and JavaScript script that include a form with three input fields. The relationship of the value of the fields is that the second field is twice the value of the first field, and the third field is the square of the first field.

If a user enters a value in the second or third field, the script should calculate the appropriate value in the other fields.

To make this script easier, you will probably want to use the `Math.sqrt()` method, which returns the square root of the argument passed to it.

CHAPTER 6

CREATING INTERACTIVE FORMS

Working with forms is the cornerstone of many of the JavaScript programs currently available on the World Wide Web. From simple spreadsheets to conversion calculators and color-pickers, many scripts use forms and their associated properties, methods, and event handlers to produce sophisticated interactive programs.

In order to effectively use forms in JavaScript, you need to understand the `form` object and its properties and methods and to have a firm command of the events generated by different form elements.

In this chapter, you will learn this through the following topics:

- The `form` object, its properties and methods
- Event handlers for form elements
- More about the `Math` object
- The `forms[]` array
- The `elements[]` array
- Limitations of event handlers

The `form` Object and Its Properties

THE `form` OBJECT

The `form` object is one of the most heavily used objects in JavaScript scripts written for Navigator. As a programmer, by using the `form` object, you have at your disposal information about the elements in a form and their values and can alter many of these values as needed.

A separate instance of the `form` object is created for each form in a document. As you learn later in the section about the `forms[]` array, forms all have a numeric index. They can also be referred to by name.

Properties of the `form` Object

Table 6-1 outlines the properties available with the `form` object.

Property	Description
`action`	String containing the value of the ACTION attribute of the FORM tag.
`elements`	Array containing an entry for each element in the form (such as checkboxes, text fields, and selection lists).
`encoding`	String containing the MIME type used for encoding the form contents sent to the server. Reflects the ENCTYPE attribute of the FORM tag.
`name`	String containing the value of the NAME attribute of the FORM tag.
`target`	String containing the name of the window targeted by a form submission.

Table 6-1 *Properties of the `form` object.*

As you learn later in the section on the `elements[]` array, each of the elements of the form is itself an object with associated properties and methods. Elements can be referred to by name, as well as through their numeric index in the `elements[]` array.

The action *Property*

With this property, you can ascertain the action specified in the form definition. For instance, in a form defined with the following:

```
<FORM METHOD=POST ACTION="/cgi-bin/test.pl">
```

the `action` property has a value of `"/cgi-bin/test.pl"`.

The elements *Property*

This property is covered in more depth later, in the section about the `elements[]` array.

The encoding *Property*

The `encoding` property reflects the MIME type, which is used to encode the data submitted from a form to the server. In practical terms, this means that the property reflects the `ENCTYPE` attribute of the `FORM` tag, and you can set the encoding of a form by changing the value of this property.

This is useful when you want to upload a file to be processed by a CGI script on the server. More details about form-based file upload are available in the *Internet Engineering Task Force's Request for Comments*, document number 1867, at the following site:

```
http://www.ics.uci.edu/pub/ietf/html/rfc1867.txt
```

The name *Property*

This property provides the programmer with the name specified in the form definition. In a form defined with the tag

```
<FORM METHOD=POST ACTION="/cgi-bin/test.pl" NAME="thisform">
```

the `name` property has a value of `"thisform"`.

Using named forms is especially useful in documents with multiple forms, where the JavaScript scripts must work with all the forms in the document.

The target *Property*

The `target` property is similar to the `action` and `name` properties and makes the content of the `TARGET` attribute available to the programmer. In the `FORM` definition

```
<FORM METHOD=POST ACTION="/cgi-bin/test.pl" NAME="thisform" TARGET="thatframe">
```

the `target` property has a value of `"thatframe"`.

Note

The **TARGET** attribute is particularly useful in the context of frames, which we discuss in Chapter 8, "Frames, Documents, and Windows."

It is possible to dynamically change the target of a form by assigning a new value to the **target** property. In the preceding example, the target could be changed from **thatframe** to **anotherframe** by using

```
document.thisform.target = "anotherframe";
```

It is important to note that target can only be assigned a string literal. It cannot be assigned an expression or a variable.

Methods of the `form` Object

There is only one method available with the **form** object: **submit()**. As mentioned in Chapter 5, "Events in JavaScript," this method emulates a click on the Submit button of a form without invoking the **onSubmit** event handler.

For instance, in the following script, the form has no Submit button and can be submitted when the user enters the correct value in the text field. The **onSubmit** event handler, which returns **false**, ensures that the form is not submitted if the user hits return in the text entry field.

```
<HTML>

<HEAD>
<TITLE>submit() Example</TITLE>

<SCRIPT LANGUAGE="JavaScript">
<!-- HIDE FROM OTHER BROWSERS

function checkValue(form) {

   if (form.answer.value == "100")
     form.submit();
   else
     form.answer.value = "";

}

// STOP HIDING FROM OTHER BROWSERS -->
</SCRIPT>

</HEAD>

<BODY>

<FORM METHOD=POST ACTION="/cgi-bin/correct.pl" onSubmit="return false;">
What is 10 * 10? <INPUT TYPE="text" NAME="answer"
_onChange="checkValue(this.form);">
</FORM>
```

```
</BODY>

</HTML>
```

Event Handlers for the form Object

Just as it has only one method, the form object has only a single event handler associated with it: onSubmit. This event handler is invoked when the user submits a form. For instance, in the following script, when the user submits the form, she is thanked for doing so.

```
<HTML>

<HEAD>
<TITLE>onSubmit Example</TITLE>
</HEAD>

<BODY>
<FORM METHOD=POST ACTION="/cgi-bin/test.pl"
_onSubmit="alert('Thanks for taking the test.');">
What is 10 * 10? <INPUT TYPE="text" NAME="answer">
<BR>

<INPUT TYPE="submit">
</FORM>
</BODY>

</HTML>
```

1. What is the action property of a form used for?
   a. It identifies the JavaScript to execute before submitting the form.
   b. To specify the program or script that accepts the contents of the form for processing.
   c. To identify the server to submit the form to.
   d. None of the above.

2. What is the name property of a form?
   a. The name of the target window for the form.
   b. The name of the server to submit the form to.
   c. The name used to identify the form.
   d. The name of the forms event handler.

3. What is the target property used for?
   a. To identify the target server to submit the form to.
   b. To identify the forms target window.

    c. To identify the window targeted by the form output.

    d. To identify the window to submit the form to.

4. The `form` object has only one method, which is

    a. `focus()`

    b. `click()`

    c. `submit()`

    d. `select()`

5. The `form` object has which of the following event handlers?

    a. `onSubmit`

    b. `onClick, onSubmit`

    c. `onLoad, onUnload`

    d. `onChange, onFocus, onSelect`

LESSON 2   Form Elements

WORKING WITH FORM ELEMENTS

Forms are made up of a variety of elements that enable users to provide information. Traditionally, the content (or value) of these elements is passed to programs on the server through an interface known as the Common Gateway Interface, or CGI for short.

Using JavaScript, though, you can write scripts into your HTML documents to work with form elements and their values. You already saw a basic example of this in Chapter 5, in Listing 5.3 where you produced an extremely simple calculator that calculated the value of a JavaScript expression and displayed the result.

In this section, you will take a look at each type of form element in detail and see what properties, methods, and event handlers are available for each.

Table 6-2 outlines the elements that make up forms. Each element has a corresponding object.

TABLE 6-2

Form Element	Description
`button`	A new element that provides a button other than a submit or reset button (`<INPUT TYPE="button">`)
`checkbox`	A checkbox (`<INPUT TYPE="checkbox">`)
`FileUpload`	A file upload element that allows the user to provide a file as input for a form submission (`<INPUT TYPE="file">`)
`hidden`	A hidden field (`<INPUT TYPE="hidden">`)
`password`	A password text field in which each keystroke appears as an asterisk (*) (`<INPUT TYPE="password">`)

Form Element	Description
radio	A radio button (`<INPUT TYPE="radio">`)
reset	A reset button (`<INPUT TYPE="reset">`)
select	A selection list (`<SELECT><OPTION>option1</OPTION>` `<OPTIONoption2</OPTION></SELECT>`)
submit	A submit button (`<INPUT TYPE="submit">`)
text	A text field (`<INPUT TYPE="text">`)
textArea	A multiline text entry field (`<TEXTAREA>default` `text</TEXTAREA>`)

Table 6-2 *Form elements.*

Each of these elements can be named and referred to by name in a JavaScript script. Each also has properties and methods associated with it.

The `type` Property

Before looking at each of the form element objects, let's take a look at the **type** property. Each of the form element objects has a **type** property, which is a string value reflecting the type of input element, such as a button, a text field, or a checkbox.

The strings reflected by the various type properties for each form element are listed below:

- Text field: `"text"`

- Radio button: `"radio"`

- Checkbox: `"checkbox"`

- Hidden field: `"hidden"`

- Submit button: `"submit"`

- Reset button: `"reset"`

- Password field: `"password"`

- Button: `"button"`

- Select list: `"select-one"`

- Multiple select lists: `"select-multiple"`

- Textarea field: `"textarea"`

The `button` **Element**

In standard HTML forms, only two buttons are available—submit and reset—because the data contained in a form must be sent to some URL (usually a CGI-BIN script) for processing or storage.

A button element is specified using the `INPUT` tag:

```
<INPUT TYPE="button" NAME="name" VALUE="buttonName">
```

In the above `INPUT` tag, a button named `name` is created. The `VALUE` attribute contains the text that the Navigator browser displays in the button.

The button element has two properties: `name` (as specified in the `INPUT` tag) and `value`, which is also specified in the `INPUT` tag.

There is a single event handler for the button element: `onClick`. Associated with this is a single method: `click()`.

The addition of the button element enables JavaScript programmers to write JavaScript code to be executed for additional buttons in a script.

For instance, in Listing 5-3, instead of using the `onChange` element, you could alter the script as shown in Listing 6-1 to evaluate the supplied expression when a button is pressed.

Input   **Listing 6-1** Evaluating a form using the `button` element.

```
<HTML>

<HEAD>
<TITLE>button Example</TITLE>

<SCRIPT LANGUAGE="JavaScript">
<!-- HIDE FROM OTHER BROWSERS

function calculate(form) {

   form.results.value = eval(form.entry.value);

}


// STOP HIDING FROM OTHER BROWSERS -->
</SCRIPT>

</HEAD>

<BODY>

<FORM METHOD=POST>
Enter a JavaScript mathematical expression:
<INPUT TYPE="text" NAME="entry" VALUE="">
<BR>
The result of this expression is:
<INPUT TYPE=text NAME="results"
        onFocus="this.blur();">
```

```
<BR>
<INPUT TYPE="button" VALUE="Calculate" onClick="calculate(this.form);">
</FORM>

</BODY>

</HTML>
```

The `checkbox` **Element**

Checkboxes are toggle switches in an HTML form. They are used to select or deselect information. Checkboxes have more properties and methods available than buttons do, as outlined in Table 6-3.

Method or Property	Description
`checked`	Indicates the current status of the checkbox element (property)
`defaultChecked`	Indicates the default status of the element (property)
`name`	Indicates the name of the element as specified in the INPUT tag (property)
`value`	Indicates the current value of the element as specified in the INPUT tag (property)
`click()`	Emulates a click in the checkbox (method)

Table 6-3 *Properties and methods for the* `checkbox` *element.*

As you might expect, there is a single event handler for checkboxes: `onClick`.

For example, you can use checkboxes to produce an alternative to the double and square exercise (Exercise 3) from Chapter 5. Instead of three fields, you can have an entry text field, a checkbox to indicate squaring (doubling will be the default action) and a results text field.

The resulting script would look like Listing 6-2.

Listing 6-2 Doubling and squaring with checkboxes.

```
<HTML>

<HEAD>
<TITLE>checkbox Example</TITLE>

<SCRIPT>
<!-- HIDE FROM OTHER BROWSERS

function calculate(form,callingField) {
```

continued on next page

continued from previous page

```
        if (callingField == "result") {
          if (form.square.checked) {
            form.entry.value = Math.sqrt(form.result.value);
          } else {
            form.entry.value = form.result.value / 2;
          }
        } else {
          if (form.square.checked) {
            form.result.value = form.entry.value * form.entry.value;
          } else {
            form.result.value = form.entry.value * 2;
          }
        }
      }

    }


    // STOP HIDING FROM OTHER BROWSERS -->
    </SCRIPT>

    </HEAD>

    <BODY>

    <FORM METHOD=POST>

    Value: <INPUT TYPE="text" NAME="entry" VALUE=0
                    onChange="calculate(this.form,this.name);">
    <BR>
    Action (default double): <INPUT TYPE=checkbox NAME=square
    _onClick="calculate(this.form,this.name);">
    Square
    <BR>
    Result: <INPUT TYPE="text" NAME="result" VALUE=0
                    onChange="calculate(this.form,this.name);">

    </FORM>

    </BODY>

    </HTML>
```

Analysis

In this script, you see an example of how to use the `onClick` event handler, as well as how the `checked` property is a Boolean value that can be used as the condition for an `if...else` statement.

You have added a checkbox named `square` to the form. If the checkbox is checked, the program will square the value. If it isn't, then the default action will be to double the value. The `onClick` event handler in the checkbox definition (`<INPUT TYPE= checkbox NAME=square onClick="calculate(this.form,this.name);">`) ensures that when the user changes the desired action, the form recalculates (as well as if the user changes the value of the entry field).

To take advantage of the checkbox, you also changed the `calculate()` function, as follows:

```
function calculate(form,callingField) {

  if (callingField == "result") {
    if (form.square.checked) {
      form.entry.value = Math.sqrt(form.result.value);
    } else {
      form.entry.value = form.result.value / 2;
    }
  } else {
    if (form.square.checked) {
      form.result.value = form.entry.value * form.entry.value;
    } else {
      form.result.value = form.entry.value * 2;
    }
  }

}
```

In this function, you use the Boolean property `checked` to determine the correct action. If `form.square.checked` is `true`, then you should be squaring; if the value is `false`, you should be doubling the value in the entry field.

The `FileUpload` Element

The file upload field in a form provides a way in which users can specify a file to be included in a form submission. File upload elements are reflected in JavaScript with the `FileUpload` object.

The `FileUpload` object has only two properties associated with it: `name` and `value`, both of which are string values like other objects. There are no methods or event handlers for the `FileUpload` object.

The `hidden` Element

The `hidden` element is unique among all the form elements in that it is not displayed by the Web browser. Hidden fields can be used to store values that need to be sent to the server along with a form submission but that shouldn't be displayed in the page. They can also be used in JavaScript to store values used throughout a script and for calculations within a form.

The `hidden` object has only two properties associated with it: `name` and `value`, both of which are string values like other objects. There are no methods or event handlers for the `hidden` object.

The `password` Element

The `password` element is a unique type of text entry field in that any keystrokes are displayed as an asterisk (*). This makes the `password` element ideal for accepting input

of confidential information, such as account passwords or bank account personal iden-
tification numbers (PINs).

The `password` object has three properties, similar to text fields: `defaultValue`, `name`,
and `value`. Unlike the previous two elements, the password fields include more
methods (`focus()`, `blur()`, and `select()`) and the corresponding event handlers: `onFocus`,
`onBlur`, and `onSelect`.

We will discuss these methods and event handlers in more detail in the section on
the `text` element.

QUIZ 2

1. Form elements can be referred to by their _____ or by their
   _____.
   a. name, subscript in the element array
   b. type, name
   c. subscript in the element array, type
   d. value, name

2. Which of the following is not a valid `button` element in a form?
   a. `<INPUT TYPE="reset">`
   b. `<INPUT TYPE="select">`
   c. `<INPUT TYPE="submit">`
   d. `<INPUT TYPE="button">`

3. What would the following button do when clicked?

   `<INPUT TYPE="button" VALUE="submit">`

   a. It submits the form.
   b. It creates an error because there is no `onClick` event handler.
   c. It calls the default `onClick` event handler for the button which does nothing.
   d. None of the above.

4. Which of the following tests would be true if a checkbox 'test' is checked?
   a. `form.test.value == form.test.checked`
   b. `form.test.checked`
   c. `form.test.value == 'checked'`
   d. none of the above

5. Hidden elements in a form are_____ and they _____.
   a. not displayed on the form, have only two properties, `name` and `value`
   b. not displayed on the form, can be used to handle hidden events
   c. not allowed, have only two properties, `name` and `value`
   d. none of the above

 3 **More form Elements**

The `radio` **Element**

The **radio** element is similar to toggle checkboxes, except that several radio buttons are combined into a group and only a single button can be selected at any given time. For instance, the following lines produce a group of three radio buttons named **test**, similar to those in Figure 6-1.

```
<INPUT TYPE="radio" NAME="test" VALUE="1" CHECKED>1<BR>
<INPUT TYPE="radio" NAME="test" VALUE="2">2<BR>
<INPUT TYPE="radio" NAME="test" VALUE="3">3<BR>
```

The group of radio buttons is formed by using a consistent name in all the **INPUT** tags.

The **radio** element is accessible in JavaScript through the **radio** object, which has several properties for checking the current status of a radio button group. Table 6-4 outlines the properties and methods available with the **radio** object.

Method or Property	Description
checked	Indicates the current status of the radio element (property)
defaultChecked	Indicates the default status of the element (property)
index	Indicates the index of the currently selected radio button in the group
length	Indicates the number of radio buttons in a group
name	Indicates the name of the element as specified in the INPUT tag (property)
value	Indicates the current value of the element as specified in the INPUT tag (property)
click()	Emulates a click in the radio button (method)

Table 6-4 *Properties and methods for the* `radio` *object.*

As is the case with checkboxes, the single event handler, **onClick**, is available for radio buttons.

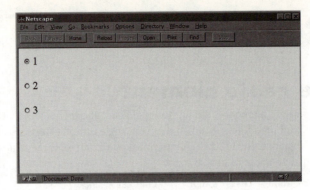

Figure 6-1
With a group of
radio buttons, only
one element can be
selected at any
given time.

The `index` and `length` properties haven't appeared in any of the form elements we have looked at so far in this chapter. Because a radio button group contains multiple elements, the `radio` object maintains an array of the radio buttons, with indexes starting at zero. In the example of a radio button group named **"test"** above, if the group were part of a form named **"testform"**, you could reference the second radio button as `testform.test[1]`, and you could check the current status of the button with `testform.test[1].checked`.

To illustrate usage of the `radio` object, you can rewrite Listing 6-2, used to demonstrate checkboxes, using radio buttons instead.

Input

Listing 6-3 Doubling and squaring with radio buttons.

```
<HTML>

<HEAD>
<TITLE>radio button Example</TITLE>

<SCRIPT>
<!-- HIDE FROM OTHER BROWSERS

function calculate(form,callingField) {

  if (callingField == "result") {
    if (form.action[1].checked) {
      form.entry.value = Math.sqrt(form.result.value);
    } else {
      form.entry.value = form.result.value / 2;
    }
  } else {
    if (form.action[1].checked) {
      form.result.value = form.entry.value * form.entry.value;
    } else {
      form.result.value = form.entry.value * 2;
    }
  }

}
```

```
// STOP HIDING FROM OTHER BROWSERS -->
</SCRIPT>

</HEAD>

<BODY>

<FORM METHOD=POST>
Value: <INPUT TYPE="text" NAME="entry" VALUE=0
              onChange="calculate(this.form,this.name);">
<BR>
Action:<BR>
<INPUT TYPE="radio" NAME="action" VALUE="twice"
_onClick="calculate(this.form,this.name);"> Double<BR>
<INPUT TYPE="radio" NAME="action" VALUE="square"
_onClick="calculate(this.form,this.name);"> Square <BR>
Result: <INPUT TYPE=text NAME="result" VALUE=0
              onChange="calculate(this.form,this.name);">

</FORM>

</BODY>

</HTML>
```

Analysis In this example, the changes from the checkbox version are subtle. Instead of one checkbox, you now have a pair of radio buttons with different values: `double` and `square`.

You know that the individual radio buttons are accessible through an array so that the double button is `action[0]` and the square button is `action[1]`. In this way, you need to change only the references in the `calculate()` function from `form.square.checked` to `form.action[1].checked`.

The `reset` **Element**

Using the `reset` object in JavaScript, you can react to clicks on the Reset button. Like the `button` object, the `reset` object has two properties (`name` and `value`) and one method (`click()`). The `onClick` event handler is also available.

A bug in Navigator 2 results in odd behavior with the Reset button: When text fields are cleared by the Reset button, this isn't reflected into the corresponding element until the field is given focus.

Although most programmers do not find a need to use the `onClick` event handler for Reset buttons or need to check the value of the button, the `reset` object can be used to clear the form to some value other than the default.

Listing 6-4 demonstrates how the Reset button can be used to clear a form to values other than the default.

Listing 6-4 Clearing a form to new values with Reset.

```html
<HTML>

<HEAD>
<TITLE>reset Example</TITLE>

<SCRIPT LANGUAGE="JavaScript">
<!-- HIDE FROM OTHER BROWSERS

function clearForm(form) {

  form.value1.value = "Form";
  form.value2.value = "Cleared";

}

// STOP HIDING FROM OTHER BROWSERS -->
</SCRIPT>

</HEAD>

<BODY>

<FORM METHOD=POST>
<INPUT TYPE="text" NAME="value1"><BR>
<INPUT TYPE="text" NAME="value2"><BR>
<INPUT TYPE="reset" VALUE="Clear Form" onClick="clearForm(this.form);">

</FORM>

</BODY>

</HTML>
```

Analysis   This script is fairly simple. You have created a form with two text fields and a Reset button. The Reset button has an `onClick` event handler, which calls `clearForm()` when the button is clicked.

The `clearForm()` function takes the `form` object as an argument and proceeds to place two new values in the two text fields of the form.

The `select` Element

Selection lists in HTML forms appear as drop-down menus or scrollable lists of selectable items. Lists are built using two tags: **SELECT** and **OPTION**. For instance, the following code snippet

```html
<SELECT NAME="test">
<OPTION SELECTED>1
<OPTION>2
```

```
<OPTION>3
</SELECT>
```

creates a three-item, drop-down menu with the choices 1, 2, and 3. Using the `SIZE` attribute, you can create a scrollable list with the number of elements visible at one time indicated by the value of the `SIZE` attribute. To turn your drop-down menu into a scrollable menu with two visible items, you could use the following:

```
<SELECT NAME="test" SIZE=2>
<OPTION SELECTED>1
<OPTION>2
<OPTION>3
</SELECT>
```

In both of these examples, the user can make only one choice. Using the `MULTIPLE` attribute, you can enable the user to select more than one choice in a scrollable selection list:

```
<SELECT NAME="test" SIZE=2 MULTIPLE>
<OPTION SELECTED>1
<OPTION>2
<OPTION>3
</SELECT>
```

Selection lists are accessible in JavaScript through the `select` object. This object bears some similarity to both the buttons you have seen, as well as to a radio button.

As with radio buttons, the list of options is maintained as an array, with indexes starting at zero. In this case, the array is a property of the `select` object called `options`.

Both selection option and the individual option elements have properties. In addition to the `options` array, the `select` object has the `selectedIndex` property, which contains the index number of the currently selected option.

Each option in a selection list also has several properties. `defaultSelected` indicates whether the option is selected by default in the `OPTION` tag. The `index` property contains the index value of the current option in the `options` array. Again, as you might expect, `selected` indicates the current status of the option, `text` contains the value of the text displayed in the menu for the specific option, and `value` contains any value indicated in the `OPTION` tag.

The `select` object has no available methods. However, the `select` object has three event handlers that don't correspond to the available event emulating method. These are `onBlur`, `onFocus`, and `onChange`—the same as for the `text` object.

In the current version of JavaScript, the `onChange` event handler is not invoked immediately after the user changes his selection. Rather, once the user leaves the selection list (that is, removes focus from the list), then the `onChange` event handler works.

For example, if you have the following selection list:

```
<SELECT NAME="example" onFocus="react();">
<OPTION SELECTED VALUE="Number One">1
```

continued on next page

continued from previous page

```
<OPTION VALUE="The Second">2
<OPTION VALUE="Three is It">3
</SELECT>
```

then when the list is first displayed, you would have access to the following information:

```
example.options[1].value = "The Second"

example.options[2].text = "3"

example.selectedIndex = 0

example.options[0].defaultSelected = true

example.options[1].selected = false
```

If the user then clicks on the menu and selects the second option, the **onFocus** event handler would execute (the `react()` function would be called), and then the values of these same properties would be as follows:

```
example.options[1].value = "The Second"

example.options[2].text = "3"

example.selectedIndex = 1

example.options[0].defaultSelected = true

example.options[1].selected = true
```

Modifying Select Lists

In Navigator 3.0, it is possible to change the content of a select list from inside JavaScript by assigning new values to the list entries' text property.

For instance, in the example earlier where you created the following selection list

```
<SELECT NAME="example" onFocus="react();">
<OPTION SELECTED VALUE="Number One">1
<OPTION VALUE="The Second">2
<OPTION VALUE="Three is It">3
</SELECT>
```

it would be possible to change the text displayed for the second entry to "two" with

```
example.options[1].text = "two";
```

New options can be added to the list using the **Option()** constructor object with the syntax:

```
newOptionName = new Option(optionText, optionValue, defaultSelected, selected);
selectListName.options[index] = newOptionName;
```

This creates an **option** object with the specified text and the **defaultSelected** and **selected** states for the option specified as Boolean values. This object is then assigned to an entry in the selection list specified by **index**.

Options can be deleted from the option list by assigning **null** to the option object for the particular entry:

```
selectListName.options[index] = null;
```

The submit **Element**

The Submit button is another special-purpose button like the Reset button. This button submits the current information from each field of the form to the URL specified in the **ACTION** attribute of the **FORM** tag using the method indicated in the **FORM** tag.

Like with the **button** object and the **reset** object, you have **name** and **value** properties available to you, along with a **click()** method and an **onClick** event handler.

The text **Element**

text elements are among the most common entry fields used in HTML forms. Similar to the password field you looked at earlier, text fields enable a single line of text entry, but unlike the password element, the text is displayed as normal type rather than as asterisks.

The **text** object has three properties: **defaultValue**, **name**, and **value**. Three methods emulate user events: **focus()**, **blur()**, and **select()** (which selects the text in the entry field). Four event handlers are available: **onBlur**, **onFocus**, **onChange**, and **onSelect** (for when the user selects some of the text in the field).

Table 6-5 outlines the properties and methods for the **text** element.

Method or Property	Description
defaultValue	Indicates the default value of the element as specified in the INPUT tag (property)
name	Indicates the name of the element as specified in the INPUT tag (property)
value	Indicates the current value of the element (property)
focus()	Emulates giving focus to the text field (method)
blur()	Emulates removing focus from the text field (method)
select()	Emulates selecting text in the text field (method)

Table 6-5 *Properties and methods for the* text *object.*

It is important to note that the content of a text field can be changed by assigning values to the **value** property. Thus, in the following example, whatever text is entered in the first field is echoed in the second field, and any text entered in the second field is echoed in the first field. By itself, this has little value, but the ability to use data from a text field and to dynamically update and change data in a text field is a powerful feature of JavaScript, as shown in Listing 6-5.

Input   **Listing 6-5** Dynamically updating text fields.

```
<HTML>

<HEAD>
<TITLE>text Example</TITLE>

<SCRIPT LANGUAGE="JavaScript">
<!-- HIDE FROM OTHER BROWSERS

function echo(form,currentField) {

  if (currentField == "first")
    form.second.value = form.first.value;
  else
    form.first.value = form.second.value;

}

// STOP HIDING FROM OTHER BROWSERS -->

</SCRIPT>

</HEAD>

<BODY>

<FORM>
<INPUT TYPE=text NAME="first" onChange="echo(this.form,this.name);">
<INPUT TYPE=text NAME="second" onChange="echo(this.form,this.name);">
</FORM>

</BODY>

</HTML>
```

In versions of Navigator 2.0, the **onChange** event handler is not invoked as soon as the user types a change. Rather, it is invoked when focus leaves the field and the text has changed.

The TEXTAREA Element

The **TEXTAREA** tag provides a custom size multiple-line text entry field defined by a container. The example in this code

```
<TEXTAREA NAME="fieldName" ROWS=10 COLS=25>
Default Text Here
</TEXTAREA>
```

creates a text entry field of 10 rows with 25 characters on each line. The words `Default Text Here` would appear in the field when it is first displayed.

Like the `text` element, JavaScript provides you with the `defaultValue`, `name`, and `value` properties, the `focus()`, `blur()`, and `select()` methods, and the `onBlur`, `onFocus`, `onChange`, and `onSelect` event handlers.

1. How are radio buttons grouped?
   a. By using the same name value in all of the `INPUT` tags.
   b. By allowing only one radio button to be selected at one time.
   c. By placing them inside a `groupbox` element.
   d. By using the `group` attribute.

2. Given the following group of radio buttons, which of the following tests would be false when the form is first loaded?

```
<INPUT TYPE="radio" NAME="test" VALUE="1" CHECKED>1
<INPUT TYPE="radio" NAME="test" VALUE="2">2
<INPUT TYPE="radio" NAME="test" VALUE="3">3
```

   a. `form.test[0].checked`
   b. `form.test.length == 3`
   c. `form.test[1].checked`
   d. `form.test[1].value == "2"`

3. Which of the following would make a scrollable selection list if there were 4 entries in the list?
   a. `<SELECT NAME="test" SIZE=2>`
   b. `<SELECT NAME="test" SCROLL="yes">`
   c. `<SELECT NAME="test" MULTIPLE>`
   d. none of the above

4. Complete the following. The text element _____
   a. can contain multiple lines of text.
   b. has only the `name` and `value` properties.
   c. is of no use on a form.
   d. enables single-line text entry on a form.

5. Which of the following would change the text displayed in a text field named 'test'?
   a. `test.text = "new text to display"`
   b. `test.name = "new text to display"`
   c. `test.value = "new text to display"`
   d. none of the above

LESSON 4   Using Tables and Arrays

USING TABLES TO CREATE A CALCULATOR

Now that we have taken a detailed look at the form object, its elements, properties, and methods, you are ready to use this information to build a somewhat more complicated script.

In this example, you will build a simple mathematical calculator using forms. That is, each number and the four mathematical functions (addition, subtraction, multiplication, and division) will each be a button. You will also have two other buttons: one to clear the running total and the other to clear the current entry.

In order to make your calculator appear more organized, you will make use of HTML tables. For those without experience using tables, tables are contained in the TABLE container tag and consist of rows contained in the TR tag and column elements contained in the TD tag. In addition, the COLSPAN attribute causes a cell to cover two columns. Similarly, ROWSPAN makes a cell two rows deep.

A more detailed discussion of HTML tables is available at Netscape's Web site at the URL: `http://home.netscape.com/assist/net_sites/tables.html`.

For instance, the HTML code in Listing 6-6 produces a simple table.

Input   **Listing 6-6** A simple table.

```
<TABLE BORDER=1>
<TR>
<TD COLSPAN=2>This is a table</TD>
</TR>
<TR>
<TD>One</TD>
<TD>Two</TD>
</TR>
<TR>
<TD>Three</TD>
<TD>Four</TD>
</TR>
</TABLE>
```

Output   The output from Listing 6-6 looks like the one in Figure 6-2.

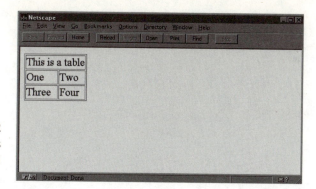

Figure 6-2
HTML tables
contain rows and
columns of cells.

Using tables, then, you are ready to work on developing your calculator.

In terms of behavior, your calculator should work the way a simple electronic calculator does: When a user enters a number, it is immediately displayed to the right of previously entered digits. Mathematical functions are executed in the order entered (no precedence here), and the effects of operations are cumulative until the clear button is pressed. Listing 6-7 is the source code for this calculator.

 Listing 6-7 Creating a calculator with tables.

```
<HTML>

<HEAD>
<TITLE>Example 6.7</TITLE>

<SCRIPT>
<!-- HIDE FROM OTHER BROWSERS

var total = 0;
var lastOperation = "+";
var newnumber = true;

function enterNumber(digit) {

  var form = digit.form;

  if (newnumber) {
    clearNumber(form);
    newnumber = false;
  }

  form.display.value = form.display.value + digit.name;

}

function clear(form) {
```

continued on next page

continued from previous page

```
        total = 0;
        lastOperation = "+";
        form.display.value = "";

}

    function clearNumber(form) {

      form.display.value = "";

}

    function calculate(operation) {

      var form = operation.form;

      var expression = total + lastOperation + form.display.value;

      lastOperation = operation.value;
      total = eval(expression);
      form.display.value = total;
      newnumber = true;

}

    // STOP HIDING FROM OTHER BROWSERS -->
    </SCRIPT>

    </HEAD>

    <BODY>

    <FORM>

    <TABLE BORDER=1>

    <TR>
    <TD COLSPAN=4>
    <INPUT TYPE=text NAME=display VALUE="" onFocus="this.blur();">
    </TD>
    </TR>


    <TR>
    <TD>
    <INPUT TYPE=button NAME="7" VALUE=" 7 " onClick="enterNumber(this);">
    </TD>
    <TD>
    <INPUT TYPE=button NAME="8" VALUE=" 8 " onClick="enterNumber(this);">
    </TD>
    <TD>
    <INPUT TYPE=button NAME="9" VALUE=" 9 " onClick="enterNumber(this);">
```

```
</TD>
<TD>
<INPUT TYPE=button NAME="+" VALUE=" + " onClick="calculate(this);">
</TD>
</TR>

<TR>
<TD>
<INPUT TYPE=button NAME="4" VALUE=" 4 " onClick="enterNumber(this);">
</TD>
<TD>
<INPUT TYPE=button NAME="5" VALUE=" 5 " onClick="enterNumber(this);">
</TD>
<TD>
<INPUT TYPE=button NAME="6" VALUE=" 6 " onClick="enterNumber(this);">
</TD>
<TD>
<INPUT TYPE=button NAME="-" VALUE="  -  " onClick="calculate(this);">
</TD>
</TR>

<TR>
<TD>
<INPUT TYPE=button NAME="1" VALUE=" 1 " onClick="enterNumber(this);">
</TD>
<TD>
<INPUT TYPE=button NAME="2" VALUE=" 2 " onClick="enterNumber(this);">
</TD>
<TD>
<INPUT TYPE=button NAME="3" VALUE=" 3 " onClick="enterNumber(this);">
</TD>
<TD>
<INPUT TYPE=button NAME="*" VALUE=" * " onClick="calculate(this);">
</TD>
</TR>

<TR>
<TD>
<INPUT TYPE=button NAME="0" VALUE=" 0 " onClick="enterNumber(this);">
</TD>
<TD>
<INPUT TYPE=button NAME="C" VALUE=" C " onClick="clear(this.form);">
</TD>
<TD>
<INPUT TYPE=button NAME="CE" VALUE="CE" onClick="clearNumber(this.form);">
</TD>
<TD>
<INPUT TYPE=button NAME="/" VALUE="  /  " onClick="calculate(this);">
</TD>
</TR>

</TABLE>
```

continued on next page

continued from previous page

```
</FORM>

</BODY>

</HTML>
```

Output

This script produces results like those in Figure 6-3.

Analysis

Several interesting techniques are used in this script. Let's take a look at selected parts of the script sequentially from the start.

```
var total = 0;
var lastOperation = "+";
var newnumber = true;
```

Here you declare the global variables to keep track of information. The `total` variable contains the current running total of the user's calculations. This is the same as the last displayed value before the user began entering a new number. `lastOperation` is used to keep track of the operation last entered by the user to be performed on the running total and the newly entered number. `newnumber` is used to keep track of when user input should be treated as a new number or part of the currently displayed number.

The initial values of these variables require some explanation. Obviously, `total` starts with a zero value. However, as you will see later in the `calculate()` function, you need a `lastOperation` value to perform on every number entered. By assigning the value `"+"` to `lastOperation`, the first number entered by the user will be added to the initial total of zero.

```
function enterNumber(digit) {

    var form = digit.form;

    if (newnumber) {
        clearNumber(form);
        newnumber = false;
```

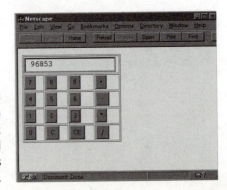

Figure 6-3
Tables make the calculator look appealing, and JavaScript makes it work.

```
  }

    form.display.value = form.display.value + digit;


}
```

You pass the currently clicked `button` object to `enterNumber()` as the argument `digit`. The line `var form = digit.form;` provides you with reference to the form containing the current button in much the same way as when you pass `this.form` to a function.

Because each new digit is added to the right side of the number, you can treat the digits as strings to concatenate.

```
function calulate(operation) {

  var form = operation.form;

  var expression = total + lastOperation + form.display.value;

  lastOperation = operation.value;
  total = eval(expression);
  form.display.value = total;
  newnumber = true;

}
```

The `calulate()` function is where the real work of the calculator script is done. The function is invoked when the user clicks on one of the operator buttons. When this happens, the line `var expression = total + lastOperation + form.display.value;` builds an expression in the form of a string.

You then use the `eval()` function to evaluate the expression you have just built. This value becomes the new value of `total`, is displayed in the text field, and the operation the user has just clicked is assigned to `lastOperation`.

One component of this calculator that is lacking is an equal (=) button. To implement it would require changing the logic of the `calulate()` function.

THE elements[] ARRAY

As mentioned in the section on the properties of the `form` object, all the elements in a form can also be referenced by the `elements[]` array. For instance, you could create the following form:

```
<FORM METHOD=POST NAME=testform>
<INPUT TYPE="text" NAME="one">
<INPUT TYPE="text" NAME="two">
<INPUT TYPE="text" NAME="three">
</FORM>
```

You can refer to the three elements as `document.testform.elements[0]`, `document.testform.elements[1]`, and `document.testform.elements[2]`, in addition to the obvious `document.testform.one`, `document.testform.two`, `document.testform.three`.

This can be useful in situations where the sequential relationship of form elements is more important than their names.

BUILDING A MULTIPLICATION TABLE

In this example, you will take advantage of the `elements[]` array to build a simple dynamic multiplication table. The form will have 11 elements. The user fills in the first field to specify which multiplication table to calculate, and the rest of the fields provide the one to ten multiplication table for that number.

Input   **Listing 6-8** Using the `elements[]` array in a multiplication table.

```
<HTML>

<HEAD>
<TITLE>Example 6.8</TITLE>

<SCRIPT LANGUAGE="JavaScript">
<!-- HIDE FROM OTHER BROWSERS

function calculate(form) {

    var num=1;
    var number=form.number.value;
    form.elements[num].value = number * num++;
    form.elements[num].value = number * num++;
    form.elements[num].value = number * num++;
    form.elements[num].value = number * num++;
    form.elements[num].value = number * num++;
    form.elements[num].value = number * num++;
    form.elements[num].value = number * num++;
    form.elements[num].value = number * num++;
    form.elements[num].value = number * num++;
    form.elements[num].value = number * num++;

}


// STOP HIDING FROM OTHER BROWSERS -->
</SCRIPT>

</HEAD>

<BODY>
```

```
<FORM METHOD=POST>
Number: <INPUT TYPE=text NAME="number" VALUE=1
_onChange="calculate(this.form);"><BR>
x 1: <INPUT TYPE=text NAME="1" VALUE=1 onFocus="blur();"><BR>
x 2: <INPUT TYPE=text NAME="2" VALUE=2 onFocus="blur();"><BR>
x 3: <INPUT TYPE=text NAME="3" VALUE=3 onFocus="blur();"><BR>
x 4: <INPUT TYPE=text NAME="4" VALUE=4 onFocus="blur();"><BR>
x 5: <INPUT TYPE=text NAME="5" VALUE=5 onFocus="blur();"><BR>
x 6: <INPUT TYPE=text NAME="6" VALUE=6 onFocus="blur();"><BR>
x 7: <INPUT TYPE=text NAME="7" VALUE=7 onFocus="blur();"><BR>
x 8: <INPUT TYPE=text NAME="8" VALUE=8 onFocus="blur();"><BR>
x 9: <INPUT TYPE=text NAME="9" VALUE=9 onFocus="blur();"><BR>
x 10: <INPUT TYPE=text NAME="10" VALUE=10 onFocus="this.blur();"><BR>
<ITEM TYPE=button NAME="calculcate" VALUE="Calculate"
_onClick="calculate(this.form);">
</FORM>


</BODY>

</HTML>
```

Output

Listing 6-8 produces results similar to those in Figure 6-4.

Analysis

Notice in this script that you can refer to form elements by number. Because the `elements[]` array starts with an index of zero, you have made the first element (index zero) the entry field and have started the multiplication table with element two (which has an index value of one).

Figure 6-4
Using the
elements[] array,
you can reference
each field in order.

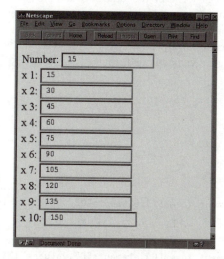

In the function `calculate()`, you use the variable `num` as a counter which starts at one. You use the following command 10 times to build the multiplication table:

```
form.elements[num].value = number * num++;
```

What this line tells you to do is assign the value of `number * num` to the current element and then increase `num` by one. This provides an excellent example of how to use the unary increment operator (`++`) to return the value of an expression and then increase it by one.

Typically, you would not write the `calculate()` function the way you have here. Instead, you would use a `for` loop:

```
function calculate(form) {

  var number=form.number.value;
  for(num = 1; num <= 10; num++) {
    form.elements[num].value = number * num;
  }

}
```

`for` loops are covered in Chapter 7, "Loops."

THE `forms[]` ARRAY

While event handlers are generally designed to work with individual forms or fields, at times, it is useful to be able to reference forms in relationship to other forms on a page.

This is where the `document.forms[]` array comes into play. It would be possible to have multiple identical forms on the same page and have information in a single field match in all three forms. This could be more easily achieved using the `document.forms[]` array than with form names. In this script, you have two text entry fields in separate forms. Using the `forms[]` array, you keep the value of the fields in each form the same when the user changes a value in one form.

```
<HTML>

<HEAD>
<TITLE>forms[] Example</TITLE>
</HEAD>

<BODY>

<FORM METHOD=POST>
<INPUT TYPE=text onChange="document.forms[1].elements[0].value = this.value;">
</FORM>

<FORM METHOD=POST>
<INPUT TYPE=text onChange="document.forms[0].elements[0].value = this.value;">
</FORM>
```

```
</BODY>

</HTML>
```

In addition to referring to forms numerically in the `forms[]` array, they can also be referred to by name. Using the `NAME` attribute of the `FORM` tag, you can assign a name to a form:

```
<FORM METHOD=POST NAME="name">
```

Then, this form can be referred to as `document.forms["name"]` or as `document.name`.

PROMPTING WITH TEXT FIELDS

Now you are going to put together some of the skills you have learned in this chapter in a different type of interactive form.

Usually, text entry forms consist of field names followed by fields. What you want to do is produce forms where the field name (that is, the prompt for the field) is the initial value of the field. This should look like the example in Figure 6-5.

If the user clicks in an unchanged field, the field clears and the user enters information. If he moves the focus out of the field and hasn't entered any information, the original content reappears.

At the same time, if the user clicks in a field that contains data entered by the user, the field is not cleared.

This can be done by developing a general-purpose set of functions, such as those in Listing 6-9.

Figure 6-5
Prompt information as a field's default value looks less cluttered on Landegg Academy's home page.

Input   **Listing 6-9** An interactive entry form.

```
<HTML>

<HEAD>
<TITLE>Listing 6-9</TITLE>

<SCRIPT LANGUAGE="JavaScript">
<!-- HIDE FROM OTHER BROWSERS

function clearField(field) {

   // Check if field contains the default value
   if (field.value == field.defaultValue) {

      // It does, so clear the field
      field.value = "";
   }

}

function checkField(field) {

   // Check if user has entered information in the field
   if (field.value == "") {

      // User has not entered anything
      field.value = field.defaultValue;
   }

}

// STOP HIDING FROM OTHER BROWSERS -->
</SCRIPT>

</HEAD>

<BODY>

<FORM METHOD=POST>
<INPUT TYPE=text NAME="name" VALUE="Name"
        onFocus="clearField(this);"
        onBlur="checkField(this);">
<BR>
<INPUT TYPE=text NAME="email" VALUE="E-mail Address"
        onFocus="clearField(this);"
        onBlur="checkField(this);">
<BR>
<INPUT TYPE=text NAME="phone" VALUE="Phone Number"
        onFocus="clearField(this);"
        onBlur="checkField(this);">
```

```
</FORM>

</BODY>

</HTML>
```

Output   This script produces a form with three text entry fields that looks like Figure 6-6. If a user clicks in the "E-mail" field, the result is similar to Figure 6-7.

Analysis   In Listing 6-9, you highlight the use of the `defaultValue` property. By using this, you are able to build two simple functions, `clearField()` and `checkField()`, to handle all the work.

`clearField()` is called when the user places focus in a field. By comparing the current value of the field with the default value, the function decides whether it should clear the field before the user starts entering information.

Similarly, `checkField()` is called when the focus leaves a field. If the content of the field is blank, then the default value is reassigned to the field.

Figure 6-6
A form with prompt information as the default value for each field.

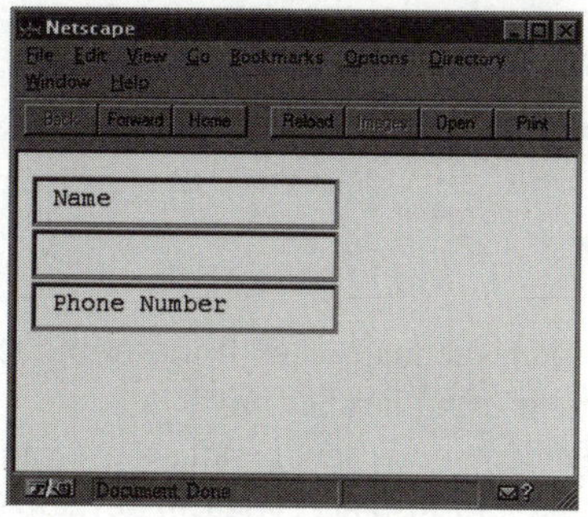

Figure 6-7
The `clearField()` function clears the content of a field if needed.

1. What is a description for a table?
   a. Tables can be used for automatically generating spreadsheets and calculators.
   b. Tables are contained in the **TABLE** container tag and consist of rows with one or more columns.
   c. Tables are the same as nested frames.
   d. None of the above.

2. The cells of a table can consist of the following.
   a. Any type of form element.
   b. Any type of form element except password fields.
   c. Text fields only.
   d. Any type of object.

3. Which of the following is invalid for referencing a form with a name of **"name"** from the **document** object?
   a. `document.forms["name"]`
   b. `document.forms[0]`
   c. `document.name`
   d. `document.forms.name`

4. Which of the following references the first element of the **elements** array?
   a. `form.elements[1]`
   b. `form.elements[0]`
   c. `form.elements.first`
   d. `form.elements[first]`

5. Complete the sentence. Each element of the **elements** array _____
   a. has only the **name** and **value** properties.
   b. has the properties appropriate for the element type.
   c. has an unknown type and properties.
   d. has the same properties.

SUMMARY

In this chapter, you have taken the major step from simple scripts to complex, interactive Web page development using JavaScript.

By working with form elements and event handlers, you can write scripts that enable sophisticated user interaction. For instance, you can develop simple spreadsheets and complex calculators and can perform error checking before sending forms to a server for processing by CGI scripts.

Event handlers are specified HTML tags. Event handlers take as their values JavaScript code, usually in the form of a function call.

To see JavaScript and forms in action, jump to Appendix C, Lab 2, Ashley Cheng's Ideal Weight Calculator.

In order to step beyond the bounds of the simple sort of processes you have been scripting up to this point, in Chapter 7 you will take a detailed look at loops, which provide you with increased control over the flow of a program.

COMMANDS AND EXTENSIONS REVIEW

Command/Extension	Type	Description
blur()	JavaScript method	Emulates removing focus from a form element
form.action	JavaScript property	String containing the value of the ACTION attribute of the FORM tag
form.elements	JavaScript property	Array containing an entry for each element in the form (such as checkboxes, text fields, and selection lists)
form.encoding	JavaScript property	String containing the MIME type used when submitting form data to the server
form.name	JavaScript property	String containing the value of the NAME attribute of the FORM tag
form.target	JavaScript property	String containing the name of the window targeted by a form submission
form.submit()	JavaScript method	Emulates the submission of an HTML form
type	JavaScript property	Reflects the type of a form element as a string

continued on next page

continued from previous page

Command/Extension	Type	Description
onSubmit	Event handler	Event handler for the submission of an HTML form
button	HTML attribute	Type attribute for HTML buttons (`<INPUT TYPE=button>`)
checkbox	HTML attribute	Type attribute for check-box toggle switches (`<INPUT TYPE=checkbox>`)
password	HTML attribute	Type attribute for pass-word text entry fields (`<INPUT TYPE=password>`)
radio	HTML attribute	Type attribute for radio button toggle switches in forms (`<INPUT TYPE=radio>`)
reset	HTML attribute	Type attribute for reset buttons (`<INPUT TYPE= reset>`)
SELECT	HTML tag	Container tag for selection lists
OPTION	HTML tag	Indicates options in a selection list (`<SELECT><OPTION>Option 1<OPTION>Option 2</SELECT>`)
submit	HTML attribute	Type attribute for Submit buttons (`<INPUT TYPE= submit>`)
text	HTML attribute	Type attribute for text fields in forms (`<INPUT TYPE=text>`)
TEXTAREA	HTML tag	Container tag for multi-line text entry field (`<TEXTAREA>default text</TEXTAREA>`)

Command/Extension	Type	Description
name	JavaScript property	String containing the name of an HTML element (button, checkbox, password, radio button, reset, submit, text, text area)
value	JavaScript property	String containing the current value of an HTML element (button, checkbox, password, radio button, reset, selection list, submit, text, text area)
click()	JavaScript method	Emulates clicking on a form element (button, checkbox, radio button, reset, selection list, submit)
onClick	JavaScript property	Event handler for a click event (button, checkbox, radio button, reset, submit)
checked	JavaScript property	Boolean value indicating if a choice is checked (checkbox, radio button)
defaultChecked	JavaScript property	Boolean value indicating if a choice is checked by default (checkbox, radio button)
defaultvalue	JavaScript property	String containing the default value of an HTML element (password, text, text area)
focus()	JavaScript method	Emulates giving focus to an element (password, text, text area)
blur()	JavaScript method	Emulates removing focus from an element (password, text, text area)

continued on next page

continued from previous page

Command/Extension	Type	Description
select()	JavaScript method	Emulates selecting text in a field (password, text, text area)
onFocus	Event handler	Event handler for a focus event (password, selection list, text, text area)
onBlur	Event handler	Event handler for a blur event (password, selection list, text, text area)
onChange	Event handler	Event handler for when the value of a field changes (password, selection list, text, text area)
onSelect	Event handler	Event handler for when the user selects text in a field (password, text, text area)
index	JavaScript property	Integer indicating the current choice from a group of choices (radio button, selection list)
length	JavaScript property	Integer indicating the number of choices in a group of choices (radio button)
defaultSelected	JavaScript property	Boolean value indicating if a choice is selected by default (selection list)
options	JavaScript property	Array of options in a selection list
text	JavaScript property	Text displayed for a menu item in a selection list

Command/Extension	Type	Description
TABLE	HTML tag	Container tag for HTML tables
TR	HTML tag	Container tag for rows of an HTML table
TD	HTML tag	Container tag for cells of an HTML table
COLSPAN	HTML attribute	Attribute of the TD tag to indicate if a cell spans multiple columns
ROWSPAN	HTML attribute	Attribute of the TD tag to indicate if a cell spans multiple rows
BORDER	HTML attribute	Attribute of the TABLE tag to indicate the width of the borders in a table
document.forms[]	JavaScript property	Array of form objects with an entry for each form in a document
string.substring()	JavaScript method	Returns a portion of the string, based on being passed the indexes of the first and last character as arguments
Math.floor()	JavaScript method	Returns the next integer value less than the argument
string.length	JavaScript property	Integer value indicating the index of the last character in a string

The **Math.floor()** and **string.substring()** methods will be used in the exercise later in this chapter.

CHAPTER EXERCISE

1. Which of these HTML tags are valid?

   a.   `<FORM METHOD=POST onClick="go();">`

   b.   `<BODY onLOAD="go();">`

   c.   `<INPUT TYPE=text onChange="go();">`

   d.   `<INPUT TYPE=checkbox onChange="go();">`

   e.   `<BODY onUnload="go();">`

   f.   `<INPUT TYPE=text onClick="go();">`

2. Take the script from Listing 6-7 (the calculator program) and extend it to add the following:

   ● A positive/negative toggle button (that is, click on the button and the currently entered number changes sign).

   ● A decimal point button, so that the user can enter floating point numbers.

   ● Check for errors as the user performs actions; specifically: check that the user is not trying to divide by zero and the user does not enter two decimal points. (If the user divides by zero, display a warning and don't perform the action; if the user enters a second decimal point, ignore it.)

3. Extend the functionality of Listing 6-9 to check optionally whether entered information is in a specific numeric range and, if not, to warn the user.

CHAPTER 7

LOOPS

U p to this point in the book, you have learned to produce fairly linear programs. That is, each line of a script gets one chance to execute (an `if...else` construct can mean certain lines don't execute), and in the case of functions, each line of the function gets only one chance to execute each time the function is called.

Most programming relies on the capability to repeat a number of lines of program code based on a condition or a counter. This is achieved by using loops.

The `for` loop enables you to count through a list and perform the specified command block for each entry in the list. The `while` loop enables you to test for a condition and repeat the command block until the condition is false.

In this chapter, we take a detailed look at loops and their applications, including the following:

- Basic concepts of loops

- The `for` and `for...in` loop

- The `while` loop

- The `break` and `continue` statements

- More about arrays

LESSON 1   Using Loops

LOOPS—BASIC CONCEPTS

Loops enable script writers to repeat sections of program code or command blocks, based on a set of criteria.

For example, a loop can be used to repeat a series of actions on each number between 1 and 10 or to continue gathering information from the user until the user indicates she has finished entering all her information.

The two main types of loops are those that are conditional (`while` loops continue until a condition is met or fails to be met) and those that iterate over a set range (the `for` and `for ... in` loops).

THE for AND for...in LOOPS

The `for` loop is the most basic type of loop and resembles similarly named loops in other programming languages including Perl, C, and BASIC.

In its most basic form, the `for` loop is used to count. For instance, in Listing 6.8 in Chapter 6, "Creating Interactive Forms," you needed to repeat a single calculation for each number between 1 and 10. This was easily achieved using a `for` loop:

```
function calculate(form) {

   var number=form.number.value;
   for(var num = 1; num <= 10; num++) {

      form.elements[num].value = number * num;
   }

}
```

What this loop says is to use the variable num as a counter. Start with num at 1, perform the command block and increment num as long as num is less than or equal to 10. In other words, count from 1 to 10 and for each number, perform the command.

In its general form, the for command looks like this:

```
for(initial value; condition; update expression)
```

The initial value sets up the counter variable and assigns the initial value. The initial value expression can declare a new variable using var. The expression is also optional.

The condition is evaluated at the start of each pass through the loop, so in this loop:

```
for(i=8; i<5; i++) {
   commands
}
```

the command block would never be executed because 8 < 5 evaluates to false. Like the initial value expression, the condition is optional, and when omitted, evaluates to true by default.

If the condition always evaluates to true, it is possible to face an infinite loop, which means the script can never end. In situations where you omit the condition on the for loop, it is important to provide some alternate means to exit the loop, such as with the break statement, which we will look at later in this chapter.

It is traditional programming to use the variables i, j, k, l, and so on as counters for loops. This is generally the practice unless a specific variable name adds clarity to the program code. Often, though, programs use general purpose counters, and these variable names are easily recognizable as counters to experienced programmers.

The third part of the for statement is the update expression. This expression is executed at the end of the command block before testing the condition again. This is generally used to update the counter. This expression is optional, and the counter updating can be done in the body of the command block, if needed.

To highlight the application of loops, the following script generates dynamic output to the display window. It asks the user for his name, followed by his 10 favorite foods for a JavaScript "top ten" list.

Input

Listing 7-1 Creating a Top Ten list with for loops.

```
<HTML>

<HEAD>
<TITLE>for Loop Example</TITLE>
</HEAD>

<BODY>

<SCRIPT LANGUAGE="JavaScript">
```

continued on next page

continued from previous page

```
<!-- HIDE FROM OTHER BROWSERS

var name = prompt("What is your name?","name");
var query = "";

document.write("<H1>" + name + "'s 10 favorite foods</H1>");

for (var i=1; i<=10; i++) {
  document.write(i + ". " + prompt('Enter food number ' + i,'food') + '<BR>');
}


// STOP HIDING FROM OTHER BROWSERS -->
</SCRIPT>

</BODY>

</HTML>
```

Output

This script produces results similar to those in Figure 7-1.

Analysis

In this example, you use the **for** loop to count from 1 (**i=1**) to 10 (**i<=10**) by increments of one (**i++**). For each turn through the loop, you prompt the user for a food
and write the food out to the window preceded by the current number using the
document.write() method.

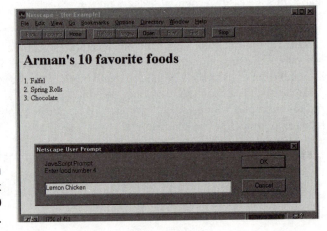

Figure 7-1
Using loops, you
can repeatedly ask
users for their 10
favorite foods.

`for` loops are not only used for counting in increments of one. They can be used for counting in larger quantities. The following line

```
for(j=2; j<=20; j+=2)
```

counts from 2 to 20 by twos. Likewise, `for` loops can be used to count backward (decrement); the following line counts down from 10 to 1:

```
for(k=10; k>=1; k--)
```

At the same time, simple addition and subtraction are not the only operations allowed in the update expression. The command

```
for(i=1; i<=256; i*=2)
```

will start with `i` equal to `1` and then proceed to double it until the value is more than 256. Similarly,

```
for(j=3; j<=81; j*=j)
```

repeatedly squares the counter.

The `for...in` Loop

Where the `for` loop is a general-purpose loop, JavaScript also has the `for ... in` loop for more specific applications. The `for ... in` loop is used to automatically step through all the properties of an object. In order to understand this, remember that each property in an object can be referred to by a number—its index. For instance, this loop

```
for (j in testObject) {
   commands
}
```

increments `j` from `0` until the index of the last property in the object `testObject`.

This is useful where the number of properties is not known or not consistent, as in a general-purpose function for an event handler.

For instance, you may want to create a simple slot machine application. The slot machine can display numbers from 0 to 9—each in a separate text field in a form. If the form is named `slotForm`, then the loop

```
for (k in slotForm) {
   code to display number
}
```

could be the basis for displaying the results of spinning the slot machine. With this type of loop, you could easily change the number of items on the slot machine so that instead of three text fields, you could have five fields, two fields, or nine fields.

USING LOOPS TO CHECK FOR NUMBERS

In this example you write a single function to check whether or not the information the user has entered in a field is a number.

In order to do this, you use the `substring()` method learned in Chapter 6, and you assume that numbers contain only the digits zero through nine plus a decimal point and a negative sign. The presence of any other character in a field indicates that the value is not numeric.

This type of function could then be used, for example, in checking form input. For instance, in Exercise 3 in Chapter 5, "Events in JavaScript" (the doubling and squaring form), you could add the function to the script, as shown in Listing 7-2.

Input

Listing 7-2 Checking input with the `isNum()` function.

```
<HTML>

<HEAD>
<TITLE>for ... in Example</TITLE>

<SCRIPT>
<!-- HIDE FROM OTHER BROWSERS

function checkNum(toCheck) {
  var isNum = true;

  if ((toCheck == null) || (toCheck == "")) {
    isNum = false;
    return isNum;
  }

  for (j = 0; j < toCheck.length; j++) {
    if ((toCheck.substring(j,j+1) != "0") &&
        (toCheck.substring(j,j+1) != "1") &&
        (toCheck.substring(j,j+1) != "2") &&
        (toCheck.substring(j,j+1) != "3") &&
        (toCheck.substring(j,j+1) != "4") &&
        (toCheck.substring(j,j+1) != "5") &&
        (toCheck.substring(j,j+1) != "6") &&
        (toCheck.substring(j,j+1) != "7") &&
        (toCheck.substring(j,j+1) != "8") &&
        (toCheck.substring(j,j+1) != "9") &&
        (toCheck.substring(j,j+1) != ".") &&
        (toCheck.substring(j,j+1) != "-")) {
      isNum = false;
    }
  }
```

```
    return isNum;

}
function calculate(form,currentField) {

  var isNum = true;
  var thisFieldNum = true;

  for (var field = 0; field < form.length; field ++) {
thisFieldNum = checkNum(field.value);
    if (!thisFieldNum)
      isNum = false;
  }

  if (isNum) {
    if (currentField == "square") {
      form.entry.value = Math.sqrt(form.square.value);
      form.twice.value = form.entry.value * 2;
    } else if (currentField == "twice") {
      form.entry.value = form.twice.value / 2;
      form.square.value = form.entry.value * form.entry.value;
    } else {
      form.twice.value = form.entry.value * 2;
      form.square.value = form.entry.value * form.entry.value;
    }
  } else {
    alert("Please Enter only Numbers!");
  }

}

// STOP HIDING FROM OTHER BROWSERS -->
</SCRIPT>

</HEAD>

<BODY>

<FORM METHOD=POST>

Value: <INPUT TYPE=text NAME="entry" VALUE=0
               onChange="calculate(this.form,this.name);">
Double: <INPUT TYPE=text NAME="twice" VALUE=0
                onChange="calculate(this.form,this.name);">
Square: <INPUT TYPE=text NAME="square" VALUE=0
                onChange="calculate(this.form,this.name);">

</FORM>

</BODY>

</HTML>
```

All the number checking takes place in the `checkNum()` function:

```
function checkNum(toCheck) {
  var isNum = true;


  if ((toCheck == null) || (toCheck == "")) {
    isNum = false;
    return isNum;
  }

  for (j = 0; j < toCheck.length; j++) {
    if ((toCheck.substring(j,j+1) != "0") &&
        (toCheck.substring(j,j+1) != "1") &&
        (toCheck.substring(j,j+1) != "2") &&
        (toCheck.substring(j,j+1) != "3") &&
        (toCheck.substring(j,j+1) != "4") &&
        (toCheck.substring(j,j+1) != "5") &&
        (toCheck.substring(j,j+1) != "6") &&
        (toCheck.substring(j,j+1) != "7") &&
        (toCheck.substring(j,j+1) != "8") &&
        (toCheck.substring(j,j+1) != "9") &&

        (toCheck.substring(j,j+1) != ".") &&
        (toCheck.substring(j,j+1) != "-")) {
      isNum = false;
    }
  }

  return isNum;

}
```

Analysis You make simple use of the `for` statement in this example. You start by assuming that the value is a number (`var isNum = true;`). First you check to make sure the value passed to the function is not the empty string or the `null` value, and then you use the loop to move from the first character in the field value to the last, and each time, check whether the given character is a numeric value. If not, you set `isNum` to `false`. After the loop, you return the value of `isNum`.

You check each character to see whether it is a number by using one `if` statement with multiple conditions. Remembering that `&&` is the symbol for logical "and," we are saying if the character doesn't match any number from 0 to 9 or the decimal point or negative sign, then the entry is not a number.

An alternative approach to comparing the number to each possible number from 0 to 9 is to use the structure `(toCheck.substring(j,j+1) <= "0" && toCheck.substring(j,j+1) >= "9"` which would check if the digit is a numeral:

```
if ((toCheck.substring(j,j+1) <= "0") &&
    (toCheck.substring(j,j+1) >= "9") &&
    (toCheck.substring(j,j+1) != ".") &&
```

```
      (toCheck.substring(j,j+1) != "-")) {
    isNum = false;
  }
```

QUIZ 1

1. Which of the following statements is false:
   a. The **for** loop is used to iterate over a set range.
   b. The **while** loop continues until a condition statement returns false.
   c. The **while** loop always executes at least once.
   d. If the condition in a loop is always true, the program may get stuck in an infinite loop.

2. Using the general form of the **for** loop: **for(initial value; condition; update expression)**, which of the following is true:
   a. The condition statement gets executed only once.
   b. The initial value can only use i, j, k, or l for counter variables.
   c. The update expression is always executed at least once.
   d. The condition statement gets executed at least once.

3. Given the following **for** loop, which of the following is true?

```
for( j in testObject ) { alert( testObject[j].value ); }
```

   a. This loop would automatically step through all of the properties of testObject and display the value in the alert dialog box.
   b. The counter variable j would start from 1 and increment by 1 to the number of properties of testObject.
   c. The alert dialog would display the values of the properties of testObject in a random order.
   d. There is no test condition for this loop.

4. Which of the following is valid for a loop construct?
   a. `for( var i in testObject ) { alert(" [i] = " + i); i++; }`
   b. `for( i in testObject; ) { alert( testObject[i].value ); }`
   c. `for( var i = 0; i < 10; ) { alert(" [i] = " + i); i++; }`
   d. none of the above.

5. How many times would the command block for the following loop execute?

```
for( j = 0; j <= 10; j += 5; ) {...}
```

   a. two times
   b. once
   c. three times
   d. four times

LESSON 2 — The while Loop and the break and continue Statements

THE while LOOP

In addition to the for loop, the while loop provides a different, but similar, function. The basic structure of a while loop is

```
while (condition) {
   JavaScript commands
}
```

where the condition is any valid JavaScript expression that evaluates to a Boolean value. The command block executes as long as the condition is true. For instance, the following loop counts until the value of num is 11:

```
var num = 1;

while (num <= 10) {
  document.writeln(num);
  num++;
}
```

A while loop could easily be used in a testing situation where the user must answer a question correctly to continue:

```
var answer = "";
var correct = 100;
var question = "What is 10 * 10?";
while (answer != correct) {
   answer = prompt(question,"0");
}
```

In this example, you simply set answer to an empty string, so that at the start of the while loop, the condition would evaluate to true and the question would be asked at least once.

Now that you have learned both the for loop and the while loop, you are ready to build a more complex program.

As an educational tool for children, you are going to build a calculator to solve the typical problems children get on tests: If a leaves b at speed c and d leaves e at speed f and they travel in a straight line toward each other, when will they meet?

The student simply enters the required information into the form and then either selects the Calculate button to see the correct answer or a Test button to be tested on the problem. Listing 7-3 contains the code for this program.

Input   **Listing 7-3** Travel problem tester.

```
<HTML>

<HEAD>
```

```
<TITLE>Listing 7-3</TITLE>

<SCRIPT LANGUAGE="JavaScript">
<!-- HIDE FROM OTHER BROWSERS

function checkNum(toCheck) {
   var isNum = true;

   if ((toCheck == null) || (toCheck == "")) {
isNum = false;
      return isNum;
   }

   for (j = 0; j < toCheck.length; j++) {
      if ((toCheck.substring(j,j+1) != "0") &&
          (toCheck.substring(j,j+1) != "1") &&
          (toCheck.substring(j,j+1) != "2") &&
          (toCheck.substring(j,j+1) != "3") &&
          (toCheck.substring(j,j+1) != "4") &&
          (toCheck.substring(j,j+1) != "5") &&
          (toCheck.substring(j,j+1) != "6") &&
          (toCheck.substring(j,j+1) != "7") &&
          (toCheck.substring(j,j+1) != "8") &&
          (toCheck.substring(j,j+1) != "9") &&
          (toCheck.substring(j,j+1) != ".") &&
          (toCheck.substring(j,j+1) != "-")) {
        isNum = false;
      }
   }

   return isNum;

}

function checkFieldNum(field) {

   if (!checkNum(field.value)) {

      alert("Please enter a number in this field!");

   }

}

function checkFormNum(form) {

   var isNum = true;

   for (field = 0; field <=2; field ++) {
      if (!checkNum(form.elements[field].value)) {
        isNum = false;
      }
   }
```

continued on next page

continued from previous page

```
      if (!isNum) {
        alert("All Fields Must Be Numbers!");
      }

      return isNum;

    }

    function calculate(form) {

      if (checkFormNum(form)) {
        with (form) {
          var time = distance.value / (eval(speedA.value) + eval(speedB.value));
          result.value = "" + time + " hour(s)";
        }
      }

    }

    function test(form) {

      if (checkFormNum(form)) {
        with (form) {
          var time = distance.value / (eval(speedA.value) + eval(speedB.value));
          var answer = "";
          while (eval(answer) != time) {
            answer = prompt("What is the answer to the problem?","0");
          }
          result.value = "" + time + " hour(s)";
        }
      }

    }

// STOP HIDING FROM OTHER BROWSERS -->
</SCRIPT>

</HEAD>

<BODY>

<FORM METHOD=POST>
Distance: <INPUT TYPE=text NAME="distance" onChange="checkFieldNum(this);"><BR>
Speed of Person A: <INPUT TYPE=text NAME="speedA" ⇐
onChange="checkFieldNum(this);"><BR>
Speed of Person B: <INPUT TYPE=text NAME="speedB" ⇐
onChange="checkFieldNum(this);"><BR>
<INPUT TYPE=button Name="Calculate" VALUE="Calculate" ⇐
onClick="calculate(this.form);">
```

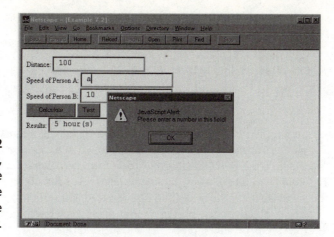

Figure 7-2
Using the for loop, you can test the form entries before calculating the result.

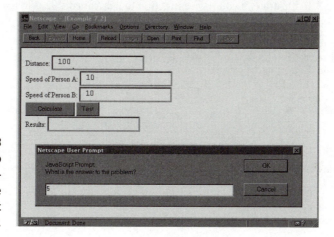

Figure 7-3
The while loop enables you to continually test the user for the correct answer.

```
<INPUT TYPE=button Name="Test" VALUE="Test" onClick="test(this.form);"><BR>
Results: <INPUT TYPE=text NAME=result onFocus="this.blur();">
</FORM>

</BODY>

</HTML>
```

Output   This script produces results like those in Figures 7-2 and 7-3.

Analysis   You make several different uses of loops in this example.

In the `checkFormNum()` function, you use the `for` loop to cycle through the first three form elements:

```
for (field = 0; field <=2; field ++) {
   if ((!checkNum(form.elements[field].value)) {
      isNum = false;
   }
}
```

You can then simply check whether the field contains a numeric.

You also use a `while` loop in the `test()` function to perform the testing of the student. In both the `test()` and `calculate()` functions, you use a new statement: `with`. This command is used where numerous references to an object are made in a block of code to make the code shorter and easier to read. For instance, in this script, you refer to the `form` object. By using `with (form)`, you can then write a block of code without the `form` prefix on all the properties and method calls.

To illustrate, if you have a function that assigned values to five fields in a form, you could write it two different ways:

```
function assign(form) {
   form.one.value = 1;
   form.two.value = 2;
   form.three.value = 3;
   form.four.value = 4;
   form.five.value = 5;
}
```

or

```
function assign(form) {
   with (form) {
      one.value = 1;
      two.value = 2;
      three.value = 3;
      four.value = 4;
      five.value = 5;
   }
}
```

THE break AND continue STATEMENTS

To add even more utility to the `for` and `while` loops, JavaScript includes the **break** and **continue** statements. These statements can be used to alter the behavior of the loops beyond a simple repetition of the related command block.

The **break** command does what the name implies—it breaks out of the loop completely, even if the loop isn't complete. For instance, if you want to give students three chances to get a test question correct, you could use the **break** statement:

```
var answer = "";
var correct = "100";
var question = "What is 10 * 10?";
```

```
for (k = 1; k <= 3; k++) {
  answer = prompt(question,"0");
  if (answer == correct) {
    alert ("Correct!");
    break;
  }
}
```

In this loop, the command block gets performed three times only if the first two answers are incorrect. A correct answer simply ends the loop prematurely.

The `continue` statement is slightly different. It is used to jump to the next repetition of the command block without completing the current pass through the command block. For instance, if you want to total three numbers input with a `prompt` statement but want to simply ignore a value if it is not a number, you might use the following structure (you are assuming the existence of a similar `checkNum()` function to the one you used before):

```
var total = 0;
var newNumber = 0;
for (i=1; i <=3; i++) {
  newNumber = prompt ("Enter a number","0");
  if (!checkNum(newNumber))
    continue;
  total = eval(total) + eval(newNumber);
  alert ("You entered " + newNumber + " and the total is " +
          total + ".");
}
```

This loop could be extended to add numbers until the user enters **0** as the new value. You do this by using a `while` loop instead of a `for` loop:

```
var total = 0;
var newNumber = "";
while ((newNumber = prompt ("Enter a number","0")) != 0) {
  if (!checkNum(newNumber))
    continue;
  total = eval(total) + eval(newNumber);
  alert ("You entered " + newNumber + " and the total is " +
          total + ".");
}
```

The reason you use the prompt in the while loop's condition is related to when the condition is tested. In this way, if the user enters 0 at the first prompt, the alert dialog box is never displayed.

CREATING A GAME OF TIC-TAC-TOE

In this example, you write a script to play a simple game of tic-tac-toe.

In order to do this, you use nine text entry fields in a single form to contain the nine spaces of the tic-tac-toe board.

The basic approach is as follows: The user plays first. After each play by the user, the relevant rows, columns, and diagonals are checked for a win. If there is no win, you scan each row, column, and diagonal to see if the computer can win. Then you check all rows, columns, and diagonals to see if there is a chance for the user to win. Failing both these scenarios, the computer simply takes any available space.

In order to easily implement the game, you use a standard naming system for the fields, such as 11 for the top left corner, 13 for the top right corner, and 33 for the bottom right corner. In this way, you will be able to use loops to quickly scan the board for combinations.

If you find the task a bit overwhelming, skip ahead to the analysis section following the source code to get a better feel of what's being done.

| Input |

Listing 7-4 Tic-tac-toe with `for` loops.

```
<HTML>

<HEAD>
<TITLE>Listing 7-4</TITLE>

<SCRIPT LANGUAGE="JavaScript">
<!-- HIDE FROM OTHER BROWSERS

var row = 0;
var col = 0;
var playerSymbol = "X";
var computerSymbol = "0";
board = new createArray(3,3);

function createArray(row,col) {

  var index = 0;
  this.length = (row * 10) + col;
  for (var x = 1; x <= row; x ++) {
    for (var y = 1; y <= col; y++) {
      index = (x*10) + y;
      this[index] = "";
    }
  }

}

function buildBoard(form) {

  var index = 0;
  for (var field = 0; field <= 8; field ++) {
    index = eval(form.elements[field].name);
    form.elements[field].value = board[index];
  }
```

```
}

function clearBoard(form) {

  var index = 0;
  for (var field = 0; field <= 8; field ++) {
    form.elements[field].value = "";
    index = eval(form.elements[field].name);
    board[index] = "";
  }

}

function win(index) {

  var win = false;

  // CHECK ROWS
  if ((board[index] == board[(index < 30) ? index + 10 : index - 20]) &&
      (board[index] == board[(index >  11) ? index - 10 : index + 20])) {
    win = true;
  }

  // CHECK COLUMNS
  if ((board[index] == board[(index%10 < 3) ? index + 1 : index - 2]) &&
      (board[index] == board[(index%10 > 1) ? index - 1 : index + 2])) {
    win = true;
  }

  // CHECK DIAGONALS
  if (Math.round(index/10) == index%10) {
    if ((board[index] == board[(index < 30) ? index + 11 : index - 22]) &&
        (board[index] == board[(index >  11) ? index - 11 : index + 22])) {
      win = true;
    }
    if (index == 22) {
      if ((board[index] == board[13]) && (board[index] == board[31])) {
        win = true;
      }
    }
  }
  if ((index == 31) || (index == 13)) {
    if ((board[index] == board[(index < 30) ? index + 9 : index - 18]) &&
        (board[index] == board[(index >  11) ? index - 9 : index + 18])) {
      win = true;
    }
  }

  // RETURN THE RESULTS
  return win;

}
```

continued on next page

continued from previous page

```
function play(form,field) {

    var index = eval(field.name);
    var playIndex = 0;
    var winIndex = 0;
    var done = false;
    field.value = playerSymbol;
    board[index] = playerSymbol;

    //CHECK FOR PLAYER WIN
if (win(index)) {
    // PLAYER WON
    alert("Good Play! You Win!");
    clearBoard(form);
} else {
    // PLAYER LOST, CHECK FOR WINNING POSITION
    for (row = 1; row <= 3; row++) {
      for (col = 1; col <= 3; col++) {
         index = (row*10) + col;
         if (board[index] == "") {
            board[index] = computerSymbol;
            if(win(index)) {
              playIndex = index;
              done = true;
              board[index] = "";
              break;
            }
            board[index] = "";
         }
      }
      if (done)
         break;
    }
    // CHECK IF COMPUTER CAN WIN
    if (done) {
      board[playIndex] = computerSymbol;
      buildBoard(form);
      alert("Computer Just Won!");
      clearBoard(form);
    } else {
      // CAN'T WIN, CHECK IF NEED TO STOP A WIN
      for (row = 1; row <=3; row++) {
        for (col = 1; col <= 3; col++) {
           index = (row*10) + col;
           if (board[index] == "") {
              board[index] = playerSymbol;
              if (win(index)) {
                playIndex = index;
                done = true;
                board[index] = "";
                break;
              }
```

```
                        board[index] = "";
                    }
                }
                if (done)
                    break;
            }
            // CHECK IF DONE
            if (done) {
                board[playIndex] = computerSymbol;
                buildBoard(form);
            } else {
                // NOT DONE, CHECK FOR FIRST EMPTY SPACE
                for (row = 1; row <= 3; row ++) {
                    for (col = 1; col <= 3; col ++) {
                        index = (row*10) + col;
                        if (board[index] == "") {
                            playIndex = index;
                            done = true;
                            break;
                        }
                    }
                    if (done)
                        break;
                }
                board[playIndex] = computerSymbol;
                buildBoard(form);
            }
        }
    }

}

// STOP HIDING HERE -->
</SCRIPT>

</HEAD>

<BODY>

<FORM METHOD = POST>

<TABLE>

<TR>
<TD>
<INPUT TYPE=text SIZE=3 NAME="11"
        onFocus="if (this.value != '') {blur();}"
        onChange="play(this.form,this);">
</TD>
<TD>
<INPUT TYPE=text SIZE=3 NAME="12"
        onFocus="if (this.value != '') {blur();}"
```

continued on next page

continued from previous page

```
            onChange="play(this.form,this);">
    </TD>
    <TD>
    <INPUT TYPE=text SIZE=3 NAME="13"
            onFocus="if (this.value != '') {blur();}"
            onChange="play(this.form,this);">
    </TD>
    </TR>

    <TR>
    <TD>
    <INPUT TYPE=text SIZE=3 NAME="21"
            onFocus="if (this.value != '') {blur();}"
            onChange="play(this.form,this);">
    </TD>
    <TD>
    <INPUT TYPE=text SIZE=3 NAME="22"
            onFocus="if (this.value != '') {blur();}"
            onChange="play(this.form,this);">
    </TD>
    <TD>
    <INPUT TYPE=text SIZE=3 NAME="23"
            onFocus="if (this.value != '') {blur();}"
            onChange="play(this.form,this);">
    </TD>
    </TR>

    <TR>
    <TD>
    <INPUT TYPE=text SIZE=3 NAME="31"
            onFocus="if (this.value != '') {blur();}"
            onChange="play(this.form,this);">
    </TD>
    <TD>
    <INPUT TYPE=text SIZE=3 NAME="32"
            onFocus="if (this.value != '') {blur();}"
            onChange="play(this.form,this);">
    </TD>
    <TD>
    <INPUT TYPE=text SIZE=3 NAME="33"
            onFocus="if (this.value != '') {blur();}"
            onChange="play(this.form,this);">
    </TD>
    </TR>

    </TABLE>


    <INPUT TYPE=button VALUE="I'm Done-Your Go">
    <INPUT TYPE=button VALUE="Start Over" onClick="clearBoard(this.form);">
```

```
</FORM>

</BODY>

</HTML>
```

Output

This script produces results similar to those in Figure 7-4.

Analysis

This is the most complex example you have worked on. You combine what you have learned about objects as arrays, loops, and expressions to produce a functional tic-tac-toe game.

To better understand exactly what the script does, let's take a look at each section in turn.

```
var row = 0;
var col = 0;
var playerSymbol = "X";
var computerSymbol = "0";
board = new createArray(3,3);
```

Here you declare the global variables and the array object that you use throughout the script. The **board** object is an instance of the **createArray** object, which you define using a function later in the script.

You use the **board** array to hold an image of the values displayed in the form because it is easier to work with indexes of an array than the sequential order of elements in a form.

```
function createArray(row,col) {

  var index = 0;
  this.length = (row*10) + col
  for (var x = 1; x <= row; x ++) {
    for (var y = 1; y <= col; y++) {
      index = (x*10) + y;
```

continued on next page

Figure 7-4
This tic-tac-toe game makes extensive use of loops.

continued from previous page

```
      thisCindex] = "";
    }
  }
}
```

The `createArray()` function defines the array object you use in this script. Notice the use of **for** loops to define the object. This type of array definition will be discussed in further detail later in this chapter. It is important to notice how you are building the two-digit numeric indexes by multiplying the row number by 10 and adding it to the column number to produce indexes such as 11, 12, 13, 21, 22, 23, 31, 32, and 33.

```
function buildBoard(form) {

  var index = 0;
  for (var field = 0; field <= 8; field ++) {
    index = eval(form.elements[field].name);
    form.elements[field].value = boardCindex];
  }

}
```

`buildBoard()` displays the values in the **board** object in the form. By cycling through all the elements in the form using a **for** loop, you can get the relevant index from the **field.name** using the **eval()** function, which converts the name (a string) into a numeric value.

```
function win(index) {

var win = false;

  // CHECK ROWS
  if ((boardCindex] == boardC(index < 30) ? index + 10 : index - 20]) &&
      (boardCindex] == boardC(index >  11) ? index - 10 : index + 20])) {
    win = true;
  }

  // CHECK COLUMNS
  if ((boardCindex] == boardC(index%10 < 3) ? index + 1 : index - 2]) &&
      (boardCindex] == boardC(index%10 > 1) ? index - 1 : index + 2])) {
    win = true;
  }

  // CHECK DIAGONALS
  if (Math.round(index/10) == index%10) {
    if ((boardCindex] == boardC(index < 30) ? index + 11 : index - 22]) &&
        (boardCindex] == boardC(index >  11) ? index - 11 : index + 22])) {
      win = true;
    }
    if (index == 22) {
      if ((boardCindex] == boardC13]) && (boardCindex] == boardC31])) {
        win = true;
```

```
      }
    }
  }
  if ((index == 31) || (index == 13)) {
    if ((board[index] == board[(index < 30) ? index + 9 : index - 18]) &&
        (board[index] == board[(index > 11) ? index - 9 : index + 18])) {
      win = true;
    }
  }

  // RETURN THE RESULTS
  return win;

}
```

The **win()** function requires more explanation. The function is designed to check all rows, columns, and diagonals crossing the space indicated by **index** to see if there is a win.

For instance, to check the row that **index** is in, you need to compare the value of **board[index]** with the value to its immediate right and to its immediate left. At first, it would seem that you could use a statement such as

```
if ((board[index] == board[index+10]) && (board[index] == board[index-10]))
```

to do this. The problem with this is that if the **index** passed to the function is the third space in a row, you will be attempting to look at a fourth, non-existent space in the first condition. Similarly, if **index** represents the first space in a row, the second condition will try looking at **board[index-10]**, which doesn't exist.

You remedy this situation through the use of conditional expressions. For instance **board[(index < 30) ? index + 10 : index - 20]** evaluates to **board[31]** if **index** is **21** but evaluates to **board[12]** if **index** is **32**.

The testing of diagonals also requires some explanation. You start by checking whether **index** represents any space on the diagonal from the top left to the bottom right. If it does, you check that diagonal, and then if the space is the middle space on the board, you also check the diagonal from the top right to bottom left. You finish by checking whether the top right or bottom left corner is represented by **index**; if it is, you check the second diagonal.

The **play()** function, which comes next, is somewhat more complex and also requires more detailed explanation.

```
function play(form,field) {

  var index = eval(field.name);
  var playIndex = 0;
  var winIndex = 0;
  var done = false;
  field.value = playerSymbol;
  board[index] = playerSymbol;
```

You start by declaring global variables and assigning the correct symbols to the appropriate field form and property of the **board** object. You do this so that the user can type any character in the field she wants to mark for her play.

After this, you use the **win()** function to check if the play makes the user a winner.

```
//CHECK FOR PLAYER WIN
if (win(index)) {
    // PLAYER WON
    alert("Good Play! You Win!");
    clearBoard(form);
} else {
```

If the user has not won, you need to start checking for the best move by the computer. The first thing to do is to look for a position that lets the computer win. You do this with a pair of embedded **for** loops. These loops enable you to cycle through each position on the playing board. For each position, if the value is an empty string (meaning no play has been made there), you temporarily play the computer's symbol there and check if that produces a win. If it does, you set the appropriate variables and break out of the inside **for** loop.

Because the **break** statement breaks out of the innermost loop only, you end the outer loop with an **if** statement to break out of the outer loop if you have found the winning play.

At the end of the inner loop, you assign the empty string back to the current position because it did not produce a win, and you are not going to play there at this point.

```
// PLAYER LOST, CHECK FOR WINNING POSITION
for (row = 1; row <= 3; row++) {
    for (col = 1; col <= 3; col++) {
        index = (row*10) + col;
        if (board[index] == "") {
            board[index] = computerSymbol;
            if(win(index)) {
                playIndex = index;
                done = true;
                board[index] = "";
                break;
            }
            board[index] = "";
        }
    }
    if (done)
        break;
}
```

If you have found a winning position, you simply display the play with **buildBoard()** and then inform the user that the computer won.

```
// CHECK IF COMPUTER CAN WIN
if (done) {
    board[playIndex] = computerSymbol;
    buildBoard(form);
    alert("Computer Just Won!");
```

```
      clearBoard(form);
} else {
```

> Next, having failed to find a winning position, it is necessary to look for potential wins by the user in the form of complete rows, columns, or diagonals missing only one play by the user. This is achieved in exactly the same way you looked for a winning computer play, except this time, you check for plays that would generate a winning play by the user.

```
// CAN'T WIN, CHECK IF NEED TO STOP A WIN
for (row = 1; row <=3; row++) {
  for (col = 1; col <= 3; col++) {
    index = (row*10) + col;
    if (board[index] == "") {
      board[index] = playerSymbol;
      if (win(index)) {
        board[index] = computerSymbol;
        playIndex = index;
        done = true;
        board[index] = "";
        break;
      }
      board[index] = "";
    }
  }
  if (done)
    break;
}
// CHECK IF DONE
if (done) {
  board[playIndex] = computerSymbol;
  buildBoard(form);
} else {
```

> Having failed to find a winning play for the computer or identified a potential win on the part of the user, you simply proceed to find the first empty position and play there. You do this with another set of embedded **for** loops and break out of the loops once you have found the first empty space.

```
// NOT DONE, CHECK FOR FIRST EMPTY SPACE
for (row = 1; row <= 3; row ++) {
  for (col = 1; col <= 3; col ++) {
    index = (row*10) + col;
    if (board[index] == "") {
      playIndex = index;
      done = true;
      break;
    }
  }
  if (done)
    break;
}
```

continued on next page

continued from previous page

```
        board[playIndex] = computerSymbol;
        buildBoard(form);
    }
  }
 }

}
```

Now that you've studied the functions that drive the game, let's take a look at how you use event handlers in the form. The form consists of nine identical fields (except for their names), named according to the scheme of 11, 12, 13, 21, 22, 23, and so on. Each **INPUT** tag contains the same two event handlers:

```
<INPUT TYPE=text SIZE=3 NAME="31"
    onFocus="if (this.value != '') {blur();}"
    onChange="play(this.form,this);">
```

In the **onFocus** event handler, you are simply checking whether the field the user has selected is empty. If not, you remove the focus immediately so that the user is free to play in empty fields only and cannot alter the content of used spaces.

The **onChange** event handler simply calls the **play()** function, which records the user's play, checks if the user has won, and if necessary, chooses a play for the computer.

CREATING ARRAYS WITH for LOOPS

Now that you have a firm grasp on the concept of loops, you can look at how **for** loops can create the equivalent of one-dimensional arrays in JavaScript.

As you saw in Chapter 4, "Functions and Objects—The Building Blocks of Programs," JavaScript has provisions for associative arrays in that object properties can be referred to as a numeric index of the object. However, programmers who have studied C, Perl, or Pascal are aware of the value of arrays of the same type.

That is, you need to be able to define an array as an ordered set of elements of the same type where the number of elements can vary each time the array is defined. You can do this using objects by defining the object function using a **for** loop.

JavaScript provides a pre-built constructor object called **Array** which does just this. However, in order to understand how this is done, you will build your own here. Some early versions of JavaScript did not provide the **Array()** object.

For instance, to define a numeric array of an unknown number of elements, you might write the object definition function createArray() like this:

```
function createArray(num) {

  this.length = num;
  for (var j = 0; j < num; j++) {
    this[j] = 0;
  }

}
```

This function creates an array starting with index 0 and assigns all values of the new array to 0. Using this object, you could then use newArray = new createArray(4) to create an array of four elements called newArray. You would refer to the elements in the array as newArray[0], newArray[1], and so on.

1. The **break** statement does which of the following?
   a. Breaks out of the outer-most enclosing loop.
   b. Breaks out of the inner-most enclosing loop.
   c. Continues execution at the top of the loop.
   d. Gets confused with nested loops.

2. The **continue** statement does which of the following?
   a. Continues execution at the next statement after the loop.
   b. Skips the next statement.
   c. Continues execution at the next iteration of the loop.
   d. Does not work inside a **for** loop.

3. How many times would the command block of the following **while** loop get executed?

```
while( num < 10 ) { ...; num++;  }
```

   a. It is impossible to tell without knowing the initial value of **num**.
   b. Ten times.
   c. Nine times.
   d. At least ten times.

4. Which of the following is equivalent to the following `while` loop?

```
i = 0; while( i != 5 ) { ... i++; }
```

     a. `for( var i = 0; i <= 5; i++ ) { ... }`
     b. `for( var i  = 0; i < 5; i++) { ... }`
     c. `i = 1; while( i <= 5 ) { ... i++; }`
     d. `until( i == 5 ) { ... i++; }`

5. Which of the following is equivalent to

```
with( form ) { elements[0].value = 'testvalue'; }
```

     a. `form = elements[0].value`
     b. `with( i form ) { elements[0].value = 'testvalue'; }`
     c. `for( i in form ) { form.elements[i].value = 'testvalue'; }`
     d. `form.elements[0].value = 'testvalue';`

SUMMARY

In this chapter you have learned how to use loops to achieve sophisticated control over the flow of a function or script. Using `for` loops, you can repeat a command block several times, based on a range and an expression to move through the range. The `for ... in` loop enables you to cycle through all the properties in an object. The `while` loop works differently in that the associated command block is executed if a condition is true; otherwise the loop finishes. The `break` and `continue` statements enable you to alter the flow of a loop by either breaking out of the loop completely, or prematurely moving on to the next cycle through the loop. You also learned that loops can be used to create `array` objects.

In Chapter 8, "Frames, Documents, and Windows," you will take a close look at the document window, the methods it offers, and how to manipulate it. You will also learn to use frames and take a detailed look at the `frames` object.

COMMANDS AND EXTENSIONS REVIEW

Command/Extension	Type	Description
for	Statement	Loops based on an initial value, a condition, and an expression
for ... in	Statement	Loops through all the properties in an object, returning the index of the property
while	Statement	Loops based on a condition; continues until the condition is false

Command/Extension	Type	Description
with	Statement	Enables a command block to omit an object prefix
break	Statement	Breaks out of the current loop
continue	Statement	Jumps to the next iteration of the current loop

CHAPTER EXERCISE

1. Write `while` loops to emulate each of these `for` loops:

   a.
   ```
   for (j = 4; j > 0; j --) {
          document.writeln(j + "<BR>");
   }
   ```

   b.
   ```
   for (k = 1; k <= 99; k = k*2) {
     k = k/1.5;
   }
   ```

   c.
   ```
   for (num = 0; num <= 10; num ++) {
     if (num == 8)
       break;
   }
   ```

2. In Chapter 4 you learned about recursion and how to use it for a variety of purposes, including calculating factorials and exponents. With loops, it is possible to make the same calculations. Write a function that doesn't use recursion to calculate factorials.

3. In Listing 7-4, the `play()` function works but is not too intelligent. Specifically, if the computer has no obvious winning play and does not immediately need to prevent the user from winning, no strategy is applied to the computer's selection.

   Rewrite the `play()` function so that in this situation, the computer first tries to find a space so that playing there creates a row or column with two of the computer's symbols and an empty space.

CHAPTER 8

FRAMES, DOCUMENTS, AND WINDOWS

Now that you have learned the basics of JavaScript and how to work with forms, you are ready to look at another advanced feature of JavaScript: frames.

Frames provide the ability to divide a document window into distinct sections, each of which contains different HTML files that can also be manipulated using JavaScript.

Besides the capability to manipulate frames, JavaScript also provides the `document` object, which provides properties and methods for dealing with anchors, links and colors, and the `window` object—the top level object of a web document window.

In this chapter we cover these topics:

- An introduction to frames
- Working with frames in JavaScript
- The `document` object
- The `window` object

● Working with the status bar

● Controlling the timing of scripts with `setTimeout()`

LESSON 1 Setting Up Frames

AN INTRODUCTION TO FRAMES

Frames are one of the most widely used new features of Navigator 2.0 and 3.0.

By using a few simple extensions to the HTML standard, Web authors are able to achieve sophisticated control over the layout of information in the Web browser window by dividing the window into rectangular sections and loading separate HTML files into each section of the window.

In addition, links in one frame can update another frame, and the result of processing form data in a CGI script on a server can be targeted at another frame.

Even without the addition of JavaScript, frames have enabled the addition of a type of interactivity that wasn't possible before, using regular HTML. For instance, sites now feature fixed tool bars and permanent search forms such as the one in Figure 8-1.

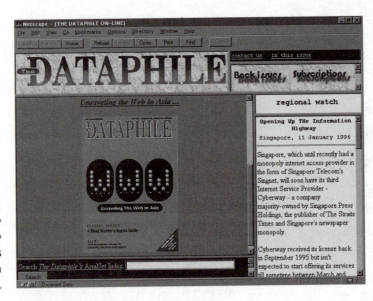

Figure 8-1
Using frames, *The Dataphile On-line* in Hong Kong has permanent search forms at its site.

THE FRAMESET TAG

A page is divided into frames using the FRAMESET tag. The tag is used in the top-level document defining a window containing frames and is used to specify how to divide the document window.

Because windows divided into frames are created from multiple HTML files, it is important to keep the hierarchical relationship of documents in mind. In a document window divided into frames, the *top-level document* is the HTML document that defines the frames and files that will load into those frames.

The FRAMESET container tag takes several attributes. The two basic ones are ROWS and COLS. A FRAMESET tag takes either one of these or both to divide a document into a set of rows or columns. For instance,

```
<FRAMESET COLS="25,*,25">
```

would define three columns. The two outer columns would each be 25 pixels wide, and the middle column would take the remaining space, depending on the size of the window. In this example, the asterisk (*) represents the remaining available space after the space is allocated for the other frames.

In addition to specifying the size of frames in pixels, the size of columns and rows can be defined using percentages relative to the space available to the document:

```
<FRAMESET ROWS="35%,*">
```

The use of percentages to define the size of frames is useful when you consider that different users will have different size monitors running at different resolutions. If you normally use a very high resolution, you may feel it is okay to define the width of a column as 700 pixels, but to a user running at standard 640×480 VGA resolution, this frame would be wider than his display allows.

The preceding FRAMESET tag would divide the display into two rows. The top row would be 35 percent of the height of the display area, and the bottom row would fill the remaining space (using the asterisk again).

The FRAMESET tag replaces the BODY tag in a file. Files with FRAMESET containers are not used to directly display HTML data in Navigator.

THE FRAME TAG

Inside a FRAMESET container, the FRAME tag is used to specify which files should be displayed in each frame. The URLs of the files—which can be relative or absolute—should be specified using the SRC attribute in the same way as the IMG tag is used to include images in an HTML document.

The terms *relative* and *absolute* refer to two different ways of indicating the location of files in HTML. In absolute URLs, the complete protocol (the part before the colon), domain name, and path of a file are provided. For instance,

```
http://wwww.juxta.com/juxta/docs/prod.htm
```

is an absolute URL.

In relative URLs, the protocol, domain name, and complete path are not indicated. Instead, the location of the file relative to the current file is indicated. If the file indicated the URL is in the same directory, then just the filename is needed. If the file is in a subdirectory, then the path from the current directory is needed.

For example, the following creates a document with two rows.

```
<FRAMESET ROWS="35%,*">
  <FRAME SRC="menu.html">
  <FRAME SRC="welcome.html">
</FRAMESET>
```

The top is 35 percent of the available space, and the bottom takes up the remaining 65 percent. The file `menu.html` is loaded into the top frame, and the file `welcome.html` is displayed in the lower frame.

In addition to the `SRC` attribute, the `FRAME` tag can take several other attributes, as outlined in Table 8-1.

Attribute	Description
SRC	Specifies the URL of the HTML file to be displayed in the frame.
NAME	Specifies the name of the frame so that it can be referenced by HTML tags and JavaScript scripts.
NORESIZE	Specifies that the size of a frame is fixed and cannot be changed by the user.
SCROLLING	Specifies whether scroll bars are available to the user. This can take a value of YES, NO, or AUTO.
MARGINHEIGHT	Specifies the vertical offset in pixels from the border of the frame.
MARGINWIDTH	Specifies the horizontal offset in pixels from the border of the frame.

Table 8-1 *Attributes for the* FRAME *tag.*

To illustrate these attributes, look at the earlier example. The user can resize the frames by dragging on the border between the frames. By adding NORESIZE to either of the frames, this is prevented:

```
<FRAMESET ROWS="35%,*">
  <FRAME SRC="menu.html" NORESIZE>
  <FRAME SRC="welcome.html">
</FRAMESET>
```

or

```
<FRAMESET ROWS="35%,*">
  <FRAME SRC="menu.html">
  <FRAME SRC="welcome.html" NORESIZE>
</FRAMESET>
```

Typically, if a document fills more space than the frame it is assigned to, Navigator will add scroll bars to the frame. If you don't want scroll bars to appear, regardless of the size of the frame, you can use SCROLLING=NO to prevent them from being used:

```
<FRAMESET ROWS="35%,*">
  <FRAME SRC="menu.html">
  <FRAME SRC="welcome.html" SCROLLING=NO>
</FRAMESET>
```

As you can see in Figure 8-2, by using SCROLLING=NO, no scroll bars appear in the lower frame, even though the graphic is larger than the frame.

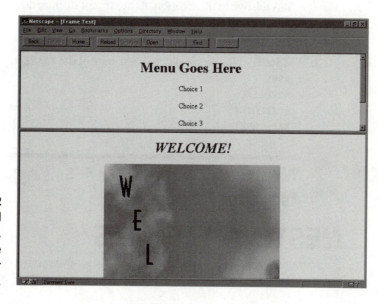

Figure 8-2
Preventing scroll bars in a frame, even when the document is larger than the frame.

QUIZ 1

1. The size of a frame can be specified in _____ or by using _____.
   a. pixels, percentages
   b. rows, columns
   c. percentages, number of rows or columns
   d. wildcards, number of rows or columns

2 The page displayed within a frame is specified by
   a. the `SRC` attribute of the `FRAMESET` tag.
   b. the `HREF` attribute of the `FRAME` tag.
   c. the `SRC` attribute of the `FRAME` tag.
   d. the `NAME` attribute of the `FRAME` tag.

3. Where is the `FRAMESET` tag placed?
   a. Before the `HEAD` tag.
   b. It replaces the `BODY` tag in the `HTML` file.
   c. Only inside a `FRAME` tag.
   d. Anywhere in the document.

4. What is a relative URL relative to?
   a. It is relative to the location of the previous document.
   b. It is relative to the location of the current document.
   c. It is relative to the `FRAMESET`.
   d. It is relative to the document in the previous frame.

5. Which of the following is not an attribute of the `FRAME` tag.
   a. `ROWS`
   b. `NORESIZE`
   c. `SCROLLING`
   d. `MARGINHEIGHT`

LESSON 2 Nesting, the NOFRAMES Tag, and Naming Frames

NESTING FRAMES

Looking at examples of frames on the Web, it quickly becomes obvious that many sites have more complex layouts than simply dividing the window into rows or columns.

For instance, in Figure 8-1 you saw an example of a site that has rows and columns combined to produce a very complex layout.

This is achieved by nesting, or embedding, FRAMESET containers within each other. For instance, if you want to produce a document with three frames where you have two rows and the bottom row is further divided in two columns (to produce three frames), you could use a structure like this:

```
<FRAMESET ROWS="30%,*">
  <FRAME SRC="menu.html">
  <FRAMESET COLS="50%,50%">
    <FRAME SRC="welcome.html">
    <FRAME SRC="pic.html" SCROLLING=AUTO>
  </FRAMESET>
</FRAMESET>
```

A similar result can be achieved by using separate files. For instance, if the first file contains

```
<FRAMESET ROWS="30%,*">
  <FRAME SRC="menu.html">
  <FRAME SRC="bottom.html">
</FRAMESET>
```

and the file bottom.html contains

```
<FRAMESET COLS="50%,50%">
  <FRAME SRC="welcome.html">
  <FRAME SRC="pic.html" SCROLLING=AUTO>
</FRAMESET>
```

then you would get the same result as the previous example where both FRAMESET containers appeared in the same file.

To get a better idea of how this works, you can look at the source code for *The Dataphile On-line*, which you saw in Figure 8-1. The following source code in Listing 8-1 combines the nested framesets from multiple files into a single file:

| Input |

Listing 8-1 The source code for *The Dataphile On-line* frames.

```
<FRAMESET ROWS="100,*">
  <FRAMESET COLS="500,*">
    <FRAME SRC="banner.htm" NORESIZE MARGINHEIGHT=0 ⇐
MARGINWIDTH=0 SCROLLING="no">
    <FRAMESET ROWS="30,*">
      <FRAME SRC="constant.htm" NORESIZE MARGINHEIGHT=0 ⇐
MARGINWIDTH=0 SCROLLING="no">
      <FRAME SRC="menu.htm" NORESIZE MARGINHEIGHT=0 ⇐
MARGINWIDTH=0 SCROLLING="auto">
    </FRAMESET>
  </FRAMESET>
```

continued on next page

continued from previous page

```
<FRAMESET COLS="*,250">
  <FRAMESET ROWS="*,50">
    <FRAME SRC="welcome.htm" NAME="middle" SCROLLING="auto">
    <FRAME SRC="search.htm" MARGINHEIGHT=2 MARGINWIDTH=2 SCROLLING="auto">
  </FRAMESET>
  <FRAMESET ROWS="50,*">

    <FRAME SRC="newshead.htm" SCROLLING="no" MARGINHEIGHT=0 MARGINWIDTH=0>
    <FRAME SRC="newstory.htm" SCROLLING="auto" MARGINGHEIGHT=2 MARGINWIDTH=2>
  </FRAMESET>
</FRAMESET>
</FRAMESET>
```

You start by dividing the window into two rows. The top row is divided into two columns, and the right column is further divided into two rows. Likewise, the bottom row is divided into two columns. The left column is divided into two rows, as is the right column.

THE NOFRAMES TAG

You may have noticed that the one problem with files containing **FRAMESET** containers is that they will go undisplayed on a non-Netscape browser, because other browsers don't support this extension to HTML.

This is addressed by the **NOFRAMES** container tag. Any HTML code contained between the **NOFRAMES** tags is ignored by the Navigator browser but will be displayed by any other browser.

For instance, this code

```
<HTML>

<HEAD>
<TITLE>NOFRAMES Example</TITLE>
</HEAD>

<FRAMESET ATTRIBUTES>
  <FRAME SRC="filename">
  <FRAME SRC="filename">
</FRAMESET>

<NOFRAMES>
  HTML code for other browsers
</NOFRAMES>

</HTML>
```

could be used to produce output like Figure 8-3 in Navigator 2.0 or 3.0 but like Figure 8-4 in another browser.

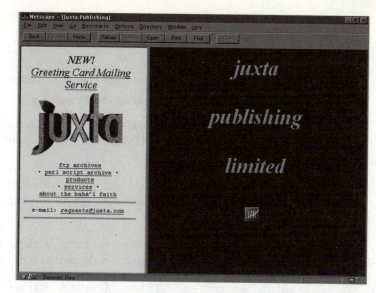

Figure 8-3
Only Navigator 2.0 recognizes the FRAMESET tag.

Figure 8-4
The NOFRAMES tag provides an alternative page for users of other browsers.

NAMING FRAMES

In order to place (or target) the result of links or form submissions in specific frames, you can name frames, using the **NAME** attribute of the **FRAME** tag. For instance,

```
<FRAMESET COLS="50%,*">
  <FRAME SRC="menu.html" NAME="menu">
  <FRAME SRC="welcome.html" NAME="main">
</FRAMESET>
```

would create two named frames called `menu` and `main`. In the file `menu.html`, you could have hypertext references target the `main` frame using the `TARGET` attribute:

```
<A HREF="choice1.html" TARGET="main">
```

Likewise, the result of a form submission could be targeted the same way:

```
<FORM METHOD=POST ACTION="/cgi-bin/test.pl" TARGET="main">
```

The `TARGET` attribute can also be used in the `BASE` tag to set a global target for all links in a document. For instance, if an HTML document has this `BASE` tag in its header

```
<BASE TARGET="main">
```

then all hypertext and results of form processing will appear in the `FRAME` named `"main"`. This global targeting is overridden by using a `TARGET` attribute in an `A` tag or `FORM` tag in the body of the HTML document.

Naming and targeting are not only relevant to frames. Windows can also be named and targeted as you learn later in this chapter, in the section about the `window` object.

In addition to targeting named frames, there are several special terms which can be used in the `TARGET` attributes. These are outlined in Table 8-2.

Value	Description
_blank	Causes a link to load in a new, unnamed window.
_self	Causes a link to load in the same window the anchor was clicked in. (This can be used to override a target specified in a BASE tag.)
_parent	Causes a link to load in the immediate FRAMESET parent.
_top	Causes a link to load in the full body of the window, regardless of the number of nested FRAMESET tags.

Table 8-2   *Special values for the* TARGET *attribute.*

1. How is a frame created that is subdivided into frames?
   a. By properly specifying both rows and columns in a frameset.
   b. By embedding a `FRAMESET` container inside another `FRAMESET` container.
   c. By placing a table inside of the frame.
   d. None of the above.

2. If content in a frameset is not displayed in a browser that is unaware of this tag, then how can this browser display what is between the NOFRAMES tags?
   a. Because Netscape ignores what is between the NOFRAMES tags.
   b. It is an error in the implementation of other browsers.
   c. Other browsers display an error message when they see a tag they do not understand.
   d. Other browsers will ignore the NOFRAMES tag but will still interpret what is between them.

3. What is the NAME attribute of a frame used for?
   a. So that the browser title bar will display the correct title.
   b. Because the only way to reference a specific frame is by its name.
   c. The NAME attribute makes it easier to target a specific frame with the result of a link or form submission.
   d. None of the above.

4. If a hypertext link inside a frame has no target attribute, then which frame will be its target frame?
   a. Either the base target specified for the current frame or the current frame, in that order.
   b. The current frame.
   c. Either the base target specified for the document or the current frame, in that order.
   d. The frame identified by _self.

5. Which of the following is not a special value for referencing a frame?
   a. _top
   b. _bottom
   c. _parent
   d. _self

 **Using Frames and Nested Framesets**

WORKING WITH FRAMES IN JAVASCRIPT

JavaScript provides the frames property of the window object for working with different frames from a script.

The frames property is an array of objects with an entry for each child frame in a parent frameset. The number of frames is provided by the length property.

For instance, in a given window or frameset with two frames, you could reference the frames as `parent.frames[0]` and `parent.frames[1]`. The index of the last frame could be `parent.frames.length`.

By using the `frames` array, you can access the functions and variables in another frame, as well as objects, such as forms and links, contained in another frame. This is useful when building an application that spans multiple frames but that also must be able to communicate between the frames.

Each frame has a different `document`, `location`, and `history` object associated with it. This is because each frame contains a separate HTML document and has a separate history list. You will learn about the `document` object later in this chapter and about the `history` object in Chapter 10, "Strings, Math, and the History List."

For example, if you have two frames, you could create a form in the first frame to provide the user with a field to enter an expression. Then you could display the results in a form in the other frame.

This cross-frame communication is achieved by referencing the `document` object's `forms[]` array in the second frame with `parent.frames[1].document.forms[0]`. In Listing 8-2 you build a simple calculator to evaluate expressions entered by users and use frames to display the output.

Input　**Listing 8-2** Cross-frame communication.

```html
<!-- HTML CODE FOR PARENT FRAMESET (this is a separate file) -->

<HTML>
<HEAD>
<TITLE>Listing 8-2</TITLE>
</HEAD>

<FRAMESET COLS="50%,*">
  <FRAME SRC="input.html">
  <FRAME SRC="output.html">
</FRAMESET>

</HTML>

<!-- HTML FOR INPUT FRAME (this is a separate file called input.html-->
<HTML>

<HEAD>
<SCRIPT LANGUAGE="JavaScript">
<!-- HIDE FROM OTHER BROWSERS
function update(field) {
  var result = field.value;
  var output = "" + result + " = " + eval(result);


  parent.frames[1].document.forms[0].result.value = output;
}
```

```
// STOP HIDING FROM OTHER BROWSERS -->
</SCRIPT>
</HEAD>

<BODY>
<FORM METHOD=POST>
<INPUT TYPE=text NAME="input" onChange="update(this);">
</FORM>
</BODY>

</HTML>

<HTML>

<!-- HTML FOR OUTPUT FRAME (this is a separate file called output.html)-->

<BODY>
<FORM METHOD=POST>
<TEXTAREA NAME=result ROWS=2 COLS=20 WRAP=SOFT></TEXTAREA>


</FORM>
</BODY>

</HTML>
```

In this example, it is important to note two things in the `update()` function. First, the `eval()` function used to evaluate the expression provided by the user doesn't work properly on the Windows 3.11 version of Navigator 2.0. Second, when you evaluate the expression and store the result in the variable `output`

```
var output = "" + result + " = " + eval(result);
```

you start the expression with " " to ensure a string value is assigned to the variable `output`.

In addition to specifying `frames` using the frames array, if you name the frames, you can specify certain frames using the form `parent.framename`. In the example you just saw, if you name the frames `input` and `output`, you could rewrite the `update()` function:

```
function update(field) {
  var result = field.value;
  var output = "" + result + " = " + eval(result);
  parent.output.form[0].result.value = output;
}
```

The frameset in this example would look like

```
<FRAMESET COLS="50%,*">
  <FRAME SRC="input.html" NAME="input">
  <FRAME SRC="output.html" NAME="output">
</FRAMESET>
```

The naming of elements can be taken one step further, and the forms can be named. For instance, if you name the forms `inputForm` and `outputForm`, then the files `input.html` and `output.html` can look like this:

```
<!-- HTML FOR INPUT FRAME (this is a separate file called input.html-->
<HTML>

<HEAD>
<SCRIPT LANGUAGE="JavaScript">
<!-- HIDE FROM OTHER BROWSERS
function update(field) {
  var result = field.value;
  var output = "" + result + " = " + eval(result);

  parent.output.document.outputForm.result.value = output;
}
// STOP HIDING FROM OTHER BROWSERS -->
</SCRIPT>
</HEAD>

<BODY>
<FORM METHOD=POST NAME="inputForm">
<INPUT TYPE=text NAME="input" onChange="update(this);">
</FORM>
</BODY>

</HTML>

<HTML>

<!-- HTML FOR OUTPUT FRAME (this is a separate file called output.html)-->

<BODY>
<FORM METHOD=POST NAME="outputForm">
<TEXTAREA NAME=result ROWS=2 COLS=20 WRAP=SOFT></TEXTAREA>
</FORM>
</BODY>

</HTML>
```

Notice, then, how the output field can be referred to with

```
parent.output.document.-outputForm.result
```

Nested Frames in JavaScript

With nested frames, cross-frame communication gets a little bit more complicated.

When building nested framesets, you can use subdocuments for each frameset. When you do this, the *parent will only refer back to the document containing the parent frameset and not the top-level frameset.*

For example, referring to the previous expression evaluation example, if you want to divide the display into four equal quarters (as shown in Figure 8-5) and then use only two of them, you would have to change the **FRAMESET** to be something like this

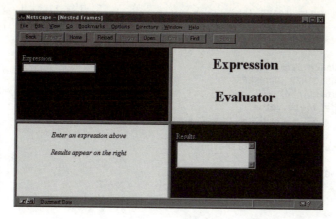

Figure 8-5
Using nested framesets produces complex screen layouts.

```
<FRAMESET ROWS="50%,*">
  <FRAME SRC="top.html">
  <FRAME SRC="bottom.html">
</FRAMESET>
```

where `top.html` and `bottom.html` contain further nested framesets as follows:

```
<!-- HTML FOR top.html -->

<FRAMESET COLS="50%,*">
    <FRAME SRC="input.html" NAME="input">
    <FRAME SRC="logo.html">
  </FRAMESET>

<!-- HTML FOR bottom.html -->

  <FRAMESET COLS="50%,*">
    <FRAME SRC="about.html">
    <FRAME SRC="output.html" NAME="output">
  </FRAMESET>
```

If `input.html` and `output.html` are still the files where the work is being done (`logo.html` and `about.html` are cosmetic), then you can't use the `update()` function you were using, because `parent.frame[1]` in the script will be referring to the frame containing `logo.html`—the parent of the `input` frame is the first nested frameset. You want to reference the frame containing `output.html`, which is in the second nested frameset. To reference this document, you need to go up two parent levels and then down two frames to reach `output.html`:

```
parent.parent.frame[1].frame[1]
```

With the named frame, this would become `parent.parent.frame[1].output`.

In addition to referring to variables and objects in other frames, the same technique can be used to invoke functions in other frames. For instance, you could add a function to `output.html` to handle displaying the results in the appropriate text field. Then, in `input.html` you could simply call the function and pass it the value of the variable `output`:

```
<!-- HTML FOR INPUT FRAME (this is a separate file called input.html-->
<HTML>

<HEAD>
<SCRIPT LANGUAGE="JavaScript">
<!-- HIDE FROM OTHER BROWSERS
function update(field) {
  var result = field.value;
  var output = "" + result + " = " + eval(result);

  parent.output.displayResult(output);
}
// STOP HIDING FROM OTHER BROWSERS -->
</SCRIPT>
</HEAD>

<BODY>
<FORM METHOD=POST NAME="inputForm">
<INPUT TYPE=text NAME="input" onChange="update(this);">
</FORM>
</BODY>

</HTML>

<HTML>

<!-- HTML FOR OUTPUT FRAME (this is a separate file called output.html)-->

<HEAD>
<SCRIPT LANGUAGE="JavaScript">
<!-- HIDE FROM OTHER BROWSERS

function displayResult(output) {

  document.ouputForm.result.value = output;

}

// STOP HIDING -->
</SCRIPT>
</HEAD>

<BODY>
<FORM METHOD=POST NAME="outputForm">
<TEXTAREA NAME=result ROWS=2 COLS=20 WRAP=SOFT></TEXTAREA>
</FORM>
</BODY>

</HTML>
```

Bill Dortch's hIdaho Frameset

It quickly becomes obvious that any program can get tangled up in deeply nested frames, all of which must interact with each other to produce an interactive application. This can quickly lead to confusing references to

```
parent.parent.frameA.frameB.frameC.form1.fieldA.value
```

or

```
parent.frameD.frameE.functionA()
```

To make this easier, Bill Dortch has produced the hIdaho Frameset. This is a set of freely available JavaScript functions to make dealing with functions in nested framesets easier. Dortch has made the hIdaho Frameset available for others to use in their scripts. Full information about the Frameset is on-line at

```
http://www.hidaho.com/frameset/
```

Using this Frameset, it is possible to register functions in a table and then call them from anywhere in a nested frameset without needing to know which frames they are defined in and without needing to use a long, and often confusing, sequence of objects and properties to refer to them. In addition, frames and framesets can be easily moved without having to recode each call to the affected functions across all your documents.

The hIdaho Frameset also provides a means of managing the timing of functions so you can ensure that a function has been loaded and registered before attempting to call it. This is especially useful during window and frame refreshes, when documents are reevaluated. The source code is reproduced on the CD-ROM:

```
<script language="JavaScript">
<!-- begin script
//*****************************************************************
// The hIdaho Frameset. Copyright©  1996 Bill Dortch, hIdaho Design
// Permission is granted to use and modify the hIdaho Frameset code,
// provided this notice is retained.
//*****************************************************************
var debug = false;
var amTopFrameset = false;
// set this to true for the topmost frameset⇐
var thisFrame = (amTopFrameset) ? null : self.name;
var maxFuncs = 32;
function makeArray (size) {
  this.length = size;
  for (var i = 1; i <= size; i++)
    this[i] = null;
  return this;
}
var funcs = new makeArray ((amTopFrameset) ? maxFuncs : 0);
function makeFunc (frame, func) {
  this.frame = frame;
  this.func = func;
  return this;
}
```

continued on next page

continued from previous page

```
function addFunction (frame, func) {
  for (var i = 1; i <= funcs.length; i++)
    if (funcs[i] == null) {
      funcs[i] = new makeFunc (frame, func);
      return true;
    }
  return false;
}
function findFunction (func) {
  for (var i = 1; i <= funcs.length; i++)
    if (funcs[i] != null)
      if (funcs[i].func == func)
        return funcs[i];
  return null;
}
function Register (frame, func) {
  if (debug) alert (thisFrame + ": ⇐
Register(" + frame + "," + func + ")");
  if (Register.arguments.length < 2)
    return false;
  if (!amTopFrameset)
    return parent.Register (thisFrame + "." + frame, func);
  if (findFunction (func) != null)
    return false;
  return addFunction (frame, func);
}
function UnRegister (func) {
  if (debug) alert (thisFrame + ": UnRegister(" + func + ")");
  if (UnRegister.arguments.length == 0)
    return false;
  if (!amTopFrameset)
    return parent.UnRegister (func);
  for (var i = 1; i <= funcs.length; i++)
    if (funcs[i] != null)
      if (funcs[i].func == func) {
        funcs[i] = null;
        return true;
      }
  return false;
}
function UnRegisterFrame (frame) {
  if (debug) alert (thisFrame + ": UnRegisterFrame(" + frame + ")");
  if (UnRegisterFrame.arguments.length == 0)
    return false;
  if (!amTopFrameset)
    return parent.UnRegisterFrame (thisFrame + "." + frame);
  for (var i = 1; i <= funcs.length; i++)
    if (funcs[i] != null)
      if (funcs[i].frame == frame) {
        funcs[i] = null;
      }
  return true;
}
```

```
function IsRegistered (func) {
  if (debug) alert (thisFrame + ": IsRegistered(" + func + ")");
  if (IsRegistered.arguments.length == 0)
    return false;
  if (!amTopFrameset)
    return parent.IsRegistered (func);
  if (findFunction (func) == null)
    return false;
  return true;
}
function Exec (func) {
  if (debug) alert (thisFrame + ": Exec(" + func + ")");
  var argv = Exec.arguments;
  if (argv.length == 0)
    return null;
  var arglist = new makeArray(argv.length);
  for (var i = 0; i < argv.length; i++)
    arglist[i+1] = argv[i];
  var argstr = "";
  for (i = ((amTopFrameset) ? 2 : 1); i <= argv.length; i++)
    argstr += "arglist[" + i + "]" + ((i < argv.length) ? "," : "");
  if (!amTopFrameset)
    return eval ("parent.Exec(" + argstr + ")");
  var funcobj = findFunction (func);
  if (funcobj == null)
    return null;
  return eval ("self." + ((funcobj.frame == null) ? "" : ⇐
(funcobj.frame + "."))+ funcobj.func + "(" + argstr + ")");
}
//****************************************************************
// End of hIdaho Frameset code.
//****************************************************************
// end script -->
</script>
```

The source code should be included in each frameset document in your hierarchy of nested framesets. The only important distinction is that the `amTopFrameset` variable should be set to `false` for all framesets except the top.

Each of the functions is used for a different purpose.

The `Register()` function.

The `Register()` function is used to register functions in the function table. It is called from the function's frame by referring to the function in the immediate parent frameset as follows: `parent.Register(self.name,"functionName")`.

`self` refers to the currently opened frame or window. You learn more about it later in this chapter.

The function will return `true` if there is room in the function table and the name is not currently registered. Otherwise, it will return `false`.

The `Unregister()` function.

This function does exactly what its name suggests: It removes a specific function from the registration table. It takes a single argument: `UnRegister("functionName")`.

continued on next page

continued from previous page

The `UnRegisterFrame()` function.

This function unregisters all functions registered for a specified frame. It takes the frame name as a single argument.

The `IsRegistered()` function.

A call to `IsRegistered("frameName")` returns `true` if the function is registered and `false` if it isn't.

The `Exec()` function.

The `Exec()` function is used to call a specific function. It takes at least one argument—the name of the function—but can take more in the form of parameters to pass to the called function as arguments. For instance, if you want to call the function `functionA` and pass two arguments, `arg1` and `arg2`, you could call

```
parent.Exec("functionA",arg1,arg2);
```

The `Exec()` function returns the value returned by the specified function.

It is not considered harmful to call an unregistered function using `Exec()`. If you do, a `null` value is returned. This can cause confusion, of course, if a legitimate value returned by the specified function could be the `null` value. This can happen when the frame containing the desired function has not finished loading when another frame's script tries to call it.

One way that Dortch suggests dealing with this timing problem is to use the `IsRegsistered()` function to ensure a function exists before calling it:

```
function intialize() {
  if (!parent.IsRegistered("functionA")) {
    setTimeout("initialize()",250);
    return;
  }
  JavaScript code
  parent.Exec("functionA",arg1,arg2);
  JavaScript code
}
```

In this example, the function `initialize()` will not get past the first `if` statement unless the function `functionA` has been registered. The function uses the `setTimeout()` method to cause a pause for 250 milliseconds after which `initialize()` is to be called again.

`setTimeout()` is a method of the `window` object that enables a pause to be specified before executing a command or evaluating an expression. We will look at the `setTimeout()` method, and the related `clearTimeout()` method, later in this chapter when we cover the `window` object.

The `initialize()` function is a recursive function that will continue to call itself every quarter second until the desired function is registered.

As indicated on the hIdaho Frameset Web page, Dortch has purposely not written functions to provide access to variables and other objects and properties in other frames because he feels that well-designed, multi-frame applications should use function calls to access information in other frames. Look for an updated version coming soon to his Web page.

PUTTING NESTED FRAMESETS TO WORK

Now that you know how to work with frames, you are going to produce a testing tool that teachers can use to easily produce a test in any given subject.

To do this, you will use nested framesets. The top-level frameset will produce three rows: one for the title, one for the work area, and one for a level selector.

The middle row, the work area, will be split into two equal columns. The left side will contain a form for the student to enter his answer as well as a field to display the current score. The right column will be used to display the questions and the result of a student's answer.

For these purposes, you only need to look at the source code for the student entry form and the level selection tool in the bottom frame. You will use Bill Dortch's hIdaho Frameset to make working with the nested framesets easier.

The frameset is defined by two files: the top-level `test.htm` (Listing 8-3) and `work.htm` (Listing 8-4) which defines the workspace in the middle row. `work.htm` contains the nested frameset referred to in `test.htm` (`<FRAME SRC="work.htm" NAME="work">`):

Input **Listing 8-3** Top-level frameset (`test.htm`).

```
<!-- FRAMESET FROM test.htm -->
<FRAMESET ROWS="20%,*,20%">
  <FRAME SRC="title.htm">
  <FRAME SRC="work.htm" NAME="work">
  <FRAME SRC="level.htm" NAME="level">
</FRAMESET>
```

Input **Listing 8-4** The nested frameset (`work.htm`).

```
<!-- FRAMESET FROM work.htm -->
<FRAMESET COLS="50%,*">
  <FRAME SRC="form.htm" NAME="form">
  <FRAME SRC="output.htm" NAME="output">
</FRAMESET>
```

Both `test.htm` and `work.htm` would include the source code of the hIdaho Frameset so that the programs can easily call functions in other frames. In the file `test.htm`, `amTopFrameset` should be set to `true` with the statement `amTopFrameset = true`. All of the functions and information are kept in the file `form.htm` (Listing 8-5). `form.htm` is one of the frames in the nested frameset.

Input **Listing 8-5** The entry form (`form.htm`).

```
<!-- SOURCE CODE OF form.htm -->
<HTML>

<HEAD>
<SCRIPT LANGUAGE="JavaScript">
```

continued on next page

continued from previous page

```
<!-- HIDE FROM OTHER BROWSERS

var currentLevel=1;
var currentQuestion=1;
var toOutput = "";

// DEFINE LEVEL ONE
q1 = new question("1 + 3",4);
q2 = new question("4 + 5",9);
q3 = new question("5 - 4",1);
q4 = new question("7 + 3",10);
q5 = new question("4 + 4",8);
q6 = new question("3 - 3",0);
q7 = new question("9 - 5",4);
q8 = new question("8 + 1",9);
q9 = new question("5 - 3",2);
q10 = new question("8 - 3",5);
levelOne = new level(q1,q2,q3,q4,q5,q6,q7,q8,q9,q10);

// DEFINE LEVEL TWO
q1 = new question("15 + 23",38);
q2 = new question("65 - 32",33);
q3 = new question("99 + 45",134);
q4 = new question("34 - 57",-23);
q5 = new question("-34 - 57",-91);
q6 = new question("23 + 77",100);
q7 = new question("64 + 32",96);
q8 = new question("64 - 32",32);
q9 = new question("12 + 34",46);
q10 = new question("77 + 77",154);
levelTwo = new level(q1,q2,q3,q4,q5,q6,q7,q8,q9,q10);

// DEFINE LEVEL THREE
q1 = new question("10 * 7",70);
q2 = new question("15 / 3",5);
q3 = new question("34 * 3",102);
q4 = new question("33 / 2",16.5);
q5 = new question("100 / 4",25);
q6 = new question("99 / 6",16.5);
q7 = new question("32 * 3",96);
q8 = new question("48 / 4",12);
q9 = new question("31 * 0",0);
q10 = new question("45 / 1",45);
levelThree = new level(q1,q2,q3,q4,q5,q6,q7,q8,q9,q10);

// DEFINE TEST
test = new newTest(levelOne,levelTwo,levelThree);

function newTest(levelOne,levelTwo,levelThree) {
  this[1] = levelOne;
  this[2] = levelTwo;
  this[3] = levelThree;
```

```
}

function level(q1,q2,q3,q4,q5,q6,q7,q8,q9,q10) {
   this[1] = q1;
   this[2] = q2;
   this[3] = q3;
   this[4] = q4;
   this[5] = q5;
   this[6] = q6;
   this[7] = q7;
   this[8] = q8;
   this[9] = q9;
   this[10] = q10;
}

function question(question,answer) {
   this.question = question;
   this.answer = answer;
}

parent.Register(self.name,"startTest");
function startTest(newLevel) {
   currentLevel=newLevel;
   currentQuestion=1;
   document.forms[0].answer.value="";
   document.forms[0].score.value=0;
   displayQuestion();
}

function displayQuestion() {
   ask = test[currentLevel][currentQuestion].question;
   answer = test[currentLevel][currentQuestion].answer;
   toOutput = "" + currentQuestion + ". What is " + ask + "?";
   document.forms[0].answer.value = "";
   window.open("display.htm","output");
}

parent.Register(self.name,"output");
function output() {
   return toOutput;
}

function checkAnswer(form) {


   answer = form.answer.value;

   if (answer == "" || answer == null) {
     alert("Please enter an answer.");
      return;
   }

   correctAnswer = test[currentLevel][currentQuestion].answer;
```

continued on next page

continued from previous page

```
        ask = test[currentLevel][currentQuestion].question;
        score = form.score.value;
        if (eval(answer) == correctAnswer) {
          toOutput = "Correct!";
          score ++;
          form.score.value = score;
        } else {
          toOutput = "Sorry! " + ask + " is " + correctAnswer + ".";
        }
        window.open("display.htm","output");
        if (currentQuestion < 10) {
          currentQuestion ++;
          setTimeout("displayQuestion()",3000);
        } else {
          toOutput = "You're Done!<BR>You're score is " + score + " out of 10.";
          setTimeout("window.open('display.htm','output')",3000);
          form.answer.value="";
          form.score.value="0";
        }
      }


      function welcome() {
        toOutput = "Welcome!";
        window.open("display.htm","output");
      }


      // STOP HIDING FROM OTHER BROWSERS -->
      </SCRIPT>

      </HEAD>

      <BODY BGCOLOR="#FFFFFF" TEXT="#0000FF" onLoad="welcome();">

      <FORM METHOD=POST>
      <CENTER>
      <STRONG>Type You're Answer Here:</STRONG><BR>
      <INPUT TYPE=text NAME=answer SIZE=30><P>
      <INPUT TYPE=button NAME=done VALUE="Check Answer" ⇐
      onClick="checkAnswer(this.form);"><P>
      Correct Answers So Far:<BR>
      <INPUT TYPE=text NAME=score VALUE="0" SIZE=10>
      </FORM>

      </BODY>

      </HTML>
```

The file `level.htm` (Listing 8-6) provides users with three buttons to select different levels. `level.htm` is the bottom frame in the parent frameset:

Input

Listing 8-6 Level selection controls.

```
<!-- SOURCE CODE OF level.htm -->
<HTML>

<BODY BGCOLOR="#000000" TEXT="#FFFFFF">
<CENTER>
<STRONG>
Select a level here:
<FORM METHOD=POST>
<INPUT TYPE=button NAME="one" VALUE="Level One" ⇐
onClick="parent.Exec('startTest',1);">
<INPUT TYPE=button NAME="two" VALUE="Level Two" ⇐
onClick="parent.Exec('startTest',2);">
<INPUT TYPE=button NAME="three" VALUE="Level Three" ⇐
onClick="parent.Exec('startTest',3);">
</FORM>
</STRONG>
</CENTER>
</BODY>

</HTML>
```

All display in the frame named `output` is done by reloading the file `display.htm` (Listing 8-7):

Input

Listing 8-7 `display.htm` is reloaded to update the output.

```
<!-- SOURCE CODE OF display.htm -->
<HTML>

<BODY BGCOLOR="#0000FF" TEXT="#FFFFFF">
<H1>
<SCRIPT LANGUAGE="JavaScript">
<!-- HIDE FROM OTHER BROWSERS

document.write(parent.Exec("output"));

// STOP HIDING FROM OTHER BROWSERS -->
</SCRIPT>
</H1>
</BODY>

</HTML>
```

Finally, `title.htm` (Listing 8-8) contains the information displayed in the top frame of the parent frameset:

Listing 8-8 The title frame.

```
<!-- SOURCE CODE OF title.htm -->
<HTML>

<BODY BGCOLOR="#000000" TEXT="#00FFFF">
<CENTER>
<H1>
<STRONG>
The Math Test
</STRONG>
</H1>
</CENTER>
</BODY>

</HTML>
```

The final product would look something like Figure 8-6.

As you can see in the source code listings, the file **form.htm** (Listing 8-5) is the centerpiece of the entire application. It is in this file that all the work of checking answers, displaying questions and results, and resetting the test is done.

Let's look at the document section by section.

```
var currentLevel=1;
var currentQuestion=1;
var toOutput = "";
```

These are the key global variables in the script which are used to keep track of the current level being tested, the current question being tested, and what should next be displayed in the **output** frame.

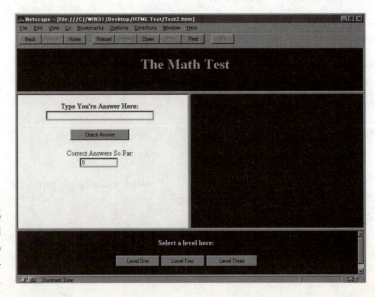

Figure 8-6
Using nested framesets to produce a multi-level math test.

Next the questions and answers for the three levels are defined:

```
// DEFINE LEVEL ONE
q1 = new question("1 + 3",4);
q2 = new question("4 + 5",9);
q3 = new question("5 - 4",1);
q4 = new question("7 + 3",10);
q5 = new question("4 + 4",8);
q6 = new question("3 - 3",0);
q7 = new question("9 - 5",4);
q8 = new question("8 + 1",9);
q9 = new question("5 - 3",2);
q10 = new question("8 - 3",5);
levelOne = new level(q1,q2,q3,q4,q5,q6,q7,q8,q9,q10);


// DEFINE LEVEL TWO
q1 = new question("15 + 23",38);
q2 = new question("65 - 32",33);
q3 = new question("99 + 45",134);
q4 = new question("34 - 57",-23);
q5 = new question("-34 - 57",-91);
q6 = new question("23 + 77",100);
q7 = new question("64 + 32",96);
q8 = new question("64 - 32",32);
q9 = new question("12 + 34",46);
q10 = new question("77 + 77",154);
levelTwo = new level(q1,q2,q3,q4,q5,q6,q7,q8,q9,q10);


// DEFINE LEVEL THREE
q1 = new question("10 * 7",70);
q2 = new question("15 / 3",5);
q3 = new question("34 * 3",102);
q4 = new question("33 / 2",16.5);
q5 = new question("100 / 4",25);
q6 = new question("99 / 6",16.5);
q7 = new question("32 * 3",96);
q8 = new question("48 / 4",12);
q9 = new question("31 * 0",0);
q10 = new question("45 / 1",45);
levelThree = new level(q1,q2,q3,q4,q5,q6,q7,q8,q9,q10);


// DEFINE TEST
test = new newTest(levelOne,levelTwo,levelThree);

function newTest(levelOne,levelTwo,levelThree) {
   this[1] = levelOne;
   this[2] = levelTwo;
   this[3] = levelThree;
}

function level(q1,q2,q3,q4,q5,q6,q7,q8,q9,q10) {
   this[1] = q1;
   this[2] = q2;
   this[3] = q3;
```

continued on next page

continued from previous page

```
      this[4] = q4;
      this[5] = q5;
      this[6] = q6;
      this[7] = q7;
      this[8] = q8;
      this[9] = q9;
      this[10] = q10;
   }



function question(question,answer) {
   this.question = question;
   this.answer = answer;
}
```

The test consists of three levels with 10 questions each. You store all this information in a series of objects. The **question** object has two properties: **question** and **answer**. The **level** object consists of 10 questions as properties. The **test** object has three properties—each level of the test.

Notice that you only name the properties in the **question** object. This is because you will want to access the level and particular question using numeric indexes rather than names. For instance, you could refer to level one as **test[1]** and question three of level one as **test[1][3]** (notice the use of two indexes next to each other) and the answer to question three of level one as **test[1][3].answer**.

The structure described here is known as a *nested object construct*. In this example, **test** is an object. It has a set of properties (all objects in this case) which can be referred to by their numerical index. So, **test[1]** is a property of **test** and an object in its own right. Because **test[1]** is an object, it can also have properties, in this case, referred to by numerical index. So, **test[1][3]** is a property of **test[1]** and, again, this property is itself an object. Once again, as an object, **test[1][3]** can have properties—in this case, **answer**, referenced by name as **test[1][3].answer**.

The next function in Listing 8-5 is the **startTest()** function:

```
parent.Register(self.name,"startTest");
function startTest(newLevel) {
   currentLevel=newLevel;
   currentQuestion=1;
   document.forms[0].answer.value="";
   document.forms[0].score.value=0;
   displayQuestion();
}
```

The **startTest()** function is one of the functions you register with the **parent.Register()** function from the hIdaho Frameset. You do this because you want to be able to call the function from the **level** frame.

The function accepts a single argument—the level of the new test—and sets **currentLevel** and **currentQuestion** appropriately, as well as clearing the fields of the form. Then the function calls **displayQuestion()** to start the test.

```
function displayQuestion() {
  ask = test[currentLevel][currentQuestion].question;
  answer = test[currentLevel][currentQuestion].answer;
  toOutput = "" + currentQuestion + ". What is " + ask + "?";
  document.forms[0].answer.value = "";
  window.open("display.htm","output");
}
```

This function is used to display each successive question. It takes no arguments but gets its information from the global variables `currentLevel` and `currentQuestion`. In this way, it can get the current text of the question by using `test[currentLevel][currentQuestion].question`.

The function then stores the complete output in `toOutput` and uses the method `window.open()` to open `display.htm` in the frame named `output`. As you will learn later in the section on the `window` object, `open()` can be used to open files in named frames and windows.

```
parent.Register(self.name,"output");
function output() {
  return toOutput;
}
```

Like the `startTest()` function, you register the `output()` function with `parent.Register()`. The function simply returns the value of `toOutput` and is used to update the display in the output frame, as you will see when you look at the source code of the file `display.htm`.

```
function checkAnswer(form) {
  answer = form.answer.value;

  if (answer == "" || answer == null) {
    alert("Please enter an answer.");
      return;
  }

  correctAnswer = test[currentLevel][currentQuestion].answer;
  ask = test[currentLevel][currentQuestion].question;
  score = form.score.value;
  if (eval(answer) == correctAnswer) {
    toOutput = "Correct!";
    score ++;
    form.score.value = score;
  } else {
    toOutput = "Sorry! " + ask + " is " + correctAnswer + ".";
  }
  window.open("display.htm","output");
  if (currentQuestion < 10) {
    currentQuestion ++;
    setTimeout("displayQuestion()",3000);
  } else {
    toOutput = "You're Done!<BR>You're score is " + score + " out of 10.";
    setTimeout("window.open('display.htm','output')",3000);
    form.answer.value="";
```

continued on next page

continued from previous page

```
        form.score.value="0";
    }
}
```

`checkAnswer()` is where the bulk of the work is done in the script.

Because `checkAnswer()` is called from the form, it takes a single argument for the `form` object. The function compares the student's answer stored in the field `form.answer` with the correct answer taken from the `test` object.

If the student answered correctly, an appropriate message is stored in `toOutput`, and the score is incremented and displayed. If the answer is wrong, an appropriate message is stored in `toOutput`, but the score is left untouched. Once the answer is checked, the message is displayed using `window.open()` to open `display.htm` in the `output` frame.

The function then uses the condition `currentQuestion < 10` to check if the question just answered is the last question in the test. If it is not the last question, then the `currentQuestion` variable is increased by one to go to the next question and `setTimeout()` is used to wait three seconds (3000 milliseconds) before displaying the new question with `displayQuestion()`.

Otherwise, the function stores the results of the test in `toOutput`, displays them with a similar three-second delay using `setTimeout()`, and then clears the `answer` and `score` fields of the form.

```
function welcome() {
  toOutput = "Welcome!";
  window.open("display.htm","output");
}
```

The function `welcome()` stores a welcome message in `toOutput` and then displays it by loading `display.htm` into the `output` frame.

```
<BODY BGCOLOR="#FFFFFF" TEXT="#0000FF" onLoad="welcome();">
```

After the document finishes loading, the `welcome()` function is called using the `onLoad` event handler.

Note

In the preceding segment of the `BODY` tag, you will notice the use of RGB triplets to define color for the background and text in the document. The RGB triplets (such as `FFFFFF` and `00FFFF`) define colors as combinations of red, blue, and green. The six hexadecimal digits consist of three pairs of the form: `RRGGBB`. The use of colors in documents is discussed in more detail later in this chapter in the section about the `document` object.

```
<FORM METHOD=POST>
<CENTER>
<STRONG>Type You're Answer Here:</STRONG><BR>
<INPUT TYPE=text NAME=answer SIZE=30><P>
<INPUT TYPE=button NAME=done VALUE="Check Answer" ⇐
onClick="checkAnswer(this.form);"><P>
Correct Answers So Far:<BR>
<INPUT TYPE=text NAME=score VALUE="0" SIZE=10 onFocus="this.blur();">
</FORM>
```

This form is where most user interaction takes place—with the exception of the **level** frame. It has a text entry field named **answer** where users type their answers to each question, a button they click on to check their answers, and a text field to display the current score.

Only two event handlers are used: **onClick="checkAnswer(this.form);"** to check the users' answer and **onFocus="this.blur;"** to ensure users don't try to cheat by changing their own scores.

The file **level.htm** (Listing 8-6) contains a simple three-button form to start a new test at any of the three levels:

```
<FORM METHOD=POST>
<INPUT TYPE=button NAME="one" VALUE="Level One" ⇐
onClick="parent.Exec('startTest',1);">
<INPUT TYPE=button NAME="two" VALUE="Level Two" ⇐
onClick="parent.Exec('startTest',2);">
<INPUT TYPE=button NAME="three" VALUE="Level Three" ⇐
onClick="parent.Exec('startTest',3);">
</FORM>
```

Each button has a similar **onClick** event handler which uses **parent.Exec()** to call the **startTest()** function from the **form** frame and pass it a single integer argument for the level.

The only other file involving JavaScript scripting is **display.htm** which sets up the body of the document and then uses **document.write()** to display the result returned by **output()** from the **form** frame. The function is called using **parent.Exec()**. In this way, every time the main script in **form.htm** reloads **display.htm**, the current value of **toOutput** is returned by **output()** and displayed as the body text for **display.htm**.

You could have written the output directly to the output frame using **document.write()**. You will see an example of this later in the chapter.

1. What is the **frames** property of the **window** object?
   a. An array of objects with an entry for each child frame in a parent frameset.
   b. An object containing the top-level frameset.
   c. An object containing the first frame in the document.
   d. An object with an entry for each frameset in the document.

2. How can a script in one frame access another frame?
   a. This cannot be done.
   b. By using the **TARGET** attribute.
   c. This can be done by referencing the **frames** property of the parent window.
   d. None of the above.

3. What does the parent attribute refer to?
   a. The top-level frameset.
   b. The document containing the parent frameset.
   c. The document containing the current frameset.
   d. The `navigator` object.

4. Using the hIdaho Frameset scripts, what value will `Exec()` return if it is used to call a function that has not been registered yet?
   a. null
   b. an arbitrary value
   c. zero
   d. the default value

5. In the test example, `test` is a nested object construct. What does this mean?
   a. It means that you can refer to the properties of `test` by their array locations.
   b. It means that you can refer to the properties of `test` by double array indexes.
   c. It means that `test` is an object that is nested inside another object.
   d. It means that some of the properties of `test` are objects themselves.

 **LESSON 4** ## The document **Object and its Properties**

THE document OBJECT

In any given window or frame, one of the primary objects is the **document** object. The **document** object provides the properties and methods to work with numerous aspects of the current document, including information about anchors, forms, links, the title, the current location and URL, and the current colors.

You already have been introduced to some of the features of the **document** object in the form of the **document.write()** and **document.writeln()** methods, as well as the **form** object and all of its properties and methods.

The **document** object is defined when the **BODY** tag is evaluated in an HTML page and the object remains in existence as long as the page is loaded. Because many of the properties of the **document** object are reflections of attributes of the **BODY** tag, you should have a complete grasp of all the attributes available in the **BODY** tag in Navigator 2.0.

The BODY Tag

The **BODY** tag defines the main body of an HTML document. Its attributes enable the HTML author to define colors for text and links, as well as background colors or patterns for the document.

In addition, as you have already learned, there are two event handlers, onLoad and onUnload, that can be used in the BODY tag.

The following is a list of available attributes for the BODY tag:

- BACKGROUND—Specifies the URL of a background image.

- BGCOLOR—Specifies a background color for the document as a hexadecimal RGB triplet or a color name. Color names available in Navigator 2.0 are listed at the end of the chapter.

- FGCOLOR—Specifies the foreground (and text) color as a hexadecimal triplet.

- LINK—Specifies the color for links as a hexadecimal triplet.

- ALINK—Specifies the color for an active link (when the user has the mouse clicked on a link until the user releases the mouse button) as a hexadecimal triplet.

- VLINK—Specifies the color for a followed link as a hexadecimal triplet.

Properties of the document Object

Table 8-3 outlines the properties of the document object.

Property	Description
alinkColor	The RGB value for the color of activated links expressed as a hexadecimal triplet.
anchors	Array of objects corresponding to each named anchor in a document.
applets	Array of objects corresponding to each Java applet included in a document. The applets array will be discussed in detail in Chapter 14.
bgColor	The RGB value of the background color as a hexadecimal triplet.
cookie	Contains the value of the cookies for the current document. Cookies are discussed in depth in Chapter 9.
embeds	Array of objects reflecting each plug-in in a document. The embeds array will be discussed in detail in Chapter 14.
fgColor	The RGB value of the foreground color as a hexadecimal triplet.

continued on next page

continued from previous page

Property	Description
forms	Array of objects corresponding to each form in a document.
images	Array of objects corresponding to each in-line image included in a document.
lastModified	A string containing the last date the document was modified.
linkColor	The RGB value of links as a hexadecimal triplet.
links	An array of objects corresponding to each link in a document. Links can be hypertext links or clickable areas of an imagemap.
location	The full URL of the document. This is the same as the URL property. URL should be used instead of location.
referrer	Contains the URL of the document that called the current document.
title	A string containing the title of the document.
URL	The full URL of the document.
vlinkColor	The RGB value of followed links as a hexadecimal triplet.

Table 8-3 *Properties of the* document *object.*

Some of these properties are obvious. For instance, in a document containing the tag

```
<BODY BGCOLOR="#FFFFFF" FGCOLOR="#000000" LINK="#0000FF">
```

document.bgColor would have a value of "#FFFFFF", document.fgColor would equal "#000000", and document.linkColor would be "#0000FF".

In addition, you have already learned to use the forms array.

However, the anchors, images, and links arrays, along with the location object, deserve a closer look.

The anchors *Array*

While the <A> tag in HTML is usually used to define hypertext links to other documents, it can also be used to define named anchors in a document so that links within a document can jump to other places in the document.

For instance, in the HTML page

```
<HTML>

<HEAD>
```

```
<TITLE>Anchors Example</TITLE>
</HEAD>

<BODY>
<A NAME="one">Anchor one is here
HTML Code
<A NAME="two">Anchor two is here
More HTML Code
<A HREF="#one">Go back to Anchor One</A><BR>
<A HREF="#two">GO back to Anchor Two</A>
</BODY>

</HTML>
```

two anchors are defined using **<A NAME="anchorName">** (**<A NAME="one">** and **<A NAME="two">**), and links to those anchors are created using **<A HREF="#anchorName">** (**<A HREF="#one">** and **<A HREF="#two">**).

JavaScript provides the **anchors** array as a means to access information and methods related to anchors in the current document. Each element in the array is an **anchor** object, and like all arrays, the array has a **length** property.

The order of anchors in the array follows the order of appearance of the anchors in the HTML document.

Therefore, in the example, **document.anchors.length** would have a value of **1** (since the **anchors** array, like the **forms** array and **frames** array, starts with a zero index), and **document.anchors[0]** would refer to the anchor named **one**.

The images *Array*

The **images** array is only implemented in Navigator 3.0. It was unavailable in Navigator 2.0.

Any image included in an HTML document with the **IMG** tag is accessible through the **images** array. Like the **anchors** array, the **images** array has a **length** property.

Each entry in the array is an **Image** object, which has nine properties that reflect information about the image and information in the **IMG** tag:

- **src:** A string reflecting the SRC attribute of the IMG tag.

- **lowsrc:** A string reflecting the LOWSRC attribute of the IMG tag. The LOWSRC attribute specifies a low-resolution version of the image file included in the SRC tag.

- **name:** A string reflecting the NAME attribute of the IMG tag.

- **height:** An integer reflecting the height of the image in pixels. This reflects the value of the HEIGHT attribute of the IMG tag.

- **width:** An integer reflecting the width of the image in pixels. This reflects the value of the WIDTH attribute in the IMG tag.

- **border:** An integer indicating the width of the image border in pixels. This reflects the value of the BORDER attribute of the IMG tag.

- .vspace: An integer reflecting the vertical space, in pixels, around an image. This reflects the value of the vSPACE attribute of the IMG tag.

- hspace: An integer reflecting the horizontal space, in pixels, around an image. This will reflect the value of the HSPACE attribute of the IMG tag.

- complete: A Boolean value indicating whether Navigator has finished downloading the image.

Most of these properties are read-only—that is, their values cannot be set in a script. src and lowsrc, however, can be dynamically changed. The result of changing these values will update the display with the new image specified.

When an new image is specified by changing the value of src or lowsrc, it is scaled to fit into the space used by the original image.

Images also have three event handlers associated with them:

- onLoad: Indicates JavaScript code to execute when an image finishes loading.

- onError: Indicates JavaScript code to execute when there is an error loading the image.

- onAbort: Indicates JavaScript code to execute when the user aborts loading an image (for instance, when the user clicks on the Stop button).

In addition to instances of the **Image** object in the **images** array, it is possible to create additional **Image** objects using the **Image()** constructor.

This causes an image to be loaded across the network, but the image will not be displayed until the object is assigned to one of the **Image** objects in the **images** array. To create an **Image** object using the constructor function, use the following syntax:

```
newImageName = new Image();
newImageName.src = "filename";
```

Then, the image could be displayed in place of an image already rendered to the window by using

```
document.images[index].src = myImage.src;
```

The links *Array*

Just as the **anchors** array provides a sequential list of all the anchors in a document, the **links** array offers an entry for each hypertext link defined by **<A HREF="URL">** in an HTML document or as a clickable area in an imagemap using the **AREA** tag.

Also like the **anchors** array, each element in the **links** array is a **link** object or an **Area** object, and the array has a **length** property.

The **link** object has a several properties and event handlers, as defined in the following list:

- ● hash: A string reflecting the anchor portion of the link URL (the portion after the "#" symbol)

- ● host: A string reflecting the host and domain name of the link URL

- ● hostname: A string reflecting the host, domain name, and port number of the link URL (includes the colon)

- ● href: A string reflecting the entire link URL

- ● pathname: A string reflecting the path portion of the link URL

- ● port: A string reflecting the port number from the link URL

- ● protocol: A string reflecting the protocol from the link URL, including the trailing colon

- ● search: A string reflecting the query portion of the link URL (the portion after the "?" symbol)

- ● target: A string reflecting the TARGET attribute

- ● onClick: Specifies code to execute when the user clicks on the link—use return false in the event handler's code to cancel the click event

- ● onMouseOut: Specifies code to execute when the user moves the mouse pointer off the link

- ● onMouseOver: Specifies code to execute when the user moves the mouse pointer onto the link

The **Area** object offers the same properties and event handlers with the exception of onClick.

Methods of the document **Object**

In addition to the **write()** and **writeln()** methods which you have been using throughout the book, the **document** object provides three other methods: **open()**, **close()**, and **clear()**.

The **open()** method is used to open the document window for writing a MIME type. It takes a single argument: the **MIME** type (such as **text/html**). You can also use the **window.open()** method to open a window or frame for writing a document, as you will see in the section on the **window** object.

MIME stands for Multi-purpose Internet Mail Extensions. MIME provides a way to exchange files in any format between computers using Internet mail standards. MIME supports pre-defined file types and allows the creation of custom types. MIME types are specified using two-part codes, such as **text/html** for HTML files and **image/gif** for GIF bitmap graphics.

Furthermore, `close()` closes the document window for writing, and the `clear()` method clears the current document window. Document output is not actually rendered (displayed) until `document.close()` is called.

USING THE document OBJECT IN A COLOR TESTER

For this example, you are going to build a simple utility to demonstrate what different combinations of text, link, and background colors look like.

The application will use two frames: The top frame contains five text entry fields for the background color, text color, link color, active link color, and followed link color, plus a button to enable users to test their color combinations.

When users press the button, the script loads a simple document, using the specified colors, into the lower frame. The users should be able to specify colors by hexadecimal triplets or by name.

To do this, you don't need to use the hIdaho Frameset you used in Listings 8-3 through 8-8 because you won't be using nested framesets or making cross-frame function calls.

The parent frameset is defined in Listings 8-9 and 8-10.

| Input |

Listing 8-9 The parent frameset for the color tester.

```
<HTML>

<HEAD>
<TITLE>Example 8.9</TITLE>
</HEAD>

<FRAMESET ROWS="45%,*">
  <FRAME SRC="pick.htm">
  <FRAME SRC="blank.htm" NAME="output">
</FRAMESET>

</HTML>
```

The source code for the file `pick.htm`, where all the processing occurs, is in Listing 8-10.

| Input |

Listing 8-10 The `pick.htm` file.

```
<HTML>

<HEAD>

<SCRIPT LANGUAGE="JavaScript">
<!-- HIDE FORM OTHER BROWSERS

function display(form) {
  doc = open("","output");
  doc.document.write ('<BODY BGCOLOR="' + form.bg.value);
```

```
    doc.document.write ('" TEXT="' + form.fg.value);
    doc.document.write ('" LINK="' + form.link.value);
    doc.document.write ('" ALINK="' + form.alink.value);
    doc.document.write ('" VLINK="' + form.vlink.value);
    doc.document.writeln ('">');
    doc.document.write("<H1>This is a test</H1>");
    doc.document.write("You have selected these colors.<BR>");
    doc.document.write('<A ⇐
HREF="#">⇐
    This is a test link</A>');
    doc.document.write("</BODY>");
    doc.document.close();
}

// STOP HIDING SCRIPT -->
</SCRIPT>

</HEAD>

<BODY>

<CENTER>

<SCRIPT LANGUAGE="JavaScript">
<!-- HIDE FROM OTHER BROWSERS

document.write('<H1>The Colour Picker</H1>');
document.write('<FORM METHOD=POST>');
document.write('Enter Colors:<BR>');

document.write('Background: <INPUT TYPE=text NAME="bg" ⇐
VALUE="' + document.bgColor + '"> ... ');
document.write('Text: <INPUT TYPE=text NAME="fg" ⇐
VALUE="' + document.fgColor + '"><BR>');
document.write('Link: <INPUT TYPE=text NAME="link" ⇐
VALUE ="' + document.linkColor + '"> ...');
document.write('Active Link: <INPUT TYPE=text NAME="alink" ⇐
VALUE="' + document.alinkColor + '"><BR>');
document.write('Followed Link: <INPUT TYPE="text" NAME="vlink" ⇐
VALUE ="' + document.vlinkColor + '"><BR>');
document.write('<INPUT TYPE=button VALUE="TEST" ⇐
onClick="display(this.form);">');

document.write('</FORM>');

display(document.forms[0]);

// STOP HIDING FROM OTHER BROWSERS -->
</SCRIPT>

</CENTER>

</BODY>

</HTML>
```

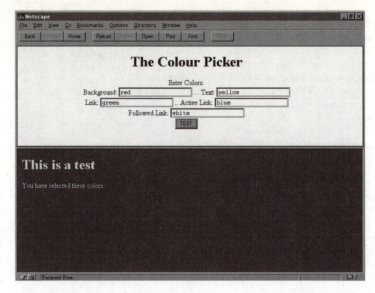

Figure 8-7
With JavaScript,
you can
dynamically
test color
combinations.

The program produces results like those in Figure 8-7.

As you can see in this example, all the work is being done in the top frame, which contains the document `pick.htm`.

The file has two main components: a JavaScript function and the body of the document, which is almost entirely generated by another JavaScript script using the `document.write()` and `document.writeln()` methods.

The interface consists of a single form containing five fields for each of the color values, plus a button that calls the function `display()`.

```
function display(form) {
   doc = open("","output");
   doc.document.write ('<BODY BGCOLOR="' + form.bg.value);
   doc.document.write ('" TEXT="' + form.fg.value);
   doc.document.write ('" LINK="' + form.link.value);
   doc.document.write ('" ALINK="' + form.alink.value);
   doc.document.write ('" VLINK="' + form.vlink.value);
   doc.document.writeln ('">');
   doc.document.write("<H1>This is a test</H1>");
   doc.document.write("You have selected these colors.<BR>");
   doc.document.write('<A ⇐
HREF="#">⇐
      This is a test link</A>');

   doc.document.write("</BODY>");
   doc.document.close();
}
```

The function is fairly simple: An empty document is opened in the `output` frame using the `window.open()` method, and the name `doc` is assigned for JavaScript to refer to that window (frame).

The commands `doc.document.write()` and `doc.document.writeln()` can then be used to write HTML to the newly opened window. The values of the five form fields are then used to build a custom `BODY` tag that defines all the colors for the document. After the text has been output, the method `doc.document.close()` is used to close the open document and finish displaying it in the frame.

With this single function, you can build a simple form in the body of the document. The form is built by a JavaScript script that assigns initial values to the five fields using properties of the `document` object to set the values to the current browser defaults. Then the script calls `display()` so that an initial sample is displayed in the lower frame.

As with many programs, there is more than one way to achieve a desired effect. For instance, the `display()` function could be rewritten to change the colors dynamically—without rewriting the content of the frame—by using the color properties of the document object:

```
function display(form) {
   parent.output.document.bgColor = form.bg.value;
   parent.output.document.fgColor = form.fg.value;
   parent.output.document.linkClor = form.link.value;
   parent.output.document.alinkColor = form.alink.value;
   parent.output.document.vlinkColor = form.vlink.value;
}
```

Then you simply can remove the call to `display()` in the body of the HTML document, make the content of the output frame a separate HTML document, and load the sample document into the lower frame in the parent frameset.

1. What does the `document` object represent?
    a. It is an array representing the collection of documents currently loaded.
    b. The document loaded in the current frame or window.
    c. The top-level document.
    d. A generic HTML document.

2. When is the `document` object created?
    a. When the `window` object is created.
    b. When Netscape is loaded.
    c. When the `<BODY>` tag is evaluated.
    d. When the document is loaded.

3. What is the `anchors` array?
    a. An `array` property of the `document` object with an entry for each `<A>` tag in the document.
    b. An array of all of the named anchors in the document.

c. A property of the document named **"anchor"**.

d. A array containing an entry for each anchor in all of the active documents.

4. Which of the following is a false statement about the `images` array?

a. It contains an entry for each image included in the HTML document with the `IMG` tag.

b. All of its properties are read-only.

c. An entry may be reassigned to display a different image.

d. Each entry is an `Image` object.

5. When using the document methods to output to the document window, at what point is the output rendered?

a. When `document.close()` is called.

b. After `document.clear()` but before `document.close()`.

c. After each `document.write()` or `document.writeln()`.

d. When `document.paint()` is called.

The `window` Object and the Status Bar

THE `window` OBJECT

As you learned in Chapter 1, "Where Does JavaScript Fit In?", when you were first introduced to the Navigator Object Hierarchy, the `window` object is the parent object of each loaded document.

Because the `window` object is the parent object for loaded documents, you usually do not explicitly refer to the `window` object when referring to its properties or invoking its methods. For this reason, `window.alert()` can be called by using `alert()`.

Table 8-4 outlines the properties and methods of the `window` object. You have seen many of these, including the `frames` array and the `parent` object, as well as the `alert()`, `confirm()`, `open()`, `prompt()`, and `setTimeout()` methods.

Name	Description
frames	Array of objects containing an entry for each child frame in a frameset document.
document	The document object for the document currently loaded in the window.
location	An object reflecting the current URL loaded in the window.
opener	Refers to the window containing the document that opened the current document. This only has a value if the current window was opened or created with the open() method.

Name	Description
parent	The frameset in a frameset-frame relationship.
self	The current window—use this to distinguish between windows and forms of the same name.
top	The top-most parent window.
status	The value of the text displayed in the window's status bar. This can be used to display status messages to the user.
defaultStatus	The default value displayed in the status bar.
alert()	Displays a message in a dialog box with an OK button.
blur()	Removes focus from a window. In most versions of Navigator, this sends the window to the background.
confirm()	Displays a message in a dialog box with OK and Cancel buttons. This returns true when the user clicks on OK, false otherwise.
close()	Closes the current window.
focus()	Gives input focus to a window. In most versions of Navigator, this brings the window to the front.
open()	Opens a new window with a specified document or opens the document in the specified named window.
prompt()	Displays a message in a dialog box along with a text entry field.
scroll()	Scrolls the window to a coordinate specified by an x,y coordinate passed as an argument to the method.
setTimeout()	Sets a timer for a specified number of milliseconds and then evaluates an expression when the timer has finished counting. Program operation continues while the timer is counting down.
clearTimeout()	Cancels a previously set timeout.

Table 8-4 *Properties and methods of the `window` object.*

The `location` Object

The `location` object provides several properties and methods for working with the location of the current object.

Table 8-5 outlines these properties and methods.

Name	Description
hash	The anchor name (the text following a # symbol in an HREF attribute)
host	The hostname and port of the URL
hostname	The hostname of the URL
href	The entire URL as a string
pathname	The file path (the portion of the URL following the third slash)
port	The port number of the URL (if there is no port number, then the empty string)
protocol	The protocol part of the URL (such as http:, gopher:, or ftp:—including the colon)
reload()	Reloads the current URL
replace()	Loads a new URL over the current entry in the history list
search	The form data or query following the question mark (?) in the URL

Table 8-5 *Properties and methods of the* location *object.*

Working with the Status Bar

The status bar—the strip at the bottom of the Navigator window where you are told about the current status of document transfers and connections to remote sites—can be used by JavaScript programs to display custom messages to the user.

This is primarily done using the **onMouseOver** event handler, which is invoked when the user points at a hypertext link. By setting the value of **self.status** to a string, you can assign a value to the status bar (you could also use **window.status** or **status** here). In the program

```
<HTML>

<HEAD>
<TITLE>Status Example</TITLE>
</HEAD>

<BODY>
<A HREF="home.html" onMouseOver="self.status='Go Home!'; return true;">Home</A>
<A HREF="next.html" onMouseOver="self.status='Go to the next Page!'; ⇐
return true;">Next</A>
</BODY>

</HTML>
```

two different messages are displayed when the user points the mouse at the links. This can be more informative than the URLs that Navigator normally displays when a user points at a link.

Notice that both of the onMouseOver event handlers in the script return a **true** value after setting the status bar to a new value. This is necessary to display a new value in the status bar using the onMouseOver event handler.

Opening and Closing Windows

By using the open() and close() methods, you have control over what windows are open and which documents they contain.

The open() method is the more complex of the two. It takes two required arguments and an optional feature list in the following form:

```
open("URL", "windowName", "featureList");
```

Here the featureList is a comma-separated list containing any of the entries in Table 8-6.

Name	Description
toolbar	Creates the standard toolbar
location	Creates the location entry field
directories	Creates the standard directory buttons
status	Creates the status bar
menubar	Creates the menu at the top of the window
scrollbars	Creates scroll bars when the document grows beyond the current window
resizable	Enables resizing of the window by the user
copyhistory	Indicates whether the history list of the current window should be copied to the new window
width	Specifies the window width in pixels
height	Specifies the window height in pixels

Table 8-6 *Windows features used in the* open() *method.*

With the exception of **width** and **height**, which take integer values, all of these features can be set to **true** with a value of **yes** or **1** or set to **false** with a value of **no** or **0**.

For example, to open a document called **new.html** in a new window named **newWindow** and to make the window 200 pixels by 200 pixels with all window features available except **resizable**, you could use the command

```
window.open("new.html","newWindow","toolbar=yes,⇐
location=1,directories=yes,status=yes,menubar=1,⇐
scrollbars=yes,resizable=0,copyhistory=1,width=200,height=200");
```

which would produce a window like the one in Figure 8-8.

Note that you can open a window and then write HTML into that window using `document.writeln()` and `document.write()`. You saw an example of this in Listings 8-6 through 8-8.

For instance, the function `newwindow()` opens a new window and writes several lines of HTML into it.

```
function newwindow() {
  newWindow = open("","New_Window");

  newWindow.document.write("<H1>Testing ...</H1>");
  newWindow.document.writeln("1... 2... 3...");
  newWindow.document.close();

}
```

Notice the command `newWindow = open("",:New Window");` which opens an instance of the `window` object and names it `newWindow` so that you can then use commands such as `newWindow.document.write()`.

The `close()` method is simpler to use:

```
window.close();
```

simply closes the current window.

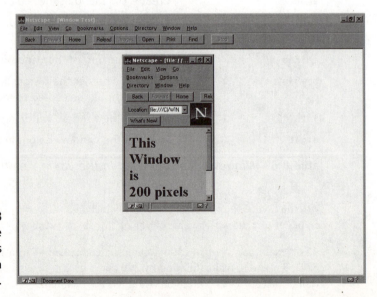

Figure 8-8
You control the size of new windows, as well as which elements to display.

Pausing with Timeouts

You already saw an example of using `setTimeout()` in Bill Dortch's hIdaho Frameset earlier in this chapter where he suggests using a `setTimeout()` call to make sure a function is registered before trying to call the function.

The `setTimeout()` method takes the form

```
ID=setTimeout("expression",milliseconds)
```

where `expression` is any string expression, including a call to a function, `milliseconds` is the number of milliseconds—expressed as an integer—to wait before evaluating the expression, and `ID` is an identifier that can be used to cancel the `setTimeout()` before the expression is evaluated.

`clearTimeout()` is passed a single argument: the identifier of the timeout setting to be canceled.

For instance, if you want to create a page that displays a welcome message to the user and then automatically goes to a new page five seconds later if the user hasn't clicked on the appropriate button, you could write a script like Listing 8-11.

Input

Listing 8-11 Creating an automatic pause.

```
<HTML>

<HEAD>
<TITLE>Timeout Example</TITLE>

<SCRIPT LANGUAGE="JavaScript">
<!-- HIDE FROM OTHER BROWSERS

function go() {
  open("new.html","newWindow");
}

// STOP HIDING FROM OTHER BROWSERS -->
</SCRIPT>

</HEAD>

<BODY onLoad="timeout = setTimeout('go()',5000);">
<IMG SRC="welcome.gif">
<H1>Click on the button or wait five seconds to continue ...</H1>
<FORM METHOD=POST>
<INPUT TYPE=button VALUE="Continue ..." onClick="clearTimeout(timeout); go();">
</FORM>
</BODY>

</HTML>
```

CREATING A STATUS BAR MESSAGE HANDLER

In this example, you produce a simple function to implement status bar help in any HTML document. The function can be called from any event handler and will display a message in the status bar.

```
function help(message) {
  self.status = message;
  return true;
}
```

With this function, you can then implement full on-line pointers and help systems. For instance, if you use this in the math test from Listings 8-3 through 8-8, you can add help messages with only slight modifications to both `form.htm` and `level.htm`. See Listing 8-12 for the new version.

Input | **Listing 8-12** Updating the math test program.

```
<!-- SOURCE CODE OF form.htm -->
<HTML>

<HEAD>
<SCRIPT LANGUAGE="JavaScript">
<!-- HIDE FROM OTHER BROWSERS

var currentLevel=1;
var currentQuestion=1;
var toOutput = "";

// DEFINE LEVEL ONE
q1 = new question("1 + 3",4);
q2 = new question("4 + 5",9);
q3 = new question("5 - 4",1);
q4 = new question("7 + 3",10);
q5 = new question("4 + 4",8);
q6 = new question("3 - 3",0);
q7 = new question("9 - 5",4);
q8 = new question("8 + 1",9);
q9 = new question("5 - 3",2);
q10 = new question("8 - 3",5);
levelOne = new level(q1,q2,q3,q4,q5,q6,q7,q8,q9,q10);

// DEFINE LEVEL TWO
q1 = new question("15 + 23",38);
q2 = new question("65 - 32",33);
q3 = new question("99 + 45",134);
q4 = new question("34 - 57",-23);
q5 = new question("-34 - 57",-91);
q6 = new question("23 + 77",100);
q7 = new question("64 + 32",96);
```

```
q8 = new question("64 - 32",32);
q9 = new question("12 + 34",46);
q10 = new question("77 + 77",154);
levelTwo = new level(q1,q2,q3,q4,q5,q6,q7,q8,q9,q10);

// DEFINE LEVEL THREE
q1 = new question("10 * 7",70);
q2 = new question("15 / 3",5);
q3 = new question("34 * 3",102);
q4 = new question("33 / 2",16.5);
q5 = new question("100 / 4",25);
q6 = new question("99 / 6",16.5);
q7 = new question("32 * 3",96);
q8 = new question("48 / 4",12);
q9 = new question("31 * 0",0);
q10 = new question("45 / 1",45);
levelThree = new level(q1,q2,q3,q4,q5,q6,q7,q8,q9,q10);

// DEFINE TEST
test = new newTest(levelOne,levelTwo,levelThree);

function newTest(levelOne,levelTwo,levelThree) {
   this[1] = levelOne;
   this[2] = levelTwo;
   this[3] = levelThree;
}

function level(q1,q2,q3,q4,q5,q6,q7,q8,q9,q10) {
   this[1] = q1;
   this[2] = q2;
   this[3] = q3;
   this[4] = q4;
   this[5] = q5;
   this[6] = q6;
   this[7] = q7;
   this[8] = q8;
   this[9] = q9;
   this[10] = q10;
}

function question(question,answer) {
   this.question = question;
   this.answer = answer;
}

parent.Register(self.name,"startTest");
function startTest(newLevel) {
   currentLevel=newLevel;
   currentQuestion=1;
   document.forms[0].answer.value="";
   document.forms[0].score.value=0;
   displayQuestion();
}
```

continued on next page

continued from previous page

```
function displayQuestion() {
  ask = test[currentLevel][currentQuestion].question;
  answer = test[currentLevel][currentQuestion].answer;
  toOutput = "" + currentQuestion + ". What is " + ask + "?";
  document.forms[0].answer.value = "";
  window.open("display.htm","output");
}

parent.Register(self.name,"output");
function output() {
  return toOutput;
}

function checkAnswer(form) {
  answer = form.answer.value;
  correctAnswer = test[currentLevel][currentQuestion].answer;
  ask = test[currentLevel][currentQuestion].question;
  score = form.score.value;
  if (eval(answer) == correctAnswer) {
    toOutput = "Correct!";
    score ++;
    form.score.value = score;
  } else {
    toOutput = "Sorry! " + ask + " is " + correctAnswer + ".";
  }
  window.open("display.htm","output");
  if (currentQuestion < 10) {
    currentQuestion ++;
    setTimeout("displayQuestion()",3000);
  } else {
    toOutput = "You're Done!<BR>You're score is " + score + " out of 10.";
    setTimeout("window.open('display.htm','output')",3000);
    form.answer.value="";
    form.score.value="0";
  }
}

function welcome() {
  toOutput = "Welcome!";
  window.open("display.htm","output");
}

parent.Register(self.name,"help");
function help(message) {
  self.status = message;
  return true;
}

// STOP HIDING FROM OTHER BROWSERS -->
</SCRIPT>

</HEAD>
```

```
<BODY BGCOLOR="#FFFFFF" TEXT="#0000FF" onLoad="welcome();">

<FORM METHOD=POST>
<CENTER>
<STRONG>Type You're Answer Here:</STRONG><BR>
<INPUT TYPE=text NAME=answer SIZE=30 ⇐
onFocus="help('Enter your answer here.');"><P>
<A HREF="#" onClick="checkAnswer(document.forms[0]);"⇐
onMouseOver="return help('Click here to check your answer.');">⇐
Check Answer</A><P>
<INPUT TYPE=text NAME=score VALUE="0" SIZE=10 onFocus="this.blur();">
</FORM>

</BODY>

</HTML>
```

Similarly, `level.htm` requires changes:

| Input |

Listing 8-13 Updating the `level.htm` file.

```
<!-- SOURCE CODE OF level.htm -->
<HTML>

<HEAD>
<SCRIPT LANGUAGE="JavaScript">
<!-- HIDE FROM OTHER BROWSERS

function help(message) {
  self.status = message;
  return true;
}

// STOP HIDING FROM OTHER BROWSERS -->
</SCRIPT>

</HEAD>

<BODY BGCOLOR="#000000" TEXT="#FFFFFF" LINK="#FFFFFF" ⇐
ALINK="#FFFFFF" VLINK="#FFFFFF">
<CENTER>
<STRONG>
Select a level here:<BR>
<A HREF="#" onClick="parent.Exec('startTest',1);"⇐
onMouseOver="return ⇐
parent.Exec('help','Start test at level one.');">LEVEL ONE</A>
<A HREF="#" onClick="parent.Exec('startTest',2);"⇐
onMouseOver="return parent.Exec('help',⇐
'Start test at level two.');">LEVEL TWO</A>
<A HREF="#" onClick="parent.Exec('startTest',3);"⇐
onMouseOver="return parent.Exec('help',⇐
'Start test at level three.');">LEVEL THREE</A>
</STRONG>
</CENTER>
```

continued on next page

continued from previous page
```
</BODY>

</HTML>
```

Output

These changes produce results like those in Figure 8-9.

Analysis

In order to implement the interactive help in the math test, you have to make only minor changes to both HTML files.

In **form.htm**, you have added the **help()** function to the header and made two changes in the body of the document. You have added an **onFocus** event handler to the answer field. The event handler calls **help()** to display a help message.

You have also changed the button to a hypertext link so that you can use the **onMouseOver** event handler to display another help message. There are several points to note in the following line:

```
<A HREF="#" onClick="checkAnswer(document.forms[0]);"⇐
onMouseOver="return help('Click here to check your answer.');">⇐
Check Answer</A>
```

First, in the call to **checkAnswer()**, you can't pass the argument **this.form** because the hypertext link is not a form element. For this reason, you use **document.forms[0]** to explicitly identify the form.

The second point to notice is that you have an empty anchor in the attribute **HREF="#"**. When a user clicks on the link, only the **onClick** event handler executes, but because there is no URL specified, the page doesn't change.

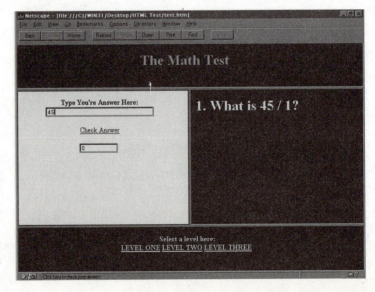

Figure 8-9
Using onMouseOver and the status property to display help messages in the Navigator window's status bar.

Note

For changes to the status bar to take effect in an onMouseOver event, you need to return a value of **true** from the event handler. This isn't true in other event handlers, such as onFocus.

Tip

Instead of using the onClick event handler, you can use a special type of URL to call JavaScript functions and methods:

```
<A HREF="JavaScript:checkAnswer(document.forms[0])">
```

In level.htm, you make similar changes. You simply have added the help function to the file's header and changed the three form buttons to three hypertext links with appropriate onMouseOver event handlers.

Note

Notice when you try these scripts that status messages stay displayed until another message is displayed in the status bar, even when the condition that caused the message to be displayed has ended.

COLORS IN NAVIGATOR

The various HTML color attributes and tags (BGCOLOR, FGCOLOR, VLINKCOLOR, ALINKCOLOR, LINKCOLOR, FONT COLOR) and their related JavaScript methods (bgColor(), fgColor(), vlinkColor(), alinkColor(), linkColor(), fontColor()) can take both RGB triplets and selected color names as their values.

Table 8-7 is a list of selected Netscape color words and their corresponding RGB triplets. The complete list of color words can be found in the JavaScript document at the Netscape Web site (see Appendix A).

Table 8-7

Color Name	RGB Triplet	Color Name	RGB Triplet
antiquewhite	FA EB D7	ivory	FF FF F0
aqua	00 FF FF	lemonchiffon	FF FA CD
azure	F0 FF FF	lightblue	AD D8 E6
beige	F5 F5 DC	lightyellow	FF FF E0
black	00 00 00	magenta	FF 00 FF
blue	00 00 FF	maroon	80 00 00
brown	A5 2A 2A	mediumpurple	93 70 DB
chartreuse	7F FF 00	mediumturquoise	48 D1 CC
cornflowerblue	64 95 ED	moccasin	FF E4 B5
crimson	DC 14 3C	navy	00 00 80
darkcyan	00 8B 8B	orange	FF A5 00

continued on next page

continued from previous page

Color Name	RGB Triplet	Color Name	RGB Triplet
darkgray	A9 A9 A9	papayawhip	FF EF D5
darkgreen	00 64 00	pink	FF C0 CB
darkpink	FF 14 93	rosybrown	BC 8F 8F
firebrick	B2 22 22	salmon	FA 80 72
floralwhite	FF FA F0	silver	C0 C0 C0
fuchsia	FF 00 FF	slateblue	6A 5A CD
gold	FF D7 00	tan	D2 B4 8C
greenyellow	AD FF 2F	tomato	FF 63 47
hotpink	FF 69 B4	yellow	FF FF 00
indigo	4B 00 82		

Table 8-7   *Color words in Navigator 2.0.*

1. Why can methods of the `window` object usually be referenced without using `window.method()`?
   a. Because JavaScript defaults every method to window.
   b. Because `window` is usually the current object.
   c. Because the window methods are unique.
   d. None of the above.

2. When using the `window.open()` method, how would you specify a blank window named `test` with default features?
   a. `window.open("test")`
   b. `window.open("", "test", "default")`
   c. `window.open("", "test")`
   d. `window.open()`

3. Given the following timeout, how would you cancel it?

```
timeoutID = setTimeout('go()', 5000);
```

   a. `cancel( timeoutID )`.
   b. Wait five seconds.
   c. `cancel( 5000 )`.
   d. Tell the user to click on the Cancel button.

4. In the following function, what does `self` refer to?

```
function test( msg ) { self.status = msg; return true; }
```

  a. It refers to the function itself.
  b. It refers to the `window` object of the current document.
  c. It refers to the current document.
  d. It refers to the status bar.

5. Given the following anchor, what will display on the status line when the `onMouseOver` event gets signaled?

```
<A HREF="#" onMouseOver="status='test';">
```

  a. `test`.
  b. The status bar display will not change.
  c. The URL for the current document with a `#` after it will display in the status bar.
  d. None of the above.

SUMMARY

In this chapter you have covered several significant topics.

You now know how to divide the Navigator window into multiple independent sections and how to work with functions and values in different windows using the hIdaho Frameset.

In addition, you have taken a detailed look at the `document` object and learned about its properties, which gives you information about colors used in a document, as well as information about the last modification date of a document and the location of a document.

The `window` object, which is the parent object of the `document` object, provides you the ability to work with various aspects of windows and frames, including altering the text displayed in the window's status bar, setting timeouts to pause before evaluating expressions or calling functions, and opening and closing named windows.

To see a great example of how to combine frames with JavaScript, jump to Appendix C, Lab 3, Michael Yu's Civic Car Viewer.

In Chapter 9, "Remember Where You've Been with Cookies," you are going to take a look at cookies—a feature of Navigator that enables you to store information about a page and recall it later when the user returns to the page.

COMMANDS AND EXTENSIONS REVIEW

Command/Extension	Type	Description
FRAMESET	HTML tag	Defines a window or frame containing frames
ROWS	HTML attribute	Defines the number of rows in a FRAMESET tag
COLS	HTML attribute	Defines the number of columns in a FRAMESET tag
FRAME	HTML tag	Defines the source document for a frame defined in a FRAMESET container
SRC	HTML attribute	Indicates the URL of a document to load into a frame
NORESIZE	HTML attribute	Specifies that a frame is fixed in size and cannot be resized by the user
SCROLLING	HTML attribute	Indicates whether scroll bars are to be displayed in a frame (takes the value YES, NO, or AUTO)
MARGINHEIGHT	HTML attribute	Specifies the vertical offset in pixels from the border of the frame
MARGINWIDTH	HTML attribute	Specifies the horizontal offset in pixels from the border of the frame
TARGET	HTML attribute	Indicates the frame or window for a document to load into—used with the A, FORM, BASE, and AREA tags

Command/Extension	Type	Description
NOFRAMES	HTML tag	Indicates HTML code to be displayed in browsers that don't support frames; used in documents containing the FRAMESET container tags
frames	JavaScript property	Array of objects for each frame in a Navigator window
parent	JavaScript property	Indicates the parent frameset document of the currently loaded document
BODY	HTML tag	Defines the main body of an HTML document
BACKGROUND	HTML attribute	Specifies the URL of a background image in the BODY tag
BGCOLOR	HTML attribute	Specifies the background color for a document as a hexadecimal triplet or color name
FGCOLOR	HTML attribute	Specifies the foreground color for a document as a hexadecimal triplet or color name
LINK	HTML attribute	Specifies the color of link text
ALINK	HTML attribute	Specifies the color of active link text
VLINK	HTML attribute	Specifies the color of followed link text
alinkColor	JavaScript property	The color value of active links
anchors	JavaScript property	Array of objects corresponding to each named anchor in a document

continued on next page

continued from previous page

Command/Extension	Type	Description
applets	JavaScript property	Array of objects corresponding to each Java applet in a document
bgColor	JavaScript property	The background color value of a document
embeds	JavaScript property	Array of objects corresponding to each plug-in in a document
fgColor	JavaScript property	The foreground color value of a document
forms	JavaScript property	Array of objects corresponding to each form in a document
images	JavaScript property	Array of objects corresponding to each image in a document
lastModified	JavaScript property	As a string, the last date the document was modified
linkColor	JavaScript property	The color value of link text
links	JavaScript property	Array of objects corresponding to each link in a document
location	JavaScript property	Object defining the full URL of the document
title	JavaScript property	Title of the document represented as a string
vlinkColor	JavaScript property	The color value of followed links
hash	JavaScript property	An anchor name (location object)
host	JavaScript property	Hostname and port of a URL (location object)
href	JavaScript property	Hostname of a URL (location object)

Command/Extension	Type	Description
opener	JavaScript property	Refers to the window containing the script that opened the current window (window object)
pathname	JavaScript property	File path from the URL (location object)
port	JavaScript property	Port number from the URL (location object)
protocol	JavaScript property	Protocol part of the URL (location object)
search	JavaScript property	Form data or query from the URL (location object)
URL	JavaScript property	The full URL of a document
blur()	JavaScript method	Removes input focus from a window (window object)
open()	JavaScript method	Opens a document for a particular MIME type (document object)
close()	JavaScript method	Closes a document for writing (document object)
clear()	JavaScript method	Clears a document window (document object)
focus()	JavaScript method	Gives input focus to a window (window object)
reload()	JavaScript method	Reloads the current URL
replace()	JavaScript method	Loads a new URL in the place of the current document
scroll()	JavaScript method	Scrolls the window to a specified location
self	JavaScript property	Refers to the current window
top	JavaScript property	The top-most parent window

continued on next page

continued from previous page

Command/Extension	Type	Description
status	JavaScript property	Text displayed in the status bar represented as a string
defaultStatus	JavaScript property	Default text displayed in the status bar
close()	JavaScript method	Closes the window (window object)
open()	JavaScript method	Opens a document in a named window (window object)
setTimeout()	JavaScript method	Pauses for a specified number of milliseconds and then evaluates an expression
clearTimeout()	JavaScript method	Cancels a previously set timeout
onMouseOver	Event handler	Specifies script to execute when the mouse pointer is over a hypertext link
location	JavaScript property	The location of the document currently loaded in a window

CHAPTER EXERCISE

1. Expand the math test example so that it presents the questions in a random order each time the user runs through the test.

2. Design a program that does the following:

   Splits the screen into two frames.

   In the first, enables the user to indicate a URL.

   Loads the URL into the second frame, and once it's loaded, displays the following information about it in the first frame: all color attributes, the title of the document, and the last date of modification.

3. What happens on the status bar in this script?

```
<HTML>

<HEAD>
<TITLE>Exercise 8.3</TITLE>

<SCRIPT LANGUAGE="JavaSCript">
<!-- HIDE FROM OTHER BROWSERS

function help(message) {
  self.status = message;
  return true;
}

function checkField(field) {
  if (field.value == "")
    help("Remember to enter a value in this field");
  else
    help("");
  return true;
}
// STOP HIDING FROM OTHER BROWSERS ñ>
</SCRIPT>

</HEAD>

<BODY>

<FORM METHOD=POST>
Name: <INPUT TYPE=text NAME="name" onFocus="help('Enter your name');"
                onBlur="checkField(this);">
Email: <INPUT TYPE=text NAME="email" ⇐
onFocus="help('Enter your email address');"
                onBlur="checkField(this);">
</FORM>

</BODY>

</HTML>
```

4. Extend Listing 8-9 and Listing 8-10 so that the user can specify any URL to be displayed using the specified color scheme. You will want to consider using the alternative method for the display() function.

CHAPTER 9

REMEMBER WHERE YOU'VE BEEN WITH COOKIES

One of the challenges of writing applications for the World Wide Web has been the inability of the Web to maintain *state*. That is, after a user sends a request to the server and a Web page is returned, the server forgets all about the user and the page she has just downloaded.

If the user clicks on a link, the server doesn't have background information about what page the user is coming from, and more importantly, if the user returns to the page at a later date, there is no information available to the server about the user's previous actions on the page.

Maintaining state can be important to developing complex interactive applications. Several sites work around this problem using complex server-end CGI scripts. However, Navigator 2.0 and 3.0 address the problem with *cookies*: a method of storing information locally in the browser and sending it to the server whenever the appropriate pages are requested by the user.

JavaScript provides the capability to work with client-side state information stored as cookies.

In addition to cookies, JavaScript offers the `navigator` object, which provides information about the version of the browser a user has and, in the future, will likely include methods to customize the browser.

The information available in the `navigator` object can be useful for a number of purposes, including ensuring that users are using a version of the browser that supports all the features of a script. The `navigator` object also includes properties for working with file types and installed plug-ins.

In this chapter, we take a detailed look at using cookies in the JavaScript applications as well as how to use the `navigator` object, including

- What cookies are
- Examples of using cookies
- Cookies and CGI
- Using cookies in JavaScript
- Information provided by the `navigator` object

LESSON 1 Cookies and How to Use Them

WHAT ARE COOKIES?

Cookies provide a method to store information at the client side and have the browser provide that information to the server along with a page request.

The term *cookies* has no special significance. It is just a name in the same way Java is just a name for Sun's object-oriented programming language.

In order to understand how the mechanism works, it is important to have a basic understanding of how servers and clients communicate on the World Wide Web using the *hypertext transfer protocol* (HTTP).

HTTP and How It Works

The hypertext transfer protocol is fairly simple. When a user requests a page, an HTTP request is sent to the server. The request includes a header that defines several pieces of information, including the page being requested.

The server returns an HTTP response that also includes a header. The header contains information about the document being returned, including its MIME type (such as `text/html` for a standard HTML page or `image/gif` for a GIF file).

These headers all contain one or more fields of information in a basic format:

```
Field-name: Information
```

Cookies and HTTP Headers

Cookie information is shared between the client browser and a server using fields in the HTTP headers. The way it works is fairly simple—in theory.

When the user requests a page for the first time, a cookie (or more than one cookie) can be stored in the browser by a `Set-Cookie` entry in the header of the response from the server. The `Set-Cookie` field includes the information to be stored in the cookie along with several optional pieces of information, including an expiry date, path, and server information, and if the cookie requires security.

Then, when the user requests a page in the future, if a matching cookie is found among all the stored cookies, the browser sends a `Cookie` field to the server in a request header. The header will contain the information stored in that cookie.

Cookie **and** Set-Cookie

The `Set-Cookie` and `Cookie` fields use a fairly simple syntax to transfer significant information between the client and server.

`Set-Cookie` takes the form:

```
Set-Cookie: name=VALUE; expires=DATE; path=PATH; domain=DOMAIN; secure
```

The `name=VALUE` entry is the only required piece of information that must be included in the `Set-Cookie` field. This is simply a string of characters defining information to be stored in the cookie for later transmission back to the server. The string cannot contain semicolons, commas, or spaces.

All other entries in the `Set-Cookie` field are optional and are outlined in Table 9-1.

Name	Description
expires=DATE	Specifies the expiry date of a cookie. After this date the cookie will no longer be stored by the client or sent to the server (DATE takes the form Wdy, DD-Mon-YY HH:MM:SS GMT—dates are only stored in Greenwich Mean Time). By default, the value of expires is set to the end of the current Navigator session.

continued on next page

continued from previous page

Name	Description
path=PATH	Specifies the path portion of URLs for which the cookie is valid. If the URL matches both the `path` and `domain`, then the cookie is sent to the server in the request header. (If left unset, the value of `path` is the same as the document that set the cookie.)
domain=DOMAIN	Specifies the domain portion of URLs for which the cookie is valid. The default value for this attribute is the domain of the current document setting the cookie.
secure	Specifies that the cookie should only be transmitted over a secure link (i.e., to HTTP servers using the SSL protocol—known as HTTPS servers).

Table 9-1 *Optional attributes for* Set-Cookie.

By comparison, the **Cookie** field in a request header contains only a set of name-value pairs for the requested URL:

```
Cookie: name1=VALUE1; name=VALUE2 ...
```

It is important to realize that multiple **Set-Cookie** fields can be sent in a single response header from the server.

A cookie that has the same path and name as an existing cookie will overwrite the old one—this can be used as a way of erasing cookies—by writing a new one with an expiry date that has already passed.

There are some limitations on the use of cookies. Navigator will store only 300 cookies in total. Within that 300, each cookie is limited to four kilobytes in length, including all the optional attributes, and only 20 cookies will be stored for each domain. When the number of cookies is exceeded, the browser will delete the least recently used, and when the length of a cookie is too long, the cookie is trimmed to fit.

EXAMPLES OF HOW COOKIES ARE USED

There are several ways that cookies can be used to enhance interactive applications.

For instance, there are sites using cookies to implement shopping carts. That is, a user traverses multiple pages at a site and selects items he wants to buy. The selections are stored in cookies until a JavaScript script or CGI script is executed to total up the purchases.

Other applications that could use cookies include

- Reminder calendars that use cookies to store appointments and other messages.

- Country tours that users can take during several visits to a Web site—cookies are used to remember where the user left off.

- Adventure games that use cookies to keep track of pertinent character data and the current state of the game.

COOKIES AND CGI SCRIPTS

In order for cookies to be useful, it is necessary for the server to be able to take advantage of the cookie information it receives and for the server to be able to generate cookie headers if they are needed.

This is primarily done by using CGI scripts.

For instance, if you want to provide a custom search tool that would search World Wide Web indexes selected by the user, you would need to develop a system that follows this basic pattern:

1. The user calls the site by using a URL that requests a CGI script.

2. The script checks whether it is the user's first time at the site by checking whether there is a `Cookie` field in the HTTP request header.

3. If there is no cookie, the script sends back a new search page with all choices unselected and an empty search field.

4. If there is a `Cookie` field, the script interprets the cookie and returns a page with all the user's previous choices selected.

5. When the user conducts a search, the script returns the search results along with a `Set-Cookie` field in the header to reset the cookie to the newly selected values that the user used for the search.

This type of application could produce results similar to Figures 9-1 and 9-2.

To implement this type of server-side processing for cookies may require significant increases in the load on a Web server. With this model, most pages are being built dynamically based on receiving cookie information in the header.

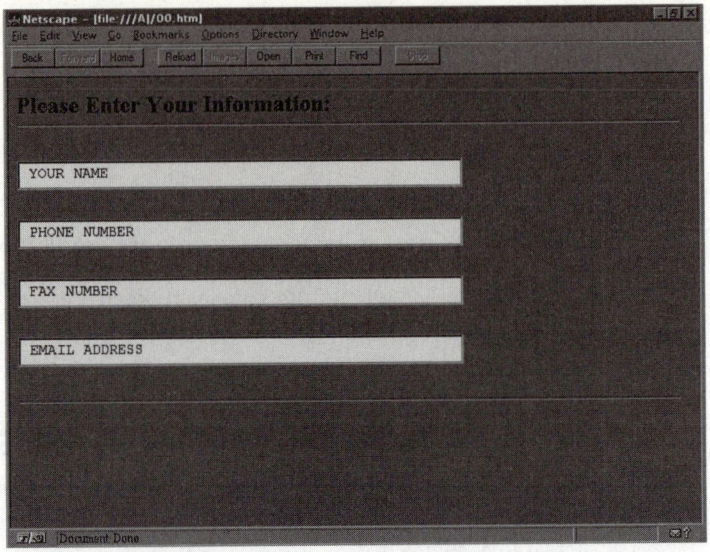

Figure 9-1
If the user has never visited the URL, a page with a new form is sent to the user.

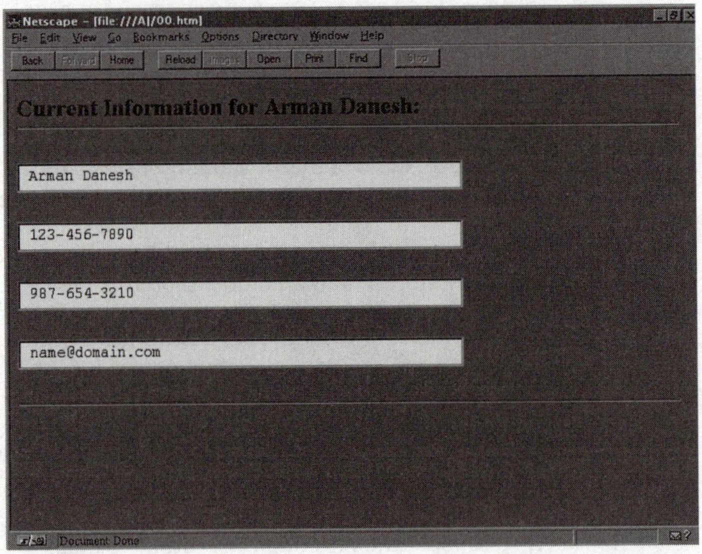

Figure 9-2
On subsequent visits, the user receives a page in the same state as he or she last left it.

This is in contrast to typical Web pages, which are static and all the server needs to do is send the correct file to the client without any additional processing.

Quiz 1

1. What is a cookie?
    a. The MIME type of a document sent down in the HTTP header.
    b. A bribe to the HTTP server to get it to send down a requested HTML document.
    c. A field in the HTTP header containing document-specific information.
    d. None of the above.

2. When do cookies expire?
    a. Always at the end of the Navigator session.
    b. After the expire date which defaults to the end of the current Navigator session.
    c. When the `expire()` method is executed.
    d. When they haven't been used for 30 days.

3. Where would you find a `Set-Cookie` entry?
    a. In the JavaScript code for a page.
    b. In the response header from the HTTP server.
    c. In the request header sent to the HTTP server.
    d. None of the above.

4. When is a `Cookie` field sent to the HTTP server?
    a. Each time a page is requested using the HTTP protocol.
    b. After a page is sent down that contains `Set-Cookie` information.
    c. When the HTTP server requests it.
    d. If a page is being requested and a cookie is found for it, then the HTTP request header will contain the cookie information.

5. What are the limitations on the use of cookies?
    a. Navigator has a limit of 300 cookies total and 20 per domain.
    b. The number of cookies is limited only by the local disk space.
    c. The number of cookies is not limited.
    d. There is a limit of 300 cookies total with a total length of 4K bytes.

Lesson 2 Cookies in JavaScript and Storing User Choices

USING COOKIES IN JAVASCRIPT

In JavaScript, however, cookies become available for processing by the *client*.

JavaScript makes the `cookie` property of the `document` object available for processing. The `cookie` property exposes all the attributes of cookies for the page to the script and enables the script to set new cookies. In this way much, if not all, of the server-end processing that would be done to take advantage of cookies can now be done by the client in a JavaScript script.

The `cookie` property simply contains a string with the value that would be sent out in a `Cookie` field for that page.

As a string, it can be manipulated like any other string, literal, or variable using the methods and properties of the `string` object.

In Chapter 10, "Strings, Math, and the History List," we will take a detailed look at the `string` object and all of its methods and properties.

By assigning values to `document.cookie`, it is possible to create new cookies. The value of the string assigned to the `cookie` property should be the same as what would be sent by the server in the `Set-Cookie` header field.

For instance, if you create two cookies named `cookie1` and `cookie2` as follows:

```
document.cookie = "cookie1=First_cookie";
document.cookie = "cookie2=Second_cookie";
```

then `document.write(document.cookie)` would produce output that looks like this:

```
cookie1=First_cookie; cookie2=Second_cookie
```

If you want to set optional properties such as the expiry date or path, you can use a command like:

```
document.cookie = 'cookie1=First_cookie; ⇐
expires=Mon, 01-Jul-95 12:00:00 GMT; path="/"';
```

This would create a cookie named `cookie1` that expires at noon on 1 July 1995 and is valid for all documents in the default domain because the path is set to the top-level directory for the domain.

Of course, times are likely to be set using offsets from the current time. For instance, you may want an expiry date one day or one year from the current date. You can use the methods of the `Date` object to achieve this:

```
expires = new Date();
expires.setTime (expires.getTime() + 24 * 60 * 60 * 365 * 1000);
document.cookie = "cookie2=Second_cookie; expires=" + expires.toGMTString();
```

These commands use the `Date` object to set a time one year after today by adding 24×60×60×365×1000 (the number of milliseconds in one year) to the current date and time. You can then use `expires.toGMTString()` to return the date string in GMT time as required by the cookie.

`setTime()`, `getTime()`, and `toGMTString()` are methods of the `Date()` object, which is discussed in more detail later in this chapter.

STORING USER CHOICES IN COOKIES

In this example, you are going to use cookies to expand the functionality of the script you created in Exercise 8-4 in the previous chapter.

In Exercise 8-4, you extended the simple color testing application to include the capability for the user to select a URL to test the colors.

In this example you further extend the script so that if a user has entered a URL, it is stored in a cookie, as are the colors. The next time the user returns to the page, the URL is recalled, loaded, and displayed with the stored colors. The expiry date for a cookie should be 30 days from the current date.

In order to achieve this, you need to do several things. You need to save the colors and URLs as cookies whenever they are changed. You also need a function that can decode the cookie when the page is loaded for the first time.

Listing 9-1 includes these additions.

 Listing 9-1 Keeping track of the user's color choices.

```
<HTML>

<HEAD>

<SCRIPT LANGUAGE="JavaScript">
<!-- HIDE FROM OTHER BROWSERS

var expires = new Date();
expires.setTime (expires.getTime() + 24 * 60 * 60 * 30 * 1000);
var expiryDate = expires.toGMTString();

function display(form) {
  parent.output.document.bgColor = form.bg.value;
  parent.output.document.fgColor = form.fg.value;
  parent.output.document.linkColor = form.link.value;
  parent.output.document.alinkColor = form.alink.value;
  parent.output.document.vlinkColor = form.vlink.value;
}

function loadPage(url) {
  var toLoad = url.value;
  if (url.value == "")
    toLoad = "sample.htm";
  open (toLoad,"output");
}

function newCookie(name,value) {
  document.cookie = name + "=" + value + "; expires=" + expiryDate;
}
```

continued on next page

continued from previous page

```
function getCookie(name) {
  var cookieFound = false;
  var start = 0;
  var end = 0;
  var cookieString = document.cookie;

  var i = 0;

  // SCAN THE COOKIE FOR name
  while (i <= cookieString.length) {
    start = i;
    end = start + name.length;
    if (cookieString.substring(start,end) == name) {
      cookieFound = true;
      break;
    }
    i++;
  }

  // IS name FOUND?
  if (cookieFound) {
    start = end + 1;
    end = document.cookie.indexOf(";",start);
    if (end < start)
      end = document.cookie.length;
    return document.cookie.substring(start,end);
  }
  return "";
}

// STOP HIDING SCRIPT -->
</SCRIPT>

</HEAD>

<BODY onLoad="loadPage(document.forms[0].url); display(document.forms[0]);">

<CENTER>

<SCRIPT LANGUAGE="JavaScript">
<!-- HIDE FROM OTHER BROWSERS

document.write('<H1>The Color Picker</H1>');
document.write('<FORM METHOD=POST>');
document.write('Enter Colors:<BR>');

var thisCookie = ((document.cookie != "") && (document.cookie != null));

var bg = (thisCookie) ? getCookie("bg") : document.bgColor;
var fg = (thisCookie) ? getCookie("fg") : document.fgColor;
var link = (thisCookie) ? getCookie("link") : document.linkColor;
var alink = (thisCookie) ? getCookie("alink") : document.alinkColor;
var vlink = (thisCookie) ? getCookie("vlink") : document.vlinkColor;
```

```
var url = (thisCookie) ? getCookie("url") : "sample.htm";

document.write('Background: <INPUT TYPE=text NAME="bg" VALUE="' + bg + '" ⇐
onChange="newCookie(this.name,this.value);"> ... ');
document.write('Text: <INPUT TYPE=text NAME="fg" VALUE="' + fg + '" ⇐
onChange="newCookie(this.name,this.value);"><BR>');
document.write('Link: <INPUT TYPE=text NAME="link" VALUE ="' + link + '" ⇐
onChange="newCookie(this.name,this.value);"> ...');
document.write('Active Link: <INPUT TYPE=text NAME="alink" VALUE="' + alink + '" ⇐
onChange="newCookie(this.name,this.value);"><BR>');
document.write('Followed Link: <INPUT TYPE="text" NAME="vlink" VALUE ="' + vlink ⇐
+ '" onChange="newCookie(this.name,this.value);"><BR>');
document.write('Test URL: <INPUT TYPE="text" SIZE=40 NAME="url" VALUE="' + url + ⇐
'" onChange="newCookie(this.name,this.value); loadPage(this);"><BR>');
document.write('<INPUT TYPE=button VALUE="TEST" ⇐
onClick="display(this.form);">');

document.write('</FORM>');

// STOP HIDING FROM OTHER BROWSERS -->
</SCRIPT>

</CENTER>

</BODY>

</HTML>
```

Analysis   In order to use cookies to store the current state for the color tester application, you have to add two new functions (`newCookie()` and `getCookie()`) to the header, as well as alter the script that dynamically generates the HTML form in the upper frame. The other two functions remain unchanged.

The `newCookie()` Function

The `newCookie()` function is the simpler of the two new functions. It stores a cookie given a name and value as arguments. The `expiryDate` variable is a global variable created by taking the current date, adding 30 days, and then converting it to a string in Greenwich Mean Time using `toGMTString()`:

```
var expires = new Date();
expires.setTime (expires.getTime() + 24 * 60 * 60 * 30 * 1000);
var expiryDate = expires.toGMTString();
```

The `getCookie()` Function

The `getCookie()` function is designed to return a particular cookie value. What makes this somewhat complicated is that `document.cookie` contains a string of name-value pairs separated by a semicolon followed by a space.

In order to find the particular value you want and return it, you need to do some relatively sophisticated processing on the **document.cookie** string.

```
function getCookie(name) {
  var cookieFound = false;
  var start = 0;
  var end = 0;
  var cookieString = document.cookie;
```

You start by declaring the variables. **cookieFound** is a Boolean variable, which you use to keep track of whether a name-value pair matching the argument has been found. **start** and **end** are used to hold indexes for the **substring()** function, and **cookieString** holds the value of **document.cookie** simply because it is a little easier to read—it's my personal preference.

```
  var i = 0;

// SCAN THE COOKIE FOR name
  while (i <= cookieString.length) {
    start = i;
    end = start + name.length;
    if (cookieString.substring(start,end) == name) {
      cookieFound = true;
      break;
    }
    i++;
  }
```

This loop is fairly simple. You use **i** as the counter, and simply loop through **cookieString** character by character and check the **substring** starting at **i** that is the length of the name you're looking for. If there is a match, you set **cookieFound** to **true** and break out of the loop.

```
// IS name FOUND?
  if (cookieFound) {
    start = end + 1;
    end = document.cookie.indexOf(";",start);
    if (end < start)
      end = document.cookie.length;
    return document.cookie.substring(start,end);
  }
```

If you've found a cookie that matches the name you are looking for, then you set **start** to the value of **end + 1**—this means you are starting after the equal sign that follows the name. Next you use **indexOf()** to look for the semicolon that may be ending the cookie (unless it is the last cookie in the string). You store the value in **end**.

We will see more of the **string.indexOf()** method in Chapter 10 when we discuss the **string** object in more detail. The method takes two arguments— **indexOf(string,startIndex)**—and starts searching for **string** from the index **startIndex**. The value returned is the index where **string** first occurs. If **indexOf()** doesn't find the character it is looking for, it returns a value of zero.

Once you have a value for **end**, you check if a semicolon was found. If not, you know the name-value pair is the last in the list, and you can set **end** to the last character in **cookieString**, which is the value of **cookieString.length**.

Finally, you return the substring indicated by **start** and **end**.

```
  return "";
}
```

If you haven't found a cookie, you simply return an empty string.

The Body of the Document

All of the HTML output is done from a JavaScript script in the body of the document.

```
<BODY onLoad="loadPage(document.forms[0].url); display(document.forms[0]);">

<CENTER>

<SCRIPT LANGUAGE="JavaScript">
<!-- HIDE FROM OTHER BROWSERS

document.write('<H1>The Color Picker</H1>');
document.write('<FORM METHOD=POST>');
document.write('Enter Colors:<BR>');
```

Here you output the title and set up the form.

```
var thisCookie = ((document.cookie != "") && (document.cookie != null));

var bg = (thisCookie) ? getCookie("bg") : document.bgColor;
var fg = (thisCookie) ? getCookie("fg") : document.fgColor;
var link = (thisCookie) ? getCookie("link") : document.linkColor;
var alink = (thisCookie) ? getCookie("alink") : document.alinkColor;
var vlink = (thisCookie) ? getCookie("vlink") : document.vlinkColor;
var url = (thisCookie) ? getCookie("url") : "sample.htm";
```

The form elements are built dynamically so that the contents of each field match any existing cookies. If there is no cookie, then the contents of the color fields will match the defaults for the browser.

You do this by checking whether the cookie exists and then using conditional expressions to assign values to several variables, which will be used later to build the actual form elements. If cookies exist, you get the values by calling **getCookie()**. If not, you use the appropriate color properties of the **document** object, except in the case of **url** which you assign to a default URL.

```
document.write('Background: <INPUT TYPE=text NAME="bg" VALUE="' + bg + '" ⇐
onChange="newCookie(this.name,this.value);"> ... ')
document.write('Text: <INPUT TYPE=text NAME="fg" VALUE="' + fg + '" ⇐
onChange="newCookie(this.name,this.value);"><BR>');
document.write('Link: <INPUT TYPE=text NAME="link" VALUE ="' + link + '" ⇐
onChange="newCookie(this.name,this.value);"> ...');
```

continued on next page

continued from previous page

```
document.write('Active Link: <INPUT TYPE=text NAME="alink" VALUE="' + alink + '" ⇐
onChange="newCookie(this.name,this.value);"><BR>');
document.write('Followed Link: <INPUT TYPE="text" NAME="vlink" VALUE ="' + vlink ⇐
+ '" onChange="newCookie(this.name,this.value);"><BR>');
document.write('Test URL: <INPUT TYPE="text" SIZE=40 NAME="url" VALUE="' + url + ⇐
'" onChange="newCookie(this.name,this.value); loadPage(this);"><BR>');
document.write('<INPUT TYPE=button VALUE="TEST" ⇐
 onClick="display(this.form);">');
```

Once you have calculated the initial values for the form fields, you use `document.write()` to output the HTML for each field. In each text entry field you use `onChange` to store a new cookie when the user changes the value of the field. The button calls `display()` on a click event.

1. The `cookie` property contains a string and is part of the _____.
   a. `navigator` object
   b. `cookie` object
   c. `document` object
   d. `string` object

2. How is a new cookie created?
   a. By resetting the expiration date on an existing cookie.
   b. By copying another cookie.
   c. By assigning values to the `document.cookie` property.
   d. By using the `document.newCookie()` method.

3. How are the optional attributes of a cookie set?
   a. By assigning the values to the cookie.
   b. By assigning the values when you assign the cookie value.
   c. Set them using `document.cookie.attribute = 'attribute value';`.
   d. Set them using the optional arguments for the `document.setCookie()` method.

4. How is the value of a cookie determined?
   a. By scanning the cookie property for the cookie string you are interested in.
   b. By getting the value of `document.cookie.attribute;`.
   c. By using the `document.getCookie()` method.
   d. By requesting it again from the HTTP server.

5. What are `newCookie()` and `getCookie()`?
   a. New methods of the `document` object.
   b. Methods of the `navigator` object.
   c. Functions created for the `document` object.
   d. JavaScript functions created to simplify the handling of cookies.

 **Encoding Cookies and the**
navigator **Object**

ENCODING COOKIES

As I mentioned earlier, the information stored in the name-value pair of a cookie cannot contain any spaces. This poses something of a limitation because many applications will need to store complete phrases or strings containing spaces in cookies.

The solution to this lies in encoding the illegal characters in a cookie. Netscape suggests using an encoding scheme such as that used in URL strings.

However, any coding scheme will work. For instance, alternative characters such as % or + could be used for spaces and a similar approach could be taken for other illegal characters, such as semicolons.

Any script that is going to build cookies using white spaces and other illegal characters, or that is going to read similar cookies, will need to include methods for dealing with these characters.

JavaScript provides the `escape()` and `unescape()` methods, which take a string as an argument. `escape()` returns the string encoded like a URL, and `unescape()` translates it back from this encoding.

An easier recipe for cookies

It should be clear now that some type of standardized method for creating new cookies, reading existing cookies, and encoding cookies would make writing scripts much easier. Just as he wrote the hIdaho Frameset, Bill Dortch has developed a set of freely available functions to perform all these tasks. The functions are available at
`http://www.hidaho.com/cookies/cookie.txt`.
The source code is reproduced on the CD-ROM:

```
<script language="javascript">
<!-- begin script
//
//    Cookie Functions - Second Helping  (21-Jan-96)
//    Written by:  Bill Dortch, hIdaho Design <bdortch@netw.com>
//    The following functions are released to the public domain.
//
//    The Second Helping version of the cookie functions dispenses with
//    my encode and decode functions, in favor of JavaScript's new ⇐
//    built-in
//    escape and unescape functions, which do more complete encoding, ⇐
//    and
//    which are probably much faster.
//
//    The new version also extends the SetCookie function, though in
//    a backward-compatible manner, so if you used the First Helping of
```

continued on next page

continued from previous page

```
//   cookie functions as they were written, you will not need to ⇐
     change any
//   code, unless you want to take advantage of the new capabilities.
//
//   The following changes were made to SetCookie:
//
//   1.   The expires parameter is now optional - that is, you can omit
//        it instead of passing it null to expire the cookie at the end
//        of the current session.
//
//   2.   An optional path parameter has been added.
//
//   3.   An optional domain parameter has been added.
//
//   4.   An optional secure parameter has been added.
//
//   For information on the significance of these parameters, and
//   and on cookies in general, please refer to the official cookie
//   spec, at:
//
//        http://www.netscape.com/newsref/std/cookie_spec.html
//
//
// "Internal" function to return the decoded value of a cookie
//
function getCookieVal (offset) {
  var endstr = document.cookie.indexOf (";", offset);
  if (endstr == -1)
    endstr = document.cookie.length;
  return unescape(document.cookie.substring(offset, endstr));
}


//
//   Function to return the value of the cookie specified by "name".
//      name - String object containing the cookie name.
//      returns - String object containing the cookie value, or null if
//        the cookie does not exist.
//
function GetCookie (name) {
  var arg = name + "=";
  var alen = arg.length;
  var clen = document.cookie.length;
  var i = 0;
  while (i < clen) {
    var j = i + alen;
    if (document.cookie.substring(i, j) == arg)
      return getCookieVal (j);
    i = document.cookie.indexOf(" ", i) + 1;
    if (i == 0) break;
  }
```

```
    return null;
}


//
//   Function to create or update a cookie.
//     name - String object containing the cookie name.
//     value - String object containing the cookie value.  May contain
//       any valid string characters.
//     [expires] - Date object containing the ⇐
expiration date of the cookie.  If
//       omitted or null, expires the cookie ⇐
at the end of the current session.
//     [path] - String object indicating the path ⇐
for which the cookie is valid.
//       If omitted or null, uses the path of the calling document.
//     [domain] - String object indicating ⇐
the domain for which the cookie is
//       valid.  If omitted or null, ⇐
uses the domain of the calling document.
//     [secure] - Boolean (true/false) value ⇐
Indicating whether cookie transmission
//       requires a secure channel (HTTPS).
//
//   The first two parameters are required.  ⇐
The others, if supplied, must
//   be passed in the order listed above.  ⇐
To omit an unused optional field,
//   use null as a place holder.  ⇐
For example, to call SetCookie using name,
//   value and path, you would code:
//
//       SetCookie ("myCookieName", "myCookieValue", null, "/");
//
//   Note that trailing omitted parameters ⇐
do not require a placeholder.
//
//   To set a secure cookie for path "/myPath", that expires after the
//   current session, you might code:
//
//       SetCookie (myCookieVar, cookieValueVar, null, ⇐
"/myPath", null, true);
//
function SetCookie (name, value) {
  var argv = SetCookie.arguments;
  var argc = SetCookie.arguments.length;
  var expires = (argc > 2) ? argv[2] : null;
  var path = (argc > 3) ? argv[3] : null;
  var domain = (argc > 4) ? argv[4] : null;
  var secure = (argc > 5) ? argv[5] : false;
  document.cookie = name + "=" + escape (value) +
    ((expires == null) ? "" : ⇐
("; expires=" + expires.toGMTString())) +
```

continued on next page

continued from previous page

```
    ((path == null) ? "" : ("; path=" + path)) +
       ((domain == null) ? "" : ("; domain=" + domain)) +
       ((secure == true) ? "; secure" : ""));
    }


    //   Function to delete a cookie. ⇐
    (Sets expiration date to current date/time)
    //     name - String object containing the cookie name
    //
    function DeleteCookie (name) {
      var exp = new Date();
      exp.setTime (exp.getTime() - 1);  // This cookie is history
      var cval = GetCookie (name);
      document.cookie = name + "=" + cval + "; ⇐
    expires=" + exp.toGMTString();
    }


    // end script -->
    </script>
```

The source code should be included in the header of any document that includes scripts that work with cookies.

Although Dortch has done a good job of documenting each of the functions in the comments of the source code, we will run through them all in the next few sections.

The `getCookieVal()` function.

This function is an internal function called by `GetCookie()`. Given the index of the first character of the value of a name-value pair in a cookie, it returns the value as an unencoded string. The function uses the `unescape` method to decode the value.

The `GetCookie()` function.

The `getCookie()` function is used to retrieve the value of a particular cookie. It takes the name of the cookie as an argument and returns the value. If the cookie doesn't exist, the function returns a `null` value.

The `SetCookie()` function.

This function can be used to create a new cookie or to update an existing cookie. The function requires two arguments and can take several optional arguments:

```
setCookie(name,value,expires,path,domain,secure)
```

where `expires`, `path`, `domain`, and `secure` are optional parameters, and `name` and `value` are required. `name`, `value`, `path`, and `domain` should be strings. `expires` should be passed as a `Date` object, and `secure` should be a Boolean value.

The order of the arguments is important, so if you want to leave out a particular value in the middle of the order, you should pass the `null` value as a placeholder.

The `DeleteCookie()` function.
This function does just what the name suggests: deletes the cookies specified by a `name` argument. The cookie is deleted by updating it with an expiry date equal to the current date and time.

BUILDING A NEWS SEARCH PAGE

You are now going to use cookies to develop a more sophisticated application.

Most users of the World Wide Web are well aware that the Web can be a great source of the latest news. However, finding just the right news can be a little daunting. The process can take loading a variety of news providers' Web pages to get all the information you want.

Using a combination of cookies and frames, you are going to build an application that provides news from multiple sources in one browser window.

The concept is simple: The screen is divided into two main sections—the left side contains a form for manipulating the application, and the right side contains three frames displaying the news sources selected by the user.

In the control frame, users should be provided with three drop-down selection lists to enable them to select the news sources for each of the three frames on the right. In addition, users should be able to add news sources to the list, as well as delete sources from the list.

Cookies are used to store the list of news sources, as well as the currently selected sources for each frame.

The application is created using scripts in two files: the top-level frameset called `news.htm` (see Listing 9-2) and the main control file that you will call `control.htm` (see Listing 9-3). The file `wait.htm` is a placeholder that is displayed when the three news source frames on the right side are first created (see Listing 9-4).

Input   **Listing 9-2** The parent frameset (`news.htm`).

```
<!-- SOURCE CODE FOR TOP-LEVEL FRAMESET -->
<HTML>

<HEAD>
<TITLE>Example 9.2</TITLE>

<SCRIPT LANGUAGE="JavaScript">
<!-- HIDE FROM OTHER BROWSERS
//
//   WE NEED TO INCLUDE THE COOKIE FUNCTIONS
//
//
//   Cookie Functions - Second Helping  (21-Jan-96)
//   Written by:  Bill Dortch, hIdaho Design <bdortch@netw.com>
```

continued on next page

continued from previous page

```
//   The following functions are released to the public domain.
//

// "Internal" function to return the decoded value of a cookie
//
function getCookieVal (offset) {
  var endstr = document.cookie.indexOf (";", offset);
  if (endstr == -1)
    endstr = document.cookie.length;
  return unescape(document.cookie.substring(offset, endstr));
}


//
//   Function to return the value of the cookie specified by "name".
//
function GetCookie (name) {
  var arg = name + "=";
  var alen = arg.length;
  var clen = document.cookie.length;
  var i = 0;
  while (i < clen) {
    var j = i + alen;
    if (document.cookie.substring(i, j) == arg)
      return getCookieVal (j);
    i = document.cookie.indexOf(" ", i) + 1;
    if (i == 0) break;
  }
  return null;
}


//
//   Function to create or update a cookie.
//
function SetCookie (name, value) {
  var argv = SetCookie.arguments;
  var argc = SetCookie.arguments.length;
  var expires = (argc > 2) ? argv[2] : null;
  var path = (argc > 3) ? argv[3] : null;
  var domain = (argc > 4) ? argv[4] : null;
  var secure = (argc > 5) ? argv[5] : false;
  document.cookie = name + "=" + escape (value) +
    ((expires == null) ? "" : ("; expires=" + expires.toGMTString())) +
    ((path == null) ? "" : ("; path=" + path)) +
    ((domain == null) ? "" : ("; domain=" + domain)) +
    ((secure == true) ? "; secure" : "");
}


//   Function to delete a cookie. (Sets expiration date to current date/time)
//
function DeleteCookie (name) {
  var exp = new Date();
  exp.setTime (exp.getTime() - 1);   // This cookie is history
  var cval = GetCookie (name);
```

```
      document.cookie = name + "=" + cval + "; expires=" + exp.toGMTString();
}


//
//   END OF THE COOKIE FUNCTIONS. OUR SCRIPT STARTS HERE.
//

function getURL(frame) {
   var name = GetCookie(frame);
   return GetCookie(name);
}

function initialize() {
   if (GetCookie("sites") == null) {
      var expiryDate = new Date();
      expiryDate.setTime(expiryDate.getTime() + (365 * 24 * 60 * 60 * 1000));
      SetCookie("sites","CNN,USA-Today,Yahoo",expiryDate,"/");
      SetCookie("CNN","http://www.cnn.com/",expiryDate,"/");
      SetCookie("USA-Today","http://www.usatoday.com/",expiryDate,"/");

      SetCookie("Yahoo","http://www.yahoo.com/headlines/news/",expiryDate,"/");
      SetCookie("frameOne","CNN",expiryDate,"/");
      SetCookie("frameTwo","USA-Today",expiryDate,"/");
      SetCookie("frameThree","Yahoo",expiryDate,"/");
      SetCookie("number","3",expiryDate,"/");
   }
}



initialize();

var frameOne = getURL("frameOne");
var frameTwo = getURL("frameTwo");
var frameThree = getURL("frameThree");

// STOP HIDING HERE -->
</script>

</HEAD>

<FRAMESET COLS="35%,*" onLoad="parent.frames['frameOne'].location=frameOne; ⇐
parent.frames['frameTwo'].location=frameTwo; ⇐
parent.frames['frameThree'].location=frameThree;">
   <FRAME SRC="control.htm" NAME="control">
   <FRAMESET ROWS="33%,33%,*">
      <FRAME SRC="wait.htm" NAME="frameOne">
      <FRAME SRC="wait.htm" NAME="frameTwo">
      <FRAME SRC="wait.htm" NAME="frameThree">
   </FRAMESET>
```

continued on next page

continued from previous page

```
</FRAMESET>


</HTML>
```

Input   **Listing 9-3** The source code for `control.htm`.

```html
<!-- SOURCE CODE FOR control.htm -->
<HTML>

<HEAD>
<TITLE>Example 9.3</TITLE>

<SCRIPT LANGUAGE="JavaScript">
<!-- HIDE FROM OTHER BROWSERS
//
//   WE NEED TO INCLUDE THE COOKIE FUNCTIONS
//
//
//   Cookie Functions - Second Helping   (21-Jan-96)
//   Written by:  Bill Dortch, hIdaho Design <bdortch@netw.com>
//   The following functions are released to the public domain.
//

// "Internal" function to return the decoded value of a cookie
//
function getCookieVal (offset) {
  var endstr = document.cookie.indexOf (";", offset);
  if (endstr == -1)
    endstr = document.cookie.length;
  return unescape(document.cookie.substring(offset, endstr));
}


//
//   Function to return the value of the cookie specified by "name".
//
function GetCookie (name) {
  var arg = name + "=";
  var alen = arg.length;
  var clen = document.cookie.length;
  var i = 0;
  while (i < clen) {
    var j = i + alen;
    if (document.cookie.substring(i, j) == arg)
      return getCookieVal (j);
    i = document.cookie.indexOf(" ", i) + 1;
    if (i == 0) break;
  }
  return null;
}

//
```

```
//   Function to create or update a cookie.
//
function SetCookie (name, value) {
  var argv = SetCookie.arguments;
  var argc = SetCookie.arguments.length;
  var expires = (argc > 2) ? argv[2] : null;
  var path = (argc > 3) ? argv[3] : null;
  var domain = (argc > 4) ? argv[4] : null;
  var secure = (argc > 5) ? argv[5] : false;
  document.cookie = name + "=" + escape (value) +
    ((expires == null) ? "" : ("; expires=" + expires.toGMTString())) +
    ((path == null) ? "" : ("; path=" + path)) +
    ((domain == null) ? "" : ("; domain=" + domain)) +
    ((secure == true) ? "; secure" : "");
}


//   Function to delete a cookie. (Sets expiration date to current date/time)
//
function DeleteCookie (name) {
  var exp = new Date();
  exp.setTime (exp.getTime() - 1);   // This cookie is history
  var cval = GetCookie (name);
  document.cookie = name + "=" + cval + "; expires=" + exp.toGMTString();
}


//
//   END OF THE COOKIE FUNCTIONS. OUR SCRIPT STARTS HERE.
//

function getURL(frame) {
  var name = GetCookie(frame);
  return GetCookie(name);
}


var expiryDate = new Date();
expiryDate.setTime(expiryDate.getTime() + (365 * 24 * 60 * 60 * 1000));

var number = parseInt(GetCookie("number"));
var siteList = GetCookie("sites");
var sites = new createArray(number);
sites = extractSites(siteList,number);

function createArray(num) {
  for (var i=1; i <= num; i++)
    this[i] = "";
  this.length = num;
}

function extractSites(list,num) {
  var results = new createArray(num);
  var first = 0;
  var last = 0;
  for (var i = 1; i <= num; i ++) {
```

continued on next page

continued from previous page

```
      first = (i == 1) ? 0 : last+1;
      last = (i == num) ? list.length : list.indexOf(",",first+1);
      results[i] = list.substring(first,last);
   }
   return results;
}

function makeList() {
  var result = "";
  for (var i = 1; i <= number; i++) {
    result += sites[i];
    result += (i == number) ? "" : ",";
  }
  return result;
}

function getList(frame) {
  var result = '<SELECT NAME="' + frame + '" onChange="loadURL(this);">';
  for (var i = 1; i<=number; i++) {
    result += '<OPTION';
    result += (GetCookie(frame) == sites[i]) ? " SELECTED" : "";
    result += ">" + sites[i] + "\n";
  }
  result += "</SELECT>";
  return result;
}

function addURL(form) {
  if ((form.name.value == "") || (form.name.value == null)) {
    returnl
  }
  var name = form.name.value;
  var url = form.url.value;
  SetCookie(name,url,expiryDate,"/");
  sites[++number] = name;
  SetCookie("sites",makeList(),expiryDate,"/");
  SetCookie("number",number,expiryDate,"/");
  window.open("control.htm","control");
}

function deleteURL(form) {
  var name = form.name.value;
  var gone = false;
  for (var i=1; i<=number; i++) {
    if (sites[i] == name) {
      gone = true;
      number--;
      for (var j=i; j<=number; j++) {
        sites[j] = sites[j+1];
      }
      sites[number+1] = null;
      break;
    }
```

```
    }
    if (gone) {
      SetCookie("number",number,expiryDate,"/");
      SetCookie("sites",makeList(),expiryDate,"/");
      var today = new Date();
      SetCookie(name,GetCookie(name),today,"/");
    }
    window.open("control.htm","control");
}

function loadURL(field) {
  var frame = field.name;
  var index = field.selectedIndex;
  var name = field.options[index].text;
  var url = GetCookie(name);
  window.open(url,frame);
  SetCookie(frame,name,expiryDate,"/");
}

// Set things up before building forms
var oneList = "";
var twoList = "";
var threeList = "";

oneList = getList("frameOne");
twoList = getList("frameTwo");
threeList = getList("frameThree");

// STOP HIDING HERE -->
</script>

</HEAD>

<BODY>

<H1>The<BR>News<BR>Source</H1>

<SCRIPT LANGUAGE="JavaScript">
<!-- HIDE FROM OTHER BROWSERS

document.write("<FORM METHOD=POST>");
document.write("Source One:");
document.write(oneList);
document.write("</FORM>");
document.write("<FORM METHOD=POST>");
document.write("<BR>");
document.write("Source Two:")
document.write(twoList);
document.write("</FORM>");
document.write("<FORM METHOD=POST>");
document.write("<BR>");
document.write("Source Three:");
```

continued on next page

continued from previous page

```
        document.write(threeList);
        document.write("</FORM>");

        // STOP HIDING -->
        </SCRIPT>

        <BR>
        <FORM METHOD=POST>

        Name:
        <INPUT TYPE="text" NAME="name">
        <BR>
        URL:
        <INPUT TYPE="text" NAME="url">
        <BR>
        <INPUT TYPE="button" VALUE="Add URL" onClick="addURL(this.form);">
        <BR>
        <INPUT TYPE="button" VALUE="Delete URL" onClick="deleteURL(this.form);">

        </FORM>

        </BODY>

        </HTML>
```

| Input |

Listing 9-4 Creating a Wait message.

```
<!-- SOURCE CODE FOR wait.htm -->
<HTML>

<BODY>
<H1>Please Wait ...</H1>
</BODY>

</HTML>
```

The results should look like Figures 9-3 and 9-4.

This program is somewhat complex in that it uses dynamically generated HTML, both in the parent frameset and the main HTML file in the control frame. Both files include Bill Dortch's cookie functions because the scripts in both files need to access the cookies.

In order to understand how the application works, you need to understand how you are using cookies to store all the information.

You need to keep track of the following information:

● A name and URL for each option in the selection lists

● The last loaded (selected) option for each of the three frames

●   A list of all the names of the options

●   The number of options currently available

All this information is stored in cookies. You keep an `optionName=url` cookie for each option. In addition, you have three cookies of the form `frameName=optionName`

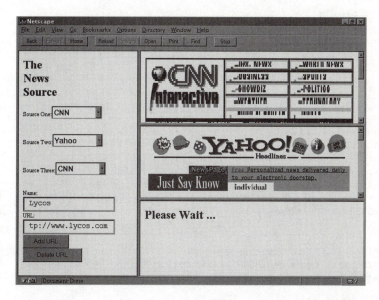

Figure 9-3
Using cookies
to create a
user-oriented cus-
tom news sources
Web page.

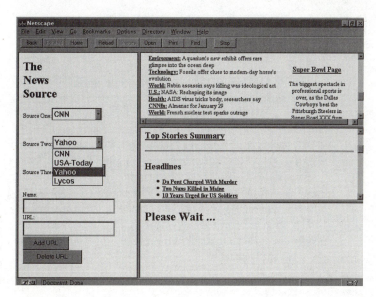

Figure 9-4
Users can add a
new URL and auto-
matically update
selection lists.

for each of the frames. The list of all names is stored in the form `sites=optionName1, optionName2,optionName3`, and so on, where the list is comma-separated and encoded using Bill Dortch's functions. The number of options is stored in the cookie `number=numberOfOptions`.

In the parent frameset, you have written two functions of your own, as well as built the HTML for the entire frameset using the `document.write()` method.

```
function getURL(frame) {
  var name = GetCookie(frame);
  return GetCookie(name);
}
```

The `getURL()` function accepts a frame name as a parameter. It first gets the name of the option for the frame from the appropriate cookie and then gets the URL for that option name with another call to `GetCookie()`. The URL is returned.

```
function initialize() {
  if (GetCookie("sites") == null) {
    var expiryDate = new Date();
    expiryDate.setTime(expiryDate.getTime() + (365 * 24 * 60 * 60 * 1000));
    SetCookie("sites","CNN,USA-Today,Yahoo",expiryDate,"/");
    SetCookie("CNN","http://www.cnn.com/",expiryDate,"/");
    SetCookie("USA-Today","http://www.usatoday.com/",expiryDate,"/");

    SetCookie("Yahoo","http://www.yahoo.com/headlines/news/",expiryDate,"/");
    SetCookie("frameOne","CNN",expiryDate,"/");
    SetCookie("frameTwo","USA-Today",expiryDate,"/");

    SetCookie("frameThree","Yahoo",expiryDate,"/");
    SetCookie("number","3",expiryDate,"/");
  }
}
```

The `initialize()` function is the first function called in the script. It simply checks whether any sites are currently stored as cookies using `if (GetCookies("sites") == null)`. If there are no sites stored, the function defines an initial list of three options and stores all the relevant information in the appropriate cookies.

After calling `initialize()` to ensure you have sites stored in cookies, you use `getURL()` to extract the URLs for the three news frames from the cookies.

Finally, the three URLs are loaded into their respective frames by using an `onLoad` event handler in the `FRAMESET` tag. This ensures that all the frames are loaded and ready when you attempt to open the URLs in them. The parent frameset itself divides the right-hand column into three frames where you load `wait.htm` as a placeholder until the various news sources begin to load. In the left-column frame you load `control.htm`, which is the main application:

```
<FRAMESET COLS="35%,*" onLoad="parent.frames['frameOne'].location=frameOne; ⇐
parent.frames['frameTwo'].location=frameTwo; ⇐
parent.frames['frameThree'].location=frameThree;">
```

```
  <FRAME SRC="control.htm" NAME="control">
  <FRAMESET ROWS="33%,33%,*">
    <FRAME SRC="wait.htm" NAME="frameOne">
    <FRAME SRC="wait.htm" NAME="frameTwo">
    <FRAME SRC="wait.htm" NAME="frameThree">
  </FRAMESET>
</FRAMESET>
```

Once the frameset is built, you use `getURL()` to extract the URLs for the three news frames from the cookies. Then you use `window.open()` to open the appropriate URL in each frame.

The file `control.htm` (refer back to Listing 9-3) is where all the interactive work of the application takes place. The file includes several HTML forms that provide the three drop-down selection lists—one for each of the three news frames—and a simple form to add and remove URLs from the list.

In order to implement all of the functionality you need, `control.htm` includes several additional functions in the header of the file.

```
var expiryDate = new Date();
expiryDate.setTime(expiryDate.getTime() + (365 * 24 * 60 * 60 * 1000));

var number = parseInt(GetCookie("number"));
var siteList = GetCookie("sites");
var sites = new createArray(number);
sites = extractSites(siteList,number);

function createArray(num) {
  for (var i=1; i <= num; i++)
    this[i] = "";
  this.length = num;
}
```

You start by setting up all the global variables you are going to need throughout the script. `expiryDate` is set to one year after the current date and is used whenever you create new cookies or update existing ones.

The variable `number` contains the number of options in the selection lists and is initially extracted from the appropriate cookie using `GetCookie()`. Also, `siteList` is the string of option names from the `sites` cookie. It is passed to `extractSites` to fill up the array `sites`, which is used throughout the script to reference option names.

You have used a standard `createArray()` type function to build the array `sites`.

```
function extractSites(list,num) {
  var results = new createArray(num);
  var first = 0;
  var last = 0;
  for (var i = 1; i <= num; i ++) {
    first = (i == 1) ? 0 : last+1;
    last = (i == num) ? list.length : list.indexOf(",",first+1);
    results[i] = list.substring(first,last);
  }
  return results;
}
```

The `extractSites()` function accepts two arguments: the string of comma-separated option names and the number of options in the list. It returns an array of option names.

The real work of the function all takes place in the **for** loop. The loop is repeated once for each of the options in the list. The first step is to figure out the index of the first character of the next option name in the list. The command `first = (i == 1) ? 0 : last+1;` does this by checking whether the loop counter is still at the start (equal to 1). If it is, the value of **first** is zero; otherwise, it is one character past the last character of the previous name, which was stored in **last**.

The index of the last character is calculated in a similar way using the command:

```
last = (i == num) ? list.length : list.indexOf(",",first+1);
```

This command checks whether the counter is at its final value. If it is, then **last** should be set to the last character in the string using **list.length**. Otherwise, the **indexOf()** method is used to find the next comma in the string.

These two lines are a good example of using conditional expressions to write what would otherwise be a set of bulkier **if-else** statements.

Once **first** and **last** are calculated, then the next entry in the array is set using **list.substring()** to extract the option name from the string.

Finally, the array **results** is returned as the result of the function.

```
function makeList() {
  var result = "";
  for (var i = 1; i <= number; i++) {
    result += sites[i];
    result += (i == number) ? "" : ",";
  }
  return result;
}
```

makeList() is used to perform exactly the opposite function of **extractSites()**. Given the array of option names stored in the global array **sites**, it returns a single string containing a comma-separated list of options.

This is done, again, in a single **for** loop that loops through each entry in the array and adds it to the **result** variable using the **+=** concatenation operator. The command

```
result += (i == number) ? "" : ",";
```

uses a conditional expression to make sure that a comma is added only after an entry from the array, if it is not the last entry in the array.

```
function getList(frame) {
  var result = '<SELECT NAME="' + frame + '" onChange="loadURL(this);">';
  for (var i = 1; i<=number; i++) {
    result += '<OPTION';
    result += (GetCookie(frame) == sites[i]) ? " SELECTED" : "";
    result += ">" + sites[i] + "\n";
  }
  result += "</SELECT>";
  return result;
}
```

The `getList()` function is used to build the drop-down selection menus for each of the three frames based on the current cookie settings. The function accepts a frame name as an argument and returns, as a single string, the **SELECT** HTML container, complete with all options set and the appropriate one preselected.

The function uses the `frame` argument to correctly set the **NAME** attribute of the **SELECT** tag. The `onChange` event handler contains the function call to load a new URL when the user chooses a new option.

The `for` loop in the function builds the list of options. It does this by looping through each option and adding an **OPTION** tag to the string. It then uses `sites[i]` to add the name to be displayed for each option. The command

```
result += (GetCookie(frame) == sites[i]) ? " SELECTED" : "";
```

checks if the current option is stored in the cookie for the frame. If it is, then the **SELECTED** attribute is added to the **OPTION** tag so that that option will appear selected initially.

```
function addURL(form) {
  if ((form.name.value == "") || (form.name.value == null)) {
    returnl
  }
  var name = form.name.value;
  var url = form.url.value;
  SetCookie(name,url,expiryDate,"/");
  sites[++number] = name;
  SetCookie("sites",makeList(),expiryDate,"/");
  SetCookie("number",number,expiryDate,"/");
  window.open("control.htm","control");
}
```

`addURL()` is invoked when the user clicks on the Add URL button near the bottom of the frame. It adds a new entry to the selection lists for each frame.

Given the `form` object as an argument, the `addURL()` function extracts the name and URL from the fields in the form and then sets the cookie for that name, as well as updates the `sites` array and stores new `sites` and `number` cookies.

Notice the use of the unary increment operator in `sites[++number] = name;` to increment the value of the `number` variable before using it as an index to `sites`. This effectively adds a new entry to `sites` before the next line:

```
SetCookie("sites",makeList(),expiryDate,"/");
```

This line updates the `sites` cookie by calling `makeList()` to build a comma-separated string out of the updated array.

Finally, the function reloads `control.htm` into `control` to rebuild the selection menus.

```
function deleteURL(form) {
  var name = form.name.value;
  var gone = false;
  for (var i=1; i<=number; i++) {
    if (sites[i] == name) {
```

continued on next page

continued from previous page

```
        gone = true;
        number--;
        for (var j=i; j<=number; j++) {
          sites[j] = sites[j+1];
        }
        sites[number+1] = null;
        break;
    }
  }
  if (gone) {
    SetCookie("number",number,expiryDate,"/");
    SetCookie("sites",makeList(),expiryDate,"/");
    var today = new Date();
    SetCookie(name,GetCookie(name),today,"/");
  }
  window.open("control.htm","control");
}
```

In this excerpt, the deleteURL() function removes an entry from the list of options. This process is actually a bit more complicated than adding a new URL to the list because a little bit of work needs to be done to remove an entry from the middle of the array and then close up the hole that this creates in the array.

The function uses a for loop to move through the array. The if statement checks whether the current entry matches the one you want to delete.

If there is a match, then the work begins. gone is set to true so that later in the function you know a match was found—after all, the user could incorrectly type the name of the entry to delete. Next, number is decreased to reflect the fact that the number of entries in the list will decrease by one. Another for loop is used to count from the current index of the entry you are deleting to the new value of number (that is, one before the current last entry in the array).

The command sites[j] = sites[j+1]; copies the array entry immediately following the current entry into the current entry. In this way, you fill in the hole created by removing an entry.

Finally, after the for loop finishes, you set the previous last entry to the null value with sites[number+1] = null;.

Once you finish the for loop, if you have found an entry to delete, you update the sites and number cookies just as you did in addURL(), and then you remove the cookie for the deleted entry by updating it with an expiry date equal to the current date and time.

```
function loadURL(field) {
  var frame = field.name;
  var url = GetURL(frame);
  open(url,frame);
  SetCookie(frame,name,expiryDate,"/");
}
```

The loadURL() function is invoked when the user changes the value of one of the selection lists. It receives the field object for the selection list as an argument.

Based on this information, it can extract the frame name, which is actually the **NAME** value of the selection element. Using this information, you can call **getURL()** to get the URL for that frame.

Once you have this information, you can open the URL in the frame and then update the cookie for that frame to reflect the new selection by the user.

```
// Set things up before building forms
var oneList = "";
var twoList = "";
var threeList = "";

oneList = getList("frameOne");
twoList = getList("frameTwo");
threeList = getList("frameThree");
```

The last thing you do in the header of the document is set up three variables containing the selection lists for the three different news source frames by calling `getList()`.

```
document.write("<FORM METHOD=POST>");
document.write("Source One:");
document.write(oneList);
document.write("</FORM>");
document.write("<FORM METHOD=POST>");
document.write("<BR>");
document.write("Source Two:")
document.write(twoList);
document.write("</FORM>");
document.write("<FORM METHOD=POST>");
document.write("<BR>");
document.write("Source Three:");
document.write(threeList);
document.write("</FORM>");
```

In the body of the document, you use scripts to build each of the three drop-down selection lists. Each list is a separate form, but could just as easily have been a single form.

```
<FORM METHOD=POST>

Name:
<INPUT TYPE="text" NAME="name">
<BR>
URL:
<INPUT TYPE="text" NAME="url">
<BR>
<INPUT TYPE="button" VALUE="Add URL" onClick="addURL(this.form);">
<BR>
<INPUT TYPE="button" VALUE="Delete URL" onClick="deleteURL(this.form);">

</FORM>
```

The last element in the document is the form used to add and delete entries from the list of options. The form contains two text entry fields and two buttons that invoke either `addURL()` or `deleteURL()` in their `onClick` event handlers.

THE navigator OBJECT

As mentioned at the beginning of this chapter, the `navigator` object makes information about the current version of Navigator available to scripts.

The properties of the `navigator` object are outlined in Table 9-2.

Name	Description
appName	The name of the application in which the page is loaded represented as a string (such as `"Netscape"`).
appVersion	The version information of the current browser as a string in the form `"2.0 (Win16; I)"` where 2.0 is the version number, `Win16` is the platform, and `I` indicates the international version (as opposed to `U` for the domestic version).
appCodeName	The code name of the current browser (such as `"Mozilla"`).
mimeTypes	An array of objects reflecting the MIME types supported by the browser. The `mimeTypes` property is discussed in more detail in Chapter 14.
plugins	An array of objects reflecting the plug-ins installed in the browser. The `plugins` property is discussed in more detail in Chapter 14.
userAgent	The user agent for the current browser as a string in the form `"Mozilla/ 2.0 (Win16; I)"`.

Table 9-2 *Properties of the* navigator *object.*

In order to understand the significance of this information, it is important to understand the concept of the user agent. In the initial communication between the client and the server during an HTTP request, the browser sends the user agent string to the server. That information becomes available on the server for a number of uses, including processing by CGI scripts or for delivering specific versions of the pages based on the nature of the client browser.

The user agent information has two parts separated by a slash: a code name for the browser and the version information for the browser. This is the information stored in the `appCodeName` and `appVersion` properties.

Using the `navigator` **Properties**

At first, it may seem as though this information serves little practical use—but it can be very useful.

For instance, during the beta development of the Navigator 2.0 and 3.0 browsers, releases of new versions of the betas were quite frequent. Each version supported new features of JavaScript and fixed problems with earlier implementations, which sometimes created incompatibilities.

Many page authors are now using the properties of the **navigator** object to check whether the browsers being used will support the features used in the script. If not, users are alerted so that they don't try to run the script and get errors—or even find Netscape, or their PCs, crashing.

For example, if a page should only be run with Navigator 2.0 beta 6a on any platform and beta 6a is the latest version, the HTML file should look like this:

```
<HTML>

<HEAD>
<TITLE>navigator Example</TITLE>

<SCRIPT LANGUAGE="JavaScript">
<!-- HIDE FROM OTHER BROWSERS

function checkBrowser() {
  if ((navigator.appVersion.substring(0,6) != "2.0b6a") && ⇐
(navigator.appName != "Netscape"))
alert("Please use version 2.0b6a of the Netscape Navigator ⇐
web browser with this page.");
}


Rest of script

// STOP HIDING FROM OTHER BROWSERS -->
</SCRIPT>

</HEAD>

<BODY onLoad="checkBrowser();">

HTML code

</BODY>

</HTML>
```

Similarly, in the future, if different browsers support JavaScript, they may offer different features or additional objects, and the use of the **navigator** object can help script authors ensure that their scripts run on the largest number of browsers while also taking advantage of the unique features of each.

Quiz 3

1. Why is it necessary to encode a cookie?
   a. To prevent others from viewing your information.
   b. To be able to handle values with embedded spaces.
   c. To make the cookie compatible with non-cookie browsers.
   d. Encoding of cookies is never necessary.

2. What does the following statement do?

```
unescape( argument );
```

   a. It returns back a string that is the input string argument after it has been decoded.
   b. It removes the escape characters from the string argument.
   c. It adds spaces to the string argument and returns the result.
   d. It prevents the user from escaping out of the current document.

3. What is the user agent information?
   a. It is the `navigator` object.
   b. It is information contained in a search request.
   c. It is a property of the `navigator` object that is sent to the HTTP server during a request.
   d. It identifies the user to the HTTP server.

4. Where can you get the name and version of the browser being used?
   a. By decoding the cookies stored by the browser.
   b. From the `appName` and `appVersion` properties of the `navigator` object.
   c. By looking in the current user directory for a configuration file.
   d. This information is not readily available.

5. Where can you get information on what plug-ins are installed for the browser being used?
   a. From the `plugins` property of the `navigator` object.
   b. From the local configuration file for the browser.
   c. From the JavaScript method `getPlugins()`.
   d. By prompting the user and asking if a plug-in is installed.

SUMMARY

In this chapter, you learned about an extremely useful feature of JavaScript: the `cookie` property.

Using the `cookie` property, scripts can be set to read cookies that store state information in the client browser. Using cookies, you can retain information between sessions to produce applications that outlive the currently loaded document and even the current browser session.

To see an example of using cookies in JavaScript, jump to Appendix C, Lab 4, James Thiele's Reminder Calendar.

Once again, Bill Dortch has provided the JavaScript community with a set of freely available functions that make setting and retrieving cookies easier.

In addition to cookies, you took a look at the `navigator` object and how it can be used to ensure that users are using the appropriate browser for your scripts.

In the next chapter, we take a look at a variety of objects and features of JavaScript that we haven't covered in detail yet, including the `string` object, the `Math` object, and the `history` object.

COMMANDS AND EXTENSIONS REVIEW

Command/Extension	Type	Description
Set-Cookie	HTTP header	Sets cookies in the client browser—part of an HTTP response header
Cookie	HTTP header	Returns cookies to the server—part of an HTTP request header
expires	Set-Cookie attribute	Indicates the expiry date for a cookie (in GMT)
path	Set-Cookie attribute	Used to set the path for files applicable to a cookie
domain	Set-Cookie attribute	Used to set the domain for files applicable to a cookie
secure	Set-Cookie attribute	Specifies that a cookie should be transmitted only on secure links

continued on next page

continued from previous page

Command/Extension	Type	Description
`cookie`	JavaScript property	String containing the value of cookies for the current document
`indexOf()`	JavaScript method	A method of the `string` object that returns the index of the next occurrence of a substring in a string
`escape()`	JavaScript method	Encodes a string using URL encoding
`unescape()`	JavaScript method	Decodes a string encoded using URL encoding
`appName`	JavaScript property	The name of the browser application as a string
`appVersion`	JavaScript property	The version number and platform of the browser as a string
`appCodeName`	JavaScript property	The code name of the browser as a string
`mimeTypes`	JavaScript property	An array of objects reflecting the MIME types supported by the browser
`plugins`	JavaScript property	An array of objects reflecting the plug-ins installed in the browser
`userAgent`	JavaScript property	The user agent string for the browser
`link()`	JavaScript method	Method of the `string` object that encloses the string in an `<A>` HTML tag
`fontcolor()`	JavaScript method	Method of the `string` object that sets the HTML font color for the string

CHAPTER EXERCISE

1. A user loads the page `http://sample.page/sample/file.html` on 1 January 1996 at noon (GMT), and a script in it contains the following lines:

```
document.cookie = "user=joe; expires=Wed, ⇐
31-Jan-96 00:00:00 GMT; path=/";
document.cookie = "message=hello";
document.cookie = "food=lasagna; expires=Wed, ⇐
31-Jan-96 00:00:00 GMT; domain=another.site; path=/anotherpath/";
document.cookie = "color=blue; expires=Tue, ⇐
02-Jan-96 12:00:00 GMT; domain=sample.page; path=/sample/";
```

If the user accesses the following pages at the following times, what will be displayed by the command `document.write(document.cookie)`?

a. `http://sample.page/otherfile.html` on 3 January

b. `http://sample.page/sample/file.html` on 31 January at noon (GMT)

c. `http://another.site/anotherfile.html` on 31 January at 11:59 a.m.

2. Extend your script in Listings 9-2 through 9-4 (the news sources example) so that some sort of error checking takes place. If the user tries to add an entry with no URL, the user should get an error. In addition, if the user tries to add more than 10 entries to the list, prompt the user for the name of an entry to replace and check the name to make sure it is valid before proceeding.

3. Design a page that asks questions of first-time visitors (or those who haven't visited for more than 30 days). Ask for their favorite color and their favorite food (from a list of options) and then customize the Web page to include the specified background color and a picture of the food indicated.

Every time users come to the page within 30 days of their last visit, build the specified page without asking for the information.

CHAPTER 10

STRINGS, MATH, AND THE HISTORY LIST

U p to this point in the book, you have learned about the major objects and tools of JavaScript. Even so, this leaves several useful objects undiscovered.

In this chapter you are going to take a detailed look at some of the objects that you have been introduced to only briefly earlier in the book. These include the `string` object, the `Math` object, and the `history` object.

Every string in JavaScript is an object. The `string` object offers properties and methods to perform a variety of manipulations on a given string. These include methods for searching a string, extracting substrings, and applying HTML tags to the content of the string.

The `Math` object provides those functions and methods necessary to perform mathematical calculations. These range from the `PI` value to methods for all the trigonometric functions.

The `history` object is a bit different in that it doesn't involve the manipulation of information the way the `string` and `Math` objects do. The `history` object reflects the information in the browser's history list.

In this chapter you will learn the details of each of these object's properties and methods plus:

- How to manipulate the content of strings

- How to perform advanced mathematical calculations with the `Math` object

- How to build dynamic forward and back buttons—in any frame

LESSON 1 — The Property and Methods of the `string` Object

THE `string` OBJECT

You already have considerable experience working with strings. You have used them throughout the book, you understand how to represent string literals, and you even know some of the basic techniques for examining the content of strings.

Even with the `substring()` and `indexOf()` methods which you saw earlier, though, you haven't reached the true possibilities of working with the `string` object.

The `length` Property

The `string` object has only one property: `length`. The `length` property is an integer value reflecting the number of characters in the string. Because the index of the first character in a string is zero, this means the `length` property is one greater than the index of the last character in the string.

For example, the string `"Hello"` has a length of five. The index of the first character (`"H"`) is `0`, and the index of the last character (`"o"`) is `4`.

Methods of the `string` Object

The flexibility and power of the `string` object rest in the wide variety of methods available to manipulate the content of the string. Table 10-1 outlines the methods available in the `string` object.

TABLE 10-1

Name	Description
`anchor()`	Surrounds the string with an anchor `A` tag.
`big()`	Surrounds the string with the HTML `BIG` tag.

Name	Description
`blink()`	Surrounds the string with the HTML BLINK tag.
`bold()`	Surrounds the string with the HTML B tag.
`charAt()`	Given an index as an argument, returns the character at the specified index.
`fixed()`	Surrounds the string with the HTML TT tag to make it display as a fixed-width font.
`fontcolor()`	Surrounds the string with the HTML <FONT COLOR=color> and </FONT> tags to make it display in the specified color.
`fontsize()`	Surrounds the string with the HTML <FONT SIZE=size> and </FONT> tags to make it display in the desired font size.
`indexOf()`	Given a string and an initial index, returns the index of the next occurrence of the string after the initial index.
`italics()`	Surrounds the string with the HTML I tag.
`lastIndexOf()`	Given a string and a starting index, returns the index of the last occurrence of the string searching backwards from the starting index.
`link()`	Given a URL, surrounds the string with an A tag to create a hypertext link.
`small()`	Surrounds the string with the HTML SMALL tag.
`split()`	Returns an array of strings by splitting the string into substrings at a separator passed to the method as an argument.
`strike()`	Surrounds the string with the HTML STRIKE tag.
`sub()`	Surrounds the string with the HTML SUB tag.
`substring()`	Given two indexes, returns the substring starting at the first index and ending with the character before the last index. If the second index is greater, the substring starts with the second index and ends with the character before the first index; if the two indexes are equal, returns the empty string.
`sup()`	Surrounds the string with the HTML SUP tag.
`toLowerCase()`	Makes the entire string lowercase.
`toUpperCase()`	Makes the entire string uppercase.

Table 10-1 *Methods of the* `string` *object.*

The HTML Methods

As you can see in Table 10-1, many of the methods of the `string` object are designed to add HTML tags to the content of the string so that when you display the string, it is suitably formatted. This can make the JavaScript code easier to read than if all the string assignments contained HTML tags, with the actual text to be displayed using `document.write()` or `document.writeln()`.

The way these functions work is to return a new string containing the additional HTML tags. So, if you have a string variable named `sample` with the value `"test"`, `sample.big()` returns `"<BIG>test</BIG>"`, but `sample` still has a value of `"test"`.

For instance, the following JavaScript commands output the text `"Hello!"` in large, blinking, bold letters:

```
var sample = "Hello!";
var sampleBig = sample.big();
var sampleBlink = sampleBig.blink();
var sampleBold = sampleBlink.bold();
document.write(sampleBold);
```

The following text displays the same word but as a hypertext link to the file `http:// some.domain/some/file.html`.

```
var sample = "Hello!";
sample = sample.link("http://some.domain/some/file.html");
document.write(sample);
```

Because these methods return strings, you can also string together a series of methods and rewrite the first example as

```
var sample = "Hello!";
document.write(sample.big().blink().bold());
```

To give you a better idea of what these methods actually do to the content of your strings, the script in Listing 10-1 displays the actual content of the strings using the `XMP` tag to force the browser not to interpret any HTML in the output.

Listing 10-1 Applying HTML tags with JavaScript's `string` object.

```
<HTML>

<HEAD>
<TITLE>HTML method example</TITLE>
</HEAD>

<BODY>

<SCRIPT LANGUAGE="JavaScript">
<!-- HIDE FROM OTHER BROWSERS

var sample = "hello";
```

```
document.write("<XMP>" + sample.italics() + "</XMP>");
document.write(sample.italics());

document.write("<XMP>" + sample.blink() + "</XMP>");
document.write(sample.blink());

document.write("<XMP>" + sample.anchor("test") + "</XMP>");
document.write(sample.anchor("test"));

document.write("<XMP>" + sample.fontsize(7) + "</XMP>");
document.write(sample.fontsize(7));

document.write("<XMP>" + sample.bold().strike() + "</XMP>");
document.write(sample.bold().strike());

document.write("<XMP>" + sample.fontcolor("iceblue").big().sup() + "</XMP>");
document.write(sample.fontcolor("iceblue").big().sup());

// STOP HIDING FROM OTHER BROWSERS -->
</SCRIPT>

</BODY>

</HTML>
```

Output   The script produces results like those in Figure 10-1.

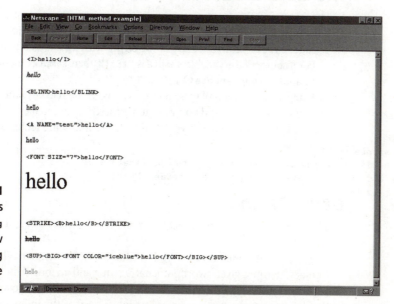

Figure 10-1
The HTML methods of the `string` object return new strings containing the appropriate HTML tags.

Analysis   In this script, you are using various methods of the **string** object and the value returned by these methods. The script contains the examples in pairs of **document.write()** statements. The first output is the result of a method call surrounded by the **XMP** HTML container tags. The **XMP** tag ensures that any content inside the container is displayed without any processing. In this way, any HTML inside the container is simply displayed as regular text rather than treated as HTML.

The second line of each pair calls the same method but this time without the surrounding **XMP** tags so that the user can see what the result looks like when it is treated as HTML.

The substring() *Method*

You have seen the **substring()** method several times in previous chapters. You first saw the **substring()** method in Exercise 6-3 when you used it to verify input in a form.

To review, the method takes two integer arguments and returns the string starting at the first argument and ending at the character before the second argument. Where the first argument is larger, the process is reversed, and the substring starts at the second argument and continues until one before the first argument. When both arguments are equal, an empty string is returned.

For instance, if you have a string named **sample** with a value **"Hello!"**, then **sample.substring(0,3)** is **"Hel"**, **sample.substring(3,0)** is **"Hel"**, and **sample.substring(2,4)** has the value **"ll"**.

The Case Methods

The **string** object has two methods for changing the case of characters in a string. **toLowerCase()** returns a new string with all characters in lowercase. Similarly, **toUpperCase()** returns a copy of the string with all characters uppercase.

For instance, if the variable **sample** is **"tEsT"**, then **sample.toLowerCase()** is **"test"**, and **sample.toUpperCase()** is **"TEST"**.

Using a combination of these methods and the **substring()** method, you can achieve more interesting results. If you want to take a string and make the first character uppercase and the rest lowercase, you could use the following technique:

```
var sample = "tEsT";
var newSample = sample.substring(0,1).toUpperCase() + ⇐
sample.substring(1,sample.length).toLowerCase();
```

Other Methods

The **string** object has three other methods: **indexOf()**, **lastIndexOf()**, and **charAt()**.

You saw the **indexOf()** method in Chapter 9, "Remember Where You've Been with Cookies." Simply, given two arguments (a string and an index) the method starts searching the **string** object from the index and looks for the first occurrence of the string that has been passed to it as an argument. It returns the index of this occurrence.

This is best understood by example: If you have a string named `sample` with the value `"Greetings! Welcome to Navigator 3.0! Enjoy!"`, then `sample.indexOf("Wel",2)` would return a value of **13** and `sample.lastIndexOf("!",sample.length – 3)` would return a value of **35**.

What happens in the first example is that the method starts searching the string sample from index **2** (the first `"e"` in `"Greetings"`). It checks if the phrase `"Wel"` starts at that index and if not, it moves to the next character (index **3**) and tries again. This is repeated until the character at index **13**, where a match is found.

The send example is similar, but it moves backwards through the string looking for a match. In this case it starts at the **3** character from the end (`"o"` in `"Enjoy"`) and moves back until it finds a `"!"`.

The other method, `charAt()`, is almost the reverse of this process. Given an index as an argument, it returns the character at that location. This is easier to use to extract a single character from a string than the `substring()` method.

For instance, with the above string, both `sample.charAt(3)` and `sample.substring(3,4)` have the value of `"e"`.

With these methods, you can now develop tools to enable users to play with HTML to see how it looks. Using two frames, you will build an application that enables users to enter text in the left frame and select from a list of HTML attributes. They will see the text displayed with the combined attributes in the right frame, along with the actual HTML code needed to produce the results. Listings 10-2 through 10-4 contain the script files for the program.

In order to do this, you need a top-level frameset which looks like Listing 10-2.

| Input |

Listing 10-2 Top-level frameset.

```
<HTML>

<HEAD>
<TITLE>Listing 10-2</TITLE>
</HEAD>

<FRAMESET COLS="50%,*">
   <FRAME SRC="htmlform.html" NAME="choose">
   <FRAME SRC="sample.html" NAME="output">
</FRAMESET>

</HTML>
```

The `htmlform.html` file is where all the work is done.

| Input |

Listing 10-3 The htmlform.html file.

```
<HTML>

<HEAD>

<SCRIPT LANGUAGE="JavaScript">
```

continued on next page

continued from previous page

```
<!-- HIDE FROM OTHER BROWSERS

function display(form) {
  var format = form.toDisplay.value;
  var doc = parent.output;

  format = (form.big.checked) ? format.big() : format;
  format = (form.blink.checked) ? format.blink() : format;
  format = (form.bold.checked) ? format.bold() : format;
  format = (form.fixed.checked) ? format.fixed() : format;
  format = (form.italics.checked) ? format.italics() : format;
  format = (form.small.checked) ? format.small() : format;
  format = (form.strike.checked) ? format.strike() : format;
  format = (form.sup.checked) ? format.sup() : format;
  format = (form.sub.checked) ? format.sub() : format;
  format = (form.color.value == "") ? format.fontcolor("black")⇐
  format.fontcolor(form.color.value);
  format = (form.size.value == "") ? format.fontsize(3) : ⇐
  format.fontsize(form.size.value);

  var result = "<CENTER>The HTML code: <XMP>";
  result += format;
  result += "</XMP> looks like:<P>"
  result += format;
  result += "</CENTER>";

  doc.document.open("text/html");
  doc.document.write(result);
  doc.document.close();

}


// STOP HIDING -->
</SCRIPT>

<BODY BGCOLOR="aquamarine">

<CENTER>
<H1>The HTML tester page</H1>
Please enter some text, select some attributes and ⇐
enter a color and size (from 1 to 7).
The display will update dynamically.
<BR>
</CENTER>
<FORM METHOD=POST>

<TEXTAREA NAME="toDisplay" ROWS=10 COLS=35 WRAP=SOFT ⇐
onChange="display(this.form);">
Enter Text Here
</TEXTAREA><BR>
<INPUT TYPE="checkbox" NAME="big" onClick="display(this.form);">Big<BR>
<INPUT TYPE="checkbox" NAME="blink" onClick="display(this.form);">Blinking<BR>
<INPUT TYPE="checkbox" NAME="bold" onClick="display(this.form);">Bold<BR>
```

```
<INPUT TYPE="checkbox" NAME="fixed" ⇐
onClick="display(this.form);">Fixed Width<BR>
<INPUT TYPE="checkbox" NAME="italics" onClick="display(this.form);">Italics<BR>
<INPUT TYPE="checkbox" NAME="small" onClick="display(this.form);">Small<BR>
<INPUT TYPE="checkbox" NAME="strike" ⇐
onClick="display(this.form);">Striked Out<BR>
<INPUT TYPE="checkbox" NAME="sub" onClick="display(this.form);">Subscript<BR>
<INPUT TYPE="checkbox" NAME="sup" onClick="display(this.form);">SuperScript<BR>
Font Color: <INPUT TYPE="text" NAME="color" VALUE="black" ⇐
onChange="display(this.form);"><BR>
Font Size (1 to 7): <INPUT TYPE="text" NAME="size" VALUE="3" ⇐
onChange="display(this.form);">

</FORM>

<SCRIPT LANGUAGE="JavaScript">
<!-- HIDE FROM OTHER BROWSERS

display(document.forms[0]);

// STOP HIDING -->
</SCRIPT>

</BODY>

</HTML>
```

The file `sample.html` (Listing 10-4) is just a blank HTML file to fill the window when the frame is initially loaded.

Input

Listing 10-4 The source code for `sample.html`.

```
<HTML>

<BODY BGCOLOR="#FFFFFF">
</BODY>

</HTML>
```

Output

This script produces results like those in Figure 10-2.

Analysis

This program not only highlights the effect of the previous example but also some of the methods and techniques you learned in previous chapters.

All the work is done in the file `htmlform.html` (Listing 10-3). The program only really does one task—displays information based on the content of a form—so only one function, `display()`, is necessary.

```
function display(form) {
  var format = form.toDisplay.value;
  var doc = parent.output;
```

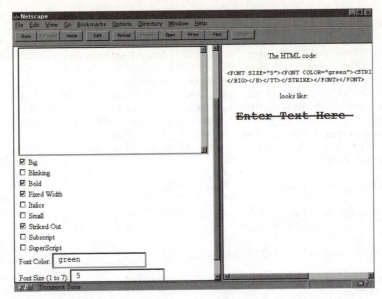

Figure 10-2
Using methods from the string object to dynamically test different combinations of HTML attributes.

You start by setting up the global variable **format**. You use this variable to hold the entire text and HTML tags to be tested. You start by assigning the content of the **textarea** input field, which contains the text you are going to test.

You also define **doc** to be equal to the object **parent.output**. **parent.output** refers to the second frame in the frameset and is effectively the **window** object for that frame. In this way, you can use **doc** instead of **parent.output**. For instance, **doc.document.write()** is the same as **parent.output.document.write()**.

```
format = (form.big.checked) ? format.big() : format;
format = (form.blink.checked) ? format.blink() : format;
format = (form.bold.checked) ? format.bold() : format;
format = (form.fixed.checked) ? format.fixed() : format;
format = (form.italics.checked) ? format.italics() : format;
format = (form.small.checked) ? format.small() : format;
format = (form.strike.checked) ? format.strike() : format;
format = (form.sup.checked) ? format.sup() : format;
format = (form.sub.checked) ? format.sub() : format;
format = (form.color.value == "") ? format.fontcolor("black") :⇐
format.fontcolor(form.color.value);
format = (form.size.value == "") ? format.fontsize(3) : ⇐
format.fontsize(form.size.value);
```

This section of code looks complex at first glance, but in reality, it is simple. You start by checking whether any of the checkboxes are checked. Because the **checkbox** object's **checked** property is a Boolean value, you can use it as the condition for a conditional expression, which performs the appropriate method and then assigns the result back to **format**.

Next, you apply the appropriate `fontcolor()` and `fontsize()` methods based on the form content. If either field is empty, you use a default value.

```
var result = "<CENTER>The HTML code: <XMP>";
result += format;
result += "</XMP> looks like:<P>"
result += format;
result += "</CENTER>";

doc.document.open("text/html");
doc.document.write(result);
doc.document.close();
```

The final task is to output the results. The string `result` holds the complete output for the second frame. Then you use `document.open()` to open a new output stream in the second frame for the HTML MIME type. You write the results to the frame and close the stream with `document.close()`.

```
<FORM METHOD=POST>

<TEXTAREA NAME="toDisplay" ROWS=10 COLS=35 WRAP=SOFT ⇐
onChange="display(this.form);">
Enter Text Here
</TEXTAREA><BR>
<INPUT TYPE="checkbox" NAME="big" onClick="display(this.form);">Big<BR>
<INPUT TYPE="checkbox" NAME="blink" onClick="display(this.form);">Blinking<BR>
<INPUT TYPE="checkbox" NAME="bold" onClick="display(this.form);">Bold<BR>
<INPUT TYPE="checkbox" NAME="fixed" ⇐
onClick="display(this.form);">Fixed Width<BR>
<INPUT TYPE="checkbox" NAME="italics" onClick="display(this.form);">Italics<BR>
<INPUT TYPE="checkbox" NAME="small" onClick="display(this.form);">Small<BR>
<INPUT TYPE="checkbox" NAME="strike" ⇐
onClick="display(this.form);">Striked Out<BR>
<INPUT TYPE="checkbox" NAME="sub" onClick="display(this.form);">Subscript<BR>
<INPUT TYPE="checkbox" NAME="sup" onClick="display(this.form);">SuperScript<BR>
Font Color: <INPUT TYPE="text" NAME="color" VALUE="black" ⇐
onChange="display(this.form);"><BR>
Font Size (1 to 7): <INPUT TYPE="text" NAME="size" VALUE="3" ⇐
onChange="display(this.form);">
```

The form is simple. When any text field changes, you call `display()`, and when any checkbox is clicked, you also call `display()`. No buttons are needed.

 When using a form with no buttons like this, realize that in the version of Navigator currently available, it is necessary to remove focus from a text field for a change event to be triggered.

```
<SCRIPT LANGUAGE="JavaScript">
<!-- HIDE FROM OTHER BROWSERS

display(document.forms[0]);
```

```
// STOP HIDING -->
</SCRIPT>
```

You end the body of the HTML file with a one-line script that calls `display()` for the first time to update the second frame with the contents of the form. This also could have been done in the `onLoad` event handler.

QUIZ 1

1. The `string` object has only one property:
   - a. `value`
   - b. `substring`
   - c. `size`
   - d. `length`

2. What are the HTML methods of the `string` object used for?
   - a. To read strings from HTML documents.
   - b. To insert HTML tags into the `string` object.
   - c. To return a new string containing the additional HTML tags.
   - d. None of the above.

3. If a string variable named `sample` has the value `'test'`, then what does `sample.big()` do?
   - a. It returns `'TEST'`.
   - b. It returns `'<BIG>test</BIG>'`.
   - c. It is the same as `sample.toUpperCase()`.
   - d. It changes the value of `test` to `'<BIG>test</BIG>'`.

4. If the variable test has the value `'Navigator'`, what does `test.substring(3,0)` return?
   - a. `'avi'`
   - b. `'vaN'`
   - c. `'Nav'`
   - d. `'iva'`

5. If the string named `sample` has the value `'big-red-bird'`, what does `sample.indexOf('big', 2)` return?
   - a. `0`
   - b. `1`
   - c. `2`
   - d. `-1`

LESSON 2   Using the search, replace, **and** space Functions

CREATING SEARCH AND REPLACE TOOLS

Anyone familiar with UNIX will miss many of the powerful text searching and matching tools found in the operating system and in scripting languages such as Perl, Awk, and sed. Although JavaScript provides the `indexOf()`, `lastIndexOf()`, `charAt()`, and `substring()` methods to help manipulate string contents, it doesn't provide powerful search and replace capabilities.

In this example, you extend the functionality of JavaScript's text manipulation capabilities with simple `search` and `replace` functions.

The `search` function should be able to search for words both in a case-sensitive and case-insensitive manner and should be able to search for whole words or substrings in words. Likewise, the `replace` function should be able to replace a word or substring, paying attention to case in the original text or ignoring it.

The `search` function should return `true` or `false`, and the `replace` function should return a new string with the result of the replace.

Listing 10-5 is the source code for these `search` and `replace` functions.

Input

Listing 10-5 Searching and replacing in JavaScript.

```
<SCRIPT LANGUAGE="JavaScript">
<!-- HIDE FROM OTHER BROWSERS

// SET UP ARGUMENTS FOR FUNCTION CALLS
//
var caseSensitive = true;
var notCaseSensitive = false;
var wholeWords = true;
var anySubstring = false;



// SEARCH FOR A TERM IN A TARGET STRING
//
// search(targetString,searchTerm,caseSensitive,wordOrSubstring)
//
// where caseSenstive is a boolean value and wordOrSubstring is a boolean
// value and true means whole words, false means substrings
//
function search(target,term,caseSens,wordOnly) {

  var ind = 0;
  var next = 0;
```

continued on next page

continued from previous page

```
      if (!caseSens) {
        term = term.toLowerCase();
        target = target.toLowerCase();
      }

      while ((ind = target.indexOf(term,next)) >= 0) {
        if (wordOnly) {
          var before = ind - 1;
          var after = ind + term.length;
          if (!(space(target.charAt(before)) && space(target.charAt(after)))) {
            next = ind + term.length;
            continue;
          }
        }
        return true;
      }

      return false;

}

// SEARCH FOR A TERM IN A TARGET STRING AND REPLACE IT
//
// replace(targetString,oldTerm,newTerm,caseSensitive,wordOrSubstring)
//
// where caseSenstive is a boolean value and wordOrSubstring is a boolean
// value and true means whole words, false means substrings
//
function replace(target,oldTerm,newTerm,caseSens,wordOnly) {

   var work = target;
   var ind = 0;
   var next = 0;

   if (!caseSens) {
     oldTerm = oldTerm.toLowerCase();
     work = target.toLowerCase();
   }

   while ((ind = work.indexOf(oldTerm,next)) >= 0) {
     if (wordOnly) {
       var before = ind - 1;
       var after = ind + oldTerm.length;
       if (!(space(work.charAt(before)) && space(work.charAt(after)))) {
         next = ind + oldTerm.length;
         continue;
       }
     }
     target = target.substring(0,ind) + newTerm + ⇐
     target.substring(ind+oldTerm.length,target.length);
```

```
     work = work.substring(0,ind) + newTerm + ⇐
     work.substring(ind+oldTerm.length,work.length);
     next = ind + newTerm.length;
     if (next >= work.length) { break; }
   }

   return target;

}

// CHECK IF A CHARACTER IS A WORD BREAK AND RETURN A BOOLEAN VALUE
//
function space(check) {

   var space = " .,/<>?!`';:@#$%^&*()=-|[]{}" + '"' + "\\\n\t";

   for (var i = 0; i < space.length; i++)
     if (check == space.charAt(i)) { return true; }

   if (check == "") { return true; }
   if (check == null) { return true; }

   return false;

}


// STOP HIDING -->
</SCRIPT>
```

To demonstrate how these functions work, you can set up a simple search and replace application using the functions in Listing 10-6.

Input   **Listing 10-6** Using the search and replace functions.

```
<HTML>

<HEAD>
<TITLE>Listing 10-6</TITLE>

<SCRIPT LANGUAGE="JavaScript">
<!-- HIDE FROM OTHER BROWSERS

// SET UP ARGUMENTS FOR FUNCTION CALLS
//
var caseSensitive = true;
var notCaseSensitive = false;
var wholeWords = true;
var anySubstring = false;


// SEARCH FOR A TERM IN A TARGET STRING
//
```

continued on next page

continued from previous page

```
// search(targetString,searchTerm,caseSensitive,wordOrSubstring)
//
// where caseSenstive is a boolean value and wordOrSubstring is a boolean
// value and true means whole words, false means substrings
//
function search(target,term,caseSens,wordOnly) {

  var ind = 0;
  var next = 0;

  if (!caseSens) {
    term = term.toLowerCase();
    target = target.toLowerCase();
  }

  while ((ind = target.indexOf(term,next)) >= 0) {
    if (wordOnly) {
      var before = ind - 1;
      var after = ind + term.length;
      if (!(space(target.charAt(before)) && space(target.charAt(after)))) {
        next = ind + term.length;
        continue;
      }
    }
    return true;
  }

  return false;

}

// SEARCH FOR A TERM IN A TARGET STRING AND REPLACE IT
//
// replace(targetString,oldTerm,newTerm,caseSensitive,wordOrSubstring)
//
// where caseSenstive is a boolean value and wordOrSubstring is a boolean
// value and true means whole words, false means substrings
//
function replace(target,oldTerm,newTerm,caseSens,wordOnly) {

  var work = target;
  var ind = 0;
  var next = 0;

  if (!caseSens) {
    oldTerm = oldTerm.toLowerCase();
    work = target.toLowerCase();
  }

  while ((ind = work.indexOf(oldTerm,next)) >= 0) {
    if (wordOnly) {
      var before = ind - 1;
```

```
      var after = ind + oldTerm.length;
      if (!(space(work.charAt(before)) && space(work.charAt(after)))) {
        next = ind + oldTerm.length;
        continue;
      }
    }
    target = target.substring(0,ind) + newTerm + ⇐
        target.substring(ind+oldTerm.length,target.length);
    work = work.substring(0,ind) + newTerm + ⇐
        work.substring(ind+oldTerm.length,work.length);
    next = ind + newTerm.length;
    if (next >= work.length) { break; }
  }

  return target;

}


// CHECK IF A CHARACTER IS A WORD BREAK AND RETURN A BOOLEAN VALUE
//
function space(check) {

  var space = " .,/<>?!`';:@#$%^&*()=-|[]{}" + '"' + "\\\n\t";

  for (var i = 0; i < space.length; i++)
    if (check == space.charAt(i)) { return true; }

  if (check == "") { return true; }
  if (check == null) { return true; }

  return false;

}

// STOP HIDING -->
</SCRIPT>

</HEAD>

<BODY>

<TABLE WIDTH=100%>

<TR>

<TD VALIGN=TOP>
<DIV ALIGN=CENTER>
<H1>Search</H1>

<FORM METHOD=POST>

<SCRIPT LANGUAGE="JavaScript">
```

continued on next page

continued from previous page

```
<!-- HIDE FROM OTHER BROWSERS

function doSearch(form) {
   var result = search(form.initial.value,form.term.value,⇐
form.casesens.checked,form.word.checked);
   alert ((result) ? "Found!" : "Not Found!");
}

// STOP HIDING -->
</SCRIPT>

<TEXTAREA NAME="initial" ROWS=2 COLS=30>Search Text</TEXTAREA><BR>
Search For: <INPUT TYPE="text" NAME="term"><BR>
<INPUT TYPE="checkbox" NAME="casesens"> Case Sensitive
<INPUT TYPE="checkbox" NAME="word"> Whole Word Search<BR>
<INPUT TYPE="button" VALUE="SEARCH" onClick="doSearch(this.form);">
</FORM>
</DIV>

</TD>

<TD VALIGN=TOP>
<DIV ALIGN=CENTER>
<H1>Replace</H1>

<FORM METHOD=POST>

<SCRIPT LANGUAGE="JavaScript">
<!-- HIDE FROM OTHER BROWSERS

function doReplace(form) {

   form.result.value =⇐
replace(form.initial.value,form.oldterm.value,form.newterm.value,⇐
form.casesens.checked,form.word.checked);

}

// STOP HIDING -->
</SCRIPT>

<TEXTAREA NAME="initial" ROWS=2 COLS=30>Search Text</TEXTAREA><BR>
<TEXTAREA NAME="result" ROWS=2 COLS=30>Result Text</TEXTAREA><BR>
Search For: <INPUT TYPE="text" NAME="oldterm"><BR>
Replace With: <INPUT TYPE="text" NAME="newterm"><BR>
<INPUT TYPE="checkbox" NAME="casesens"> Case Sensitive
<INPUT TYPE="checkbox" NAME="word"> Whole Word Search<BR>
<INPUT TYPE="button" VALUE="REPLACE" onClick="doReplace(this.form);">
</FORM>
</DIV>

</TD>
```

```
</TR>

</TABLE>

</BODY>

</HTML>
```

Output   This script produces results like those in Figure 10-3.

Analysis   You use three functions to implement the search and replace system: search(), replace(), and space().

search() and replace() use a similar approach to handling their tasks, but differ in the specific actions they take when they find the term they are looking for.

The replace() **Function**

The replace() function takes five arguments: the string to work on, the term to search for, the term to replace it with, and two Boolean values. The two Boolean values indicate whether to pay attention to the case of letters in searching and whether to search only for whole words (if not, substrings will be matched and replaced).

```
var work = target;
var ind = 0;
var next = 0;
```

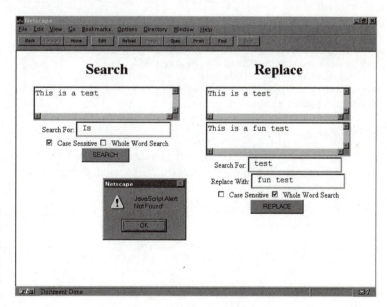

Figure 10-3
The search and replace functions can be used in any JavaScript application.

As would be expected, you start by setting up the work variables.

```
if (!caseSens) {
  oldTerm = oldTerm.toLowerCase();
  work = target.toLowerCase();
}
```

Then you check whether you are paying attention to case. If not, you change the search term and the string to search to lowercase, using the **toLowerCase()** method. This means that case is ignored in the searches because any variation in case in either string has been removed.

```
while ((ind = work.indexOf(oldTerm,next)) >= 0) {
  if (wordOnly) {
    var before = ind - 1;
    var after = ind + oldTerm.length;
    if (!(space(work.charAt(before)) && space(work.charAt(after)))) {
      next = ind + oldTerm.length;
      continue;
    }
  }
```

All the work is done in the preceding **while** loop. In the condition of the **while** loop, you search the target string for the next occurrence of the search term, store the index in **ind**, and see if it is greater than zero.

If you have found an occurrence of the term, you next check if you are searching for whole words or substrings. If you are searching for whole words, you use the **space()** function to check if the characters before and after the word boundary are word breaks. If they aren't, you update **next** to the index of the character after the term you just found and start the loop again.

```
target = target.substring(0,ind) + newTerm + ⇐
      target.substring(ind+oldTerm.length,target.length);
work = work.substring(0,ind) + newTerm + ⇐
      work.substring(ind+oldTerm.length,work.length);
next = ind + newTerm.length;
if (next >= work.length) { break; }
}
```

If you reach this point in the loop, then you have found a term you want to replace. You use the **substring** method to update both the string itself and change the variable **next** to the index of the character after the term you have just added.

Finally, you check if you have reached the end of the target string, and if not, you run the loop again to look for another occurrence.

The `search()` Function

This function is similar in structure to the `replace()` function. The differences lie in the `while` loop:

```
while ((ind = target.indexOf(term,next)) >= 0) {
  if (wordOnly) {
    var before = ind - 1;
    var after = ind + term.length;
    if (!(space(target.charAt(before)) && space(target.charAt(after)))) {
      next = ind + term.length;
      continue;
    }
  }
  return true;
}

return false;
```

As before, you perform the search for the search term using the `indexOf()` method in the condition of the `while` loop. Again, you check if you are searching for whole words, and if you are, you check for word boundaries. If you haven't found a complete word, prepare to search again and return to the top of the loop with the `continue` statement.

If you get beyond the `if` statements, you have found an occurrence of the term and return a `true` value from the function. If you finish the `while` loop without returning `true`, then you haven't found a match, and you return a `false` value.

The `space()` Function

The `space()` function plays a support role for `search()` and `replace()`.

Given a character as an argument, the function checks whether it is one of a series of characters considered word breaks or delimiters. If it is, the function returns `true`—otherwise, it returns a `false` value.

The way this is done is simple. All the possible word breaks are stored in the string `space`. A `for` loop goes through the string, character by character, and compares each character to the argument. If there is a match, a `true` result is returned.

After the loop, a comparison is made between the argument and either the empty string or the `null` value. If these are `true`, the function returns a `true` value as well.

If you have failed all these conditions, then a `false` value is returned because the argument character is not a word break.

If the programmer wants to change the definition of a word break, he or she simply has to change the declaration of the variable `space`.

1. What is the **search** function?
   a. A method of the **string** object.
   b. A JavaScript function.
   c. A JavaScript method.
   d. An object.

2. Given the statement

```
oldTerm = oldTerm.toLowerCase();
```

which of the following is equivalent?
   a. `oldTerm.toLowerCase();`
   b. `oldTerm = oldTerm.small();`
   c. `oldTerm.sub();`
   d. None of the above

3. Which of the following would count the number of characters in a string in the variable **i**?
   a. `var i = 0; for( i = 1; i < sample.length; i++ ) { i++; }`
   b. `var i = 0; while( sample.charAt(i) != "" ) { i++; }`
   c. `var i = 1; while( i++ ) { if( sample.charAt(i) == "" break; }`
   d. None of the above

4. Assuming the indexes are correct, which of the following would replace a substring in the variable sample?
   a. `sample.substring(i, j) = 'replacement';`
   b. `sample.substring = sample.substring(0, i) + 'replacement' +`
      `sample.substring(j, sample.length);`
   c. `sample = sample.substring(0, i) + 'replacement' +`
      `sample.substring(j, sample.length);`
   d. `sample = sample.substring(0, i) + 'replacement' +`
      `sample.substring(j, sample.length - 1);`

5. In the function space, the following code is found

```
for( var i = 0; i < space.length; i++ )
    if( check == space.charAt(i) ) { return true; }
```

Which of the following can be used as a replacement?
   a. `return( space.indexOf( check, 0 ) <= 0 ? false : true);`
   b. `if( space,lastIndexOf( check, check.length ) > 0 ) { return ⇐`
      `true: }`
      `return false;`

c. `return( space.lastIndexOf( check, check.length ) == 0 ? false : true );`

d. `if( space.indexOf( check, 0 ) >= 0 ) { return true; } return false;`

LESSON 3 The Math Object, the triangle Function, and the History List

THE Math OBJECT

Where the **string** object enables you to work with text literals, the **Math** object provides methods and properties to move beyond the simple arithmetic manipulations offered by the arithmetic operators.

Among the features offered by the **Math** object are several special values such as **PI**, natural logarithms, common square roots, trigonometric methods, rounding methods, an absolute value method, and more.

Table 10-2 outlines all the properties and methods of the **Math** object.

TABLE 10-2

Name	Description
E	Euler's constant—the base of natural logarithms (roughly 2.718).
LN10	The natural logarithm of 10 (roughly 2.302).
LN2	The natural logarithm of 2 (roughly 0.693).
PI	The ratio of the circumference of a circle to the diameter of the same circle (roughly 3.1415).
SQRT1_2	The square root of ½ (roughly 0.707).
SQRT2	The square root of 2 (roughly 1.414).
abs()	Calculates the absolute value of a number.
acos()	Calculates the arc cosine of a number—returns result in radians.
asin()	Calculates the arc sine of a number—returns result in radians.
atan()	Calculates the arc tangent of a number—returns result in radians.

continued on next page

continued from previous page

Name	Description
`atan2()`	Calculates the angle of a polar coordinate that corresponds to a cartesian (x,y) coordinate passed to the method as arguments.
`ceil()`	Returns the next integer greater than or equal to a number.
`cos()`	Calculates the cosine of a number.
`exp()`	Calculates e to the power of a number.
`floor()`	Returns the next integer less than or equal to a number.
`log()`	Calculates the natural logarithm of a number.
`max()`	Returns the greater of two numbers—takes two arguments.
`min()`	Returns the least of two numbers—takes two arguments.
`pow()`	Calculates the value of one number to the power of a second number—takes two arguments.
`random()`	Returns a random number between zero and one.
`round()`	Rounds a number to the nearest integer.
`sin()`	Calculates the sine of a number.
`sqrt()`	Calculates the square root of a number.
`tan()`	Calculates the tangent of a number.

Table 10-2 *Properties and methods of the* `Math` *object.*

Some of these functions require further discussion.

The Trigonometric Methods

You will notice that the trigonometric methods, such as `acos()` and `sin()`, use radians to measure the size of angles instead of the more familiar degrees.

This isn't too difficult to handle. Where you have 360 degrees in a circle, there are 2×PI (or roughly 6.283) radians in a circle.

So, where the arc tangent of 1 is 45 degrees, in radians, the result is roughly 0.785398.

The `log()` and `exp()` Methods

The `log()` and `exp()` functions are related in that they use **e**, Euler's constant, as their base.

The relationship between logarithms and exponential expressions is that if `log(a) = b`, then `exp(b) = a`.

The abs() Method

The absolute value method returns the positive value of a number. That is, it removes a negative sign from a number so that `abs(4)` and `abs(-4)` both have a value of `4`.

CALCULATING GEOMETRIC MEASUREMENTS

To highlight some of these math functions, you are going to build a simple calculator that calculates the angles and the lengths of the sides of a right angle triangle and calculates the area, diameter, and circumference of a circle.

In order to do this, you will use the trigonometric functions and `PI`.

As a reminder, with a right angle triangle, if you want to calculate the sine, cosine, or tangent of any of the other two angles, you can use the following formulas:

```
sine = opposite side / hypotenuse
cosine = adjacent side / hypotenuse
tangent = opposite side / adjacent side
```

The script should be able to fill in all the information about the shapes when there is sufficient information in the relevant form. The results of Listing 10-7 look like Figure 10-4.

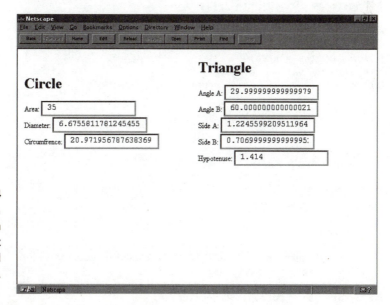

Figure 10-4
Using the Math object to perform more complex mathematical calculations.

Input   **Listing 10-7** Using the trigonometric functions.

```
<HTML>

<HEAD>
<TITLE>Example 10.7</TITLE>

<SCRIPT LANGUAGE="JavaScript">
<!-- HIDE FROM OTHER BROWSERS

function circle(form,changed) {

  with (Math) {
    var area = form.area.value;
    var diameter = form.diameter.value;
    var circumfrence = form.circumfrence.value;

    if (changed == "area") {
      var radius = sqrt(area / PI);
      diameter = 2 * radius;
      circumfrence = PI * diameter;
    }

    if (changed == "diameter") {
      area = PI * (diameter / 2) * (diameter / 2);
      circumfrence = PI * diameter;
    }

    if (changed == "circumfrence") {
      diameter = circumfrence / PI;
      area = PI * (diameter / 2) * (diameter / 2);
    }

    form.area.value = area;
    form.diameter.value = diameter;
    form.circumfrence.value = circumfrence;

  }

}

var toDegrees = 360 / (Math.PI * 2);
var toRadians = (Math.PI * 2) / 360;

function angle(form,changed) {

  with (Math) {

    var angle = (changed == "angleA") ? form.angleA.value * ⇐
    toRadians : form.angleB.value;
    var otherAngle = (90 * toRadians) - angle;
    var hypotenuse = form.hypotenuse.value;
    var sine = sin(angle);
```

```
      var opposite = sine * hypotenuse;
      var cosine = cos(angle);
      var adjacent = cosine * hypotenuse;

      if (changed == "angleA") {
        form.angleB.value = otherAngle * toDegrees;
        form.sideA.value = adjacent;
        form.sideB.value = opposite;
      } else {
        form.angleA.value = otherAngle * toDegrees;
        form.sideB.value = adjacent;
        form.sideC.value = opposite;
      }

    }

  }


function side(form,changed) {

  with (Math) {

      var side = (changed == "sideA") ? form.sideA.value : form.sideB.value;
      var hypotenuse = form.hypotenuse.value;
      var otherSide = sqrt(pow(hypotenuse,2) - pow(side,2));
      var angle = acos(side/hypotenuse);
      var otherAngle = acos(otherSide/hypotenuse);

      if (changed == "sideA") {
        form.sideB.value = otherSide;
        form.angleA.value = angle * toDegrees;
        form.angleB.value = otherAngle * toDegrees;
      } else {
        form.sideA.value = otherSide;
        form.angleB.value = angle * toDegrees;
        form.angleA.value = otherAngle * toDegrees;
      }

  }

}

function hyp(form) {

  angle(form,"angleA");

}

// STOP HIDING FROM OTHER BROWSERS -->
</SCRIPT>

</HEAD>
```

continued on next page

continued from previous page

```
<BODY>

<TABLE WIDTH="100%">

<TR>

<TD>
<H1>Circle</H1>
<FORM METHOD=POST>
Area: <INPUT TYPE="text" NAME="area" VALUE=0 ⇐
onChange="circle(this.form,this.name);"><BR>
Diameter: <INPUT TYPE="text" NAME="diameter" VALUE=0 ⇐
onChange="circle(this.form,this.name);"><BR>
Circumfrence: <INPUT TYPE="text" NAME="circumfrence" VALUE=0 ⇐
onChange="circle(this.form,this.name);">
</FORM>
</TD>

<TD>
<H1>Triangle</H1>
<FORM METHOD=POST>
Angle A: <INPUT TYPE="text" NAME="angleA" VALUE=45 ⇐
onChange="angle(this.form,this.name);"><BR>
Angle B: <INPUT TYPE="text" NAME="angleB" VALUE=45 ⇐
onChange="angle(this.form,this.name);"><BR>
Side A: <INPUT TYPE="text" NAME="sideA" VALUE=1 ⇐
onChange="side(this.form,this.name);"><BR>
Side B: <INPUT TYPE="text" NAME="sideB" VALUE=1 ⇐
onChange="side(this.form,this.name);"><BR>
Hypotenuse: <INPUT TYPE="text" NAME="hypotenuse" VALUE=1.414 ⇐
onChange="hyp(this.form);">
</FORM>
</TD>

</TR>

</TABLE>

</BODY>

</HTML>
```

Output   Figure 10-4 shows the result.

Analysis   This script is rather simple, but it shows how to use the methods and properties available in the `Math` object.

Of the two forms, the circle form is the simpler because it has less information to deal with. The following two sections analyze the two functions.

The circle() Function

The **circle()** function takes two arguments: the **form** object and the name of the field that was just changed. The calculations are based on the name of this field.

```
with (Math) {
  var area = form.area.value;
  var diameter = form.diameter.value;
  var circumfrence = form.circumfrence.value;
```

You start by extracting whatever information is in the form and storing it in local variables. Notice the use of the **with (Math)** command. This enables all of the **Math** properties and methods in the function to be used without the **Math** prefix.

 The **with** command makes it easy to write command blocks that use properties and methods of a single object repeatedly. For instance, if you use **with (object) { command block }** then inside the command block, the methods and properties of **object** can be referred to as **methodName** and **propertyName** without the leading **object**.

```
if (changed == "area") {
  var radius = sqrt(area / PI);
  diameter = 2 * radius;
  circumfrence = PI * diameter;
}

if (changed == "diameter") {
  area = PI * (diameter / 2) * (diameter / 2);
  circumfrence = PI * diameter;
}

if (changed == "circumfrence") {
  diameter = circumfrence / PI;
  area = PI * (diameter / 2) * (diameter / 2);
}
```

The three **if** statement blocks simply calculate the other two fields based on the value of the changed field. All of these use two basic formulas:

```
Area of Circle = PI×radius×radius
Circumference of Circle = PI×diameter
```

Notice the use of the **sqrt()** method without the preceding **Math** prefix, which is made possible with the earlier **with (Math)** command.

```
form.area.value = area;
form.diameter.value = diameter;
form.circumfrence.value = circumfrence;
```

Once the calculation is done, you can reassign the results to the form.

Working with the Triangle

The **triangle** function assumes that you are working with a right angle triangle. This means the angle across from the hypotenuse is always 90 degrees.

The relationship between the remaining angles and sides is that `sideA` is adjacent to `angleA` and `sideB` is adjacent to `angleB`.

Before you can proceed to calculate the information in this form, you need to be able to convert between degrees and radians. All the trigonometric functions either take a radian value as a parameter or return a radian value. Users, on the other hand, are likely to prefer working in degrees.

You get around this by using the variables `toDegrees` and `toRadians` which represent the number of degrees per radian and the number of radians per degree:

```
var toDegrees = 360 / (Math.PI * 2);
var toRadians = (Math.PI * 2) / 360;
```

The `angle()` function is called whenever you change one of the two angle values. It uses the fact that all the angles of a triangle add up to 180 degrees to calculate the remaining angle. Then, using the `sin()` and `cos()` methods and the formulas for sine and cosine, the program calculates the length of the opposite and adjacent sides for the changed angle.

Finally, based on which angle was changed, the results are assigned to the correct form field.

The `side()` function plays a similar role when either `sideA` or `sideB` is changed. Using the value of the changed side and the value of the hypotenuse, you can calculate the value of the third side using the formula:

```
sideA×sideA + sideB×sideB = hypotenuse×hypotenuse
```

Once you have the value for the three sides, you can use the `acos()` method and the formula for cosine to calculate the value of the two angles.

The `hypotenuse` function simply calculates what the value of `sideA` and `sideB` should be based on the current angle settings by calling `angle(form,"angleA")`. You could just as easily have made the call `angle(form,"angleB")`.

The forms in the body of the HTML file are fairly simple. They call the appropriate function in the `onChange` event handler for each text field.

WORKING WITH THE HISTORY LIST

When you use the Navigator browser, you will notice the history list, which is accessible under the Go menu.

The `history` object makes this list accessible in JavaScript. Early versions of JavaScript made the actual URLs in the list available to the script, but this was too large a security hole because it could be used by malicious scripts to steal information to access some secure Web sites. In addition, it could be used to breach privacy by supplying a page author with information about what sites a visitor had previously visited.

The current version of the `history` object provides methods for working with the list without actually reflecting the value of URLs and entries into a script.

Properties and Methods of the history Object

Table 10-3 outlines the properties and methods available in the history object.

Name	Description
length	The length of the history list
back()	Loads the previous URL in the history list
forward()	Loads the next URL in the history list
go()	Loads the URL indicated by an offset from the current place in the history list

Table 10-3 *Properties and methods of the history object.*

For instance, history.back() goes to the previous page while history.go(-3) goes back to the page visited three pages ago (like clicking the back button three times on the Navigator toolbar) and history.go(2) goes two URLs forward in the list.

The history.go() method can also take a string instead of an integer as an argument. When a string is used, the method loads the nearest entry in the history that contains the string as part of its URL. The matching of the string against the URL is case-insensitive.

One of the more popular uses of the history object is to provide back and forward buttons in individual frames or dynamic back buttons, which take users back to the last page they were on.

1. What is the Math object?
   a. It is a string containing numbers.
   b. It is a JavaScript object that provides methods and properties for performing mathematical operations.
   c. It is a JavaScript object that allows you to draw geometric figures in your HTML document.
   d. It is a navigator property.

2. Which of the following calculates the circumference of a circle?
   a. circumference = PI * diameter;
   b. circumference = PI + diameter;
   c. circumference = Math.PI * diameter;
   d. None of the above

3. Which of the following pairs are not equivalent?
   a. `abs( 4 )` and `abs( -4 )`
   b. `sqrt( 2 )` and `SQRT2`
   c. `ceil( 4 )` and `floor( 4 )`
   d. `max( 0, 4 )` and `min( 4, 0 )`

4. Which of the following pairs do the same thing?
   a. `history.go(-2)` and `history.back()`
   b. `history.back()` and `history.go(-1)`
   c. `history.forward()` and `history.go()`
   d. `history.go( history.length )` and `history.go(0)`

5. Which of the following is not a method of the `history` object?
   a. `previous()`
   b. `go()`
   c. `forward()`
   d. `back()`

SUMMARY

Manipulating data has been the focus of much of this chapter.

Using the `string` object, you now know how to add HTML tags using methods, how to change the case of a string, and how to search for the string and perform basic `search` and `replace` functions.

The `Math` object enables you to extend the type of mathematical calculations you can perform to include trigonometry, logarithms, and square roots and also provides several values as properties, including `PI`, `E`, and `LN2`.

The `history` object is a little different. By providing the ability to jump to URLs in the history list (without breaching security by providing the actual URL information), it is possible to build dynamic back and forward buttons into documents.

In the next chapter you will put everything you have learned together into producing a fun cartoon face drawing program.

Commands and Extensions Review

Command/Extension	Type	Description
`anchor()`	JavaScript method	Surrounds the string with an anchor A tag.
`big()`	JavaScript method	Surrounds the string with the HTML BIG tag.
`blink()`	JavaScript method	Surrounds the string with the HTML BLINK tag.
`bold()`	JavaScript method	Surrounds the string with the HTML B tag.

Command/Extension	Type	Description
charAt()	JavaScript method	Given an index as an argument, returns the character at the specified index.
fixed()	JavaScript method	Surrounds the string with the HTML TT tag to make it display as a fixed-width font.
fontcolor()	JavaScript method	Surrounds the string with the HTML <FONT COLOR=color> and </FONT> tags to make it display in the specified color.
fontsize()	JavaScript method	Surrounds the string with the HTML <FONT SIZE=size> and </FONT> tags to make it display in the desired font size.
indexOf()	JavaScript method	Given a string and an initial index, returns the index of the next occur-rence of the string after the initial index.
italics()	JavaScript method	Surrounds the string with the HTML I tag.
lastIndexOf()	JavaScript method	Given a string and a starting index, returns the index of the last occurrence of the string searching backward from the starting index.
link()	JavaScript method	Given a URL, surrounds the string with an A tag to create a hypertext link.
small()	JavaScript method	Surrounds the string with the HTML SMALL tag.
split()	JavaScript method	Returns an array by splitting a string at a specified separator.
strike()	JavaScript method	Surrounds the string with the HTML STRIKE tag.
sub()	JavaScript method	Surrounds the string with the HTML SUB tag.
substring()	JavaScript method	Given two indexes, returns the substring starting at the first index and ending with the character before the last index.

continued on next page

continued from previous page

Command/Extension	Type	Description
		If the second index is greater, the substring starts with the second index and ends with the character before the first index; if the two indexes are equal, returns the empty string.
sup()	JavaScript method	Surrounds the string with the HTML SUP tag.
toLowerCase()	JavaScript method	Makes the entire string lower-case.
toUpperCase()	JavaScript method	Makes the entire string upper-case.
E	JavaScript property	Euler's constant—the base of natural logarithms (roughly 2.718).
LN10	JavaScript property	The natural logarithm of 10 (roughly 2.302).
LN2	JavaScript property	The natural logarithm of 2 (roughly 0.693).
PI	JavaScript property	The ratio of the circumference of a circle to the diameter of the same circle (roughly 3.1415).
SQRT1_2	JavaScript property	The square root of $1/2$ (roughly 0.707).
SQRT2	JavaScript property	The square root of 2 (roughly 1.414).
abs()	JavaScript method	Calculates the absolute value of a number.
acos()	JavaScript method	Calculates the arc cosine of a number—returns result in radians.
asin()	JavaScript method	Calculates the arc sine of a number—returns result in radians.
atan()	JavaScript method	Calculates the arc tangent of a number—returns result in radians.

Command/Extension	Type	Description
`atan2()`	JavaScript method	Calculates the angle of a polar coordinate based on a Cartesian coordinate.
`ceil()`	JavaScript method	Returns the next integer greater than or equal to a number.
`cos()`	JavaScript method	Calculates the cosine of a number.
`exp()`	JavaScript method	Calculates e to the power of a number.
`floor()`	JavaScript method	Returns the next integer less than or equal to a number.
`log()`	JavaScript method	Calculates the natural logarithm of a number.
`max()`	JavaScript method	Returns the greater of two numbers—takes two arguments.
`min()`	JavaScript method	Returns the least of two numbers—takes two arguments.
`pow()`	JavaScript method	Calculates the value of one number to the power of a second number—takes two arguments.
`random()`	JavaScript method	Returns a random number between zero and one.
`round()`	JavaScript method	Rounds a number to the nearest integer.
`sin()`	JavaScript method	Calculates the sine of a number.
`sqrt()`	JavaScript method	Calculates the square root of a number.
`tan()`	JavaScript method	Calculates the tangent of a number.
`length`	JavaScript method	The length of the history list. Also used in the `string` object to provide the value of the string.
`back()`	JavaScript method	Loads the previous URL in the history list.

continued on next page

continued from previous page

Command/Extension	Type	Description
`forward()`	JavaScript method	Loads the next URL in the history list.
`go()`	JavaScript method	Loads the URL indicated by an offset from the current place in the history list.

CHAPTER EXERCISE

1. What would the output of the following code segment look like, assuming there were no HTML tags elsewhere in the file affecting the output?

```
var sample = "test.";
sample.big();
sample.blink();
sample.bold();
sample.strike();
sample.fontsize(7);
document.write(sample.italics());
```

2. In the text searching and replacing functions (Listings 10-5 through 10-6), we have left out a critical feature: a wildcard. Extend the search and replace script to add a simple wildcard capability to the `search()` function. Use the following criteria:

   - Use the asterisk character for your wildcard.

   - The wildcard represents zero or more of any letter.

   - Only one wildcard is enabled in a search term.

   - Wildcards are valid only in the middle of a search term: `"text*"` and `"*text"` are not valid—catch this and inform the user.

   If you search the string `"Hello there"` for `"lo*e"` you should get a match as you would with `"H*lo"`, but `"the*h"` would not succeed.

3. What are the lines of code necessary to implement a dynamic forward and back button in an HTML page? The buttons should work just like the ones in the Navigator toolbar. (Hint: You need only one form with two buttons to do this.)

CHAPTER 11

HAVING FUN WITH JAVASCRIPT

In this chapter you are going to apply some of what you have learned to build a simple application that demonstrates how, with very basic JavaScript, it is possible to create the impression of a sophisticated interactive application.

You are going to design an application that enables users to build their own cartoon faces out of a library of existing eyes, noses, and mouths. No drawing skill is required for the users.

THE SPECIFICATIONS

The application has several basic requirements:

- Display each piece of the face in a separate frame while the user is experimenting.

- Provide a button to build the complete face in a separate window which the user can then print out or save as a complete HTML file which displays the face.

- Provide a random face button which causes the script to build a random face from among the possible faces.

LESSON 1 Building and Extending Your Application

BUILDING THE APPLICATION

In order to build this face program, you need to define the frameset, which contains all the elements of the interface and application.

To do this, use the frameset in Listing 11-1.

Input   **Listing 11-1** The parent frameset.

```
<FRAMESET ROWS="150,150,150,*">

  <FRAMESET COLS="400,*">
    <FRAME SRC="eye1.gif" NAME="eye" MARGINHEIGHT=0 ⇐
MARGINWIDTH=0 SCROLLING="no">
    <FRAME SRC="eyes.htm" MARGINHEIGHT=0 MARGINWIDTH=0 SCROLLING="auto">
  </FRAMESET>

  <FRAMESET COLS="400,*">
    <FRAME SRC="nose1.gif" NAME="nose" MARGINHEIGHT=0 ⇐
MARGINWIDTH=0 SCROLLING="no">
    <FRAME SRC="noses.htm" MARGINHEIGHT=0 MARGINWIDTH=0 SCROLLING="auto">
  </FRAMESET>

  <FRAMESET COLS="400,*">
    <FRAME SRC="mouth1.gif" NAME="mouth" MARGINHEIGHT=0 ⇐
MARGINWIDTH=0 SCROLLING="no">
    <FRAME SRC="mouths.htm" MARGINHEIGHT=0 MARGINWIDTH=0 SCROLLING="auto">
  </FRAMESET>

  <FRAME SRC="build.htm">

</FRAMESET>
```

This sets up a four-row grid. The top three rows are each divided into two columns: The left side displays the current selection for the eyes, nose, or mouth, and the right side presents all the available choices.

The bottom row is where the control buttons to build the face and generate a random face appear.

Based on this, you need to create four other HTML files (see Listings 11-2 through 11-5) which are the basis of the program: `eyes.htm`, `noses.htm`, `mouths.htm`, and `build.htm`.

Input **Listing 11-2** The source code for `eyes.htm`.

```html
<!-- SOURCE CODE FOR eyes.htm -->

<HTML>

<BODY BGCOLOR="iceblue">

  <TABLE BORDER=0>

    <TR>

      <TD><A HREF="eye1.gif" TARGET="eye">
      <IMG SRC="eye1sample.gif" BORDER=0></A></TD>

      <TD><A HREF="eye2.gif" TARGET="eye">
      <IMG SRC="eye2sample.gif" BORDER=0></A></TD>

    </TR>

    <TR>

      <TD><A HREF="eye3.gif" TARGET="eye"">
      <IMG SRC="eye3sample.gif" BORDER=0></A></TD>

      <TD><A HREF="eye4.gif" TARGET="eye">
      <IMG SRC="eye4sample.gif" BORDER=0></A></TD>

    </TR>

  </TABLE>

</BODY>

</HTML>
```

Input **Listing 11-3** The source code for `noses.htm`.

```html
<!-- SOURCE CODE FOR noses.htm -->

<HTML>

<BODY BGCOLOR="iceblue">
```

continued on next page

continued from previous page

```
    <TABLE BORDER=0>

      <TR>

        <TD><A HREF="nose1.gif" TARGET="nose">
        <IMG SRC="nose1sample.gif" BORDER=0></A></TD>

        <TD><A HREF="nose2.gif" TARGET="nose">
        <IMG SRC="nose2sample.gif" BORDER=0></A></TD>

      </TR>

      <TR>

        <TD><A HREF="nose3.gif" TARGET="nose">
        <IMG SRC="nose3sample.gif" BORDER=0></A></TD>

        <TD><A HREF="nose4.gif" TAGRET="nose">
        <IMG SRC="nose4sample.gif" BORDER=0></A></TD>

      </TR>

    </TABLE>

</BODY>

</HTML>
```

| Input |

Listing 11-4 The source code for `mouths.htm`.

```
<!-- SOURCE CODE FOR mouths.htm -->

<HTML>

<BODY BGCOLOR="iceblue">

  <TABLE BORDER=0>

    <TR>

      <TD><A HREF="mouth1.gif" TARGET="mouth">
      <IMG SRC="mouth1sample.gif" BORDER=0></A></TD>

      <TD><A HREF="mouth2.gif" TAGRET="mouth">
      <IMG SRC="mouth2sample.gif" BORDER=0></A></TD>

    </TR>

    <TR>

      <TD><A HREF="mouth3.gif" TARGET="mouth">
      <IMG SRC="mouth3sample.gif" BORDER=0></A></TD>
```

```
      <TD><A HREF="mouth4.gif" TARGET="mouth">
      <IMG SRC="mouth4sample.gif" BORDER=0></A></TD>

   </TR>

 </TABLE>

</BODY>

</HTML>
```

The file **build.htm** (Listing 11-5) provides the controls in the bottom frame:

Input

Listing 11-5 The source code for **build.htm**.

```
<!-- SOURCE CODE FOR build.htm -->

<HTML>

<HEAD>

<SCRIPT LANGUAGE="JavaScript">
<!-- HIDE FROM OTHER BROWSERS

// Build the complete face in a separate window
function buildFace() {

  var eye = parent.eye.location;
  var nose = parent.nose.location;
  var mouth = parent.mouth.location;

  var face = window.open("","builtFace","width=400,height=450");
  face.document.open("text/html");
  face.document.write('<IMG SRC="' + eye + '">');
  face.document.write('<IMG SRC="' + nose + '">');
  face.document.write('<IMG SRC="' + mouth + '">');
  face.document.close();

}

// Build a random face in the current window
function randomFace() {

  var eye = "eye" + getRandom() + ".gif";
  var nose = "nose" + getRandom() + ".gif";
  var mouth = "mouth" + getRandom() + ".gif";

parent.eye.location = eye;
parent.nose.location = nose;
parent.mouth.location = mouth;

}
```

continued on next page

continued from previous page

```
// Generate a random number
function getRandom() {

  today = new Date();
  var bigNumber = today.getSeconds() * today.getTime() * ⇐
Math.sqrt(today.getMinutes());
  var randomNum = (bigNumber % 4) + 1;

  return Math.floor(randomNum);

}

// STOP HIDING -->
</SCRIPT>

</HEAD>

<BODY BGCOLOR="#000000" TEXT="iceblue">
<FORM METHOD=POST>
<CENTER>
<INPUT TYPE="button" VALUE="Build This Face" onClick="buildFace();">
<INPUT TYPE="button" VALUE="Make A Random Face" onClick="randomFace();">
</CENTER>
</FORM>
</BODY>

</HTML>
```

Output

The results of this application appear similar to Figures 11-1 and 11-2.

Analysis

The first thing to notice about the four HTML documents is that three of them—**eyes.htm**, **noses.htm**, and **mouths.htm**—are very similar.

This is because all three files play the same role: They present options for the user to select each of three parts of the face.

Each file displays four options in a 2×2 table. Each of the small images displayed is, in fact, a link targeted to the appropriate frame on the left. When the user clicks on one of the sample images, the full-size version of that feature is displayed in the corresponding frame on the left.

You use JavaScript in the **build.htm** document. Here you have three functions related to the two buttons displayed in the bottom frame of the frameset: **buildFace()**, **randomFace()**, and **getRandom()**.

buildFace() and **randomFace()** are called by the event handlers of the two buttons:

```
<INPUT TYPE="button" VALUE="Build This Face" onClick="buildFace();">
<INPUT TYPE="button" VALUE="Make A Random Face" onClick="randomFace();">
```

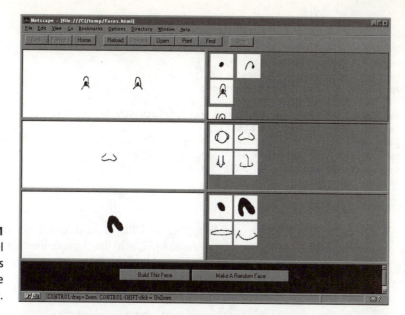

Figure 11-1
Choosing a facial
feature updates
the relevant frame
on the left.

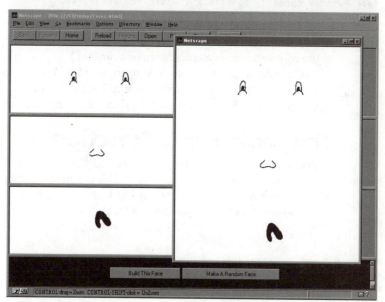

Figure 11-2
Clicking on the
build button causes
a new window to
open.

The `buildFace()` Function

The `buildFace()` function takes the three pieces of the face in the three frames and displays them in a single new window. This function needs to find out which files are displayed in each of the three left frames and then builds a single HTML file that displays the three files in a single window.

```
function buildFace() {

  var eye = parent.eye.location;
  var nose = parent.nose.location;
  var mouth = parent.mouth.location;

  var face = window.open("","builtFace","width=400,height=450");
  face.document.open("text/html");
  face.document.write('<IMG SRC="' + eye + '">');
  face.document.write('<IMG SRC="' + nose + '">');
  face.document.write('<IMG SRC="' + mouth + '">');
  face.document.close();

}
```

The function starts by getting the URLs of the three selected facial features with the
`location` property of the `frame` object, as in the example `var eye = parent.eye.loca-
tion;`. You use the fact that you can address object properties by name in the structure
`parent.eye` to reference each frame.

Once this is done, a new window of the desired size is opened using

```
var face =window.open("","builtFace","width=400,height=450");
```

This command specifies the size of the window in pixels using the optional windows
attributes argument. The new object for this window is called `face` so that you can later
use commands such as `face.document.write()`.

Once the window is open, you open an HTML output stream using `face.docu-
ment.open("text/html")` and then write out the three image tags based on the URLs
you got earlier. Finally, you close the document output stream.

The `randomFace()` Function

The `randomFace()` function simply selects three random facial features and then
opens them in the appropriate frames. This is done by calling the `getRandom()` function, which returns a number from 1 to 4, and then building three filenames, such as
`var eye = "eye" + getRandom() + ".gif"`.

```
function randomFace() {

  var eye = "eye" + getRandom() + ".gif";
  var nose = "nose" + getRandom() + ".gif";
  var mouth = "mouth" + getRandom() + ".gif";

parent.eye.location = eye;
parent.nose.location = nose;
parent.mouth.location = mouth;

}
```

Once this is done, the three files are opened using `window.open()`.

The getRandom() **Function**

The getRandom() function is designed to return a random number from one to four. This is done by creating a new **Date** object for the current date and time, getting a large number by multiplying together different elements of the **Date** object, and then taking the modulus by four and adding one, as shown in the following lines.

```
function getRandom() {

  today = new Date();
  var bigNumber = today.getSeconds() * today.getTime() * ⇐
Math.sqrt(today.getMinutes());
  var randomNum = (bigNumber % 4) + 1;

  return Math.floor(randomNum);

}
```

The result is a pseudo-random number from one to four (because the modulus returns a number greater than or equal to zero and less than four). The use of **Math.floor()** ensures that the number returned is an integer.

In Navigator 3, the **Math.random()** method could provide a random number. However, this will not work on all platforms in Navigator 2.

MOVING BEYOND THE BASIC SCRIPT

There are a couple of limitations to the current script that you might like to improve:

● You have fixed the number of available eyes, noses, and mouths at four each. The program should be easily extendible to any number of eyes, noses, and mouths, and the number of each feature should be able to vary.

● Each time you build a face, it opens in the same window as the last face you built. The program should open each face in a different window.

● Users should be able to save the current face, and when they first come to the page, that face should be loaded as the default first face.

More Than Four Choices

In order to expand the script to support more than four choices for each feature, you need to make changes to each of the HTML files, including the parent frameset.

You start by adding a small script to the parent frameset (refer to Listing 11-1).

```
SCRIPT LANGUAGE="JavaScript">
<!-- HIDE FROM OTHER BROWSERS

var numEyes = 4;
var numNoses = 4;
var numMouths = 4;

// STOP HIDING -->
</SCRIPT>
```

This script is where you set the number of options for each of the three facial features. That way, if you want to add or remove choices, you only need to change these three numbers, and the whole program will work.

Next, you need to alter the three files eyes.htm, noses.htm, and mouths.htm (refer to Listings 11-2 through 11-4) so that you use JavaScript to dynamically build two-row tables, regardless of the number of choices.

By way of example, this is what eyes.htm would look like:

```
<BODY BGCOLOR="iceblue">

   <TABLE BORDER=0>

     <TR>

     <SCRIPT LANGUAGE="JavaScript">
     <!-- HIDE FROM OTHER BROWSERS

     for (var i = 1; i <= Math.floor(parent.numEyes / 2); i ++) {
        document.write('<TD><A HREF="eye' + i + '.gif" TARGET="eye">');

        document.write('<IMG SRC="eye' + i + 'sample.gif" BORDER=0></A></TD>');
     }

     // STOP HIDING -->
     </SCRIPT>

     </TR>

     <TR>

     <SCRIPT LANGUAGE="JavaScript">
     <!-- HIDE FROM OTHER BROWSERS

     for (var i = Math.floor(parent.numEyes / 2) + 1; ⇐
i <= parent.numEyes; i ++) {
        document.write('<TD><A HREF="eye' + i + '.gif" TARGET="eye">');

        document.write('<IMG SRC="eye' + i + 'sample.gif" BORDER=0></A></TD>');
     }

     // STOP HIDING -->
```

```
    </SCRIPT>

    </TR>

  </TABLE>

</BODY>
```

What you have added are two short scripts that build the table cells for each row of the table. The first script builds cells for each image from the first to the halfway point in the available list, and the second builds from there to the end. You use `Math.floor()` to ensure that you are building filenames out of integer values.

Finally, you need to alter the `randomFace()` and `getRandom()` functions in `build.htm` (refer to Listing 11-5). `getRandom()` now takes an argument which is the range it is supposed to return (that is, from **1** to **num**). `randomFace()` passes the appropriate variable from the parent frameset for each function call to `getRandom()`.

```
function randomFace() {

  var eye = "eye" + getRandom(parent.numEyes) + ".gif";
  var nose = "nose" + getRandom(parent.numNoses) + ".gif";
  var mouth = "mouth" + getRandom(parent.numMouths) + ".gif";

parent.eye.location = eye;
parent.nose.location = nose;
parent.mouth.location = mouth;

}

function getRandom(num) {

  today = new Date();
  var bigNumber = today.getSeconds() * today.getTime() * ⇐
Math.sqrt(today.getMinutes());
  var randomNum = bigNumber % num + 1;

  return Math.floor(randomNum);

}
```

Building Faces in Multiple Windows

In order to build each face in a new window, you need to make far fewer changes than you made to support the variable number of choices for each facial attribute.

All the changes are made to the file `build.htm`. You add a global variable called `windowNumber`, which you increment for each window you open. Then you make one change to the function `buildFace()` on the line where you open the window:

```
var face = window.open("","builtFace" + windowNumber ++,"width=400,height=450");
```

This builds a new window name based on the value of `windowNumber` and then increments `windowNumber` by one. Remember that the unary increment operator (`++`) after an expression first evaluates the expression (in this case, that is simply `windowNumber`) and then increments the expression.

Note   Navigator includes a special target `_blank` which, when used in conjunction with `window.open()`, opens a new window. For instance, `window.open("","_blank")` opens a new empty window.

1. What would the following frameset look like?

```
<FRAMESET ROWS="150,150,*">
   <FRAMESET COLS="400,*">     </FRAMESET>
   <FRAMESET COLS="400,*">     </FRAMESET>
   <FRAME ...>
</FRAMESET>
```

a. This is an invalid frameset because the number of columns in all of the rows is not the same.
b. It would have three columns and three rows.
c. It would have three rows and two columns.
d. It would have two rows with two columns and a third row with one column.

2. Given the following script segment,

```
var win = window.open("", "face", "width=400,height=450");
win.document.open("text/html");
win.document.write("<IMG SRC=eye1sample.gif>");
win.document.write("<IMG SRC=nose1sample.gif>");
win.document.write("<IMG SRC=mouth1sample.gif>");
win.document.close();
```

Which of the following statements is false?
a. The `win.document.close()` closes the window so it is no longer visible.
b. The `win.document.close()` closes the document for writing and allows it to be rendered.
c. The `window.open(...)` opens a new empty window.
d. The `win.document.open("text/html")` opens the document for writing.

3. If the variable `windowNum` has the value of `4`, then what will the name of this new window be?

```
window.open( "", "window" + windowNum++ );
```

a. `'windowwindowNum'`
b. `'window4'`
c. `'window'`
d. `'window5'`

4. In the HTML example in this chapter, the function `loadFace` is called when the onLoad event for the frame is signaled. Where can you place this function so that it will be defined when it is called?

   a. Place it in the head section.
   b. Place it in the body section before the frameset.
   c. Place it anywhere in the body section.
   d. Place it at the beginning of the frameset.

5. How does the following code delete a cookie?

```
var exp = new Date();
exp.setTime( exp.getTime() - 1 );
var cval = GetCookie( name );
document.cookie = name + "=" + cval + "; expires=" + exp.toGMTString();
```

   a. It resets the expiration date to an invalid date.
   b. It creates a new cookie with the same name, so the old one gets deleted.
   c. It resets the expiration date so the cookie gets deleted by Netscape Navigator.
   d. It does not delete a cookie.

 Jump to Appendix C, Lab 5, Michal Sramka's Matches game to see another fun use of JavaScript.

SUMMARY

To help you see all the changes you have made, here is the source code including all the changes. I am only including `eyes.htm` (and not `noses.htm` or `mouths.htm`) because the changes are the same in these three files.

Input

Listing 11-6 Final version of the application.

```
<!-- SOURCE CODE FOR PARENT FRAMESET -->


<HEAD>

<SCRIPT LANGUAGE="JavaScript">
<!-- HIDE FROM OTHER BROWSERS

var numEyes = 4;
var numNoses = 4;
var numMouths = 4;

// STOP HIDING -->
</SCRIPT>

</HEAD>

<FRAMESET ROWS="150,150,150,*">
```

continued on next page

continued from previous page

```
    <FRAMESET COLS="400,*">
        <FRAME SRC="eye1.gif" NAME="eye" MARGINHEIGHT=0 ⇐
MARGINWIDTH=0 SCROLLING="no">
        <FRAME SRC="eyes.htm" MARGINHEIGHT=0 MARGINWIDTH=0 SCROLLING="auto">
    </FRAMESET>

    <FRAMESET COLS="400,*">
        <FRAME SRC="nose1.gif" NAME="nose" MARGINHEIGHT=0 ⇐
MARGINWIDTH=0 SCROLLING="no">
        <FRAME SRC="noses.htm" MARGINHEIGHT=0 MARGINWIDTH=0 SCROLLING="auto">
    </FRAMESET>

    <FRAMESET COLS="400,*">
        <FRAME SRC="mouth1.gif" NAME="mouth" MARGINHEIGHT=0 ⇐
MARGINWIDTH=0 SCROLLING="no">
        <FRAME SRC="mouths.htm" MARGINHEIGHT=0 MARGINWIDTH=0 SCROLLING="auto">
    </FRAMESET>

    <FRAME SRC="build.htm">

</FRAMESET>

<!-- SOURCE CODE FOR build.html -->

<HEAD>

<SCRIPT LANGUAGE="JavaScript">
<!-- HIDE FROM OTHER BROWSERS

var windowNumber = 1;

// Build the face in a separate window
function buildFace() {

  var eye = parent.eye.location;
  var nose = parent.nose.location;
  var mouth = parent.mouth.location;

  var face = window.open("","builtFace" + ⇐
windowNumber ++,"width=400,height=450");
  face.document.open("text/html");
  face.document.write('<IMG SRC="' + eye + '">');
  face.document.write('<IMG SRC="' + nose + '">');
  face.document.write('<IMG SRC="' + mouth + '">');
  face.document.close();

}

// Display a random face in the current window
function randomFace() {

  var eye = "eye" + getRandom(parent.numEyes) + ".gif";
```

```
    var nose = "nose" + getRandom(parent.numNoses) + ".gif";
    var mouth = "mouth" + getRandom(parent.numMouths) + ".gif";

parent.eye.location = eye;
parent.nose.location = nose;
parent.mouth.location = mouth;

}

// Generate a random number
function getRandom(num) {

  today = new Date();
  var bigNumber = today.getSeconds() * today.getTime() * ⇐
Math.sqrt(today.getMinutes());
  var randomNum = Math.floor(bigNumber % num);

  return randomNum + 1;

}

// STOP HIDING -->
</SCRIPT>

</HEAD>

<BODY BGCOLOR="#000000" TEXT="iceblue">
<FORM METHOD=POST>
<CENTER>
<INPUT TYPE="button" VALUE="Build This Face" onClick="buildFace();">
<INPUT TYPE="button" VALUE="Make A Random Face" onClick="randomFace();">
</CENTER>
</FORM>
</BODY>

<!-- SOURCE CODE FOR eyes.html -->

<BODY BGCOLOR="iceblue">

  <TABLE BORDER=0>

    <TR>

    <SCRIPT LANGUAGE="JavaScript">
    <!-- HIDE FORM OTHER BROWSERS

    for (var i = 1; i <= Math.floor(parent.numEyes / 2); i ++) {
      document.write('<TD><A HREF="eye' + i + '.gif" TARGET="eye">');

      document.write('<IMG SRC="eye' + i + 'sample.gif" BORDER=0></A></TD>');
    }

    // STOP HIDING -->
    </SCRIPT>
```

continued on next page

continued from previous page

```
        </TR>

        <TR>

        <SCRIPT LANGUAGE="JavaScript">
        <!-- HIDE FROM OTHER BROWSERS

        for (var i = Math.floor(parent.numEyes / 2) + 1; ⇐
i <= parent.numEyes; i ++) {
document.write('<TD><A HREF="eye' + i + '.gif" TARGET="eye">');

           document.write('<IMG SRC="eye' + i + 'sample.gif" BORDER=0></A></TD>');
        }

        // STOP HIDING -->
        </SCRIPT>

        </TR>

    </TABLE>

</BODY>
```

CHAPTER EXERCISE

We still have one more addition to make: the ability to save a face and have it displayed as the first face when the user returns to the site. Extend the application so that there is a third button at the bottom to save the current face and change the loading procedure so that the saved face is loaded each time the user arrives at the site.

CHAPTER 12

CREATING A SPREADSHEET IN JAVASCRIPT

n this chapter, you are going to apply what you have learned to developing another application—a general-purpose spreadsheet.

Although you have experienced creating, and have seen examples of specific-function calculators, JavaScript's capability to work with forms and its math functions are not limited to these types of applications.

Using forms and cookies, you can create a general-purpose spreadsheet that retains its formulas between sessions.

THE SPECIFICATIONS

The spreadsheet has several basic requirements:

- It should have a reasonable number of fields—not so many that users with small displays will have trouble, but not so few as to be less than useful. A good number appears to be roughly 100.

- The columns and rows should be labeled—one with numerals and one with letters.

- Users should be able to create formulas, or expressions, for any of the fields that use values from other fields to calculate their own values.

- Formulas should be able to include mathematical operators, as well as any of the methods of the `Math` object. Basically, any legal JavaScript mathematical expression should be acceptable.

- Users should be able to change or delete any expression.

- Expressions should be saved between sessions so that users can come back and continue using their spreadsheets.

LESSON 1   Defining and Designing Your Spreadsheet

WHAT YOU NEED TO DO

In order to implement a spreadsheet with these requirements, you need to do several things before you start writing the script.

You need to decide the structure of expressions, how to store expressions, and how to handle changes to information in the spreadsheet.

The obvious choice for saving expressions is using cookies, and you will use Bill Dortch's functions again to achieve this. Each function should be stored in a cookie named by the field it is attached to in the spreadsheet.

For instance, if an expression is created for field A6, then a cookie named A6 should be created with the expression stored as a string for the value of the cookie. You will use an expiry date one year in the future to ensure that cookies are available between sessions.

Of course, you are limited by the number of cookies you can store for a given page and need to keep track of them so you don't accidentally delete important expressions by enabling the user to add too many expressions. You can do this by using one cookie as a counter to keep track of how many expressions have been created so far on the page.

The syntax for expressions is simple: The value of another field can be referenced simply by using the field's name followed by a semicolon. So, the expression A1; * B7; would multiply the value in field A1 by the value in field B7.

Every time the value of a form field is changed, you need to be able to re-evaluate all expressions. Likewise, if the definition of an expression is changed, a new expression is created, or an expression is deleted, all expressions need to be reevaluated because the change could potentially affect any of the formulas. Listing 12-1 contains the script for the program.

Input

Listing 12-1 A general-purpose spreadsheet.

```
<HTML>

<HEAD>
<TITLE>Chapter 12</TITLE>

<SCRIPT LANGUAGE="JavaScript">
<!-- HIDE FROM OTHER BROWSERS
//
//  Cookie Functions - Second Helping  (21-Jan-96)
//  Written by:  Bill Dortch, hIdaho Design <bdortch@netw.com>
//  The following functions are released to the public domain.

//
// "Internal" function to return the decoded value of a cookie
//
function getCookieVal (offset) {
  var endstr = document.cookie.indexOf (";", offset);
  if (endstr == -1)
    endstr = document.cookie.length;
  return unescape(document.cookie.substring(offset, endstr));
}


//
//  Function to return the value of the cookie specified by "name".
//
function GetCookie (name) {
  var arg = name + "=";
  var alen = arg.length;
  var clen = document.cookie.length;
  var i = 0;
  while (i < clen) {
    var j = i + alen;
    if (document.cookie.substring(i, j) == arg)
      return getCookieVal (j);
    i = document.cookie.indexOf(" ", i) + 1;
    if (i == 0) break;
  }
  return null;
}
```

continued on next page

continued from previous page

```
//
//  Function to create or update a cookie.
//
function SetCookie (name, value) {
  var argv = SetCookie.arguments;
  var argc = SetCookie.arguments.length;
  var expires = (argc > 2) ? argv[2] : null;
  var path = (argc > 3) ? argv[3] : null;
  var domain = (argc > 4) ? argv[4] : null;
  var secure = (argc > 5) ? argv[5] : false;
  document.cookie = name + "=" + escape (value) +
    ((expires == null) ? "" : ("; expires=" + expires.toGMTString())) +
    ((path == null) ? "" : ("; path=" + path)) +
    ((domain == null) ? "" : ("; domain=" + domain)) +
    ((secure == true) ? "; secure" : "");
}


// Function to delete a cookie. (Sets expiration date to current date/time)
//     name - String object containing the cookie name
//
function DeleteCookie (name) {
  var exp = new Date();
  exp.setTime (exp.getTime() - 1);  // This cookie is history
  var cval = GetCookie (name);
  document.cookie = name + "=" + cval + "; expires=" + exp.toGMTString();
}


// END OF COOKIE FUNCTIONS

// SEARCH AND REPLACE FUNCTIONS
//
// SET UP ARGUMENTS FOR FUNCTION CALLS
//
var caseSensitive = true;
var notCaseSensitive = false;
var wholeWords = true;
var anySubstring = false;


// SEARCH FOR A TERM IN A TARGET STRING
//
// search(targetString,searchTerm,caseSensitive,wordOrSubstring)
//
// where caseSenstive is a boolean value and wordOrSubstring is a boolean
// value and true means whole words, false means substrings
//
function search(target,term,caseSens,wordOnly) {

  var ind = 0;
  var next = 0;
```

```
  if (!caseSens) {
    term = term.toLowerCase();
    target = target.toLowerCase();
  }

  while ((ind = target.indexOf(term,next)) >= 0) {
    if (wordOnly) {
      var before = ind - 1;
      var after = ind + term.length;
      if (!(space(target.charAt(before)) && space(target.charAt(after)))) {
        next = ind + term.length;
        continue;
      }
    }
    return true;
  }

  return false;

}

// SEARCH FOR A TERM IN A TARGET STRING AND REPLACE IT
//
// replace(targetString,oldTerm,newTerm,caseSensitive,wordOrSubstring)
//
// where caseSenstive is a boolean value and wordOrSubstring is a boolean
// value and true means whole words, false means substrings
//
function replace(target,oldTerm,newTerm,caseSens,wordOnly) {

  var work = target;
  var ind = 0;
  var next = 0;

  if (!caseSens) {
    oldTerm = oldTerm.toLowerCase();
    work = target.toLowerCase();
  }

  while ((ind = work.indexOf(oldTerm,next)) >= 0) {
    if (wordOnly) {
      var before = ind - 1;
      var after = ind + oldTerm.length;
      if (!(space(work.charAt(before)) && space(work.charAt(after)))) {
        next = ind + oldTerm.length;
        continue;
      }
    }
    target = target.substring(0,ind) + newTerm + ⇐
        target.substring(ind+oldTerm.length,target.length);
```

continued on next page

continued from previous page

```
        work = work.substring(0,ind) + newTerm + ⇐
            work.substring(ind+oldTerm.length,work.length);
  next = ind + newTerm.length;
      if (next >= work.length) { break; }
    }

    return target;

}

// CHECK IF A CHARACTER IS A WORD BREAK AND RETURN A BOOLEAN VALUE
//
function space(check) {

  var space = " .,/<>?!`';:a#$%^&*()=-|[]{}" + '"' + "\\\n\t";

  for (var i = 0; i < space.length; i++)
    if (check == space.charAt(i)) { return true; }

  if (check == "") { return true; }
  if (check == null) { return true; }

  return false;

}

// END OF SEARCH AND REPLACE FUNCTIONS

// MAIN BODY OF SCRIPT
//
// Set up global variables
//
var width = 8;
var height = 12;
var letters = "ABCDEFGHIJKLMNOPQRSTUVWXYZ";

// Set up Expiry Date for cookies
//
var expiryDate = new Date();
expiryDate.setTime(expiryDate.getTime() + 365*24*60*60*1000);
var deleteExpiry = new Date();
deleteExpiry.setTime(deleteExpiry.getTime() - 1);

// Function to calculate the spreadsheet
//
function calculate(form) {

  var expField = "";
  var expression = "";

  // Check each field for an expression and if there is one, evaluate it
  for (var x = 0; x < width; x ++) {
```

```
      for (var y = 1; y <= height; y ++) {
        expField = letters.charAt(x) + y;
        if ((expression = GetCookie(expField)) != null)
          form[expField].value = evaluateExp(form,expression);
      }
    }

}

// Function to evaluate an expression
//
function evaluateExp(form,expression) {

  var column = "";
  var index = 0;
  var nextExpField;
  var nextExpression = "";
  var nextResult = "";

  // Scan the expression for field names
  for (var x = 0; x < width; x ++) {
    column = letters.charAt(x);
    index = 0;
    index = expression.indexOf(column,index);

    // If we find a field name, evaluate it
    while(index >= 0) {

      // Check if the field has an expression associated with it
      nextExpField = expression.substring(index,expression.indexOf(";",index));

      // If there is an expression, evaluate--⇐
otherwise grab the value of the fieldif ((nextExpression = GetCookie(nextExpField))
!= null) {
        nextResult = evaluateExp(form,nextExpression);
      } else {
        nextResult = form[nextExpField].value;
        if ((nextResult == "") || (nextResult == null))
          nextResult = "0";
      }

      // Replace the field name with the result
      nextExpField = nextExpField + ";";
      nextResult = "(" + nextResult + ")";
      expression = replace(expression,nextExpField,nextResult,⇐
notCaseSensitive,anySubstring);

      // Check if we have reached the end of the expression
      index = index + nextResult.length;
      if (index >= expression.length - 1) { break; }

      // If not, search for another field name
```

continued on next page

continued from previous page

```
            index = expression.indexOf(column,index);
      }
   }

   // Evaluate the expression
   with (Math) {
      var result = eval(expression);
   }

   // Return the result
   return result;

}


// Function to save an expression
//
function saveExp(form) {

   var numExp = GetCookie("numExpressions");

   // Check the number of saved expressions
   if (numExp == "19") {
      alert("Too many expressions. Delete One first");
   } else {

      // If there is room, save the expression and update⇐
   the number of expressions
   SetCookie(form.expField.value,form.expression.value,expiryDate);
      numExp = parseInt(numExp) + 1;
      SetCookie("numExpressions",numExp,expiryDate);

      // Recalculate the spreadsheet
      calculate(document.spreadsheet);

      alert("Expession for field " + form.expField.value + " is saved.");

   }

}


// Function to delete an expression
//
function deleteExp(form) {

   var numExp = GetCookie("numExpressions");
   var expression = GetCookie(form.expField.value);

   // Check if there is an expression to delete for the field
   if (expression != null) {

      // There is, so set the expiry date
      SetCookie(form.expField.value,"",deleteExpiry);
```

```
        numExp = parseInt(numExp) - 1;
        SetCookie("numExpressions",numExp,expiryDate);

        // Update the field and recalculate the spreadsheet
        document.spreadsheet[form.expField.value].value = "";
        calculate(document.spreadsheet);

        alert("Expession for field " + form.expField.value + " is removed.");

    }

}


// Function to build form
//
function buildForm() {

   var numExp = 0;

   // Check if this is a new spreadsheet. If it is, ⇐
set the number of expressions to zero
   if ((numExp = GetCookie("numExpressions")) == null) {
        SetCookie("numExpressions",0,expiryDate);
   }

   // Build row header
   document.write("<TR><TD></TD>");
   for (var x = 0; x < width; x++) {
        document.write("<TD><DIV ALIGN=CENTER>" +⇐
letters.charAt(x) + "</DIV></TD>");
}
   document.write("</TR>");

   // Build each field -- each is the same, with a different name
   for (var y = 1; y <= height; y++) {
        document.write("<TR><TD>" + y + "</TD>");
        for (var x = 0; x < width; x++) {
           document.write('<TD><INPUT TYPE=text SIZE=10 NAME="' + ⇐
letters.charAt(x) + y + '" onChange="calculate(this.form);"></TD>');
//SetCookie(letters.charAt(x) + y,"",deleteExpiry);
        }
        document.write("</TR>");
   }

}


// STOP HIDING -->
</SCRIPT>

</HEAD>

<BODY BGCOLOR="iceblue">
```

continued on next page

continued from previous page

```
<CENTER>

<FORM METHOD=POST NAME="spreadsheet">
<TABLE BORDER=0>

<SCRIPT LANGUAGE="JavaScript">
<!-- HIDE FROM OTHER BROWSERS

buildForm();

// STOP HIDING -->
</SCRIPT>

</TABLE>
</FORM>
<HR>

<FORM METHOD=POST>
<TABLE BORDER=1>

<TR>
<TD><DIV ALIGN=CENTER>Field Name</DIV></TD>
<TD><DIV ALIGN=CENTER>Expression</DIV></TD>
</TR>

<TR>
<TD><DIV ALIGN=CENTER><INPUT TYPE=text SIZE=10 NAME="expField"
    onChange="var exp = GetCookie(this.value); this.form.expression.value = ⇐
(exp == null) ? '' : exp;"></DIV></TD>
<TD><DIV ALIGN=CENTER><INPUT TYPE=text SIZE=50 NAME="expression"></DIV></TD>
<TD><DIV ALIGN=CENTER><INPUT TYPE=button VALUE="Apply" ⇐
onClick="saveExp(this.form);"></DIV></TD>
<TD><DIV ALIGN=CENTER><INPUT TYPE=button VALUE="Delete" ⇐
onClick="deleteExp(this.form);"></DIV></TD>
</TR>

</TABLE>
</FORM>
</CENTER>

</BODY>

</HTML>
```

Output   The results of this script appear like those in Figures 12-1 and 12-2.

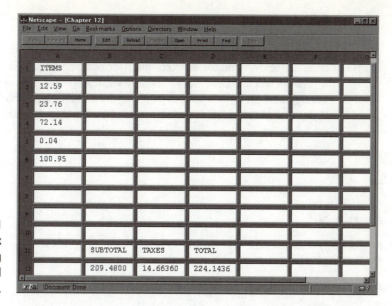

Figure 12-1
Building complex
spreadsheets using
mathematical
expressions.

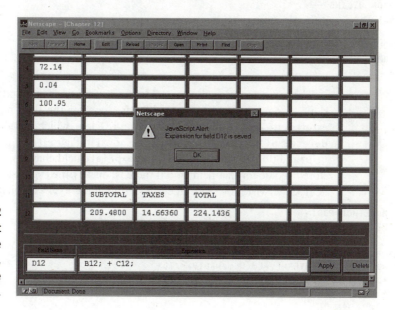

Figure 12-2
The small form at
the bottom can be
used to create,
update, and delete
expressions.

Analysis   You have used five functions to create the spreadsheet application. In addition, you have included Bill Dortch's cookie functions and the search and replace functions you built in Chapter 10, "Strings, Math, and the History List."

Using these, the `calculate()`, `evaluateExp()`, `saveExp()`, `deleteExp()`, and `buildForm()` functions do everything you need.

Before you look at the functions, you need to look at the body of the HTML document to understand the different interface components accessible to the user.

The document consists of two forms: the spreadsheet and the expression update form. The spreadsheet form is built dynamically by a small script which calls `buildForm()`. You use an HTML table to create a nicely formatted spreadsheet layout, as shown in the following segment.

```
<BODY BGCOLOR="iceblue">

<CENTER>

<FORM METHOD=POST NAME="spreadsheet">
<TABLE BORDER=0>

<SCRIPT LANGUAGE="JavaScript">
<!-- HIDE FROM OTHER BROWSERS

buildForm();

// STOP HIDING -->
</SCRIPT>

</TABLE>
</FORM>
<HR>
```

The second form is also in a table and is used to create, update, or delete expressions. It contains two text entry fields—one for the field name and one for the expression—and two buttons, Apply and Delete, which invoke the `saveExp()` and `deleteExp()` functions, respectively, (shown in Figure 12-2).

In addition, when the value of the `expField` field changes, you check if there is a stored cookie for that field, and if there is, display the expression in the `expression` field. Otherwise, you store an empty string in the `expression` field.

```
<FORM METHOD=POST>
<TABLE BORDER=1>

<TR>
<TD><DIV ALIGN=CENTER>Field Name</DIV></TD>
<TD><DIV ALIGN=CENTER>Expression</DIV></TD>
</TR>

<TR>
<TD><DIV ALIGN=CENTER><INPUT TYPE=text SIZE=10 NAME="expField"
    onChange="var exp = GetCookie(this.value); this.form.expression.value = ⇐
(exp == null) ? '' : exp;"></DIV></TD>
<TD><DIV ALIGN=CENTER><INPUT TYPE=text SIZE=50 NAME="expression"></DIV></TD>
<TD><DIV ALIGN=CENTER><INPUT TYPE=button VALUE="Apply" ⇐
onClick="saveExp(this.form);"></DIV></TD>
```

```
<TD><DIV ALIGN=CENTER><INPUT TYPE=button VALUE="Delete" ⇐
onClick="deleteExp(this.form);"></DIV></TD>
</TR>

</TABLE>
</CENTER>
</FORM>

</BODY>
```

Setting Up the Global Variables

In addition to the functions, you have several global variables you use to keep track of information throughout the script:

```
var width = 8;
var height = 12;
var letters = " ABCDEFGHIJKLMNOPQRSTUVWXYZ ";

// Set up Expiry Date for cookies
//
var expiryDate = new Date();
expiryDate.setTime(expiryDate.getTime() + 365*24*60*60*1000);
var deleteExpiry = new Date();
deleteExpiry.setTime(deleteExpiry.getTime() - 1);
```

The `width` and `height` variables define the size of the spreadsheet. Eight columns and 12 rows fit well on an 800×600 pixel display. Only notebook users with 640×480 displays may need a smaller spreadsheet.

The `letters` string contains the letters of the alphabet which are used to name the columns of the form. Each letter is extracted by its index (the column number minus one) when it is needed. You include the whole alphabet because this gives you the flexibility to increase the number of columns in the form simply by increasing the value of `width`.

`expiryDate` and `deleteExpiry` are the `Date` objects used for setting and deleting the cookies. `expiryDate` is set to one year from the current date, and `deleteExpiry` is set to one millisecond before the current time.

The `calculate()` Function

The `calculate()` function is probably the main function of the script. This function is called every time you want to reevaluate the form when a value changes or an expression is added, updated, or deleted. The function takes one argument: the `form` object for the spreadsheet form.

The structure of the function is quite simple. You have two nested `for` loops: one for each column using variable `x` and one for each row using variable `y`. For each combination of row and column you build the field name with `letters.charAt(x) + y`. Notice that the first `for` statement loops from zero to one less than the number of columns, which means `x` is the index of the appropriate letter in the `letters` string.

```
// Function to calculate the spreadsheet
//
function calculate(form) {

  var expField = "";
  var expression = "";

  // Check each field for an expression and if there is one, evaluate it
  for (var x = 0; x < width; x ++) {
    for (var y = 1; y <= height; y ++) {
      expField = letters.charAt(x) + y;
```

You then check if there is an expression stored in the cookie with the name of the field. You store the result of the `GetCookie()` call in the variable expression and compare this to `null`. If it is not `null`, you have an expression, and you evaluate the expression by calling `evaluateExp()`. `evaluateExp()` returns the evaluated expression, and you directly store that value in the appropriate field in the form.

Notice the use of the `form[expField]` structure to refer to the appropriate field in the form. As you learned earlier in the book, object properties can be referred to in three ways:

```
objectName.propertyName
```

```
objectName["propertyName"]
```

```
objectName[propertyIndexNumber]
```

The second form uses a string literal between the brackets, and in Listing 12-1, the value of `expField` is a string literal.

```
if ((expression = GetCookie(expField)) != null)
        form[expField].value = evaluateExp(form,expression);
    }
  }

}
```

The evaluateExp() **Function**

This is, perhaps, the most heavily used function in the script (with the exception of the cookie functions).

Given two arguments—the `form` object for the spreadsheet and the expression to be evaluated—the `evaluateExp()` function returns the value of the expression based on the current content of the spreadsheet.

```
// Function to evaluate an expression
//
function evaluateExp(form,expression) {

  var column = "";
```

```
var index = 0;
var nextExpField;
var nextExpression = "";
var nextResult = "";
```

You start with a **for** loop which iterates through each of the letters that name the columns. Inside that loop, you check whether there is an occurrence of the letter in the expression. If there is, it means that there is a reference to a field in that column that you need to handle.

You check for an occurrence of the letter by using **indexOf()** and storing the results in **index**.

```
// Scan the expression for field names
for (var x = 0; x < width; x ++) {
  column = letters.charAt(x);
  index = 0;
  index = expression.indexOf(column,index);
```

The **while** loop executes only when a field for the current column has been found—that is, **index** must be greater than zero.

Inside the loop, you get the field name by using **substring()** from **index** to the first occurrence of a semicolon (**;**), which marks the end of the field name. Given this value, you check whether there is an expression for that field and store the expression in **nextExpression**. If there is an expression, you call **evaluateExp()** recursively to get the value for that expression and store the result in **nextResult**.

If there is no expression for the field, you get the value of **nextResult** directly from the form. If this value is a **null** value or an empty string, you change **nextResult** to zero.

```
// If we find a field name, evaluate it
  while(index >= 0) {

    // Check if the field has an expression associated with it
    nextExpField = expression.substring(index,expression.indexOf(";",index));

    // If there is an expression, evaluate--⇐
otherwise grab the value of the field
if ((nextExpression = GetCookie(nextExpField)) != null) {
      nextResult = evaluateExp(form,nextExpression);
    } else {
      nextResult = form[nextExpField].value;
      if ((nextResult == "") || (nextResult == null))
        nextResult = "0";
    }
```

Once you have a value for **nextResult**, you can replace the occurrence of the field in the expression with the value of **nextResult** using the **replace()** function. Make sure that you also replace the semicolon after the field name and add parentheses to **nextResult** so that when the expression is evaluated, the value of **nextResult** is correctly evaluated and not affected by the rules of operator precedence.

For instance, if you have an expression `A1; * B1;` and `B1` has the value of `C1; + D1;`, then, without adding the brackets, `A1` would be multiplied by `C1` and the result added to `D1`, when what you really want is to add `C1` to `D1` first and have the result multiplied by `A1`.

```
// Replace the field name with the result
      nextExpField = nextExpField + ";";
      nextResult = "(" + nextResult + ")";
      expression = replace(expression,nextExpField,nextResult,⇐
notCaseSensitive,anySubstring);
```

Once you have updated the expression, you check whether you have reached the end of the expression by updating **index** to the character after the newly replaced value and compare this to the index of the last character in the expression.

If you haven't reached the end of the string, you check for another occurrence of the current letter with **indexOf()** and return to the condition at the top of the **while** loop.

```
// Check if we have reached the end of the expression
      index = index + nextResult.length;
      if (index >= expression.length - 1) { break; }

// If not, search for another field name
      index = expression.indexOf(column,index);
   }
}
```

Once you finish the **for** loop, you are ready to evaluate the expression. You use **with(Math)** so that any methods from the **Math** object that occurred in the expression don't require the presence of the **Math** prefix.

You evaluate the expression using the **eval()** statement.

```
// Evaluate the expression
with (Math) {
   var result = eval(expression);
}

// Return the result
return result;

}
```

The saveExp() Function

The **saveExp()** function saves an expression in a cookie when the user clicks the Apply button in the lower form, which is used to create and manipulate expressions. The function takes the **form** object for the expression as an argument.

The function starts by checking the number of expressions that have already been saved. If the number is already 19, the limit, then you inform the user that she needs to delete another expression if she wants to save this one.

```
// Function to save an expression
//
function saveExp(form) {

  var numExp = GetCookie("numExpressions");

  // Check the number of saved expressions
  if (numExp == "19") {
    alert("Too many expressions. Delete One first");
  } else {
```

If you have room to save the expression, then save it by getting the name of the cookie directly from the appropriate field in the form and getting the expression in the same way. You also update the number of expressions by one and update the cookie containing this value (notice the use of `parseInt()` to change the string returned by `GetCookie()` into an integer).

```
// If there is room, save the expression and⇐
update the number of expressions
SetCookie(form.expField.value,form.expression.value,expiryDate);
    numExp = parseInt(numExp) + 1;
    SetCookie("numExpressions",numExp,expiryDate);
```

Finally, you recalculate the spreadsheet by calling `calculate()` and then inform the user that the expression has been saved.

```
    // Recalculate the spreadsheet
    calculate(document.spreadsheet);

    alert("Expession for field " + form.expField.value + " is saved.");

  }

}
```

The `deleteExp()` Function

Just as `saveExp()` saved an expression, `deleteExp()` deletes the expression indicated by a field name in the form. Again, it takes the `form` object as an expression and is invoked when the user clicks on the Delete button.

You start by checking whether there is an expression stored in that field. If there is, you save a new cookie with the same name but use `deleteExpiry` as the expiry date. You also decrease the number of expressions by one and update the cookie containing the number.

```
// Function to delete an expression
//
function deleteExp(form) {

  var numExp = GetCookie("numExpressions");
  var expression = GetCookie(form.expField.value);
```

continued on next page

continued from previous page

```
    // Check if there is an expression to delete for the field
    if (expression != null) {

        // There is, so set the expiry date
        SetCookie(form.expField.value,"",deleteExpiry);
        numExp = parseInt(numExp) - 1;
        SetCookie("numExpressions",numExp,expiryDate);
```

Once the cookie has been deleted, you recalculate the spreadsheet and inform the user the task is done in the same way as the **saveExp()** function.

```
        // Update the field and recalculate the spreadsheet
        document.spreadsheet[form.expField.value].value = "";
        calculate(document.spreadsheet);

        alert("Expession for field " + form.expField.value + " is removed.");

    }

}
```

The buildForm() Function

The **buildForm()** function is the last function in Listing 12-1. It is called from inside the body of the HTML file and builds the HTML of the spreadsheet form, which is displayed in a table.

Using JavaScript to dynamically build the table is the best approach because each field is repetitive and because you want to be able to build the spreadsheet table to match the **width** and **height** variables if they get changed.

You start by determining whether this is a new spreadsheet by checking if there is any value stored in the cookie holding the number of expressions. If there isn't a value, you save a zero value there to initialize the spreadsheet.

```
// Function to build form
//
function buildForm() {

  var numExp = 0;

  // Check if this is a new spreadsheet. ⇐
If it is, set the number of expressions to zero
  if ((numExp = GetCookie("numExpressions")) == null) {
      SetCookie("numExpressions",0,expiryDate);
  }
```

Next, you build the header row for the table which contains a blank field at the start, and then a field for each column with the appropriate letter centered in the field. You do this with a **for** loop that extracts each letter from the **letters** string.

```
  // Build row header
  document.write("<TR><TD></TD>");
```

```
   for (var x = 0; x < width; x++) {
      document.write("<TD><DIV ALIGN=CENTER>" +⇐
letters.charAt(x) + "</DIV></TD>");
}
   document.write("</TR>");
```

Once the table header is output, you use two nested **for** loops to build each row of the table with the number in the first field and then blank text input fields in the rest of the table cells in the row.

The names of the text entry fields are created using `letters.charAt(x) + y`.

```
   // Build each field -- each is the same, with a different name
   for (var y = 1; y <= height; y++) {
      document.write("<TR><TD>" + y + "</TD>");
      for (var x = 0; x < width; x++) {
         document.write('<TD><INPUT TYPE=text SIZE=10 NAME="' + ⇐
letters.charAt(x) + y + '"onChange="calculate(this.form);"></TD>');
}
      document.write("</TR>");
   }

}
```

BEYOND THE BASIC SCRIPT

The basic script works but it has several limitations, including the following:

- Efficiency—Most users, especially those on Windows platforms, will notice that your script is a little slow and that actions create a noticeable lag to update the spreadsheet.

- Error checking—This script doesn't check that the syntax of the expressions is valid. It doesn't check that fields contain numeric values when it evaluates expressions and doesn't check for circular expressions (expressions that depend on each other to evaluate and will cause infinite recursion).

- Title—If you tried to create a spreadsheet including titles, you will notice that when you come back to the spreadsheet, the values of these title fields are lost.

In addition to these limitations, there are several features you could add to the spreadsheet to make it more useful:

- Ranges—Most spreadsheets enable formulas to include ranges in their expressions. (For instance, A1; ... A5; might be the total of the values in all fields from A1 to A5.)

- Clear—This application provides no easy way for the user to clear all the field values and all the expressions and start from scratch.

Improving Efficiency

The main efficiency bottleneck is in the `calculate()` function. In this function, you use two nested `for` loops to iterate through all 96 fields in the form. For each, you call `GetCookie()` to check whether the field has an expression, and if it does, you call `evaluateExp()`.

This is inefficient, however. You end up calling `GetCookie()` for each empty field in the form, which in the example, means at least 77 unneeded calls to `GetCookie()` each time you change a value in the form.

If you have a way to know which fields have expressions without checking each field in the spreadsheet, you could avoid all these unnecessary calls to `GetCookie()`.

To do this, you can take one more of the cookies and use it to store a list of fields that contain expressions. For instance, a semicolon-delimited list such as `A1;B11;C10;` could be used.

In order to do this, you need to make changes to `calculate()`, `saveExp()`, and `deleteExp()`.

In the `calculate()` function, you make a fundamental change to the logic of the function:

```
function calculate(form) {

   var index = 0;
   var next = 0;
   var expField = "";
   var expression = "";
   var fieldList = GetCookie("fieldList");

   if (fieldList != null) {
      while (index != fieldList.length) {
         next = fieldList.indexOf(";",index);
         expField = fieldList.substring(index,next);
         expression = GetCookie(expField);
         form[expField].value = evaluateExp(form,expression);
         index = next + 1;
      }
   }

}
```

You get the field list from the `fieldList` cookie. If it is `null`, there are no expressions and no evaluation is needed. Otherwise, you enter a `while` loop that continues until the index reaches the end of the `fieldList` string.

Inside the `while` loop, you scan for the next semicolon using `indexOf()` and extract the substring from `index` to the character before the semicolon. This value is the field name of an expression which you then get from the cookie, evaluate, and store in `form[expField].value`.

You then increment `index` to the character after the semicolon.

The `saveExp()` and `deleteExp()` functions both have similar changes. In the `saveExp()` function, you need to add a few lines to handle the extra cookie containing the field list, as well as change the maximum number of cookies to 18 to make room for the `fieldList` cookie.

You handle updating the `fieldList` cookie by first checking whether there is a list already. If not, you simply create the list with the current field name. If there is a list, you remove the field name from the list by replacing it with an empty string and then add it back in. In this way, you don't get double occurrences of any field name in the list.

```
function saveExp(form) {

  var expField = form.expField.value;
  var fieldList = GetCookie("fieldList");
  var numExp = GetCookie("numExpressions");

  // Check the number of saved expressions
  if (numExp == "18") {
    alert("Too many expressions. Delete One first");
  } else {

    // If there is room, save the expression and⇐
update the number of expressions
SetCookie(form.expField.value,form.expression.value,expiryDate);
    numExp = parseInt(numExp) + 1;
    SetCookie("numExpressions",numExp,expiryDate);
    expField += ";"
    if (fieldList == null) {
      fieldList = expField;
    } else {
      fieldList = replace(fieldList,expField,"",notCaseSensitive,anySubstring);
      fieldList += expField;
    }
    SetCookie("fieldList",fieldList,expiryDate);

    // Recalculate the spreadsheet
    calculate(document.spreadsheet);

    alert("Expession for field " + form.expField.value + " is saved.");

  }

}
```

The `deleteExp()` function works in a similar manner:

```
function deleteExp(form) {

  var fieldList = GetCookie("fieldList");
  var expField = form.expField.value;
  var numExp = GetCookie("numExpressions");
  var expression = GetCookie(form.expField.value);

  // Check if there is an expression to delete for the field
  if (expression != null) {
```

continued on next page

continued from previous page

```
        // There is, so set the expiry date
        SetCookie(form.expField.value,"",deleteExpiry);
        numExp = parseInt(numExp) - 1;
        SetCookie("numExpressions",numExp,expiryDate);
        expField += ";";
        fieldList = replace(fieldList,expField,"",notCaseSensitive,anySubstring);
        SetCookie("fieldList",fieldList,expiryDate);

        // Update the field and recalculate the spreadsheet
        document.spreadsheet[form.expField.value].value = "";
        calculate(document.spreadsheet);

        alert("Expression for field " + form.expField.value + " is removed.");

    }

}
```

To delete the entry from the field list and update the cookie, you simply use the `replace()` function to delete the name and replace it with an empty string before updating the `fieldList` cookie.

Adding Title Fields

In order to save title fields, treat them as expressions so they get saved as cookies. The structure you will use is to have the first character of the title expression be a double-quote character.

Then, you can simply update the `evaluateExp()` function to return the rest of the string when it encounters this syntax:

```
function evaluateExp(form,expression) {

  var column = "";
  var index = 0;
  var nextExpField;
  var nextExpression = "";
  var nextResult = "";

  if (expression.charAt(0) == '"') {
    return(expression.substring(1,expression.length));
  }

  // Scan the expression for field names
  for (var x = 0; x < width; x ++) {
    column = letters.charAt(x);
    index = 0;
    index = expression.indexOf(column,index);
```

```
    // If we find a field name, evaluate it
    while(index >= 0) {

        // Check if the field has an expression associated with it
        nextExpField = expression.substring(index,expression.indexOf(";",index));

        // If there is an expression, evaluate.⇐
Otherwise grab the value of the field
if ((nextExpression = GetCookie(nextExpField)) != null) {
        nextResult = evaluateExp(form,nextExpression);
    } else {
        nextResult = form[nextExpField].value;
        if ((nextResult == "") || (nextResult == null))
            nextResult = "0";
    }

        // Replace the field name with the result
        nextExpField = nextExpField + ";";
        nextResult = "(" + nextResult + ")";
        expression = replace(expression,nextExpField,⇐
nextResult,notCaseSensitive,anySubstring);

        // Check if we have reached the end of the expression
        index = index + nextResult.length;
        if (index >= expression.length - 1) { break; }

        // If not, search for another field name
        index = expression.indexOf(column,index);
    }
    }

    // Evaluate the expression
    with (Math) {
        var result = eval(expression);
    }

    // Return the result
    return result;

}
```

You have added only one step to the `evaluateExp()` function. Before you attempt to evaluate the expression as a mathematical expression, you check the first character for a double quotation mark. If you find one, you simply return the rest of the `expression` string.

Checking for Errors

By way of example, you are going to perform some very basic error checking. There are two places you need to check for errors. First, you need to make sure that the user has entered a legitimate expression in the expression field.

Here, if the user has entered a mathematical expression, you will check basic syntax—that is, that the field names use capital letters and end with a semicolon and also that you don't have a circular expression.

To make the script easier to read, do this in a separate function and call the function from the main `if` statement in **saveExp()**:

```
if (numExp == "18") {
   alert("Too many expressions. Delete One first");
} else {

   if (!checkExp(form.expression.value,expField + ";")) { return }

   // If there is room, save the expression and⇐
update the number of expressions
SetCookie(form.expField.value,form.expression.value,expiryDate);
   numExp = parseInt(numExp) + 1;
   SetCookie("numExpressions",numExp,expiryDate);
   expField += ";"
   if (fieldList == null) {
      fieldList = expField;
   } else {
      fieldList = replace(fieldList,expField,"",notCaseSensitive,anySubstring);
      fieldList += expField;
   }
   SetCookie("fieldList",fieldList,expiryDate);

   // Recalculate the spreadsheet
   calculate(document.spreadsheet);

   alert("Expession for field " + form.expField.value + " is saved.");

}
```

The line

```
if (!checkExp(form.expression.value,expField + ";")) { return }
```

calls **checkExp()** which checks the expression in question and, if it finds an error, alerts the user and returns **false**. Otherwise, it returns **true**. By checking whether you get a **false** value from **checkExp()**, you are able to exit the function before saving the new expression.

The main work of error checking takes place in the function **checkExp()**:

```
function checkExp(expression,expField) {

   var index =0;
   var next = 0;
   var checkNum = 0;
   var otherExpField = ""
   var otherExp = "";
   var lowerColumn = ""

   if (expression.charAt(0) == '"') { return true; }
```

```
for (var x = 0; x < width; x++) {
  index =0;
  column = letters.charAt(x);
  lowerColumn = column.toLowerCase();

  // Check for field in this column
  index = expression.indexOf(column,0);
  if (index < 0) {
    index = expression.indexOf(lowerColumn,0);
  }

  // If we have a reference to this column, check the syntax
  while (index >= 0) {

    next = index + 1;

    // Check if letter is followed by a number, if not assume it is a Math method
checkNum = parseInt(expression.charAt(next));
    if ((checkNum == 0) && (expression.charAt(next) != "0") && ⇐
(expression.charAt(index) == lowerColumn)) {
if (next + 1 == expression.length) { break; }
      index = expression.indexOf(column,next+1);
      if (index < 0) {
        index = expression.indexOf(lowerColumn,next+1);
      }
      continue;
    }

    // It is not a Math method so check that the letter was uppercase
    if (expression.charAt(index) == lowerColumn) {
      alert("Field names must use uppercase letters.");
      return false;
    }

    // The letter was uppercase, so check that we have ⇐
only numbers followed by a semicolon
while(expression.charAt(++next) != ";") {
      checkNum = parseInt(expression.charAt(next));
      if ((checkNum == 0) && (expression.charAt(next) != "0")) {
        alert("Field name format is incorrect (should be like A12; or B9;).");
        return false;
      }
      if (next == expression.length - 1) {
        alert("Field name format is incorrect (should be like A12; or B9;).");
        return false;
      }
    }

    otherExpField = expression.substring(index,next);

    // Check for a circular expression
    otherExp = GetCookie(otherExpField);
```

continued on next page

continued from previous page

```
        if (otherExp != null) {
          if (search(otherExp,expField,caseSensitive,anySubstring)) {
            alert("You have created a circular expression ⇐
with field " + otherExpField + ".");
return false;
          }
        }

        if (next + 1 == expression.length) { break; }

        index = expression.indexOf(column,next+1);
        if (index < 0) {
          index = expression.indexOf(lowerColumn,next+1);
        }

      }

    }

    return true;

}
```

This function is divided into several steps. It starts by checking whether you have a string expression (which starts with a double quotation mark). If you do, it returns **true**.

If you don't have a string expression, then you need to check the mathematical expression according to the criteria previously outlined. To do this, you use a **for** loop which loops through each of the letters that are column names and performs a series of checks based on that column.

```
index =0;
column = letters.charAt(x);
lowerColumn = column.toLowerCase();

// Check for field in this column
index = expression.indexOf(column,0);
if (index < 0) {
  index = expression.indexOf(lowerColumn,0);
}
```

You first assign the column name to the variable **column**. You also assign the lowercase version of the same letter to **lowerColumn** because you will also need to deal with lowercase versions of the same letter.

You then check for an occurrence of either the uppercase or lowercase letter using **indexOf()** and assign the index to the variable **index**. You then enter a **while** loop that performs the main checking. The condition of the **while** loop means it will repeat as long as you continue to find instances of the letter.

```
    // If we have a reference to this column, check the syntax
    while (index >= 0) {

      next = index + 1;

      // Check if letter is followed by a number,⇐
if not assume it is a Math method
checkNum = parseInt(expression.charAt(next));
      if ((checkNum == 0) && (expression.charAt(next) != "0") && ⇐
(expression.charAt(index) == lowerColumn)) {
if (next + 1 == expression.length) { break; }
        index = expression.indexOf(column,next+1);
        if (index < 0) {
          index = expression.indexOf(lowerColumn,next+1);
        }
        continue;
      }
```

The first check in the `while` loop is to see if the character immediately following the letter is a number. If it is not a number—which would make it the start of a field reference—you assume it refers to a method or property from the `Math` object.

This is not a perfect assumption. To correctly check, you would need to assure that whatever character string you find is actually part of the `Math` object. This could be done using the `typeof` operator.

You perform this check by passing the character through `parseInt()` and then check if the result is zero. If it is, you also check if the actual character is zero and make sure that the letter you found is a lowercase letter (since all the `Math` methods start with lowercase letters).

Having passed all these conditions, you make the assumption that this is a `Math` method and you scan forward for another occurrence of the letter and then return to the top of the loop with the `continue` statement.

```
    // It is not a Math method so check that the letter was uppercase
    if (expression.charAt(index) == lowerColumn) {
      alert("Field names must use uppercase letters.");
      return false;
    }
```

If you get by the first `if` statement, you know you have a letter followed by a number, which means the user is trying to reference a field name. The first thing you do is check if the user is using an uppercase letter; if not, you alert the user and return a `false` value.

```
    // The letter was upper case, so check that we ⇐
have only numbers followed by a semicolon
while(expression.charAt(++next) != ";") {
        checkNum = parseInt(expression.charAt(next));
        if ((checkNum == 0) && (expression.charAt(next) != "0")) {
          alert("Field name format is incorrect (should be like A12; or B9;).");
```

continued on next page

continued from previous page

```
            return false;
        }
        if (next == expression.length - 1) {
            alert("Field name format is incorrect (should be like A12; or B9;).");
            return false;
        }
    }
```

Next, you move forward through the expression, checking each character. If you find a non-numeric character before you reach a semicolon, then you know that you have an invalid reference; so you alert the user and return a **false** value. Likewise, if you reach the end of the expression without hitting a semicolon, you also know you have an incorrect form, and you do the same thing.

```
otherExpField = expression.substring(index,next);

// Check for a circular expression
otherExp = GetCookie(otherExpField);
if (otherExp != null) {
   if (search(otherExp,expField,caseSensitive,anySubstring)) {
      alert("You have created a circular expression ⇐
with field " + otherExpField + ".");
return false;
      }
   }
```

The last check you perform is to look for a circular expression. You extract the field name that you are currently looking at and use it to get any existing expression for that field. If the field has an expression, you search it using **search()** to see if the expression refers back to the field you are trying to add an expression to. If it does, you have a circular expression, and you inform the user and return a **false** value again.

For instance, if the user is trying to define the expression A1-B1 in field A1, this would create a circular expression; so the user needs to be informed, and the expression should not be saved.

```
if (next + 1 == expression.length) { break; }

    index = expression.indexOf(column,next+1);
    if (index < 0) {
       index = expression.indexOf(lowerColumn,next+1);
    }

  }
```

Finally, you check whether you have reached the end of the expression and if not, search for another occurrence of the letter, store the index in **index**, and return to the top of the **while** loop.

The other place you need to perform error checking is in the **evaluateExp()** function. Here, you need to make sure that the values of fields being used in expressions are numeric. You do this in the main **if** statement in the **while** loop:

```
if ((nextExpression = GetCookie(nextExpField)) != null) {
    nextResult = evaluateExp(form,nextExpression);
    if ("" + nextResult == "error") {
        return "error";
    }
} else {
    nextResult = form[nextExpField].value;
    if ((nextResult == "") || (nextResult == null)) {
        nextResult = "0";
    } else {
        // Check if this is a numeric expression
        var checkNum = parseInt(nextResult);
        if ((checkNum == 0) && (nextResult.charAt(0) != "0")) {
            return "error";
        }
    }
}

}
```

When you get back a value of calling **evaluateExp()**, you check that the result is not **"error"**. If it is **"error"**, you simply return **"error"** back up the chain of function calls.

If you are getting a value directly from a form field and the field is not empty, you check whether the value is a number by applying **parseInt()** to the value and checking the result. If you don't have a numeric expression, you return **"error"**.

SUMMARY

In this chapter we have put together a complete, workable spreadsheet application using only the commands and JavaScript objects learned in this book. This demonstrates the power of JavaScript as an easy-to-use and flexible scripting language.

To help you put together the program you have just built, I am including the complete source code of the program, including all the changes you just made (Listing 12-2). In the exercises later in this chapter you will extend the features of this application even further.

| Input |

Listing 12-2 The final spreadsheet script.

```
<HTML>

<HEAD>
<TITLE>Chapter 12</TITLE>

<SCRIPT LANGUAGE="JavaScript">
<!-- HIDE FROM OTHER BROWSERS
//
//  Cookie Functions - Second Helping  (21-Jan-96)
//  Written by:  Bill Dortch, hIdaho Design <bdortch@netw.com>
```

continued on next page

continued from previous page

```
//  The following functions are released to the public domain.


//
// "Internal" function to return the decoded value of a cookie
//
function getCookieVal (offset) {
  var endstr = document.cookie.indexOf (";", offset);
  if (endstr == -1)
    endstr = document.cookie.length;
  return unescape(document.cookie.substring(offset, endstr));
}


//
//  Function to return the value of the cookie specified by "name".
//
function GetCookie (name) {
  var arg = name + "=";
  var alen = arg.length;
  var clen = document.cookie.length;
  var i = 0;
  while (i < clen) {
    var j = i + alen;
    if (document.cookie.substring(i, j) == arg)
      return getCookieVal (j);
    i = document.cookie.indexOf(" ", i) + 1;
    if (i == 0) break;
  }
  return null;
}


//
//  Function to create or update a cookie.
//
function SetCookie (name, value) {
  var argv = SetCookie.arguments;
  var argc = SetCookie.arguments.length;
  var expires = (argc > 2) ? argv[2] : null;
  var path = (argc > 3) ? argv[3] : null;
  var domain = (argc > 4) ? argv[4] : null;
  var secure = (argc > 5) ? argv[5] : false;
  document.cookie = name + "=" + escape (value) +
    ((expires == null) ? "" : ("; expires=" + expires.toGMTString())) +
    ((path == null) ? "" : ("; path=" + path)) +
    ((domain == null) ? "" : ("; domain=" + domain)) +
    ((secure == true) ? "; secure" : "");
}


//  Function to delete a cookie. (Sets expiration date to current date/time)
//    name - String object containing the cookie name
//
```

```
function DeleteCookie (name) {
   var exp = new Date();
   exp.setTime (exp.getTime() - 1);   // This cookie is history
   var cval = GetCookie (name);
   document.cookie = name + "=" + cval + "; expires=" + exp.toGMTString();
}


// END OF COOKIE FUNCTIONS

// SEARCH AND REPLACE FUNCTIONS
//
// SET UP ARGUMENTS FOR FUNCTION CALLS
//
var caseSensitive = true;
var notCaseSensitive = false;
var wholeWords = true;
var anySubstring = false;


// SEARCH FOR A TERM IN A TARGET STRING
//
// search(targetString,searchTerm,caseSensitive,wordOrSubstring)
//
// where caseSenstive is a boolean value and wordOrSubstring is a boolean
// value and true means whole words, false means substrings
//
function search(target,term,caseSens,wordOnly) {

   var ind = 0;
   var next = 0;

   if (!caseSens) {
     term = term.toLowerCase();
     target = target.toLowerCase();
   }

   while ((ind = target.indexOf(term,next)) >= 0) {
     if (wordOnly) {
       var before = ind - 1;
       var after = ind + term.length;
       if (!(space(target.charAt(before)) && space(target.charAt(after)))) {
         next = ind + term.length;
         continue;
       }
     }
     return true;
   }

   return false;

}
```

continued on next page

continued from previous page

```
// SEARCH FOR A TERM IN A TARGET STRING AND REPLACE IT
//
// replace(targetString,oldTerm,newTerm,caseSensitive,wordOrSubstring)
//
// where caseSenstive is a boolean value and wordOrSubstring is a boolean
// value and true means whole words, false means substrings
//
function replace(target,oldTerm,newTerm,caseSens,wordOnly) {

  var work = target;
  var ind = 0;
  var next = 0;

  if (!caseSens) {
    oldTerm = oldTerm.toLowerCase();
    work = target.toLowerCase();
  }

  while ((ind = work.indexOf(oldTerm,next)) >= 0) {
    if (wordOnly) {
      var before = ind - 1;
      var after = ind + oldTerm.length;
      if (!(space(work.charAt(before)) && space(work.charAt(after)))) {
        next = ind + oldTerm.length;
        continue;
      }
    }
    target = target.substring(0,ind) + newTerm + ⇐
target.substring(ind+oldTerm.length,target.length);
work = work.substring(0,ind) + newTerm + ⇐
work.substring(ind+oldTerm.length,work.length);
next = ind + newTerm.length;
    if (next >= work.length) { break; }
  }

  return target;

}

// CHECK IF A CHARACTER IS A WORD BREAK AND RETURN A BOOLEAN VALUE
//
function space(check) {

  var space = " .,/<>?!`';:@#$%^&*()=-|[]{}" + '"' + "\\\n\t";

  for (var i = 0; i < space.length; i++)
    if (check == space.charAt(i)) { return true; }

  if (check == "") { return true; }
  if (check == null) { return true; }

  return false;
```

```
}

// END OF SEARCH AND REPLACE FUNCTIONS

// MAIN BODY OF SCRIPT
//
// Set up global variables
//
var width = 8;
var height = 12;
var letters = "ABCDEFGHIJKLMNOPQRSTUVWXYZ";

// Set up Expiry Date for cookies
//
var expiryDate = new Date();
expiryDate.setTime(expiryDate.getTime() + 365*24*60*60*1000);
var deleteExpiry = new Date();
deleteExpiry.setTime(deleteExpiry.getTime() - 1);

// Function to calculate the spreadsheet
//
function calculate(form) {

  var index = 0;
  var next = 0;
  var expField = "";
  var expression = "";
  var fieldList = GetCookie("fieldList");

  if (fieldList != null) {
    while (index != fieldList.length) {
      next = fieldList.indexOf(";",index);
      expField = fieldList.substring(index,next);
      expression = GetCookie(expField);
      form[expField].value = evaluateExp(form,expression);
      index = next + 1;
    }
  }

}


// Function to evaluate an expression
//


function evaluateExp(form,expression) {

  var column = "";
  var index = 0;
  var nextExpField;
  var nextExpression = "";
  var nextResult = "";
```

continued on next page

continued from previous page

```
        if (expression.charAt(0) == '"') {
          return(expression.substring(1,expression.length));
        }

        // Scan the expression for field names
        for (var x = 0; x < width; x ++) {
          column = letters.charAt(x);
          index = 0;
          index = expression.indexOf(column,index);

          // If we find a field name, evaluate it
          while(index >= 0) {

            // Check if the field has an expression associated with it
            nextExpField = expression.substring(index,expression.indexOf(";",index));

            // If there is an expression, evaluate--otherwise grab the value of the field
            if ((nextExpression = GetCookie(nextExpField)) != null) {
              nextResult = evaluateExp(form,nextExpression);
            } else {
              nextResult = form[nextExpField].value;
              if ((nextResult == "") || (nextResult == null))
                nextResult = "0";
            }

            // Replace the field name with the result
            nextExpField = nextExpField + ";";
            nextResult = "(" + nextResult + ")";
            expression = ⇐
    replace(expression,nextExpField,nextResult,notCaseSensitive,anySubstring);
            // Check if we have reached the end of the expression
            index = index + nextResult.length;
            if (index >= expression.length - 1) { break; }

            // If not, search for another field name
            index = expression.indexOf(column,index);
          }
        }

        // Evaluate the expression
        with (Math) {
          var result = eval(expression);
        }

        // Return the result
        return result;

      }
```

```
// Function to save an expression
//
function saveExp(form) {

   var expField = form.expField.value;
   var fieldList = GetCookie("fieldList");
   var numExp = GetCookie("numExpressions");

   // Check the number of saved expressions
   if (numExp == "18") {
     alert("Too many expressions. Delete One first");
   } else {

     if (!checkExp(form.expression.value,expField + ";")) { return }

     // If there is room, save the expression and⇐
update the number of expressions
SetCookie(form.expField.value,form.expression.value,expiryDate);
     numExp = parseInt(numExp) + 1;
     SetCookie("numExpressions",numExp,expiryDate);
     expField += ";"
     if (fieldList == null) {
        fieldList = expField;
     } else {
        fieldList = replace(fieldList,expField,"",notCaseSensitive,anySubstring);
        fieldList += expField;
     }
     SetCookie("fieldList",fieldList,expiryDate);

     // Recalculate the spreadsheet
     calculate(document.spreadsheet);

     alert("Expession for field " + form.expField.value + " is saved.");

   }

}

// Function to delete an expression
//
function deleteExp(form) {

   var fieldList = GetCookie("fieldList");
   var expField = form.expField.value;
   var numExp = GetCookie("numExpressions");
   var expression = GetCookie(form.expField.value);

   // Check if there is an expression to delete for the field
   if (expression != null) {

     // There is, so set the expiry date
     SetCookie(form.expField.value,"",deleteExpiry);
     numExp = parseInt(numExp) - 1;
```

continued on next page

continued from previous page

```
        SetCookie("numExpressions",numExp,expiryDate);
        expField += ";";
        fieldList = replace(fieldList,expField,"",notCaseSensitive,anySubstring);
        SetCookie("fieldList",fieldList,expiryDate);

        // Update the field and recalculate the spreadsheet
        document.spreadsheet[form.expField.value].value = "";
        calculate(document.spreadsheet);

        alert("Expession for field " + form.expField.value + " is removed.");

    }

}


// Function to build form
//
function buildForm() {

  var numExp = 0;

  // Check if this is a new spreadsheet. If it is, ⇐
set the number of expressions to zero
  if ((numExp = GetCookie("numExpressions")) == null) {
      SetCookie("numExpressions",0,expiryDate);
  }

  // Build row header
  document.write("<TR><TD></TD>");
  for (var x = 0; x < width; x++) {
     document.write("<TD><DIV ALIGN=CENTER>" +⇐
letters.charAt(x) + "</DIV></TD>");
  }
  document.write("</TR>");

  // Build each field -- each is the same, with a different name
  for (var y = 1; y <= height; y++) {
     document.write("<TR><TD>" + y + "</TD>");
     for (var x = 0; x < width; x++) {
        document.write('<TD><INPUT TYPE=text SIZE=10 NAME="' + ⇐
letters.charAt(x) + y + '" onChange="calculate(this.form);"></TD>');
  }
     document.write("</TR>");
   }

}



// Function check expressions
//
```

```
function checkExp(expression,expField) {

  var index =0;
  var next = 0;
  var checkNum = 0;
  var otherExpField = ""
  var otherExp = "";
  var lowerColumn = ""

  if (expression.charAt(0) == '"') { return true; }

  for (var x = 0; x < width; x++) {
    index =0;
    column = letters.charAt(x);
    lowerColumn = column.toLowerCase();

    // Check for field in this column
    index = expression.indexOf(column,0);
    if (index < 0) {
      index = expression.indexOf(lowerColumn,0);
    }

    // If we have a reference to this column, check the syntax
    while (index >= 0) {

      next = index + 1;

      // Check if letter is followed by a number, if not assume it is a Math method
      checkNum = parseInt(expression.charAt(next));
      if ((checkNum == 0) && (expression.charAt(next) != "0") && ⇐
(expression.charAt(index) == lowerColumn)) {
          if (next + 1 == expression.length) { break; }
          index = expression.indexOf(column,next+1);
          if (index < 0) {
            index = expression.indexOf(lowerColumn,next+1);
          }
          continue;
      }

      // It is not a Math method so check that the letter was uppercase
      if (expression.charAt(index) == lowerColumn) {
        alert("Field names must use uppercase letters.");
        return false;
      }

      // The letter was uppercase, so check that we have only numbers followed by ⇐
a semicolon
      while(expression.charAt(++next) != ";") {
        checkNum = parseInt(expression.charAt(next));
        if ((checkNum == 0) && (expression.charAt(next) != "0")) {
          alert("Field name format is incorrect (should be like A12; or B9;).");
```

continued on next page

continued from previous page

```
            return false;
         }
         if (next == expression.length - 1) {
            alert("Field name format is incorrect (should be like A12; or B9;).");
            return false;
         }
      }

      otherExpField = expression.substring(index,next);

      // Check for a circular expression
      otherExp = GetCookie(otherExpField);
      if (otherExp != null) {
        if (search(otherExp,expField,caseSensitive,anySubstring)) {
         alert("You have created a circular expression with field " + otherExpField
+ ".");
           return false;
        }
      }

      if (next + 1 == expression.length) { break; }

      index = expression.indexOf(column,next+1);
      if (index < 0) {
         index = expression.indexOf(lowerColumn,next+1);
      }

    }

  }

  return true;

}

// STOP HIDING -->
</SCRIPT>

</HEAD>

<BODY BGCOLOR="iceblue">

<CENTER>

<FORM METHOD=POST NAME="spreadsheet">
<TABLE BORDER=0>

<SCRIPT LANGUAGE="JavaScript">
<!-- HIDE FROM OTHER BROWSERS
```

```
buildForm();

// STOP HIDING -->
</SCRIPT>

</TABLE>
</FORM>
<HR>

<FORM METHOD=POST>
<TABLE BORDER=1>

<TR>
<TD><DIV ALIGN=CENTER>Field Name</DIV></TD>
<TD><DIV ALIGN=CENTER>Expression</DIV></TD>
</TR>

<TR>
<TD><DIV ALIGN=CENTER><INPUT TYPE=text SIZE=10 NAME="expField"
    onChange="var exp = GetCookie(this.value); this.form.expression.value = ⇐
(exp == null) ? '' : exp;"></DIV></TD>
<TD><DIV ALIGN=CENTER><INPUT TYPE=text SIZE=50 NAME="expression"></DIV></TD>
<TD><DIV ALIGN=CENTER><INPUT TYPE=button VALUE="Apply" ⇐
onClick="saveExp(this.form);"></DIV></TD>
<TD><DIV ALIGN=CENTER><INPUT TYPE=button VALUE="Delete" ⇐
onClick="deleteExp(this.form);"></DIV></TD>
</TR>

</TABLE>
</FORM>
</CENTER>

</BODY>

</HTML>
```

CHAPTER EXERCISE

1. Earlier in the chapter we discussed adding two additional features: the Clear button and the range capability. Extend the script to add the Clear button.

2. Extend the script you just wrote in Exercise 1 to include the following range capability: When the user specifies the range, simply add up the values in all the fields in that range. You will need to define a syntax for ranges and then adjust the script to accommodate those changes. Try to define the syntax in such a way that it does not cause problems in the existing checkExp() function.

Quiz 1

1. In designing your spreadsheet code, you will want to save expressions using cookies. What limitations on the number of expressions should you keep in mind?

   a. This is not a problem, since the page can be any size.

   b. There will be a field for every cell, and an optional expression for every field, so there will be no limitation.

   c. The number of cookies per page may be exceeded, so a counter should be kept to help enforce this limit.

   d. Every time an expression is entered, make sure the cookie has a large enough buffer for the whole expression.

2. The spreadsheet is defined as a fixed height and width; what do you need to keep in mind when setting this?

   a. The number of rows should match the number of columns.

   b. That not all users will have a large display, so defining a large spreadsheet will force some users to scroll around a lot.

   c. Some users will want to create very large spreadsheets, so you should make it as large a possible.

   d. There are no real considerations to keep in mind.

3. The following `for` loops are similar to the ones in the first version of the `calculate()` function; in what order will the cells of the spreadsheet be evaluated?

```
for( var x = 0; x < width; x++ ) {
  for( var y = 1; y <= height; y++ ) {



  }
}
```

   a. The order is A1, A2, ..., B1, B2, ...

   b. The order is A, B, C.

   c. The order is A1, B1, ..., A2, B2, ...

   d. The order is random.

4. In a subsequent version of the `calculate()` function, a cookie that has a list of the cells that contain expressions is used; in what order will the cells of the spreadsheet be evaluated?

   a. The order is A1, B1, ..., A2, B2, ...

   b. The order is A1, A2, ..., B1, B2, ...

   c. The order is the order that they are listed in the cookie.

   d. The order is random.

5. The following script segment is from the improved version of the `saveExp()` function; if fieldList contains 'A1;B11;C10;' and expField contains 'B11;' then what does fieldList contain after these two expressions are executed?

```
fieldList = replace( fieldList, expField, "", notCaseSensitive, anySubstring );
   fieldList += expField;
```

         a. A1;B11;C10;B11;
         b. A1;B11;C10;
         c. B11;C10;A1;
         d. A1;C10;B11;

CHAPTER 13

NAVIGATOR GOLD— A JAVASCRIPT DEVELOPMENT TOOL

Now that you know how to develop large applications on the World Wide Web using JavaScript, it would be useful to have sophisticated development tools for JavaScript applications similar to the large number of powerful HTML editors, validators, and assistants.

Although there are currently no editors or development tools specifically designed for JavaScript, Netscape has developed Navigator Gold. This product brings together the Navigator browser with a comprehensive editing environment for developing Netscape-specific Web pages that support all the major features of Navigator, including JavaScript.

In this chapter we take a look at Navigator Gold as a development tool, both for HTML and for JavaScript. We discuss the following:

- The features of Navigator Gold
- Using Navigator Gold to develop HTML documents
- Developing JavaScript in Navigator Gold
- Other advanced features of Navigator Gold
- Limitations of Navigator Gold

This chapter describes the features of Navigator Gold 2.0, which is in release version at the time of this writing. As of this writing, Navigator Gold 3.0 is in beta development.

LESSON 1 Navigator Gold and the Browser

AN INTRODUCTION TO NAVIGATOR GOLD 2.0

Navigator Gold could be seen as the advanced version of the Navigator Web browser. Where Netscape is trying to position Navigator as the complete Web browser and Internet tool for the Internet user, Navigator Gold is being positioned as a key application for users to develop Web applications that take advantage of the special features of Navigator.

These are the main features of Navigator Gold:

- An editing environment
- Drag-and-drop capability
- Distributed publishing
- JavaScript support
- Tutorials and guides for the novice developer

An Editing Environment

Navigator Gold adds a new editing window accessible from the File menu and from a new button on the Web browser's toolbar. Using the editor, it is possible to develop Web pages in a WYSIWYG (what you see is what you get) environment. The editor makes it easy to apply HTML tags in such a way as to completely avoid the intricacies of HTML tags. Figures 13-1 and 13-2 show what the same document looks like in the Web browser window and the editor window.

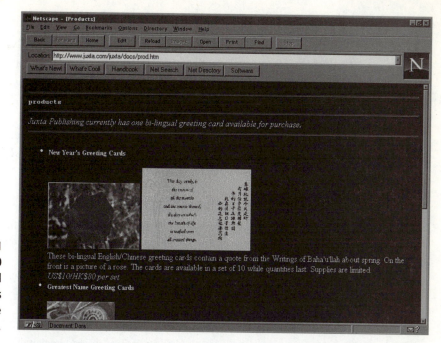

Figure 13-1
Navigator Gold 2.0
supports standard
browsing features
found in Netscape
Navigator.

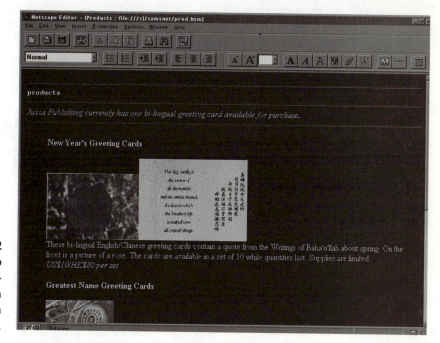

Figure 13-2
In addition to
browsing capabili-
ties, documents can
be opened in a
built-in editor.

Drag-and-Drop Capability

Netscape has implemented drag-and-drop support throughout Navigator Gold. It is possible to drag images or links from the Web browser window to the editor window to develop pages quickly.

Distributed Publishing

Netscape has indicated that Navigator Gold will include a feature called One Button Publish, which will enable the simple uploading of Web pages developed with Navigator Gold to Internet Service Providers that support this feature.

JavaScript Support

Netscape claims that Navigator Gold provides the industry's first JavaScript program editor. The built-in editor window will provide specific features and options particularly designed for JavaScript programming.

Tutorials and Guides for the Novice Developer

Netscape's promotions for Navigator Gold include several on-line services. These include the Netscape Page Starter Site, which offers resources on the Web for page authors, and the Netscape Page Wizard, which guides a novice developer through Web creation using simple questions, style guides, and pre-designed artwork. For more information about these, check out the Navigator Gold handbook at

`http://home.netscape.com/eng/mozilla/Gold/handbook.`

THE RELATIONSHIP BETWEEN THE BROWSER AND EDITOR WINDOWS

In order to take advantage of the features of Navigator Gold, it is necessary to understand the relationship between the browser and editor windows.

As with Navigator, the default window is the browser window. From the browser window, there are several ways to get to the editor window:

- Choose New Document from the File menu—This causes a new editor window to be opened with a blank document. The original browser window remains open.

- Click the Edit button—Changes the current browser window into an editor window and opens the document you were viewing. The Edit button is an addition to the toolbar in Navigator Gold's browser window.

- Choose Edit Document from the File menu—Changes the current browser window into an editor window and opens the document you were viewing.

- Choose Open File in Editor from the File menu—Opens an editor window containing the specified file. The original browser window and file remain open.

The Editor Window

The editor window is similar to the browser window. The document is displayed in a WYSIWYG mode similar to the browser window, and the user can specify the color of text, links, and other page elements.

Unlike the browser window, the editor window does not offer the same toolbar, location field, and directory buttons. Instead, the editor window offers the File|Edit toolbar, the Paragraph Format toolbar, and the Character Format toolbar, each of which can be individually displayed or hidden by the user.

The File|Edit Toolbar

The File|Edit toolbar provides buttons to perform the main file and editing functions, including opening and saving documents, switching to the browser window, cutting, copying and pasting, and printing documents. The File|Edit toolbar looks like Figure 13-3. Table 13-1 describes each button.

Button	Function
New	Opens a new document for editing
Open	Opens an existing document in a new editor window
Save	Saves the current document
Browse	Opens the current document in a new browser window
Cut	Cuts the selected items/section and saves it in the Clipboard
Copy	Copies the selected items/section to the Clipboard
Paste	Pastes the Clipboard contents into the current document
Print	Prints the current document
Search	Searches for text in the current document
Web Page Starter	Displays information about Web content creation

Table 13-1 *The buttons on the File|Edit toolbar.*

Figure 13-3
The File|Edit toolbar.

The Paragraph Format Toolbar

The Paragraph Format toolbar provides the basic buttons for applying HTML formatting tags to text. A drop-down list offers the main paragraph formats, including various header formats. Buttons offer a range of features, including unnumbered and numbered lists and paragraph alignment. The Paragraph Format toolbar looks like Figure 13-4. Table 13-2 describes each button.

Button	Function
Unnumbered List	Create or change to an unnumbered list
Numbered List	Create or change to a numbered list
Increase Indent	Increase paragraph indent by one level
Decrease Indent	Decrease paragraph indent by one level
Left	Align text to the left
Center	Align text to the center
Right	Align text to the right

Table 13-2   *The buttons on the Paragraph Format toolbar.*

The Character Format Toolbar

The Character Format toolbar offers buttons to set the font size tag, the style of type including bold, italic, and fixed-width, as well as setting font color, creating links, and inserting images and horizontal rules. The Character Format toolbar looks like Figure 13-5. Table 13-3 describes each button.

Button	Function
Decrease Font	Decrease the font size
Increase Font	Increase the font size
Bold	Apply a bold style
Italic	Apply an italic style
Fixed Width	Make the type monospaced (fixed width)
Font Color	Select a font color
Link	Create a new link or modify an existing one
Clear	Clear all styles
Image	Insert an image
Rule	Insert a horizontal line
Properties	Open the object properties dialog box for the selected object

Table 13-3   *The buttons on the Character Format toolbar.*

Figure 13-4
The Paragraph
Format toolbar.

Figure 13-5
The Character
Format toolbar.

Pop-Up Menus

The other key feature of the editor window is context-sensitive pop-up menus. Pop-up menus on different objects provide quick access to a list of relevant commands and frequently used functions. Most objects in a document generate different pop-up menus, including links, images, and horizontal rules. Pop-up menus are accessed by right clicking on an object in the editor window.

1. What is the main extended feature of Navigator Gold?
   a. Support for HTML 3.0.
   b. The edit window that allows you to develop Web pages.
   c. A JavaScript syntax checker.
   d. The ability to look at the document source.

2. Which of the following is not a way to get to the editor window?
   a. Choose Edit Document from the Edit menu.
   b. Choose New Document from the File menu.
   c. Click the Edit button in the browser toolbar.
   d. Choose Open File in Editor from the File menu.

3. How are the various toolbars displayed or hidden by the user?
   a. By right-clicking in the edit window and checking them on or off in the pop-up menu.
   b. These toolbars are always displayed.
   c. By checking them on or off in the Options menu.
   d. By setting them on or off in the HTML document.

4. What does the drop-down list in the paragraph tool bar do?
   a. It lists the paragraph formats available.
   b. It allows you to select a paragraph format.
   c. It allows you to select a list format for the current paragraph.
   d. None of the above.

5. Which of the following buttons does not belong on the character format toolbar?
   a. Decrease Font
   b. Bold
   c. Decrease Indent
   d. Fixed Width

LESSON 2 HTML and Navigator Gold

CREATING AN HTML DOCUMENT USING NAVIGATOR GOLD

In order to understand better how the editor window works, you are going to create a new document using Navigator Gold.

The document you create will include an image, a horizontal rule, a link to another page, as well as header and body text and highlighted text using different character styles and different color text. The final page should look like the one in Figure 13-6.

Figure 13-6
You are going to create this page using Navigator Gold 2.0.

Setting Up the Editor

The editor preferences dialog box can be opened from the Options menu. It offers the user the opportunity to set general options, as well as default display colors and backgrounds for the editor.

The two pages of the editor preferences dialog box look like Figures 13-7 and 13-8.

The general options include the default author of documents, as well as two options: Keep images with document (to copy all images to your local hard disk) and Maintain link integrity (to adjust links to work regardless of whether the file is saved locally or published to a Web site on the Internet).

For this file, select both Keep images with document and Maintain link integrity.

Figure 13-7
General
preferences.

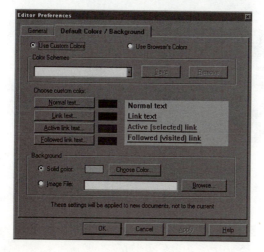

Figure 13-8
Default Colors/
Backgrounds.

The Default Colors/Backgrounds screen also enables the user to set the colors used by the editor to display everything from normal text to link text, as well as the background.

Creating the File

As mentioned earlier, you can create a new document by selecting New Document from the File menu in the browser window. This opens a new editor window with a blank document but will not close the existing browser window.

Once the file is created, you can give it a filename by saving it—this can be done in the File menu or by choosing the save button on the File/Edit toolbar. It is important to save the file for many of Gold's link-related features to function correctly.

The document properties dialog box (in the Properties menu) enables you to set up several features of your HTML document, including header information, such as the title and the color and background information for the `<BODY>` tag.

The information in the dialog box is divided into two pages which can be selected by tabs: header (document) information and color/background information.

The document properties dialog box looks like Figures 13-9 and 13-10.

The Document Information screen allows the user to set information to include in the header of the HTML document. This includes the title of the document and the author.

For your document, you want to set the Title to `Example 13.1` and the background color to whatever color you prefer.

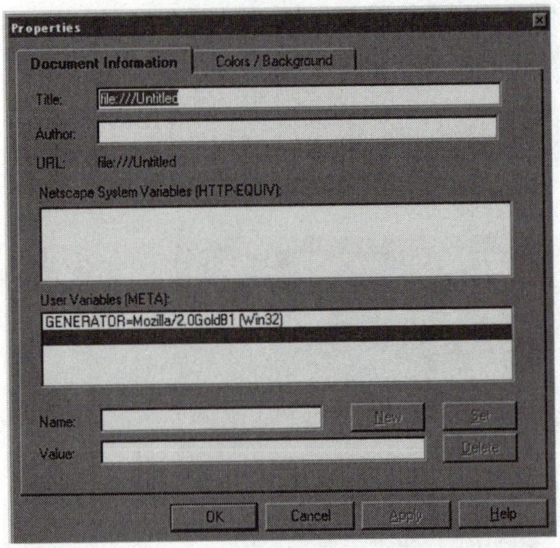

Figure 13-9
Header information.

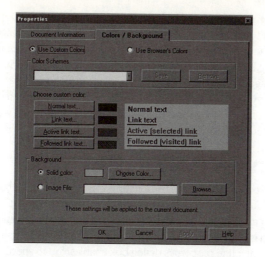

Figure 13-10
Colors/Background.

Inserting the Image

There are two ways you can insert the desired image—drag an existing image from the browser window or insert a new image by choosing Image from the Insert menu (which is the same as clicking on the insert image button on the Character Format toolbar). You will use the latter.

When you choose to insert an image, you are presented with an image properties dialog box like the one in Figure 13-11.

Figure 13-11
The image properties dialog box.

The image properties dialog box allows you to specify the image file, an alternate image file, and alternate text. In addition, the alignment of the image relative to the neighboring text, the size of the border, and the blank space around the image can be controlled.

The dialog box contains two browse buttons—one for the image file and one for the alternate image file.

If you want to, you could specify alternate text for text-based browsers, as well as the space around the image and the width of the border. If you want to make the image a link, you could select a link as well.

Inserting a Horizontal Line

You can insert a horizontal line by selecting the horizontal line button on the Character Format toolbar or by selecting Horizontal Line from the Insert menu. Once the line is inserted, you can right click on it to get a pop-up menu and then select Horizontal Line Properties to get the horizontal line properties dialog box, as shown in Figure 13-12.

The horizontal line properties dialog box enables you to specify the alignment, width, height, and other properties of a horizontal line.

You aren't selecting anything special for this example except to choose a center alignment.

Inserting a Heading

By clicking next to the horizontal line you just inserted and pressing return, you can type in the text of the header.

Next you need to apply the appropriate paragraph format. Paragraph formats apply to all paragraphs in a selection. If no text is selected, then the format applies to the paragraph where the cursor is.

By leaving the cursor in the paragraph you have just written, you can simply select the header style you like from the drop-down list on the Paragraph Format toolbar.

Figure 13-12
The horizontal line properties dialog box.

You also want to change the words **"Netscape Navigator Gold"** in the paragraph to italics and change the color to red. You can do this using character formatting features.

In order to apply character formats to selected text, you need to select the text you want to work with. Next, you can select the italic style from the Character Format toolbar. Then you can add the color red by clicking the color button on the toolbar or selecting Font Color from the Properties menu.

When you do, you get the font color dialog box, which looks like Figure 13-13.

Inserting Body Text

Next you can click after the header you have just created, hit return, and enter the body text. You need to select the normal paragraph format from the drop-down list in the Paragraph Format toolbar to switch from the header style to normal text. You also need to turn off italics by clicking on the italics button in the Character Format toolbar and set the color back to black before you start typing.

Creating a Link

You want to turn the text here into a link to Netscape's home page. You can do this by selecting the text and clicking on the link button in the Character Format toolbar. When you do this, you get the modify/insert links dialog box like the one in Figure 13-14.

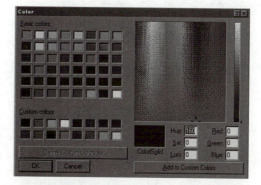

Figure 13-13
The font color
dialog box.

Figure 13-14
The modify/insert
links dialog box.

In this dialog box, you can specify a link. You can select a link by clicking on the Browser button or by typing a URL. In this case, you can enter the URL `http://home.netscape.com/`.

Save the File and View It

Now you can save the document by selecting the save button on the File|Edit toolbar or by selecting Save from the File menu.

If you want to view the source code of the document you have just created, select Document Source from the View menu. This opens a view source window, which looks like Figure 13-15.

Then you can view the document by selecting the browser button in the File|Edit dialog box. The document will be opened in the browser window.

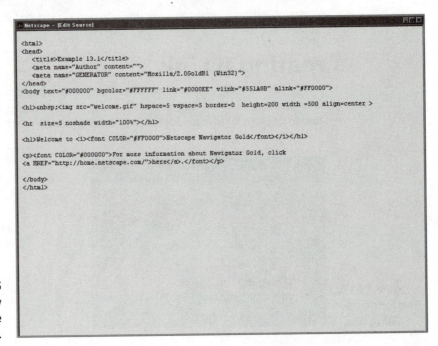

```
Netscape - [Edit Source]

<html>
<head>
    <title>Example 13.1</title>
    <meta name="Author" content="">
    <meta name="GENERATOR" content="Mozilla/2.0GoldB1 (Win32)">
</head>
<body text="#000000" bgcolor="#FFFFFF" link="#0000EE" vlink="#551A8B" alink="#FF0000">

<h1> <img src="welcome.gif" hspace=5 vspace=5 border=0  height=200 width =500 align=center >

<hr  size=5 noshade width="100%"></h1>

<h1>Welcome to <i><font COLOR="#FF0000">Netscape Navigator Gold</font></i></h1>

<p><font COLOR="#000000">For more information about Navigator Gold, click
<a HREF="http://home.netscape.com/">here</a>.</font></p>

</body>
</html>
```

Figure 13-15
You can view the source code of any project.

Quiz 2

1. Where is the editor preferences dialog opened from?
   a. By selecting Properties from the File menu.
   b. By selecting Preferences from the pop-up menu in the edit window.
   c. By selecting Preferences from the Edit menu.
   d. By selecting Editor Preferences from the Options menu.

2. What does the Default Colors/Backgrounds screen do?
   a. It allows you to set the colors used by the editor to display document items.
   b. It allows you to specify the colors of the document you are creating.
   c. It allows you to set the colors and background of your browser.
   d. None of the above.

3. What are two ways to insert an image into your document?
   a. By choosing Image from the Insert menu, and by choosing Insert from the Edit menu.
   b. By choosing Paste from the Edit menu, and by choosing Open Image from the File menu.
   c. By choosing Image from the Insert menu, and by dragging an existing image from the browser window.
   d. By choosing Insert from the Edit menu, and by dragging and dropping an image.

4. Which of the following is not a way to create a link in your document?
   a. Select the link text and click on the Link button.
   b. Select the link text and select Link from the Properties menu.
   c. Select the link text and select Link from the Insert menu.
   d. Select the link text, right-click, and select Create Link from the pop-up menu.

5. What is the easiest way to view the document you have created?
   a. Select Save from the File menu.
   b. Select View from the File menu.
   c. Select Close from the File menu.
   d. Click the View button from the File/Edit toolbar.

LESSON 3 **JavaScript and Navigator Gold**

DEVELOPING JAVASCRIPT APPLICATIONS IN NAVIGATOR GOLD

In the release version of Navigator Gold that is currently available, the JavaScript features of Gold are limited. Still, Navigator Gold does offer the first integrated tools for working with both HTML and JavaScript and offers a few basic editing features especially well-suited to JavaScript editing.

For instance, when you indent a line using the Tab key, the editor remembers the level of indent and the next line will also be indented to the same point. The Shift+Tab combination enables you to back out to a higher level (that is, indent less). This feature can be useful in maintaining well-structured, easy-to-read JavaScript programs.

In addition, JavaScript code is treated as a character style, so you can type a script without the `<SCRIPT>` tags. Then, you can highlight the text and select JavaScript (client) from the character submenu of the Properties menu, and the `<SCRIPT>` tag will be inserted (but not displayed), and the color of the script text will change.

One drawback of the editor is that you need to hit Shift+Return (a soft return) at the end of each line. Otherwise, each line of your script will be contained in separate `<SCRIPT>` container tags.

Even so, in the current beta version of Navigator Gold, it is not practical to create new JavaScript pages using the editor window. Not only is there no direct way to put scripts into the header of the document, but it is not possible to add event handlers to various HTML tags.

Nonetheless, you can use the editor to edit an existing JavaScript application by loading the page in the browser and then switching to the editor window by clicking on the Edit button. Then all of your `<SCRIPT>` containers will appear, and if you edit the existing files, they will remain properly contained in `<SCRIPT>` container tags.

Even so, event handlers in JavaScript tags will not appear, and it will be difficult to work with forms because Gold's form handling, especially related to JavaScript, is less than perfect in the current beta version. Nonetheless, these aspects of editing and creating integrated JavaScript and HTML documents should be worked out by a later release of Navigator Gold.

OTHER ADVANCED FEATURES OF NAVIGATOR GOLD

In addition to promising to offer JavaScript editing capabilities, Navigator Gold includes, or will include in a later version, several other advanced functions that can ease the Web page development process. These features include a one-button publish feature that will publish your page or pages to your service provider's Web server along with all related images and linked files.

Navigator Gold also promises to include the ability to create client-side image maps (one of the new features in Navigator 2.0), include audio files, and provide basic document management capabilities.

At the current time, Navigator Gold is still in an early public beta release and is not complete. In this stage, it has several limitations which restrict its usefulness as a complete HTML and JavaScript development tool:

● Editor window does not support frame display.

● Editor window does not display tables.

● Forms support in editor window is not stable.

● JavaScript capabilities are limited.

● Image alignment and text wrapping display support are not complete.

In addition to these shortcomings, many of which should be fixed by the release of the final version of Navigator Gold 2.0, there are several other limitations of the product, including:

● Not designed for site management: Navigator Gold 2 is designed for producing individual Web pages—it cannot be used to develop and maintain large sites with numerous internal links.

QUIZ 3

1. What is the editor provided as part of Navigator Gold used for?
   a. It is used for editing email messages.
   b. It is only used for HTML documents.
   c. It is used for editing both HTML and JavaScript documents.
   d. It is used for word processing.

2. What special feature does the editor have when using the tab key?
   a. The tab key can be used to indent lines.
   b. When a line is indented using the tab key, subsequent lines are indented to the same level.
   c. The shift-tab key can be used to un-indent a line.
   d. None of the above.

3. What special feature does the editor have for entering JavaScript code?
   a. JavaScript code is automatically displayed in a different color.
   b. The editor performs syntax checking on your JavaScript code.
   c. JavaScript code can be entered as regular text and then tagged as a script from the character submenu.
   d. The editor does not treat JavaScript differently than regular text.

4. What limitations on entering JavaScript does the editor have?
   a. The editor can only edit one script at a time.
   b. The editor does not handle scripts in the document body.
   c. There is no way to add new scripts to the document.
   d. The editor has no direct way of putting scripts into the header section of the document, and it has no way to add event handlers to various HTML tags.

5. When editing existing documents, what types of scripts will not appear?
   a. Scripts in the document header will not appear.
   b. Scripts in the body of the document will not appear.
   c. All of the scripts will appear.
   d. Event handler scripts will not appear.

SUMMARY

In this chapter, you learned the basics of using Navigator Gold to create HTML pages, and we discussed how future versions of Gold will allow for integrated development of JavaScript scripts. Navigator Gold provides a separate WYSIWYG editing window which enables drag-and-drop editing, and provides tools for easy adjustment of object properties in a page through properties dialog boxes and toolbars.

In Chapter 14, "From JavaScript to Java—Looking into the Future," you are going to take a look at the relationship of JavaScript and Java, how to move from JavaScript to Java, how to bring Java and JavaScript together in an HTML document, and future developments of JavaScript.

CHAPTER 14

FROM JAVASCRIPT TO JAVA—LOOKING INTO THE FUTURE

Now that you've mastered the essentials of JavaScript, it should be clear that JavaScript is a powerful tool for extending the functionality of basic HTML documents and creating sophisticated interactive applications.

Nonetheless, the questions remain: How do I do more? Can I move beyond JavaScript and extend its power?

In this chapter, we take a look at the relationship between JavaScript and Java and how you can quickly and easily add Java applets to your pages. We will also look at how JavaScript can interact with Navigator plug-ins. This intercommunication between Java, JavaScript, and plug-ins is known as LiveConnect, a feature of Navigator 3.

In Navigator 2.0, direct communication between Java and JavaScript was not possible. With Navigator 3.0, Netscape has added the `applets` array, which provides a mechanism for communication between JavaScript and Java.

This chapter first looks at the limited interaction possible in Navigator 2.0, and then introduces the `applets` array available in Navigator 3.0. We will go on to look at interacting with plug-ins in Navigator 3.0.

You'll learn about the following:

- ● Basic Java concepts
- ● Using the `<APPLET>` tag to use pre-built Java applets
- ● Similarities between JavaScript and Java
- ● The `applets` array
- ● The `plugins` array and the `plugin` object

LESSON 1   Java

INTEGRATING JAVA INTO JAVASCRIPT—THE applet OBJECT

When Sun and Netscape announced the creation of JavaScript in late 1995, they made a lot of noise about the role of JavaScript in gluing Java into Web pages.

Java applets, because they exist outside the context of the Web page itself, are unable to interact with the type of document, form, and window objects that JavaScript can work with. Java applets are simply assigned a space in the current page, like images are given a particular rectangle, and then they do their thing in that space.

Any interaction with the user requires the applet to provide its own alternatives to the HTML forms and links that JavaScript can so readily work with. Given this, JavaScript's role is supposed to become the link. By having access to all the document and browser objects, as well as having objects which provide hooks into each Java applet in a page, a JavaScript script can play the role of middleman and cause information generated by user or browser events outside the applet to be passed to any applet.

Pretty powerful stuff, overall.

The version of JavaScript built into version 2.0 of Netscape Navigator doesn't provide the `applet` object. Navigator 3.0 supports this feature.

Still, this doesn't prevent JavaScript-enabled Web pages from taking advantage of Java applets and even from performing some basic manipulations that would seem to the user to interact with Java applets—even in Navigator 2.0.

BASIC JAVA CONCEPTS

In order to be able to easily use in your Web pages applets that other people have written, you need to understand several fundamental things about Java.

First, Java is compiled. In order to build your own Java applets or to compile source code provided by friendly folk on the Web and in Usenet newsgroups, it is necessary to have a Java compiler.

Presently, the Java Development Kit is available for SPARC-based hardware running the Solaris operating system and 32-bit Windows platforms (namely, Windows 95 and Windows NT). The compiler and related files and documentation are available at

http://www.javasoft.com/

Other groups have ported the Java Development Kit to other platforms, such as Linux and the Mac OS.

Once the source code for an applet is compiled, it becomes a class file. Class files are not source code and contain objects that can be used in other programs or applets you build. The class file for a Java applet is what is downloaded to the browser and executed when a user loads a page containing the applet.

Presently, there are several large archives of freely available applets, which often include source code or even downloadable Java binary files. If you want to use these applets, you can download the source code and compile them yourself or download the actual class files. Information about using the Java compiler is included in the documentation at the Java Web page.

The leading archives can be found at this site:

http://www.gamelan.com/

and at the Java Web page itself.

In order to understand how to go about obtaining and preparing to use existing applets, you are going to prepare the Growing Text applet by Jamie Hall, which you will use for the rest of the chapter. This applet animates any string of text and causes it to grow from very small to very large. The page author can control several different options including color, font, and delay.

I am assuming that you have downloaded the Development Kit (which includes the compiler) from Sun's Java home page and have followed the installation instructions. The Development Kit is available for several platforms including Windows 95, the Mac OS, and Solaris. Navigator can run Java applets in its 32-bit Windows version, its UNIX versions, and the Mac version.

In looking through these archives, you will notice both Alpha and Beta applets (supported by Navigator). There have been two main stages in the development of Java. The alpha applets are supported on the HotJava browser for Solaris and 32-bit Windows. The beta applets and applets written to the final release API are supported by Netscape. Sun is encouraging Java developers to move from Alpha applets to the current specification. We will be discussing the current specification throughout this chapter.

The Growing Text applet can be found on the Web at this site:

`http://www1.mhv.net/~jamihall/java/GrowingText/GrowingText.html`

You should download the source code, which looks like Listing 14-1 (remember—this is Java code and not a JavaScript script).

Input　　**Listing 14-1** The Growing Text applet source code.

```
/*
 * GrowingText
 *
 * Feel free to re-use any part of this code.
 *
 * Jamie Hall, hallj@frb.gov   1/9/96
 *
 * Jamie Hall 2/2/96 - Added blur parameter
 */

/*
    Takes text, delay, fontName, fontBold, fontItalic, bgColor,
    and fgColor as parameters.  The following are the defaults:

    text       -    String displayed in applet    -  Growing Text
    delay      -    Milliseconds between updates   -  500
    fontName   -    Font style                     -  TimesRoman
    fontBold   -    Font boldness                  -  true
    fontItalic -    Font italics                   -  false
    bgColor    -    Background color (hex. number) -  light Gray
    fgColor    -    Foreground color (hex. number) -  black
    blur       -    Blurring effect                -  false

    Note: 'random' can be used as the background or foreground color
    to generate a random color on each update.
 */

import java.awt.*;
import java.applet.*;

public class GrowingText extends Applet implements Runnable {
   String fontName = "TimesRoman", text = "Growing Text", bgColor, fgColor;
   Thread killme = null;
   boolean threadSuspended = false, blur = false;
   int fonts[] = { 8, 12, 14, 18, 24, 36 };
   int delay = 500, numFonts = 6, fontIndex = 0, fontStyle;
   Font appFont;

   public void init() {
      String param;
      boolean fontBold = true, fontItalic = false;

      param = getParameter("text");
      if (param != null) { text = param; }
```

```
      param = getParameter("delay");
      if (param != null) { delay = Integer.parseInt(param); }

      param = getParameter("fontName");
      if (param != null) { fontName = param; }

      param = getParameter("fontBold");
      if (param != null) { fontBold = param.equals("true"); }

      param = getParameter("fontItalic");
      if (param != null) { fontItalic = param.equals("true"); }

      fontStyle = (fontBold ? Font.BOLD : Font.PLAIN) +
         (fontItalic ? Font.ITALIC : Font.PLAIN);

      bgColor = getParameter("bgColor");
      if (bgColor == null) { bgColor = "Color.lightGray"; }
      setBackground(colorFromString(bgColor, Color.lightGray));

      fgColor = getParameter("fgColor");
      if (fgColor == null) { fgColor = "Color.black"; }
      setForeground(colorFromString(fgColor, Color.black));

      param = getParameter("blur");
      if (param != null) { blur = param.equals("true"); }

      /* Resize applet to fit string with largest font.
         Only works in JDK appletviewer, Netscape ignores it */
      /* FontMetrics fm = ⇐
getFontMetrics(new Font(fontName, fontStyle, fonts[numFonts-1]));
resize(fm.stringWidth(s) + 20, appFont.getSize() + 20); */
   }

   public void start() {
      if (killme == null) {
        killme = new Thread(this);
        killme.start();
      }
   }

   public void stop() {
      if (killme != null) {
        killme.stop();
        killme = null;
      }
   }

   public void run() {
      while (killme != null) {
        repaint();
        try { Thread.sleep(delay); } catch (InterruptedException e) {};
```

continued on next page

continued from previous page

```
      }
    killme = null;
  }

  public void update(Graphics g) {
    if (blur) {
      if (fontIndex > numFonts - 1 ) {
        g.clearRect(0, 0, size().width, size().height);
      }
      paint(g);
    } else {
      g.clearRect(0, 0, size().width, size().height);
      paint(g);
    }
  }

  public void paint(Graphics g) {
    if (bgColor.equalsIgnoreCase("random")) {
      setBackground(colorFromString(bgColor, Color.lightGray));
    }

    if (fgColor.equalsIgnoreCase("random")) {
      setForeground(colorFromString(fgColor, Color.black));
    }

    if (fontIndex > numFonts - 1 ) {
      fontIndex = 0;
    }
    g.setFont(appFont = new Font(fontName, fontStyle, fonts[fontIndex++]));
    FontMetrics fm = getFontMetrics(appFont);

    g.drawString(text, (size().width - fm.stringWidth(text))/2,
      (size().height/2)+10);
  }

  public boolean mouseDown(Event evt, int x, int y) {
    if (threadSuspended) {
      killme.resume();
    } else {
      killme.suspend();
    }
    threadSuspended = !threadSuspended;
    return true;
  }

  public Color colorFromString(String str, Color defaultColor) {
    if (str.equalsIgnoreCase("random")) {
      return new Color((int)(Math.random() * 256), ⇐
```

```
(int)(Math.random() * 256), (int)(Math.random() * 256));
} else {
      try {
         Integer i = Integer.valueOf(str, 16);
         return new Color(i.intValue());
      } catch (NumberFormatException e) {
          return defaultColor;
      }
   }
 }

 public String getAppletInfo() {
    return "GrowingText effect by Jamie M. Hall, 1996";
 }

}
```

Output   The demonstration page for this applet looks like Figure 14-1.

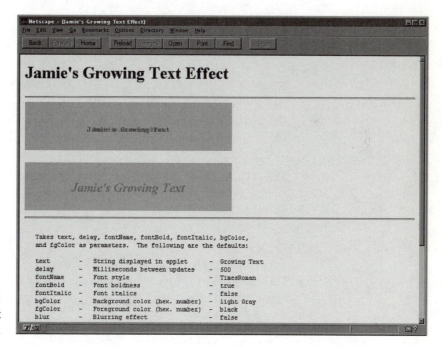

Figure 14-1
The Growing Text applet.

Once you have the source code, the next step is to compile it. On Windows 95 or NT systems, this involves running the program `javac` (which is the compiler). For instance, `javac GrowingText.java` will compile the Java source code file you downloaded. The result of this process should be a file called `GrowingText.class`. The `.class` files are Java binaries, and this is the actual executable applet used by the browser.

QUIZ 1

1. What is the intercommunication between Java, JavaScript, and plug-ins called?
   a. JavaScript
   b. LiveConnect
   c. LiveWire
   d. Internet

2. How can a Java applet interact with a Web page?
   a. Through the use of LiveWire.
   b. Java applets can integrate directly with the browser.
   c. Through the use of JavaScript to pass information from the browser to the Java applet.
   d. Through the use of special HTML tags.

3. What do you need for developing in Java applets?
   a. An HTML editor.
   b. The plug-ins development kit.
   c. The Java Development Kit from Sun.
   d. The HotJava browser.

4. What is Java source code compiled into?
   a. A class file.
   b. An object module.
   c. An executable.
   d. Binary code.

5. What is a class file?
   a. It is just a compressed version of the source code.
   b. The class file is in an executable format and is downloaded and executed by a Java-enabled browser.
   c. A class file is a machine-executable file.
   d. A class file is a Web page containing the Java applet.

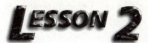

LESSON 2 Java, JavaScript, and HTML

INCORPORATING JAVA APPLETS IN HTML: THE APPLET TAG

Including a Java applet in an HTML file requires the use of the **APPLET** tag. The **APPLET** tag specifies the URL of the Java class file for the applet and tells the browser what size rectangular space to set aside for use by the applet. This is done using the attributes outlined in Table 14-1.

Name	Description
CODE	Specifies the URL binary class file for the applet (this can be relative to the base URL specified with the CODEBASE attribute).
CODEBASE	Specifies the base URL for applets (this points to the directory containing applet code).
WIDTH	Specifies the width of the rectangle set aside for the applet.
HEIGHT	Specifies the height of the rectangle set aside for the applet.

Table 14-1 *Attributes of the APPLET tag.*

The **APPLET** tag is a container tag. Any text between the opening and closing tags will be displayed by browsers that don't support the **APPLET** tag (that is, which don't support the beta version of Java).

In addition to defining the space in which the **APPLET** is able to operate, you can also pass parameters—which can be thought of as arguments—to the applet using the **PARAM** tag. You can include as many **PARAM** tags—which define name-value pairs for the parameters—as you want between the opening and closing **APPLET** tags. The **PARAM** tag takes the form:

```
<PARAM NAME="nameOfParameter" VALUE="valuePassedForParameter">
```

Using the Growing Text applet, which you compiled in Listing 14-1, you can now build a simple Web page that displays the applet in a 500×200 pixel rectangle with the words "Java Really Works" as the text used by the applet.

As you can see in the source code for the applet (Listing 14-1), several parameters are available for you to set:

```
Takes text, delay, fontName, fontBold, fontItalic, bgColor,
    and fgColor as parameters.  The following are the defaults:

    text       -    String displayed in applet    -  Growing Text
    delay      -    Milliseconds between updates   -  500
    fontName   -    Font style                      -  TimesRoman
    fontBold   -    Font boldness                   -  true
    fontItalic -    Font italics                    -  false
    bgColor    -    Background color (hex. number) -  Light Gray
    fgColor    -    Foreground color (hex. number) -  black
    blur       -    Blurring effect                 -  false

    Note: 'random' can be used as the background or foreground color
    to generate a random color on each update.
```

For your Web page, you will use a delay of 250 milliseconds and bold type to test the blurring effect. Listing 14-2 shows how to combine the applet into a Web page.

Input   **Listing 14-2** Combining the Growing Text applet into a Web page.

```
<HTML>

<HEAD>
<TITLE>Example 14.2</TITLE>
</HEAD>

<BODY>
<H1>Java Applet Example</H1>
<APPLET CODE="GrowingText.class" WIDTH=500 HEIGHT=200>
<PARAM NAME="text" VALUE="Java Really Works">
<PARAM NAME="delay" VALUE="250">
<PARAM NAME="bold" VALUE="true">
<PARAM NAME="blur" VALUE="true">
</APPLET>
</BODY>

</HTML>
```

Output   Figure 14-2 illustrates the effects of the script.

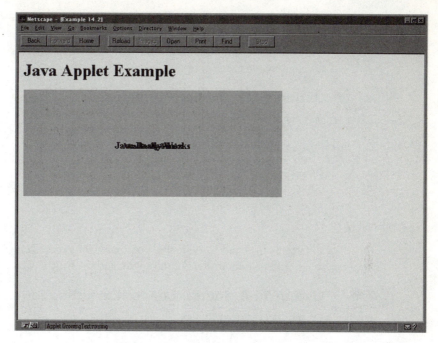

Figure 14-2
The APPLET tag lets you define the space available to the applet.

Analysis　　There are several things to notice in this example. First, there are default values for many of the parameters, so you don't actually need any parameters to get the applet to work. The parameters are like optional arguments. In this case, you can use as few or as many as you like.

The Java applet continues to run until you leave the page or close Netscape.

WORKING WITH JAVA IN NAVIGATOR 2.0

Although the `applet` object is not available in the version of JavaScript implemented in Navigator 2.0, it is still possible to create limited interaction between applets and the browser environment, using JavaScript.

For instance, with JavaScript's capability to dynamically generate HTML code, a form in one frame could easily reload a Java applet in another frame, with new parameters.

While this is not truly interacting with an applet while it is loaded and executing, it can produce the appearance that the applet is better integrated into a Web application.

To demonstrate how dynamically written HTML can be used to change the state of an applet in another frame, let's build a simple testing program for the Growing Text applet.

This program should enable the user to enter a string, select options from check-boxes, and fill in fields. When the user clicks on a Test button, the applet should be reloaded in a second frame with the new parameters. Listings 14-3 through 14-5 are the source code for this application.

Input   **Listing 14-3** The parent frameset.

```
<!-- SOURCE CODE OF PARENT FRAMESET -->

<FRAMESET ROWS="50%,*">

  <FRAME SRC="javatest.html" NAME="form">
  <FRAME SRC="blank.html" NAME="applet">


</FRAMESET>
```

Listings 14-4 and 14-5 are the source code for `javatest.html` that provides a form to test different parameters of the applet and the code to display it.

Input   **Listing 14-4** Source code for the testing form.

```
<!-- SOURCE CODE FOR JAVATEST.HTML -->

<HEAD>
<TITLE>Example 14.4</TITLE>
</HEAD>

<BODY BGCOLOR="#FFFFFF">
<H1>Growing Text Java Applet Tester</H1>
<FORM METHOD=POST>
Text to display: <INPUT TYPE=text NAME="text" SIZE=40><BR>
Delay between updates: <INPUT TYPE=text NAME="delay"><BR>
Font to use: <INPUT TYPE=text NAME="font" SIZE=40><BR>
<INPUT TYPE=checkbox NAME="bold"> Bold
<INPUT TYPE=checkbox NAME="blur"> Blur<BR>
<INPUT TYPE=button VALUE="Test Applet" ⇐
onClick="parent['applet'].location='applet.html';"> </FORM>
</BODY>

</HTML>
```

Input   **Listing 14-5** The code to display the applet.

```
<!-- SOURCE CODE FOR applet.html -->

<BODY>
<SCRIPT LANGUAGE="JavaScript">
<!-- HIDE FROM OTHER BROWSERS
```

```
  document.write('<APPLET CODE="GrowingText.class" WIDTH=500 HEIGHT=200>');
  document.write('<PARAM NAME="text" VALUE="' + ⇐
parent["form"].document.forms[0].text.value + '">');
document.write('<PARAM NAME="delay" VALUE="' + ⇐
parent["form"].document.forms[0].delay.value + '">');
document.write('<PARAM NAME="fontName" VALUE="' + ⇐
parent["form"].document.forms[0].font.value + '">');
document.write('<PARAM NAME="boldBold" VALUE="' + ⇐
parent["form"].document.forms[0].bold.value + '">');
document.write('<PARAM NAME="blur" VALUE="' + ⇐
parent["form"].document.forms[0].blur.value + '">');
document.write('</APPLET>');
// STOP HIDING -->
</SCRIPT>
</BODY>
```

Output The results appear in Figure 14-3.

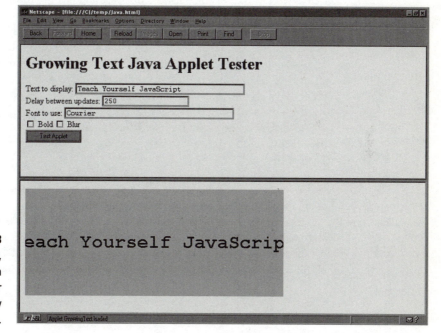

Figure 14-3
Using JavaScript,
you can reload an
applet in another
frame with new
parameters.

Analysis

The process by which you update the applet parameters is fairly straight forward: In the upper frame, you load the form, which you use to change the parameters of the applet. In the lower frame, you load the file `applet.html` which builds the `APPLET` and `PARAM` tags in a script. The script in `applet.html` assigns the relevant `PARAM` values based on the values in the form in the other frame (using `parent["form"]` to reference the named frame).

The file `javatest.html` makes minimal use of JavaScript. The only place you use JavaScript is in the `onClick` event handler in the form button where you reload `applet.html` into the lower frame to get it to restart the applet with the new parameters.

THE applets ARRAY

Starting with Navigator 3.0, Netscape has added the ability for two-way communication between Java and JavaScript. JavaScript can call public methods in Java applets as well as work with Java objects and properties, and Java applets can call JavaScript functions.

In this section we will look at how to call Java applets from JavaScript scripts since this is the key tool to making JavaScript the glue for Java applets.

Java applets are reflected into the JavaScipt environment through the `applets` array— an array of `applet` objects. Each applet is reflected by a single entry in the array in the order in which they appear in the source code of the HTML document. The `applets` array is a property of the `document` object.

For instance, the second applet in a document would be accessed with `document.applets[1]`. Applets can be named using the `NAME` attribute of the `APPLET` tag. The applet

```
<APPLET CODE="codeURL" WIDTH=width HEIGHT=height NAME=appletName>
```

could then be accessed with `document.appletName`.

Properties and methods of the applet are then reflected in JavaScript as properties and methods of the corresponding `applet` object.

The following listing includes the Growing Text applet used earlier and adds two HTML form buttons—Start and Stop—which allow the user to start and stop the applet:

```
<HTML>

<HEAD>
<TITLE>applet Example</TITLE>
</HEAD>

<BODY>

<APPLET CODE="GrowingText.class" WIDTH=500 HEIGHT=200 NAME="Growing">
<PARAM NAME="text" VALUE="Java and JavaScript">
</APPLET>
```

```
<HR>

<FORM>
<INPUT TYPE=button VALUE="Start" onClick="document.Growing.start()">
<INPUT TYPE=button VALUE="Stop" onClick="document.Growing.stop()">
</FORM>

</BODY>

</HTML>
```

Here, the `onClick` event handlers in the INPUT tags are used to call the `stop()` and `start()` methods of the Growing Text applet.

The Java Environment

In addition to being able to access properties and methods in an applet, it is possible to access any Java class or packages. However, this requires knowledge of the Java environment and how to use Java classes and packages.

More details on how to do this are available on Netscape's Web site. The subject is also covered in detail in the *JavaScript 1.1 Developer's Guide* from Sams.net Publishing.

FROM JAVASCRIPT TO JAVA

For many of you, the next step after reading this book will be to look into learning Java. This isn't that outrageous an idea.

By learning JavaScript, you have learned the fundamental syntax used throughout Java. You are familiar with how Java commands are built, how to use loops, and how to build expressions.

Of course, Java is not the same as JavaScript. Besides being compiled and having access to the same set of objects JavaScript does, there are other significant differences:

● Static Binding: In JavaScript, you are able to refer to objects in your scripts that may not exist when the script is first loaded and checked for errors. In Java, a program will not compile unless all objects being referred to exist at the time of compilation.

● Object-orientation: JavaScript implements only a limited object model. Java takes this further to include classes and inheritance—two important aspects of true object-oriented programming.

● Graphics and GUI capabilities: Java provides graphics primitives and the ability to generate GUI elements that are not available in JavaScript.

The result of these and other more subtle differences between Java and JavaScript is that Java programming can be more complex and require more rigorous debugging and organization than JavaScript scripts.

At the same time, with Java it is possible to write complete standalone applications and to perform actions not possible with JavaScript.

The types of applications and applets being developed with Java are wide and varied. A quick glance through a Java archive, such as Gamelan, shows that the major categories of Java applet development include:

Arts and Entertainment: Applets range from portrait-painting tools to interactive drag-and-drop poetry creators to simple drawing tools.

Business and Finance: Numerous applets have been created for business applications including stock ticker tapes, real estate viewing tools, shopping carts, and spreadsheets.

Education: Included in the educational applications of Java today are rotatable, three-dimensional molecular models, an interactive abacus, an animated juggling tutorial, and multilingual word-matching games.

Multimedia: Multimedia is the most talked-about area of Java development and includes animation tools, fractal drawing applets, electronic publishing systems, audio players, and MIDI applications.

Network: Applets in this area include terminal emulators and chat applications.

Utilities: Utilities developed as Java applets range from font viewers to graphical calculators to clocks.

Currently, JavaScript is limited to products from Netscape, and more recently in the Windows 95 and NT versions of Microsoft's Web browser, Internet Explorer. The most prominent use of JavaScript, which we have discussed throughout this book, is the use of the language for developing client-end applications that are integrated into HTML pages displayed in the Navigator or Internet Explorer browsers.

However, Netscape also has implemented JavaScript to use at the server end, much like CGI programming. Using the Netscape product called LiveWire—a server package for developing sophisticated interactive Web applications—it is possible to create CGI-like scripts using JavaScript. This simplifies Web development in many ways because programming at both ends can be done in the same language, rather than requiring the use of JavaScript for the client end of an application and using Perl, C, or another language for the server end.

COMMUNICATING WITH PLUG-INS

In addition to communication between JavaScript and Java applets, LiveConnect also makes it possible for JavaScript to interact with Navigator plug-ins that have been designed to provide LiveConnect support.

Navigator 3 includes several plug-ins, such as LiveVideo and LiveAudio, which provide the necessary support for LiveConnect and can be accessed from within JavaScript scripts.

A list of available plug-ins is on the Web at

http://home.netscape.com/comprod/products/navigator/version⇐
_2.0/plugins/index.html

The EMBED Tag

Plug-ins are included in an HTML file with the **EMBED** tag. The **EMBED** tag is similar to the **IMG** tag and the **APPLET** tag. It allows the embedding of a plug-in file format into a Web page to be downloaded when the page is being rendered by the browser.

The tag takes the following attributes:

- HEIGHT: Specifies the height of the space to allot for the object. HEIGHT is specified in the units defined with the UNITS attribute.

- SRC: Specifies the URL of the object to be embedded.

- WIDTH: Specifies the width of the space to allot for the object. WIDTH is specified in the units defined with the UNITS attribute.

- HIDDEN: Specifies whether the plug-in should be visible. Takes the value true or false and overrides the HEIGHT and WIDTH tags if set to true.

- PALETTE: Specifies the color palette mode for the plug-in. Can either be set to foreground or background and is only used on Windows versions of Navigator.

- PLUGINSPAGE: Specifies the URL for a page containing instructions on downloading the plug-in for the embedded type. Used by Navigator's assisted installation feature.

- TYPE: Specifies the MIME type for the <EMBED> tag. <EMBED> tags require either the SRC or TYPE attribute.

- NAME: Specifies a name for the embedded plug-in object.

- UNITS: Specifies the unit of measurement for the HEIGHT and WIDTH attributes. UNITS takes the value pixels or en—which equals half a point size. Pixels is the default value for UNITS.

Similar to frames where the <NOFRAMES> tag provided a mechanism to include alternate HTML code for browsers that don't support frames, the <NOEMBED> tag enables authors to specify HTML code to display in browsers that don't support the <EMBED> tag, and therefore don't support plug-ins.

For example, the HTML code

```
<BODY>
This is a QuickTime movie:<BR>
<EMBED SRC="sample.qt" WIDTH=100 HEIGHT=100 UNITS=pixels>
<NOEMBED>
<H1>Sorry!</H1>
You need a plug-ins capable browser.
</NOEMBED>
</BODY>
```

will display the text "Sorry! You need a plug-ins capable browser." in browsers that don't support the <EMBED> tag.

JavaScript includes two objects—mimeTypes and plug-ins—which can be used in scripts to determine if specific plug-ins or MIME types are supported. Both are properties of the navigator object.

The plugins **Object**

The plugins object is an array of plugin objects, reflecting each of the available plug-ins in the browser.

Each entry in the plugins array has five properties:

- name: The name of the plug-in.

- filename: The filename of the plug-in on the local system.

- description: The description provided by the plug-in.

- length: The number of plug-ins.

- mimeTypes: An array indicating the MIME types supported by the plug-in—this has the same characteristics as the mimeTypes object discussed later in this chapter.

It is possible to check for the existence of a particular plug-in by evaluating the plug-in object itself. The code segment

```
if (navigator.plugins["ShockWave"])
    document.writeln('<EMBED SRC="sample.dir" HEIGHT=50 WIDTH=50>');
else
    document.writeln('Install the Shockwave plug-in');
```

outputs the appropriate HTML, based on the existence of the Shockwave plug-in.

The mimeTypes Object

mimeTypes is an array of all the MIME types supported by the browser through any means, including plug-ins and helper applications. Each MIME type is represented by a mimeType object. The array itself is indexed by number or by MIME type names.

The mimeType object has three properties:

●   name: The name of the MIME type such as image/jpeg or video/avi.

●   description: A description of the MIME type.

●   suffixes: A string containing a comma-separated list of file suffixes for the MIME type.

For instance, for TIFF images, navigator.mimeTypes["image/tiff"].suffixes might have the value "tiff, tif" and navigator.mimeTypes["images/tiff"].description might be equal to "TIFF Image".

The embeds Array

Where the plugins array provided information about each plug-in supported by the browser, the embeds array reflects each of the plug-ins used by an EMBED tag in a document.

The entries in the array reflect each of the EMBED tags in their order of appearance in the HTML source code. The embeds array is a property of the document object. Each entry in the array has no properties or methods, but provides a mechanism for calling the plug-ins methods from JavaScript.

Calling Plugin Methods from JavaScript

Plug-ins that have been written to interact with JavaScript through LiveConnect make available what are known as *native methods*. These methods are available to be called by JavaScript scripts as methods of the particular entry in the embeds array.

For instance, most versions of Navigator 3.0 come with the LiveVideo plug-in. This plug-in's object is accessible in Java (and therefore in JavaScript).

The LiveVideo plug-in documentation indicates that it makes four native methods available to the Java environment:

●   play(): Start playing the source file from the current position.

●   stop(): Stop playing.

●   seek(position): Sets the current position to position where position indicates a frame number.

●   rewind(): Sets the current position to the start of the video.

Using these methods, you can use JavaScript to create a simple control panel for an embedded audio file:

```
<BODY>

<EMBED SRC="demo.avi" NAME="testVideo" HEIGHT=100 WIDTH=100>

<FORM>
<INPUT TYPE=button VALUE="Play" onClick="document.embeds[0].play(false);">
<INPUT TYPE=button VALUE="Stop" onClick="document.testVideo.stop(false);">
</FORM>

</BODY>
```

This file uses JavaScript event handlers to provide control buttons for the video file specified in the EMBED tag. Notice that the plug-in is referred to both by its position in the embeds array as well as by name.

1. Which of the following is correct for embedding the applet GrowingText into an HTML page?
   a. `<SCRIPT LANGUAGE="Java" SRC="GrowingText.class"> </SCRIPT>`
   b. `<APPLET CODE="GrowingText.class PARAM NAME="bold" VALUE="true">` `</APPLET>`
   c. `<APPLET CODE="GrowingText.class"> </APPLET>`
   d. `<APPLET CODE="GrowingText.class"> <PARAM bold="true"> </APPLET>`

2. What is the PARAM tag and what is it used for?
   a. It is used for setting parameters for a plug-in.
   b. It is used for passing named parameter values to an applet.
   c. It is used for naming the parameters of an applet.
   d. It is the tag used for identifying applet parameters for use by JavaScript.

3. What is the applets array and what methods are available?
   a. The applets array has an entry for each applet currently loaded and name and parameter are the methods available.
   b. The applets array has an entry for each applet currently available and there is only the name method.
   c. The applets array lists the applets embedded in the document and has no methods available.
   d. The applets array reflects the applets of each Java applet in the current document; while the methods available vary depending on the actual applet for the array entry.

4. In the following HTML code, what are `'document.embeds[0]'` and `'document.testVideo'`?

```
<BODY>
<EMBED SRC="demo.avi" NAME="testVideo" HEIGHT=100 WIDTH=100>
<FORM>
<INPUT TYPE=button VALUE="Play" onClick="document.embeds[0].play(false);">
<INPUT TYPE=button VALUE="Stop" onClick="document.testVideo.stop(false);">
</FORM>
</BODY>
```

    a. `'embeds[0]'` references the embedded play object, while the other references the stop object.
    b. They are both references to the same embedded video object.
    c. `embeds[0]` references the play method while `testVideo` references the stop method.
    d. None of the above.

5. Both the `plugins` array and the `embeds` array deal with plug-ins, why is there need for both of them?
    a. Because the `plugins` array tells which plug-ins are supported by the browser, the `embeds` array tells you which plug-ins are actually used by the current document.
    b. They both provide the same information so only one is really needed.
    c. The `plugins` array is the mechanism to communicate with the plug-in, while the `embeds` array just lists what plug-ins are available.
    d. The `embeds` array has no properties, while the `plugins` array does.

SUMMARY

Having learned to use JavaScript, you looked in this chapter at the relationship between JavaScript and Java and the relationship between JavaScript and plug-ins.

We discussed how the `applet` object allows JavaScript applications to interact with Java applets. You also learned how to incorporate existing Java applets into HTML pages and to use JavaScript to pass custom parameters to the applets you are using.

Finally, you took a look at how to make the move from JavaScript scripting to Java programming and considered the future development of JavaScript.

A discussion of the `mimeTypes` and `plugins` objects, plus the `embeds` array, provided an introduction to interacting with plug-ins from JavaScript.

APPENDIX A

JAVASCRIPT REFERENCE RESOURCES

The following is a list of selected JavaScript and Java reference resources on the Internet, organized by type of resource.

WORLD WIDE WEB SITES

JavaScript Overview: Netscape's brief introduction to JavaScript, which includes pointers to several examples and a link to the JavaScript documentation.

```
http://home.netscape.com/comprod/products/navigator/version_2.0/script/index.html
```

JavaScript Documentation: Netscape's official JavaScript documentation and reference materials.

```
http://home.netscape.com/eng/mozilla/Gold/handbook/javascript/index.html
```

JavaScript Index: A comprehensive index of JavaScript-related pages, including sites using JavaScript, teaching JavaScript, and offering JavaScript consulting and development services.

```
http://www.c2.org/~andreww/javascript/
```

JavaScript Library: A growing library of JavaScript examples and applications available on the Web.

```
http://www.c2.org/~andreww/javascript/lib/
```

JavaScript PDF Documentation: The JavaScript documentation from the Netscape Web site in Adobe Acrobat format for easy printing.

`http://www.ipst.com/docs.htm`

Morphic Molecules: A collection of advanced information and mini-tutorials about different aspects of JavaScript.

`http://www.txdirect.net/users/everett/`

Learning JavaScript with Windows Help: Offers a Windows help file with information for learning JavaScript.

`http://www.jchelp.com/javahelp/javahelp.htm`

JavaScript Tutorial: A growing tutorial covering many aspects of JavaScript.

`http://www.webconn.com/java/javascript/intro`

Gamelan: A leading repository of Java applets, which also includes a JavaScript section.

`http://www.gamelan.com/`

Java Home Page: Sun's source of official information about Java.

`http://www.javasoft.com`

MAILING LISTS

JavaHouse: Focuses on Java with some coverage of JavaScript.

`http://www.center.nitech.ac.jp/ml/java-house/hypermail/0000`

JavaScript List: Focuses on JavaScript (can be high volume).
Subscribe by sending an e-mail to `majordomo@obscure.org` with "subscribe JavaScript" in the message body.

NEWSGROUPS

`comp.lang.java.misc`: Discussion of Java with some JavaScript talk.

`news:comp.lang.java.misc`

`comp.lang.javascript`: Discussion of JavaScript.

`news:comp.lang.javascript`

Livesoftware's Developer Group:

`news://news.livesoftware.com/`

APPENDIX B

JAVASCRIPT LANGUAGE REFERENCE

The first part of this reference is organized by object with properties and methods listed by the object they apply to. The second part covers independent functions in JavaScript not connected with a particular object, as well as operators in JavaScript.

The following codes are used to indicate where objects, methods, properties and event handlers are implemented:

- C   Client JavaScript (Server JavaScript is not covered in this appendix)

- 2   Netscape Navigator 2

- 3   Netscape Navigator 3

- I   Microsoft Internet Explorer 3

THE anchor OBJECT [C|2|3|I]

The **anchor** object reflects an HTML anchor.

Properties

- **name**   A string value indicating the name of the anchor. [Not 2|3]

THE applet OBJECT [C|3]

The **applet** object reflects a Java applet included in a Web page with the **APPLET** tag.

Properties

- **name** A string reflecting the NAME attribute of the APPLET tag.

THE area OBJECT [C|3]

The **area** object reflects a clickable area defined in an imagemap. **area** objects appear as entries in the **links** array of the **document** object.

Properties

- **hash** A string value indicating an anchor name from the URL.

- **host** A string value reflecting the host and domain name portion of the URL.

- **hostname** A string value indicating the host, domain name, and port number from the URL.

- **href** A string value reflecting the entire URL.

- **pathname** A string value reflecting the path portion of the URL (excluding the host, domain name, port number, and protocol).

- **port** A string value indicating the port number from the URL.

- **protocol** A string value indicating the protocol portion of the URL, including the trailing colon.

- **search** A string value specifying the query portion of the URL (after the question mark).

- **target** A string value reflecting the TARGET attribute of the AREA tag.

Event Handlers

- **onMouseOut** Specifies JavaScript code to execute when the mouse moves outside the area specified in the AREA tag.

● **onMouseOver**   Specifies JavaScript code to execute when the mouse enters the area specified in the AREA tag.

THE array OBJECT [Cl3ll]

Provides a mechanism for creating and working with arrays. New arrays are created with `arrayName = new Array()` or `arrayName = new Array(arrayLength)`.

Properties

● **length**   An integer value reflecting the number of elements in an array.

● **prototype**   Provides a mechanism to add properties to an Array object.

Methods

● **join(string)**   Returns a string containing each element of the array, separated by string. [Not I]

● **reverse()**   Reverses the order of an array. [Not I]

● **sort(function)**   Sorts an array based on its function. If function is omitted, the sort defaults to dictionary order. [Not I]

THE button OBJECT [Cl2l3ll]

The **button** object reflects a push button from an HTML form in JavaScript.

Properties

● **enabled**   A Boolean value indicating if the button is enabled. [Not 2l3]

● **form**   A reference to the form object containing the button. [Not 2l3]

● **name**   A string value containing the name of the button element.

● **type**   A string value reflecting the TYPE attribute of the INPUT tag. [Not 2lI]

● **value**   A string value containing the value of the button element.

Methods

- **click()** Emulates the action of clicking on the button.

- **focus()** Gives focus to the button. [Not 2|3]

Event Handlers

- **onClick** Specifies JavaScript code to execute when the button is clicked.

- **onFocus** Specifies JavaScript code to execute when the button receives focus. [Not 2|3]

THE checkbox OBJECT [C|2|3|I]

The **checkbox** object makes a checkbox in an HTML form available in JavaScript.

Properties

- **checked** A Boolean value indicating if the checkbox element is checked.

- **defaultChecked** A Boolean value indicating if the checkbox element was checked by default (i.e., reflects the CHECKED attribute).

- **enabled** A Boolean value indicating if the checkbox is enabled. [Not 2|3]

- **form** A reference to the form object containing the checkbox. [Not 2|3]

- **name** A string value containing the name of the checkbox element.

- **type** A string value reflecting the TYPE attribute of the INPUT tag. [Not 2|I]

- **value** A string value containing the value of the checkbox element.

Methods

- **click()** Emulates the action of clicking on the checkbox.

- **focus()** Gives focus to the checkbox. [Not 2|3]

Event Handlers

- **onClick** Specifies JavaScript code to execute when the checkbox is clicked.

● **onFocus** Specifies JavaScript code to execute when the checkbox receives focus. [Not 2I3]

THE combo OBJECT [CII]

The **combo** object reflects a combo field in JavaScript.

Properties

● **enabled** A Boolean value indicating if the combo is enabled. [Not 2I3]

● **form** A reference to the form object containing the combo. [Not 2I3]

● **listCount** An integer reflecting the number of elements in the list.

● **listIndex** An integer reflecting the index of the selected element in the list.

● **multiSelect** A Boolean value indicating if the combo field is in multi-select mode.

● **name** A string value reflecting the name of the combo field.

● **value** A string containing the value of the combo field.

Methods

● **addItem(index)** Adds an item to the combo field before the item at index.

● **click()** Simulates a click on the combo field.

● **clear()** Clears the contents of the combo field.

● **focus()** Gives focus to the combo field.

● **removeItem(index)** Removes the item at index from the combo field.

Event Handlers

● **onClick** Specifies JavaScript code to execute when the mouse clicks on the combo field.

● **onFocus** Specifies JavaScript code to execute when the combo field receives focus.

THE Date OBJECT [Cl2l3ll]

The **Date** object provides mechanisms for working with dates and times in JavaScript. Instances of the object can be created with the syntax

```
newObjectName = new Date(dateInfo)
```

where **dateInfo** is an optional specification of a particular date and can be one of the following:

```
"month day, year hours:minutes:seconds"
year, month, day
year, month, day, hours, minutes, seconds
```

where the later two options represent integer values.

If no **dateInfo** is specified, the new object will represent the current date and time.

Properties

- **prototype** Provides a mechanism for adding properties to a Date object. [Not 2]

Methods

- **getDate()** Returns the day of the month for the current Date object as an integer from 1 to 31.

- **getDay()** Returns the day of the week for the current Date object as an integer from 0 to 6 (where 0 is Sunday, 1 is Monday, and so on).

- **getHours()** Returns the hour from the time in the current Date object as an integer from 0 to 23.

- **getMinutes()** Returns the minutes from the time in the current Date object as an integer from 0 to 59.

- **getMonth()** Returns the month for the current Date object as an integer from 0 to 11 (where 0 is January, 1 is February, and so on).

- **getSeconds()** Returns the seconds from the time in the current Date object as an integer from 0 to 59.

- **getTime()** Returns the time of the current Date object as an integer representing the number of milliseconds since 1 January 1970 at 00:00:00.

- **getTimezoneOffset()** Returns the difference between the local time and GMT as an integer representing the number of minutes.

- **getYear()** Returns the year for the current Date object as a two-digit integer representing the year less 1900.

- **parse(dateString)** Returns the number of milliseconds between January 1, 1970, at 00:00:00 and the date specified in dateString. dateString should take the format [Not I]

  ```
  Day, DD Mon YYYY HH:MM:SS TZN
  Mon DD, YYYY
  ```

- **setDate(dateValue)** Sets the day of the month for the current Date object. dateValue is an integer from 1 to 31.

- **setHours(hoursValue)** Sets the hours for the time for the current Date object. hoursValue is an integer from 0 to 23.

- **setMinutes(minutesValue)** Sets the minutes for the time for the current Date object. minutesValue is an integer from 0 to 59.

- **setMonth(monthValue)** Sets the month for the current Date object. monthValue is an integer from 0 to 11 (where 0 is January, 1 is February, and so forth.

- **setSeconds(secondsValue)** Sets the seconds for the time for the current Date object. secondsValue is an integer from 0 to 59.

- **setTime(timeValue)** Sets the value for the current Date object. timeValue is an integer representing the number of milliseconds since January 1, 1970, at 00:00:00.

- **setYear(yearValue)** Sets the year for the current Date object. yearValue is an integer greater than 1900.

- **toGMTString()** Returns the value of the current Date object in GMT as a string using Internet conventions in the form

  ```
  Day, DD Mon YYYY HH:MM:SS GMT
  ```

- **toLocaleString()** Returns the value of the current Date object in the local time using local conventions.

- **UTC(yearValue, monthValue, dateValue, hoursValue, minutesValue, secondsValue)** Returns the number of milliseconds since January 1, 1970, at 00:00:00 GMT. yearValue is an integer greater than 1900. monthValue is an integer from 0 to 11. dateValue is an integer from 1 to 31. hoursValue is an integer from 0 to 23. minutesValue and secondsValue are integers from 0 to 59. hoursValue minutesValue, and secondsValue, are optional. [Not I]

THE document OBJECT [Cl2l3ll]

The document object reflects attributes of an HTML document in JavaScript.

Properties

- **alinkColor**   The color of active links as a string or a hexadecimal triplet.

- **anchors**   Array of anchor objects in the order they appear in the HTML document. Use anchors.length to get the number of anchors in a document.

- **applets**   Array of applet objects in the order they appear in the HTML document. Use applets.length to get the number of applets in a document. [Not 2]

- **bgColor**   The color of the document's background.

- **cookie**   A string value containing cookie values for the current document.

- **embeds**   Array of plugin objects in the order they appear in the HTML document. Use embeds.length to get the number of plugins in a document. [Not 2ll]

- **fgColor**   The color of the document's foreground.

- **forms**   Array of form objects in the order the forms appear in the HTML file. Use forms.length to get the number of forms in a document.

- **images**   Array of image objects in the order they appear in the HTML document. Use images.length to get the number of images in a document. [Not 2ll]

- **lastModified**   String value containing the last date of modification of the document.

- **linkColor**   The color of links as a string or a hexadecimal triplet.

- **links**   Array of link objects in the order the hypertext links appear in the HTML document. Use links.length to get the number of links in a document.

- **location**   A string containing the URL of the current document. Use document.URL instead of document.location. This property is expected to disappear in a future release.

- **referrer**   A string value containing the URL of the calling document when the user follows a link.

- **title** A string containing the title of the current document.

- **URL** A string reflecting the URL of the current document. Use instead of `document.location`. [Not I]

- **vlinkColor** The color of followed links as a string or a hexadecimal triplet.

Methods

- **clear()** Clears the document window. [Not I]

- **close()** Closes the current output stream.

- **open(mimeType)** Opens a stream which allows `write()` and `writeln()` methods to write to the document window. `mimeType` is an optional string which specifies a document type supported by Navigator or a plug-in (i.e. `text/html`, `image/gif`, etc.).

- **write()** Writes text and HTML to the specified document.

- **writeln()** Writes text and HTML to the specified document followed by a newline character.

THE FILEUPLOAD [C|3]

Reflects a file upload element in an HTML form.

Properties

- **name** A string value reflecting the name of the file upload element.

- **value** A string value reflecting the file upload element's field.

THE form OBJECT [C|2|3|I]

The **form** object reflects an HTML form in JavaScript. Each HTML form in a document is reflected by a distinct instance of the **form** object.

Properties

- **action** A string value specifying the URL that the form data is submitted to.

- **elements** Array of objects for each form element in the order in which they appear in the form.

- **encoding** String containing the MIME encoding of the form as specified in the ENCTYPE attribute.

- **method** A string value containing the method of submission of form data to the server.

- **target** A string value containing the name of the window that responses to form submissions are directed to.

Methods

- **reset()** Resets the form. [Not 2II]

- **submit()** Submits the form.

Event Handlers

- **onReset** Specifies JavaScript code to execute when the form is reset. [Not 2II]

- **onSubmit** Specifies JavaScript code to execute when the form is submitted. The code should return a true value to allow the form to be submitted. A false value prevents the form from being submitted.

THE frame OBJECT [CI2I3II]

The frame object reflects a frame window in JavaScript.

Properties

- **frames** An array of objects for each frame in a window. Frames appear in the array in the order in which they appear in the HTML source code.

- **onblur** A string reflecting the onBlur event handler for the frame. New values can be assigned to this property to change the event handler. [Not 2]

- **onfocus** A string reflecting the onFocus event handler for the frame. New values can be assigned to this property to change the event handler. [Not 2]

- **parent**   A string indicating the name of the window containing the frameset.

- **self**   An alternative for the name of the current window.

- **top**   An alternative for the name of the top-most window.

- **window**   An alternative for the name of the current window.

Methods

- **alert(message)**   Displays `message` in a dialog box.

- **blur()**   Removes focus from the frame. [Not 2]

- **close()**   Closes the window.

- **confirm(message)**   Displays `message` in a dialog box with OK and CANCEL buttons. Returns `true` or `false` based on the button clicked by the user.

- **focus()**   Gives focus to the frame. [Not 2]

- **open(url,name,features)**   Opens `url` in a window named `name`. If `name` doesn't exist, a new window is created with that name. `features` is an optional string argument containing a list of features for the new window. The feature list contains any of the following name-value pairs separated by commas and without additional spaces:

`toolbar=[yes,no,1,0]`	Indicates if the window should have a toolbar.
`location=[yes,no,1,0]`	Indicates if the window should have a location field.
`directories=[yes,no,1,0]`	Indicates if the window should have directory buttons.
`status=[yes,no,1,0]`	Indicates if the window should have a status bar.
`menubar=[yes,no,1,0]`	Indicates if the window should have menus.
`scrollbars=[yes,no,1,0]`	Indicates if the window should have scroll bars.
`resizable=[yes,no,1,0]`	Indicates if the window should be resizable.
`width=pixels`	Indicates the width of the window in pixels.
`height=pixels`	Indicates the height of the window in pixels.

- **prompt(message,response)** Displays message in a dialog box with a text entry field with the default value of response. The user's response in the text entry field is returned as a string.

- **setTimeout(expression,time)** Evaluates expression after time where time is a value in milliseconds. The timeout can be named with the structure

  ```
  name = setTimeOut(expression,time)
  ```

- **clearTimeout(name)** Cancels the timeout with the name name.

Event Handlers

- **onBlur** Specifies JavaScript code to execute when focus is removed from a frame. [Not 2]

- **onFocus** Specifies JavaScript code to execute when blur is removed from a frame. [Not 2]

THE Function OBJECT [Cl3]

The Function object provides a mechanism for indicating JavaScript code to compile as a function. The syntax to use the Function object is `functionName = new Function(arg1, arg2, arg3, ..., functionCode)`. This is similar to

```
function functionName(arg1, arg2, arg3, ...) {
    functionCode
}
```

except that in the former `functionName` is variable with a reference to the function and the function is evaluated each time it is used rather than being compiled once.

Properties

- **arguments** An integer reflecting the number of arguments in a function.

- **prototype** Provides a a mechanism for adding properties to a Function object.

THE hidden OBJECT [C|2|3|I]

The **hidden** object reflects a hidden field from an HTML form in JavaScript.

Properties

- **name**   A string value containing the name of the hidden element.

- **type**   A string value reflecting the TYPE property of the INPUT tag. [Not 2|I]

- **value**   A string value containing the value of a hidden text element.

THE history OBJECT [C|2|3|I]

The **history** object allows a script to work with the Navigator browser's history list in JavaScript. For security and privacy reasons, the actual content of the list is not reflected into JavaScript.

Properties

- **length**   An integer representing the number of items on the history list. [Not I]

Methods

- **back()**   Goes back to the previous document in the history list. [Not I]

- **forward()**   Goes forward to the next document in the history list. [Not I]

- **go(location)**   Goes to the document in the history list specified by location. location can be a string or integer value. If it is a string, it represents all or part of a URL in the history list. If it is an integer, location represents the relative position of the document on the history list. As an integer, location can be positive or negative. [Not I]

THE Image OBJECT [C|3]

The **Image** object reflects an image included in an HTML document.

Properties

- **border** An integer value reflecting the width of the image's border in pixels.

- **complete** A Boolean value indicating if the image has finished loading.

- **height** An integer value reflecting the height of an image in pixels.

- **hspace** An integer value reflecting the HSPACE attribute of the IMG tag.

- **lowsrc** A string value containing the URL of the low-resolution version of the image to load.

- **name** A string value indicating the name of the Image object.

- **prototype** Provides a mechanism for adding properties as an Image object.

- **src** A string value indicating the URL of the image.

- **vspace** An integer value reflecting the VSPACE attribute of the IMG tag.

- **width** An integer value indicating the width of an image in pixels.

Event Handlers

- **onAbort** Specifies JavaScript code to execute if the attempt to load the image is aborted. [Not 2]

- **onError** Specifies JavaScript code to execute if there is an error while loading the image. Setting this event handler to null suppresses error messages if an error does occur while loading. [Not 2]

- **onLoad** Specifies JavaScript code to execute when the image finishes loading. [Not 2]

THE Link OBJECT [C|2|3|I]

The Link object reflects a hypertext link in the body of a document.

Properties

- **hash** A string value containing the anchor name in the URL.

- **host** A string value containing the hostname and port number from the URL.

● **hostname** A string value containing the domain name (or numerical IP address) from the URL.

● **href** A string value containing the entire URL.

● **pathname** A string value specifying the path portion of the URL.

● **port** A string value containing the port number from the URL.

● **protocol** A string value containing the protocol from the URL (including the colon, but not the slashes).

● **search** A string value containing any information passed to a GET CGI-BIN call (for example, any information after the question mark).

● **target** A string value containing the name of the window or frame specified in the TARGET attribute.

Event Handlers

● **moveMouse** Specifies JavaScript code to execute when the mouse pointer moves over the link. [Not 2|3]

● **onClick** Specifies JavaScript code to execute when the link is clicked.

● **onMouseOver** Specifies JavaScript code to execute when the mouse pointer moves over the hypertext link.

THE location OBJECT [C|2|3|I]

The **location** object reflects information about the current URL.

Properties

● **hash** A string value containing the anchor name in the URL.

● **host** A string value containing the hostname and port number from the URL.

● **hostname** A string value containing the domain name (or numerical IP address) from the URL.

● **href** A string value containing the entire URL.

● **pathname** A string value specifying the path portion of the URL.

- **port** A string value containing the port number from the URL.

- **protocol** A string value containing the protocol from the URL (including the colon, but not the slashes).

- **search** A string value containing any information passed to a GET CGI-BIN call (for example, any information after the question mark).

Methods

- **reload()** Reloads the current document. [Not 2II]

- **replace(url)** Loads url over the current entry in the history list, making it impossible to navigate back to the previous URL with the back button. [Not 2II]

THE Math OBJECT [Cl2l3lI]

The Math object provides properties and methods for advanced mathematical calculations.

Properties

- **E** The value of Euler's constant (roughly 2.718) used as the base for natural logarithms.

- **LN10** The value of the natural logarithm of 10 (roughly 2.302).

- **LN2** The value of the natural logarithm of 2 (roughly 0.693).

- **LOG10E** The value of the base 10 logarithm of e (roughly 0.434).

- **LOG2E** The value of the base 2 logarithm of e (roughly 1.442).

- **PI** The value of pi—used in calculating the circumference and area of circles (roughly 3.1415).

- **SQRT1_2** The value of the square root of ½ (roughly 0.707).

- **SQRT2** The value of the square root of 2 (roughly 1.414).

Methods

● `abs(number)` Returns the absolute value of `number`. The absolute value is the value of a number with its sign ignored, so `abs(4)` and `abs(-4)` both return 4.

● `acos(number)` Returns the arc cosine of `number` in radians.

● `asin(number)` Returns the arc sine of `number` in radians.

● `atan(number)` Returns the arc tangent of `number` in radians.

● `atan2(number1,number2)` Returns the angle of the polar coordinate corresponding to the Cartesian coordinate (`number1,number2`). [Not I]

● `ceil(number)` Returns the next integer greater than `number`—in other words, rounds up to the next integer.

● `cos(number)` Returns the cosine of `number` where `number` represents an angle in radians.

● `exp(number)` Returns the value of `E` to the power of `number`.

● `floor(number)` Returns the next integer less than `number`—in other words, rounds down to the nearest integer.

● `log(number)` Returns the natural logarithm of `number`.

● `max(number1,number2)` Returns the greater of `number1` and `number2`.

● `min(number1,number2)` Returns the smaller of `number1` and `number2`.

● `pow(number1,number2)` Returns the value of `number1` to the power of `number2`.

● `random()` Returns a random number between zero and one (at press time, this method was available only on UNIX versions of Navigator 2.0).

● `round(number)` Returns the closest integer to `number`—in other words rounds to the closest integer.

● `sin(number)` Returns the sine of `number` where `number` represents an angle in radians.

● `sqrt(number)` Returns the square root of `number`.

● `tan(number)` Returns the tangent of `number` where `number` represents an angle in radians.

THE mimeType OBJECT [Cl3]

The `mimeType` object reflects a Mime type supported by the client browser.

Properties

- **type** A string value reflecting the Mime type.

- **description** A string containing a description of the Mime type.

- **enabledPlugin** A reference to `plugin` object for the plug-in supporting the Mime type.

- **suffixes** A string containing a comma-separated list of file suffixes for the Mime type.

THE navigator OBJECT [Cl2l3ll]

The `navigator` object reflects information about the version of Navigator being used.

Properties

- **appCodeName** A string value containing the code name of the client (for example, "Mozilla" for Netscape Navigator).

- **appName** A string value containing the name of the client (such as, "Netscape" for Netscape Navigator).

- **appVersion** A string value containing the version information for the client in the form:

  `versionNumber (platform; country)`

  For instance, Navigator 2.0, beta 6 for Windows 95 (international version), would have an `appVersion` property with the value "2.0b6 (Win32; I)".

- **mimeTypes** An array of `mimeType` objects reflecting the Mime types supported by the client browser. [Not 2ll]

- **plugins** An array of `plugin` objects reflecting the plug-ins in a document in the order of their appearance in the HTML document. [Not 2ll]

- **userAgent** A string containing the complete value of the user-agent header sent in the HTTP request. This contains all the information in `appCodeName` and `appVersion`:

  `Mozilla/2.0b6 (Win32; I)`

Methods

- **javaEnabled()** Returns a Boolean value indicating if Java is enabled in the browser [Not 2|I].

THE Option **OBJECT [C|3]**

The Option object is used to create entries in a select list using the syntax optionName Name = new Option(optionText, optionValue, defaultSelected, selected) and then selectName.options[index] = optionName.

Properties

- **defaultSelected** A Boolean value specifying if the option is selected by default.

- **index** An integer value specifying the option's index in the select list.

- **prototype** Provides a mechanism to add properties to an Option object.

- **selected** A Boolean value indicating if the option is currently selected.

- **text** A string value reflecting the text displayed for the option.

- **value** A string value indicating the value submitted to the server when the form is submitted.

THE password **OBJECT [C|2|3|I]**

The password object reflects a password text field from an HTML form in JavaScript.

Properties

- **defaultValue** A string value containing the default value of the password element (for example, the value of the VALUE attribute).

- **enabled** A Boolean value indicating if the password field is enabled. [Not 2|3]

- **form** A reference to the form object containing the password field. [Not 2|3]

- **name** A string value containing the name of the password element.

- **value** A string value containing the value of the password element.

Methods

● **focus()**   Emulates the action of focusing in the password field.

● **blur()**   Emulates the action of removing focus from the password field.

● **select()**   Emulates the action of selecting the text in the password field.

Event Handlers

● **onBlur**   Specifies JavaScript code to execute when the password field loses focus. [Not 2|3]

● **onFocus**   Specifies JavaScript code to execute when the password field receives focus. [Not 2|3]

THE plugin OBJECT

The **plugin** object reflects a plug-in supported by the browser.

Properties

● **name**   A string value reflecting the name of the plug-in.

● **filename**   A string value reflecting the file name of the plug-in on the system's disk.

● **description**   A string value containing the description supplied by the plug-in.

THE radio OBJECT [C|2|3|I]

The **radio** object reflects a set of radio buttons from an HTML form in JavaScript. To access individual radio buttons, use numeric indexes starting at zero. For instance, individual buttons in a set of radio buttons named **testRadio** could be referenced by **testRadio[0]**, **testRadio[1]**, and so on.

Properties

● **checked**   A Boolean value indicating if a specific button is checked. Can be used to select or deselect a button.

● **defaultChecked**   A Boolean value indicating if a specific button was checked by default (that is, reflects the CHECKED attribute). [Not I]

- **enabled**   A Boolean value indicating if the radio button is enabled. [Not 2|3]

- **form**   A reference to the form object containing the radio button. [Not 2|3]

- **length**   An integer value indicating the number of radio buttons in the set. [Not I]

- **name**   A string value containing the name of the set of radio buttons.

- **value**   A string value containing the value of a specific radio button in a set (i.e. reflects the VALUE attribute).

Methods

- **click()**   Emulates the action of clicking on a radio button.

- **focus()**   Gives focus to the radio button. [Not 2|3]

Event Handlers

- **onClick**   Specifies JavaScript code to execute when a radio button is clicked.

- **onFocus**   Specifies JavaScript code to execute when a radio button receives focus. [Not 2|3]

THE reset OBJECT [C|2|3|I]

The reset object reflects a reset button from an HTML form in JavaScript.

Properties

- **enabled**   A Boolean value indicating if the reset button is enabled. [Not 2|3]

- **form**   A reference to the form object containing the reset button. [Not 2|3]

- **name**   A string value containing the name of the reset element.

- **value**   A string value containing the value of the reset element.

Methods

- **click()** Emulates the action of clicking on the reset button.

- **focus()** Specifies JavaScript code to execute when the reset button receives focus. [Not 2|3]

Event Handlers

- **onClick** Specifies JavaScript code to execute when the reset button is clicked.

- **onFocus** Specifies JavaScript code to execute when the reset button receives focus. [Not 2|3]

THE select OBJECT [C|2|3]

The **select** object reflects a selection list from an HTML form in JavaScript.

Properties

- **length** An integer value containing the number of options in the selection list.

- **name** A string value containing the name of the selection list.

- **options** An array reflecting each of the options in the selection list in the order they appear. The options property has its own properties:

defaultSelected	A Boolean value indicating if an option was selected by default (that is, reflects the SELECTED attribute).
index	An integer value reflecting the index of an option.
length	An integer value reflecting the number of options in the selection list.
name	A string value containing the name of the selection list.
selected	A Boolean value indicating if the option is selected. Can be used to select or deselect an option.
selectedIndex	An integer value containing the index of the currently selected option.

    text   A string value containing the text displayed in the selection list for a particular option.

    value   A string value indicating the value for the specified option (that is, it reflects the `VALUE` attribute).

- **selectedIndex** Reflects the index of the currently selected option in the selection list.

Methods

- **blur()** Removes focus from the select list. [Not 2|3]

- **focus()** Gives focus to the select list. [Not 2|3]

Event Handlers

- **onBlur** Specifies JavaScript code to execute when the selection list loses focus.

- **onFocus** Specifies JavaScript code to execute when focus is given to the selection list.

- **onChange** Specifies JavaScript code to execute when the selected option in the list changes.

THE String OBJECT [C|2|3|I]

The `String` object provides properties and methods for working with string literals and variables.

Properties

- **length** An integer value containing the length of the string expressed as the number of characters in the string.

- **prototype** Provides a mechanism for adding properties to a `String` object. [Not 2]

Methods

- **anchor(name)** Returns a string containing the value of the string object surrounded by an A container tag with the NAME attribute set to name.

- **big()** Returns a string containing the value of the string object surrounded by a BIG container tag.

- **blink()** Returns a string containing the value of the string object surrounded by a BLINK container tag.

- **bold()** Returns a string containing the value of the string object surrounded by a B container tag.

- **charAt(index)** Returns the character at the location specified by index.

- **fixed()** Returns a string containing the value of the string object surrounded by a FIXED container tag.

- **fontColor(color)** Returns a string containing the value of the string object surrounded by a FONT container tag with the COLOR attribute set to color where color is a color name or an RGB triplet. [Not I]

- **fontSize(size)** Returns a string containing the value of the string object surrounded by a FONTSIZE container tag with the size set to size. [Not I]

- **indexOf(findString,startingIndex)** Returns the index of the first occurrence of findString, starting the search at startingIndex where startingIndex is optional. If it is not provided, the search starts at the start of the string.

- **italics()** Returns a string containing the value of the string object surrounded by an I container tag.

- **lastIndexOf(findString,startingIndex)** Returns the index of the last occurrence of findString. This is done by searching backwards from startingIndex. startingIndex is optional and assumed to be the last character in the string if no value is provided.

- **link(href)** Returns a string containing the value of the string object surrounded by an A container tag with the HREF attribute set to href.

- **small()** Returns a string containing the value of the string object surrounded by a SMALL container tag.

- **split(separator)** Returns an array of strings created by splitting the string at every occurrence of separator. [Not 2II]

- **strike()** Returns a string containing the value of the string object surrounded by a STRIKE container tag.

- **sub()** Returns a string containing the value of the string object surrounded by a SUB container tag.

- **substring(firstIndex,lastIndex)** Returns a string equivalent to the substring starting at firstIndex and ending at the character before lastIndex. If firstIndex is greater than lastIndex, the string starts at lastIndex and ends at the character before firstIndex.

- **sup()** Returns a string containing the value of the string object surrounded by a SUP container tag.

- **toLowerCase()** Returns a string containing the value of the string object with all characters converted to lowercase.

- **toUpperCase()** Returns a string containing the value of the string object with all characters converted to uppercase.

THE submit OBJECT [Cl2l3lI]

The submit object reflects a submit button from an HTML form in JavaScript.

Properties

- **enabled** A Boolean value indicating if the submit button is enabled. [Not 2l3]

- **form** A reference to the form object containing the submit button. [Not 2l3]

- **name** A string value containing the name of the submit button element.

- **type** A string value reflecting the TYPE attribute of the INPUT tag. [Not 2lI]

- **value** A string value containing the value of the submit button element.

Methods

- **click()** Emulates the action of clicking on the submit button.

- **focus()** Gives focus to the submit button. [Not 2l3]

Event Handlers

- **onClick** Specifies JavaScript code to execute when the submit button is clicked.

- **onFocus** Specifies JavaScript code to execute when the submit button receives focus. [Not 2l3]

THE text OBJECT [Cl2l3ll]

The **text** object reflects a text field from an HTML form in JavaScript.

Properties

- **defaultValue** A string value containing the default value of the text element (that is, the value of the VALUE attribute).

- **enabled** A Boolean value indicating if the text field is enabled. [Not 2l3]

- **form** A reference to the **form** object containing the text field. [Not 2l3]

- **name** A string value containing the name of the text element.

- **type** A string value reflecting the TYPE attribute of the INPUT tag. [Not 2ll]

- **value** A string value containing the value of the text element.

Methods

- **focus()** Emulates the action of focusing in the text field.

- **blur()** Emulates the action of removing focus from the text field.

- **select()** Emulates the action of selecting the text in the text field.

Event Handlers

- **onBlur** Specifies JavaScript code to execute when focus is removed from the field.

- **onChange** Specifies JavaScript code to execute when the content of the field is changed.

- **onFocus** Specifies JavaScript code to execute when focus is given to the field.

- **onSelect** Specifies JavaScript code to execute when the user selects some or all of the text in the field.

THE textarea OBJECT [C|2|3|1]

The **textarea** object reflects a multiline text field from an HTML form in JavaScript.

Properties

- **defaultValue** A string value containing the default value of the `textarea` element (for example the value of the VALUE attribute).

- **enabled** A Boolean value indicating if the `textarea` field is enabled. [Not 2|3]

- **form** A reference to the `form` object containing the `textarea` field. [Not 2|3]

- **name** A string value containing the name of the `textarea` element.

- **type** A string value reflecting the type of the `textarea` object. [Not 2|1]

- **value** A string value containing the value of the `textarea` element.

Methods

- **focus()** Emulates the action of focusing in the `textarea` field.

- **blur()** Emulates the action of removing focus from the `textarea` field.

- **select()** Emulates the action of selecting the text in the `textarea` field.

Event Handlers

- **onBlur** Specifies JavaScript code to execute when focus is removed from the field.

- **onChange** Specifies JavaScript code to execute when the content of the field is changed.

- onFocus   Specifies JavaScript code to execute when focus is given to the field.

- onSelect   Specifies JavaScript code to execute when the user selects some or all of the text in the field.

THE window OBJECT [C|2|3|I]

The window object is the top-level object for each window or frame and is the parent object for the document, location, and history objects.

Properties

- defaultStatus   A string value containing the default value displayed in the status bar.

- frames   An array of objects for each frame in a window. Frames appear in the array in the order in which they appear in the HTML source code.

- length   An integer value indicating the number of frames in a parent window. [Not I]

- name   A string value containing the name of the window or frame.

- opener   A reference to the window object containing the open() method used to open the current window. [Not 2|I]

- parent   A string indicating the name of the window containing the frameset.

- self   An alternative for the name of the current window.

- status   Used to display a message in the status bar—this is done by assigning values to this property.

- top   An alternative for the name of the top-most window.

- window   An alternative for the name of the current window.

Methods

- alert(message)   Displays message in a dialog box.

- blur()   Removes focus from the window. On many systems, this sends the window to the background. [Not 2|I]

● `close()`   Closes the window. [Not I]

● `confirm(message)`   Displays `message` in a dialog box with OK and CANCEL buttons. Returns `true` or `false` based on the button clicked by the user.

● `focus()`   Gives focus to the window. On many systems, this brings the window to the front. [Not 2lI]

● `navigator(url)`   Loads `url` in the window. [Not 2l3]

● `open(url,name,features)`   Opens `url` in a window named `name`. If `name` doesn't exist, a new window is created with that name. `features` is an optional string argument containing a list of features for the new window. The feature list contains any of the following name-value pairs separated by commas and without additional spaces: [Not I]

`toolbar=[yes,no,1,0]`	Indicates if the window should have a toolbar.
`location=[yes,no,1,0]`	Indicates if the window should have a location field.
`directories=[yes,no,1,0]`	Indicates if the window should have directory buttons.
`status=[yes,no,1,0]`	Indicates if the window should have a status bar.
`menubar=[yes,no,1,0]`	Indicates if the window should have menus.
`scrollbars=[yes,no,1,0]`	Indicates if the window should have scroll bars.
`resizable=[yes,no,1,0]`	Indicates if the window should be resizable.
`width=pixels`	Indicates the width of the window in pixels.
`height=pixels`	Indicates the height of the window in pixels.

● `prompt(message,response)`   Displays `message` in a dialog box with a text entry field with the default value of `response`. The user's response in the text entry field is returned as a string.

● `setTimeout(expression,time)`   Evaluates `expression` after `time` where `time` is a value in milliseconds. The timeout can be named with the structure

`name = setTimeOut(expression,time)`

● `scroll(x,y)`   Scrolls the window to the coordinate `x,y`. [Not 2lI]

● `clearTimeout(name)`   Cancels the timeout with the name `name`.

Event Handlers

- **onBlur** Specifies JavaScript code to execute when focus is removed from a window. [Not 2ll]

- **onError** Specifies JavaScript code to execute when a JavaScript error occurs while loading a document. This can be used to intercept JavaScript errors. Setting this event handler to null effectively prevents JavaScript errors from being displayed to the user. [Not 2ll]

- **onFocus** Specifies JavaScript code to execute when the window receives focus. [Not 2ll]

- **onLoad** Specifies JavaScript code to execute when the window or frame finishes loading.

- **onUnload** Specifies JavaScript code to execute when the document in the window or frame is exited.

INDEPENDENT FUNCTIONS, OPERATORS, VARIABLES, AND LITERALS

Independent Functions

- **escape(character)** Returns a string containing the ASCII encoding of character in the form %xx where xx is the numeric encoding of the character. [Cl2l3ll]

- **eval(expression)** Returns the result of evaluating expression where expression is an arithmetic expression. [Cl2l3ll]

- **isNaN(value)** Evaluates value to see if it is NaN. Returns a Boolean value. [Cl2l3ll] [On UNIX platforms, Not 2]

- **parseFloat(string)** Converts string to a floating-point number and returns the value. It continues to convert until it hits a non-numeric character and then returns the result. If the first character cannot be converted to a number, the function returns "NaN" (zero on Windows platforms). [Cl2l3ll]

- `parseInt(string,base)` Converts `string` to an integer of base `base` and returns the value. It continues to convert until it hits a non-numeric character and then returns the result. If the first character cannot be converted to a number, the function returns "`NaN`" (zero on Windows platforms). [Cl2l3ll]

- `taint(propertyName)` Adds tainting to `propertyName`. [Cl3]

- `toString()` This is a method of all obejcts. It returns the object as a string or returns "`[object type]`" if no string representation exists for the object. [Cl2l3]

- `unescape(string)` Returns a character based on the ASCII encoding contained in `string`. The ASCII encoding should take the form "`%integer`" or "`hexadecimalValue`". [Cl2l3ll]

- `untaint(propertyName)` Removes tainting from `propertyName`. [Cl3]

Operators

- `Assignment` Operators   Assignment operators in JavaScript (see Table B-1). [Cl2l3ll]

Operator	Description
`=`	Assigns value of right operand to the left operand
`+=`	Adds the left and right operands and assigns the result to the left operand
`-=`	Subtracts the right operand from the left operand and assigns the result to the left operand
`*=`	Multiplies the two operands and assigns the result to the left operand
`/=`	Divides the left operand by the right operand and assigns the value to the left operand
`%=`	Divides the left operand by the right operand and assigns the remainder to the left operand

Table B-1 *Assignment operators.*

- `Arithmetic` Operators   Arithmetic operators in JavaScript (see Table B-2). [Cl2l3ll]

Operator	Description
+	Adds the left and right operands
–	Subtracts the right operand from the left operand
*	Multiplies the two operands
/	Divides the left operand by the right operand
%	Divides the left operand by the right operand and evaluates to the remainder
++	Increments the operand by one (can be used before or after the operand)
--	Decreases the operand by one (can be used before or after the operand)
–	Changes the sign of the operand

Table B-2 *Arithmetic operators.*

 Bitwise Operators   Bitwise operators deal with their operands as binary numbers but return JavaScript numerical value (see Table B-3). [Cl2l3ll]

Operator	Description
AND (or &)	Converts operands to integers with 32 bits, pairs the corresponding bits, and returns one for each pair. Returns zero for any other combination.
OR (or |)	Converts operands to integers with 32 bits, pairs the corresponding bits, and returns one for each pair where one of the two bits is one. Returns zero if both bits are zero.
XOR (or ^)	Converts operands to integers with 32 bits, pairs the corresponding bits, and returns one for each pair where only one bit is one. Returns zero for any other combination.
<<	Converts the left operand to an integer with 32 bits and shifts bits to the left of the number of bits indicated by the right operand. Bits shifted off to the left are discarded and zeros are shifted in from the right.
>>>	Converts the left operand to an integer with 32 bits and shifts bits to the right of the number of bits indicated by the right operand. Bits shifted off

Operator	Description
	to the right are discarded and zeros are shifted in from the left.
>>	Converts the left operand to an integer with 32 bits and shifts bits to the right of the number of bits indicated by the right operand. Bits shifted off to the right are discarded and copies of the leftmost bit are shifted in from the left.

Table B-3 *Bitwise Operators in JavaScript.*

 **Logical** Operators   Table B-4. Logical operators in JavaScript [Cl2l3ll]

Operator	Description
&&	Logical "and"—returns true when both operands are true, otherwise it returns false.
||	Logical "or"—returns true if either operand is true. It only returns false when both operands are false.
!	Logical "not"—returns true if the operand is false and false if the operand is true. This is a unary operator and precedes the operand.

Table B-4 *Logical operators.*

 Comparison Operators   Table B-5. Comparison Operators in JavaScript [Cl2l3ll]

Operator	Description
==	Returns true if the operands are equal
!=	Returns true if the operands are not equal
>	Returns true if the left operand is greater than the right operand
<	Returns true if the left operand is less than the right operand
>=	Returns true if the left operand is greater than or equal to the right operand
<=	Returns true if the left operand is less than or equal to the right operand

Table B-5 *Logical (comparison) operators.*

● `Conditional` Operators   Conditional expressions take one form:

`(condition) ? val1 : val2`

If `condition` is true, the expression evaluates to `val1`, otherwise it evaluates to `val2`. [Cl2l3ll]

● `String` Operators   The concatenation operator (+) is one of two string operators. It evaluates to a string combining the left and right operands. The concatenation assignment operator (+=) is also available. [Cl2l3ll]

● `typeof` Operator   The `typeof` operator returns the type of its single operand. Possible types are `object`, `string`, `number`, `boolean`, `function`, and `undefined`. [Cl3ll]

● `void` Operator   The `void` operator takes an expression as an operand but returns no value. [Cl3]

● `Operator Precedence`   JavaScript applies the rules of operator precedence as follows (from lowest to highest precedence):

comma (,)

assignment operators (= += -= *= /= %=)

conditional (? :)

logical or (||)

logical and (&&)

bitwise or (|)

bitwise xor (^)

bitwise and (&)

equality (== !=)

relational (< <= > >=)

shift (<< >> >>>)

addition/subtraction (+ -)

multiply/divide/modulus (* / %)

negation/increment (! - ++ ñ)

call, member (() [])

APPENDIX C

FROM THE WEB

 LAB 1

DAVE EISENBERG'S CALENDAR

Dave Eisenberg's calendar (`http://www.best.com/~nessus/js-today.html`) is a good example of the use of expressions and variables, as well as functions and objects. The program generates a dynamic Web page that includes a greeting suited to the time of day (such as "Good Evening!"), the time of day, and the current month's calendar with the current date highlighted.

In addition, the page includes an image suited to the current time of day.

In doing this, Eisenberg makes use of several techniques that we haven't seen yet. His script uses the `Date` object, as well as several new methods including `Math.floor()` from the `Math` object and others from the `Date` object.

The source code for the page is in Listing L1-1.

Input   **Listing L1-1** Dave Eisenberg's calendar.

```html
<HTML>
<HEAD>
<TITLE>Greetings from Dave Eisenberg</TITLE>
</HEAD>

<BODY>

<SCRIPT LANGUAGE="JavaScript">
<!--  to hide script contents from old browsers

function greeting()
{
    var today = new Date();
    var hrs = today.getHours();

    document.writeln("<CENTER>");
    if ((hrs >=6) && (hrs <=18))
    {
        document.writeln("<IMG SRC=\"daypix/day");
        document.write(Math.floor(hrs / 10));
        document.write(Math.floor(hrs % 10));
        document.write("00.gif\">");
    }
    else
        document.write("<IMG SRC=\"daypix/night1.gif\">");

    document.writeln("<BR>");
    document.write("<H1>Good ");
    if (hrs < 6)
        document.write("(Early) Morning");
    else if (hrs < 12)
        document.write("Morning");
    else if (hrs <= 18)
        document.write("Afternoon");
    else
        document.write("Evening");
    document.writeln("!</H1>");
    document.write("You entered this page at ");
    dayStr = today.toLocaleString();
    i = dayStr.indexOf(' ');
    n = dayStr.length;
    document.write(dayStr.substring(i+1, n));
    document.writeln("</CENTER>");
}

function montharr(m0, m1, m2, m3, m4, m5, m6, m7, m8, m9, m10, m11)
{
    this[0] = m0;
    this[1] = m1;
```

```
    this[2] = m2;
    this[3] = m3;
    this[4] = m4;
    this[5] = m5;
    this[6] = m6;
    this[7] = m7;
    this[8] = m8;
    this[9] = m9;
    this[10] = m10;
    this[11] = m11;
}

function calendar()
{
    var monthNames = "JanFebMarAprMayJunJulAugSepOctNovDec";
    var today = new Date();
    var thisDay;
    var monthDays = new montharr(31, 28, 31, 30, 31, 30, 31, 31, 30,
        31, 30, 31);

    year = today.getYear() + 1900;
    thisDay = today.getDate();

    // do the classic leap year calculation
    if (((year % 4 == 0) && (year % 100 != 0)) || (year % 400 == 0))
        monthDays[1] = 29;

    // figure out how many days this month will have...
    nDays = monthDays[today.getMonth()];

    // and go back to the first day of the month...
    firstDay = today;
    firstDay.setDate(1);
    // and figure out which day of the week it hits...
    startDay = firstDay.getDay();

    document.writeln("<CENTER>");
    document.write("<TABLE BORDER>");
    document.write("<TR><TH COLSPAN=7>");
    document.write(monthNames.substring(today.getMonth() * 3,
        (today.getMonth() + 1) * 3));
    document.write(". ");
    document.write(year);
    document.write("<TR><TH>Sun<TH>Mon<TH>Tue<TH>Wed<TH>Thu<TH>Fri<TH>Sat");

    // now write the blanks at the beginning of the calendar
    document.write("<TR>");
    column = 0;
    for (i=0; i<startDay; i++)
    {
        document.write("<TD>");
```

continued on next page

continued from previous page

```
        column++;
    }

    for (i=1; i<=nDays; i++)
    {
        document.write("<TD>");
        if (i == thisDay)
            document.write("<FONT COLOR=\"#FF0000\">")
document.write(i);
        if (i == thisDay)
            document.write("</FONT>")
column++;
        if (column == 7)
        {
            document.write("<TR>"); // start a new row
            column = 0;
        }
    }
    document.write("</TABLE>");
    document.writeln("</CENTER>");
}
document.write(greeting());
document.write("<HR>");
document.write(calendar());
document.write("<HR>");
document.write("<A HREF=\"http://www.best.com/~nessus\">");
document.write("Back to Dave Eisenberg's resume<\A>");

<!-- end hiding contents from old browsers  -->
</SCRIPT>

</BODY>
</HTML>
```

Output   The code produces results like those in Figures L1-1 and L1-2.

Analysis   The first thing you notice about this script is that it is not placed inside the header of the HTML file. The author does this because there is no chance of events triggering calls to functions which have not yet been defined.

In addition, all HTML code is dynamically generated by the script.

The calendar program uses three functions. The calls are made in sequence by the main body of the script:

```
document.write(greeting());
document.write("<HR>");
document.write(calendar());
document.write("<HR>");
document.write("<A HREF=\"http://www.best.com/~nessus\">");
document.write("Back to Dave Eisenberg's resume<\A>");
```

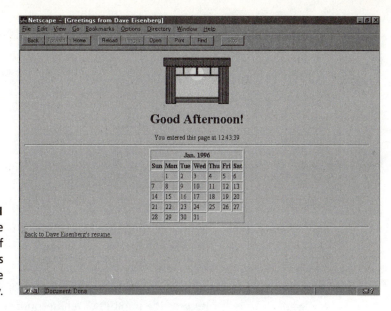

Figure L1-1
During the day, the user gets one of several images depicting the time of day.

Jan. 1996						
Sun	Mon	Tue	Wed	Thu	Fri	Sat
	1	2	3	4	5	6
7	8	9	10	11	12	13
14	15	16	17	18	19	20
21	22	23	24	25	26	27
28	29	30	31			

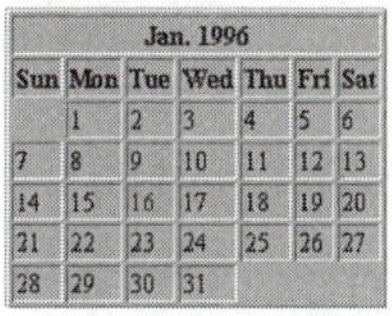

Figure L1-2
Using the `Date` object, the program builds a calendar for the current month.

At the top of the script, two global declarations (**`today`** and **`hrs`**) occur. The command **`var today = new Date();`** creates an instance of the system's **`Date`** object in much the same way you could create an instance of any object you defined yourself.

The **`Date`** object enables programmers to create an object that contains information about a particular date and provides a set of methods to work with that information.

In order to create an instance of the **`Date`** object, you use the form: **`variable = new Date(parameters)`** where the parameters can be any of the following:

- Empty to create today's date and the current time
- A string of the form "*Month day, year hours:minutes:seconds*" (for example `"May 11, 1979 8:00:00"`)
- Integer values for the current year, month, and day as in `Date(79,5,11)`
- Integer values for the current year, month, day, and time as in `Date(79,5,11,8,0,0)`

In JavaScript, it is not possible to create dates before 1 January 1970. The date 1 January 1970 at 00:00:00 is known as the epoch.

The `Date` object provides the methods outlined in Table L1-1.

Name	Description
getDate	Returns the day of the month as an integer from 1 to 31
getDay	Returns the day of the week as an integer where zero is Sunday and one is Monday
getHours	Returns the hour as an integer between 0 and 23
getMinutes	Returns the minutes as an integer from 0 to 59
getMonth	Returns the month as an integer from 0 to 11 where zero is January and 11 is December
getSeconds	Returns the seconds as an integer between 0 and 59
getTime	Returns the number of milliseconds since 1 January 1970 at 00:00:00
getTimezoneOffset	Returns the difference between the local time and Greenwich Mean Time in minutes
getYear	Returns the year as a two-digit integer
parse	Returns the number of milliseconds since 1 January 1970 at 00:00:00 for the date string passed to it
setDate	Sets the day of the month based on an integer argument from 1 to 31
setHours	Sets the hour based on an argument from 0 to 23
setMinutes	Sets the minutes based on an argument from 0 to 59
setMonth	Sets the month based on an argument from 0 to 11
setSeconds	Sets the seconds based on an argument between 0 and 59
setTime	Sets the time based on an argument representing the number of milliseconds since 1 January 1970 at 00:00:00
setYear	Sets the year based on a four-digit integer greater than 1900
toString	Returns the current date as a string
toGMTString	Returns the current date and time using the Internet GMT conventions (that is, in the form "Mon, 18 Dec 1995 17:28:35 GMT")

Name	Description
toLocaleString	Returns the date as a string in the form *"MM/DD/YY HH:MM:SS"*
UTC	Takes a comma delimited date and returns the number of milliseconds since 1 January 1970 at 00:00:00 GMT time

Table L1-1 *Methods of the* Date *object.*

Based on this information, the variable declaration var hrs = today=getHours() will contain the current hour when the user loads the page.

The first function the script calls is **greeting()**, which displays the appropriate image and welcome message along with the current time:

```
function greeting()
{
    var today = new Date();
    var hrs = today.getHours();

    document.writeln("<CENTER>");
    if ((hrs >=6) && (hrs <=18))
    {
        document.writeln("<IMG SRC=\"daypix/day");
        document.write(Math.floor(hrs / 10));
        document.write(Math.floor(hrs % 10));
        document.write("00.gif\">");
    }
    else
        document.write("<IMG SRC=\"daypix/night1.gif\">");

    document.writeln("<BR>");
    document.write("<H1>Good ");
    if (hrs < 6)
        document.write("(Early) Morning");
    else if (hrs < 12)
        document.write("Morning");
    else if (hrs <= 18)
        document.write("Afternoon");
    else
        document.write("Evening");
    document.writeln("!</H1>");
    document.write("You entered this page at ");
    dayStr = today.toLocaleString();
    i = dayStr.indexOf(' ');
    n = dayStr.length;
    document.write(dayStr.substring(i+1, n));
    document.writeln("</CENTER>");
}
```

The function determines that it is daytime if `hrs` is between 6 and 18 and then builds an `image` tag. The filename includes a number built out of the `hrs` variable using `Math.floor()`. This method returns the closest integer less than the argument. In that way, if `hrs` is 12, the image's filename would be `day1200.gif`.

`Math.ceil()` is similar to `Math.floor()` except it returns the nearest integer greater than the value of the argument.

The current time, which is output at the end of the function, is obtained from the string returned by the `Date.toLocaleString()` method. This string contains the date and time separated by a single space. The function uses the `indexOf()` method of the `string` object to locate the index of the space in the string. The `length` property of the `string` object is used to determine the index of the last character in the string.

The `substring()` method then returns the portion of the string after the index up to the end of the string. The `string` object, and in particular the `substring()` method, are discussed in more detail in later chapters. The `string` object is covered in depth in Chapter 10, "Strings, Math, and the History List."

The next function to be called is the `calendar()` function, which does the more complex job of building the calendar. The calendar is designed using HTML tables, which are discussed further in Chapter 7, "Loops."

```
function calendar()
{
    var monthNames = "JanFebMarAprMayJunJulAugSepOctNovDec";
    var today = new Date();
    var thisDay;
    var monthDays = new montharr(31, 28, 31, 30, 31, 30, 31, 31, 30,
        31, 30, 31);

    year = today.getYear() + 1900;
    thisDay = today.getDate();

    // do the classic leap year calculation
    if (((year % 4 == 0) && (year % 100 != 0)) || (year % 400 == 0))
        monthDays[1] = 29;

    // figure out how many days this month will have...
    nDays = monthDays[today.getMonth()];

    // and go back to the first day of the month...
    firstDay = today;
    firstDay.setDate(1);
    // and figure out which day of the week it hits...
    startDay = firstDay.getDay();
```

```
document.writeln("<CENTER>");
document.write("<TABLE BORDER>");
document.write("<TR><TH COLSPAN=7>");
document.write(monthNames.substring(today.getMonth() * 3,
    (today.getMonth() + 1) * 3));
document.write(". ");
document.write(year);
document.write("<TR><TH>Sun<TH>Mon<TH>Tue<TH>Wed<TH>Thu<TH>Fri<TH>Sat");

// now write the blanks at the beginning of the calendar
document.write("<TR>");
column = 0;
for (i=0; i<startDay; i++)
{
    document.write("<TD>");
    column++;
}

for (i=1; i<=nDays; i++)
{
    document.write("<TD>");
    if (i == thisDay)
        document.write("<FONT COLOR=\"#FF0000\">")
    document.write(i);
    if (i == thisDay)
        document.write("</FONT>")
    column++;
    if (column == 7)
    {
        document.write("<TR>"); // start a new row
        column = 0;
    }
}
document.write("</TABLE>");
document.writeln("</CENTER>");
}
```

The function starts by defining variables that will be used later in the function, as well as defining an instance of the **Date** object called **today** and an instance of the **montharr** object (defined by the **montharr()** function), which contains 12 properties with the number of days in each month of the year.

The first step is to determine whether it is a leap year so that the value of **monthDays[1]** (for February) can be adjusted. This is done by using **today.getYear()** to get the current year and then using the following **if** statement to check whether the year is a leap year:

```
if (((year % 4 == 0) && (year % 100 != 0)) || (year % 400 == 0))
    monthDays[1] = 29;
```

Next, the variable `nDays` is assigned the number of days in the current month. The index used in `monthDays` is the value returned by `today.getMonth()` because it returns an integer that corresponds to the indexes of the `monthDays` object.

A copy of `today`, called `firstDay`, is created, and the date is set to the first of the month using `firstDay.setDate(1)`, in order to figure out the day of the week using `startDay = firstDay.getDay()`. You could have used `today.setDate(1)` and `today.getDay()`, but that would have made the script harder to read and understand.

The function then outputs the opening tags of the table and writes out the current month by using the `substring()` method on the variable `monthNames`. This is followed by writing the number of blank calendar spaces needed in the first row, using a `for` loop, which is covered in Chapter 7.

Next, another `for` loop is used to write out the dates of the month in sequence. The `if` statements with the `condition (i== thisDay)` are used to determine whether the text color should be changed for the current table cell.

The variable `column` is incremented throughout both `for` loops to keep track of which column of the seven-column table the current date is written into. If the date has been written into the seventh column, then the last `if` statement in the second loop starts a table row with the `TR` tag and resets `column` to zero.

Finally, the function writes out all the closing HTML for the table.

ASHLEY CHENG'S IDEAL WEIGHT CALCULATOR

Hong Kong's Dr. Ashley Cheng has produced a JavaScript page that contains an example of how JavaScript and forms can be combined to create special-purpose calculators and mini-spreadsheets. It's located at this site:

`http://www.iohk.com/UserPages/acheng/javascript.html`

Cheng's example is a calculator that, given a user's height and weight, calculates the individual's Body Mass Index and then makes a comment (usually light-hearted) about the implications of the calculated index. The comments range from `"Umm_You are obese, want some liposuction?"` to `"You are starving. Go find some food!"`

The interface is simple: a form with four fields—the user fills in the height and weight fields and the remaining two fields are filled in by the script with the user's BMI and the relevant comment. Two buttons are provided. One calculates the results and displays them in the appropriate fields, and the other enables the user to reset the form.

In addition, Dr. Cheng has added basic form checking to the script so that if either of the user's entry fields is empty, an appropriate alert is displayed. In addition, the script checks whether the height and weight values are totally illogical. For instance, if the weight value is less than zero kilograms or more than 500 kilograms, the program assumes that the user has made a mistake.

This script uses kilograms and centimeters for the user's weight and height. One kilogram is roughly equal to 2.2 pounds and 100 centimeters is roughly the same as 3.3 feet.

The source code for the program is in Listing L2-1.

Listing L2-1 Source code for Dr. Cheng's Ideal Weight Calculator.

```
<HTML>

<HEAD>
<TITLE>Ashley's JavaScript(tm) Examples</TITLE>

<SCRIPT LANGUAGE="JAVASCRIPT">
<!-- hide this script tag's contents from old browsers

function ClearForm(form){

    form.weight.value = "";
    form.height.value = "";
```

continued on next page

continued from previous page

```
        form.bmi.value = "";
        form.my_comment.value = "";


}

function bmi(weight, height) {

        bmindx=weight/eval(height*height);
        return bmindx;
}

function checkform(form) {

        if (form.weight.value==null||form.weight.value.length==0 || ⇐
form.height.value==null||form.height.value.length==0){
alert("\nPlease complete the form first");
            return false;
        }

        else if (parseFloat(form.height.value) <= 0||
                parseFloat(form.height.value) >=500||
                parseFloat(form.weight.value) <= 0||
                parseFloat(form.weight.value) >=500){
                alert("\nReally know what you're doing? \nPlease enter values⇐
                again. \nWeight in kilos and \nheight in cm");
                ClearForm(form);
                return false;
        }
        return true;


}

function computeform(form) {

        if (checkform(form)) {

        yourbmi=Math.round(bmi(form.weight.value, form.height.value/100));
        form.bmi.value=yourbmi;

        if (yourbmi >40) {
            form.my_comment.value="You are grossly obese, ⇐
consult your physician!";
        }

        else if (yourbmi >30 && yourbmi <=40) {
            form.my_comment.value="Umm... You are obese, want some liposuction?";
        }

        else if (yourbmi >27 && yourbmi <=30) {
            form.my_comment.value="You are very fat, ⇐
do something before it's too late";
        }
```

```
        else if (yourbmi >22 && yourbmi <=27) {
            form.my_comment.value="You are fat, need dieting and exercise";
        }

        else if (yourbmi >=21 && yourbmi <=22) {
            form.my_comment.value="I envy you. Keep it up!!";
        }

        else if (yourbmi >=18 && yourbmi <21) {
            form.my_comment.value="You are thin, eat more.";
        }

        else if (yourbmi >=16 && yourbmi <18) {
            form.my_comment.value="You are starving. Go Find some food!";
        }

        else if (yourbmi <16) {
            form.my_comment.value="You're grossly undernourished, ⇐
need hospitalization ";
        }

    }
    return;
}
 // -- done hiding from old browsers -->
</SCRIPT>
</HEAD>



<BODY BACKGROUND="background.gif">
<CENTER>

<H1>Ashley's JavaScript(tm) Examples:</H1>
<HR SIZE=3>

<UL>
<LI><A HREF="#HK1997">Hong Kong and 1997</A>
<LI><A HREF="#Calc">Want to know whether your weight is ideal?</A>
</UL>


<A NAME="HK1997">
<HR>


<P>
<SCRIPT LANGUAGE="JAVASCRIPT">

<!-- hide this script tag's contents from old browsers
```

continued on next page

continued from previous page

```
document.write('<IMG SRC="hkf.jpg"> <P>');

today = new Date();

document.write("Today is <B>"+today+"</B><P>");
BigDay = new Date("July 1, 1997")
msPerDay = 24 * 60 * 60 * 1000 ;
timeLeft = (BigDay.getTime() - today.getTime());
e_daysLeft = timeLeft / msPerDay;
daysLeft = Math.floor(e_daysLeft);
e_hrsLeft = (e_daysLeft - daysLeft)*24;
hrsLeft = Math.floor(e_hrsLeft);
minsLeft = Math.floor((e_hrsLeft - hrsLeft)*60);
document.write("There are only<BR> <H3>" + daysLeft + " days " ⇐
+ hrsLeft +" hours and " + minsLeft + " minutes left ⇐
</H3><BR> before Hong Kong revert from British to Chinese ⇐
rule <BR> on the <B>1st of July 1997!</B><P>");

 // -- done hiding from old browsers -->
</SCRIPT>

<FORM>
<input type=button name="Refresh"  value="Refresh" onclick="window.location= ⇐
'http://www.iohk.com/UserPages/acheng/javascript.html'">
</FORM>
</A>

<HR>
<A NAME="Calc">

<H2><IMG SRC="scale.jpg" ALIGN=MIDDLE> Do you have an ideal weight??</H2>
Enter your weight in kilograms and your height in centimeters<BR>
in the form below and press the "Let's see" button<BR>
(Please read disclaimer below before using this form)<BR>

<FORM NAME="BMI" method=POST>
<TABLE border=1>
<TR>
<TD><DIV ALIGN=CENTER>Your Weight (kg)</DIV></TD>
<TD><DIV ALIGN=CENTER>Your Height (cm)</DIV></TD>
<TD><DIV ALIGN=CENTER>Your BMI</DIV></TD>
<TD><DIV ALIGN=CENTER>My Comment</DIV></TD>
</TR>

<TR>
<TD><INPUT TYPE=TEXT NAME=weight   SIZE=10 ⇐
onfocus="this.form.weight.value=''"></TD>
<TD><INPUT TYPE=TEXT NAME=height   SIZE=10 ⇐
onfocus="this.form.height.value=''"></TD>
<TD><INPUT TYPE=TEXT NAME=bmi       SIZE=8 ></TD>
<TD><INPUT TYPE=TEXT NAME=my_comment   SIZE=35 ></TD>
```

```
</TABLE>

<P>
<INPUT TYPE="button" VALUE="Let's see" onclick="computeform(this.form)">
<INPUT TYPE="reset"  VALUE="Reset" onclick="ClearForm(this.form)">
</FORM>

</A>

<HR>


</CENTER>

<B>Disclaimer</B>: This form is based on the calculation of
<A HREF="http://www.iohk.com/UserPages/acheng/bmi.html"> ⇐
<I>"Body Mass Index"</I></A>
and is only meant to be a demonstration of how Javascript(tm) could be used
on a Web Page. Information it contains may not be accurate and is not designed
or intended to serve as medical advice. You should not act in accordance to the
"comment" provided in this form and I shall not be liable for any physical or
psychological damages suffered as a result of using this form or script.

<HR>
Access: <IMG SRC="http://www.iohk.com/cgi-bin/nph-count? ⇐
link=ashleycheng&width=6"> <P>
<IMG SRC="cheng3.gif" ALIGN="LEFT" HSPACE=15><BR>
Author: Ashley Cheng (<A HREF="mailto:ackcheng@ha.org.hk"> ⇐
ackcheng@ha.org.hk</A>) Jan 1996<BR>
Go back to <A HREF="http://www.iohk.com/UserPages/acheng"> ⇐
my Home-Page</A> or see ⇐
<A HREF="http://www.wahyan.edu.hk/ashleyticker.html"> ⇐
Java(tm) applets written by me</A>. <P>


</BODY>
</HTML>
```

| Output | The script produces results similar to those in Figures L2-1 and L2-2. |

| Analysis | Dr. Cheng's page has two JavaScript applications on it: a countdown to China's take-over of Hong Kong and the weight calculator in which we are interested. |

Cheng places all the functions for the weight calculator in the header, but because the countdown application involves dynamic HTML content based on the date and time, that script is contained in the body of the HTML document.

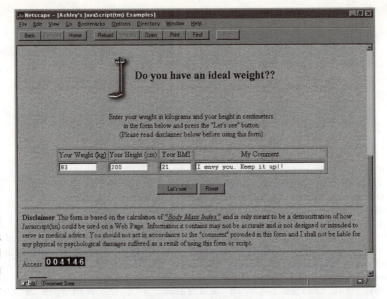

Figure L2-1
Calculators and
mini-spreadsheets
can be created
using
JavaScript.

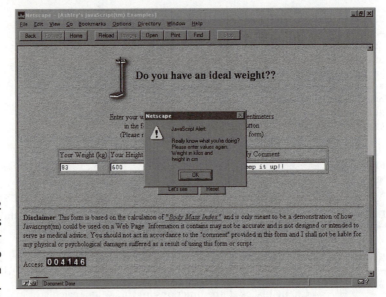

Figure L2-2
Dr. Cheng uses
simple error
checking to
ensure data
is valid.

The weight calculator is built out of four functions: `ClearForm()`, `bmi()`, `checkform()`, and `computeform()`.

Before looking at each function and how it works, we need to understand the HTML form that provides the interface to the script:

```
<FORM NAME="BMI" method=POST>
<TABLE border=1>
<TR>
<TD><DIV ALIGN=CENTER>Your Weight (kg)</DIV></TD>
<TD><DIV ALIGN=CENTER>Your Height (cm)</DIV></TD>
<TD><DIV ALIGN=CENTER>Your BMI</DIV></TD>
<TD><DIV ALIGN=CENTER>My Comment</DIV></TD>
</TR>

<TR>
<TD><INPUT TYPE=TEXT NAME=weight   SIZE=10 ⇐
onfocus="this.form.weight.value=''"></TD>
<TD><INPUT TYPE=TEXT NAME=height   SIZE=10 ⇐
onfocus="this.form.height.value=''"></TD>
<TD><INPUT TYPE=TEXT NAME=bmi      SIZE=8 ></TD>
<TD><INPUT TYPE=TEXT NAME=my_comment  SIZE=35 ></TD>
</TABLE>

<P>
<INPUT TYPE="button" VALUE="Let's see" onclick="computeform(this.form)">
<INPUT TYPE="reset"  VALUE="Reset" onclick="ClearForm(this.form)">
</FORM>
```

For appearance, Dr. Cheng has put the four text fields into a table. He uses the `<DIV ALIGN=CENTER> ... </DIV>` structure to center text inside the table cells. `<DIV ALIGN= CENTER>` is the HTML 3 method for centering text and is supported by Navigator 2.0 along with Netscape's own methods, such as the `CENTER` tag.

The form contains four text fields: `weight`, `height`, `bmi`, and `my_comment`. The two that the user uses—`weight` and `height`—are cleared when the user clicks in them simply by setting the value of the field to an empty string in the `onFocus` event handler:

```
onfocus="this.form.height.value=''"
```

The Let's See button uses the `onClick` event handler to call `computeform()` and passes it the `form` object as an argument using `this.form`. The Reset button calls the `ClearForm()` function.

The next four sections elaborate on the `ClearForm()`, `bmi()`, `checkform()`, and `computeform()` functions.

The `ClearForm()` Function

This function simply sets the values of the four fields in the form to the empty string.

The `bmi()` Function

The `bmi()` function is used to calculate the Body Mass Index using the formula `bmi = weight/(height¥height)`, where the weight is in kilograms and the height is in meters (not centimeters). The function accepts `weight` and `height` as arguments and then simply calculates the BMI and returns it.

The `checkform()` **Function**

`checkform()` accepts the `form` object as an argument and performs two error checks on the data. The function is called from the `computeform()` function.

First, the function checks whether either the `weight` or `height` field in the form contains a `null` value or an empty string:

```
if (form.weight.value==null||form.weight.value.length==0 || ⇐
form.height.value==null||form.height.value.length==0){
        alert("\nPlease complete the form first");
        return false;
    }
```

If either field is not filled in, then an alert is displayed and the function returns a `false` value.

If both fields are filled in, the function then checks to see whether the values make sense. If they seem out of a reasonable range, then an alert is displayed, and the function returns a `false` value. Notice the use of `\n` in the alert message to perform basic formatting of the text:

```
else if (parseFloat(form.height.value) <= 0||
        parseFloat(form.height.value) >=500||
        parseFloat(form.weight.value) <= 0||
        parseFloat(form.weight.value) >=500){
        alert("\nReally know what you're doing? \nPlease enter values ⇐
        again.\nWeight in kilos and \nheight in cm"); ClearForm(form);
return false;
    }
```

If the data is acceptable following both these checks, then the function simply returns a `true` value.

The `computeform()` **Function**

The `computeform()` function is where the primary work of the script is done. This function is called when the user clicks on the Let's See button, and it accepts the `form` object as an argument.

The script starts by calling `checkform()` to be sure the data is valid. If the data passes muster in the `checkform()` function, the `ComputeForm()`function proceeds to make the necessary calculations:

```
yourbmi=Math.round(bmi(form.weight.value, form.height.value/100));
form.bmi.value=yourbmi;
```

The program first calls `bmi()` and passes the weight and height entered by the user. The height is divided by 100 because the `bmi()` function expects the height in meters, and there are 100 centimeters in a meter. `Math.round()` is used to round the results to the nearest integer and then the value is assigned to `yourbmi`.

Notice that **yourbmi** is not defined using the **var** statement. As you learned in Chapter 4, "Functions and Objects—The Building Blocks of Programs," JavaScript is perfectly happy to define variables when they are first used, without the **var** statement.

```
if (yourbmi >40) {
    form.my_comment.value="You are grossly obese, ⇐
        consult your physician!";
}        else if (yourbmi >30 && yourbmi <=40) {
    form.my_comment.value="Umm... You are obese, want some liposuction?";
}

else if (yourbmi >27 && yourbmi <=30) {
    form.my_comment.value="You are very fat, ⇐
        do something before it's too late";
}

else if (yourbmi >22 && yourbmi <=27) {
    form.my_comment.value="You are fat, need dieting and exercise";
}

else if (yourbmi >=21 && yourbmi <=22) {
    form.my_comment.value="I envy you. Keep it up!!";
}

else if (yourbmi >=18 && yourbmi <21) {
    form.my_comment.value="You are thin, eat more.";
}

else if (yourbmi >=16 && yourbmi <18) {
    form.my_comment.value="You are starving. Go Find some food!";
}

else if (yourbmi <16) {
    form.my_comment.value="You're grossly undernourished, ⇐
need hospitalization ";
}

}
```

The rest of the function simply consists of a long **if ...else** construct that checks the value of **yourbmi** against different ranges and places the appropriate message in the **my_comment** field in the form.

MICHAEL YU'S CIVIC CAR VIEWER

Michael Yu's Civic Car viewing program provides you with a good example of how to combine frames with JavaScript. It's located at

```
http://www-leland.stanford.edu/~guanyuan/public/car/car.html
```

The premise behind the program is simple: In one frame, a view of a Honda Civic is displayed. In the other frame, the user has four directional controls to rotate the view in steps in any direction: up, down, left, or right.

In achieving this, Yu has made use of a simple file-naming scheme, the `windows.location` property, and the `frames` array.

The program in Listing L3-1 produces results similar to those shown in Figures L3-1 and L3-2.

Input   **Listing L3-1** Source code for Michael's Civic Car Viewer page.

Parent frameset:
```
<HTML>
<head>
<title> Car View 3D</title>
</head>

<FRAMESET ROWS="18%, 72%, 10%">
```

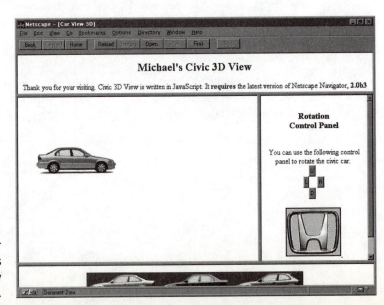

Figure L3-1
Michael's Civic Car Viewer provides interactivity between frames.

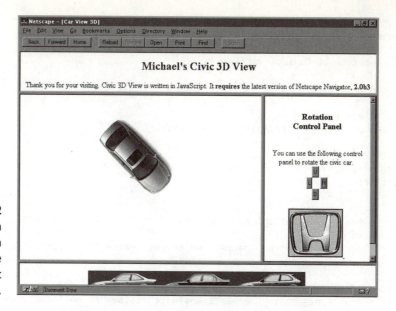

Figure L3-2
The user selects a rotation control on the right, and the image on the left updates.

```
<FRAME SRC="head.html" NAME="head" TARGET="head" SCROLLING="no">

<FRAMESET COLS="68%, 32%">
    <FRAME NAME="left" SRC="left.html" NORESIZE>
    <FRAME NAME="right" SRC="right.html" NORESIZE>

</FRAMESET>
    <FRAME SRC="tail.html" NAME="tail" SCROLLING="no">
</FRAMESET>

<noframes>

<h2 align="center">Sorry, Netscape 2.0b3 (Beta 3) required.</h2>

</noframes>

</BODY></HTML>
```

The file `right.html`:
```
<html>
<title>control pad</title>

<BODY BGCOLOR="ffffff" LINK="#0000FF" ALINK="#D9D919" VLINK="#871F78">

<form method="post">
```

continued on next page

continued from previous page

```html
<center>
<br>
<h3> Rotation<br>Control Panel</h3>
<br>
You can use the following control panel to rotate the civic car.
<br>
<div align="center">
<table border=0 cellspacing=0 cellpadding=0>
<tr>
  <td></td>
  <td><input type="button" name="upmiddle" value="U" onclick="up()"></td>
  <td></td>
</tr>
<tr>
  <td><input type="button" name="middleleft" value="L" onclick="left()"></td>
  <td></td>
  <td><input type="button" name="middleright" value="R" onclick="right()"></td>
</tr>
<tr>
  <td></td>
  <td><input type="button" name="downmiddle" value="D" onclick="down()">
  <td></td>
</tr>
</table>
</div>
<br>
<a href="http://www-leland.stanford.edu/~guanyuan/michael.html" target="_top">
<img src="cycleimages.gif">
</a>

</center>

</form>

<script language="LiveScript">
  var ud=0;
  var lr=0;
  var chars="012345678";

function up(){
  getcar(1,0);
  return 0;
}

function down(){
  getcar(-1,0);
  return 0;
```

```
}

function left(){
  getcar(0,1);
  return 0;
}

function right(){
 getcar(0,-1);
  return 0;
}

function getcar( myud, mylr){

  ud=ud+myud;
  lr=lr+mylr;
  if (lr == 8) { lr=0;};
  if (lr == -1) { lr=7;};
  if (ud == 3) { ud=1; lr=4+lr;};
  if (ud == -1) { ud=1; lr=lr+4;};
  if (lr > 7) { lr=lr-8;};


  parent.frames[1].location="http://www-leland.stanford.edu/~guanyuan/public/ ⇐
car/car"+chars.substring(ud,ud+1)+ "_"+chars.substring(lr,lr+1)+".html";
return 0;
}

</script>

</body>
</html>
```

The Civic Car Viewer uses two main working frames across the center of the window: The car is displayed on the left, and the rotation controls are in the right-hand frame.

Analysis   Although the Civic Car Viewer may seem simple at first glance, it provides a good example of how to build easy-to-use programs using multiple frames. It is interesting to note that the program does not follow Netscape's recommendation of placing function definitions in the header of the HTML file. This means it is possible that a user could press one of the four buttons before a function has been evaluated.

All the image files are named `carA_B.html` where A and B are integers. A represents the up-down axis and can have values from 1 to 3, and B represents the left-right axis and can have values from 0 to 7.

The script uses three global variables:

```
var ud=0;
var lr=0;
var chars="012345678";
```

`ud` and `lr` are used to keep track of the current viewing angle of the car. The variable `chars` is used to build the URL for a new view, as you will see later.

The primary function is `getcar()`. This function accepts two arguments— `myud` and `mylr`, which represent changes to the values of **ud** and **lr**:

```
ud=ud+myud;
lr=lr+mylr;
```

Once the changes to the values are made, a series of `if` statements check whether the new value is outside the acceptable range for each variable; if it is, the command block of the `if` statement wraps the value around to the other end of the range. For instance, if **lr** is **8**, it becomes **0**:

```
if (lr == 8) { lr=0;};
if (lr == -1) { lr=7;};
if (ud == 3) { ud=1; lr=4+lr;};
if (ud == -1) { ud=1; lr=lr+4;};
if (lr > 7) { lr=lr-8;};
```

Once this has been done, the function is ready to open the new view in the left frame using

```
parent.frames[1].location= ⇐
"http://www-leland.stanford.edu/~guanyuan/public/car/car" ⇐
+chars.substring(ud,ud+1)+"_"+chars.substring(lr,lr+1)+".html";
```

The command uses **parent** to look at the parent frameset and the **frames** array to explicitly choose the desired frame. It then sets the **location** property to the new URL.

An easy way to load a new page in a window or frame is to set the **location** property. This automatically causes the new URL to load into the window or frame.

Because the left frame is named, the script could just as easily have used the form `parent.left.location`.

The actual filename is built with the portion of the URL expression which reads:

```
car"+chars.substring(ud,ud+1)+"_"+chars.substring(lr,lr+1)+".html"
```

The **substring()** method is used to select single digits from the **chars** variable based on the values of **ud** and **lr**, respectively.

Each of the four buttons in the form calls one of four functions: **up()**, **down()**, **left()**, or **right()**. These functions all work in the same way. They call **getcar()** with appropriate arguments based on the direction, and then they return a value of **0**. The value returned by the function is incidental because the value is never used anywhere in the script.

Michael Yu's Civic Car Viewer is a concrete example of how combining frames and JavaScript makes it possible to create interactive applications. By taking advantage of frames to build sophisticated interfaces and combining that with JavaScript's ability to generate dynamic URLs, it is possible to extend the simple Web metaphor into something more diverse and powerful.

JAMES THIELE'S REMINDER CALENDAR

James Thiele has designed a simple reminder calendar as an example of using cookies in JavaScript. The calendar is available at

`http://www.eskimo.com/~jet/javascript/calendar_js.html`

Rather than being a full-fledged application, this page provides simple functionality, yet is a compelling example of how cookies can extend the value of a script beyond time and session constraints.

The program (see Listing L4-1) displays a calendar of the current month, much the same as in Dave Eisenberg's calendar example. When users click on any of the days in the calendar, they either can enter a reminder for that day, or are alerted of their previously entered reminder.

When the user reloads the page or returns to it later in the month, the days with reminders are displayed in a different color.

Input **Listing L4-1** Source code for James Thiele's Reminder Calendar.

```
<HTML>
<HEAD>
<SCRIPT LANGUAGE="JavaScript">


<!--  to hide script contents from old browsers

//
//  Cookie Functions
//  Written by:  Bill Dortch, hIdaho Design
//  The following functions are released to the public domain.
//

//
// "Internal" function to encode cookie value.  This permits cookies to
// contain whitespace, comma and semicolon characters.
//
function encode (str) {
  var dest = "";
  var len = str.length;
  var index = 0;
  var code = null;
  for (var i = 0; i < len; i++) {
    var ch = str.charAt(i);
    if (ch == " ") code = "%20";
```

continued on next page

continued from previous page

```
        else if (ch == "%") code = "%25";
        else if (ch == ",") code = "%2C";
        else if (ch == ";") code = "%3B";
        else if (ch == "\b") code = "%08";
        else if (ch == "\t") code = "%09";
        else if (ch == "\n") code = "%0A";
        else if (ch == "\f") code = "%0C";
        else if (ch == "\r") code = "%0D";
        if (code != null) {
          dest += str.substring(index,i) + code;
          index = i + 1;
          code = null;
        }
      }
      if (index < len)
        dest += str.substring(index, len);
      return dest;
    }


    //
    // "Internal" function to decode cookie values.
    //
    function decode (str) {
      var dest = "";
      var len = str.length;
      var index = 0;
      var code = null;
      var i = 0;
      while (i < len) {
        i = str.indexOf ("%", i);
        if (i == -1)
          break;
        if (index < i)
          dest += str.substring(index, i);
        code = str.substring (i+1,i+3);
        i += 3;
        index = i;
        if (code == "20") dest += " ";
        else if (code == "25") dest += "%";
        else if (code == "2C") dest += ",";
        else if (code == "3B") dest += ";";
        else if (code == "08") dest += "\b";
        else if (code == "09") dest += "\t";
        else if (code == "0A") dest += "\n";
        else if (code == "0C") dest += "\f";
        else if (code == "0D") dest += "\r";
        else {
          i -= 2;
          index -= 3;
        }
      }
      if (index < len)
```

```
      dest += str.substring(index, len);
   return dest;
}


//
// "Internal" function to return the decoded value of a cookie
//
function getCookieVal (offset) {
   var endstr = document.cookie.indexOf (";", offset);
   if (endstr == -1)
     endstr = document.cookie.length;
   return decode(document.cookie.substring(offset, endstr));
}


//
//   Function to return the value of the cookie specified by "name".
//      name - String object containing the cookie name.
//
function GetCookie (name) {
   var arg = name + "=";
   var alen = arg.length;
   var clen = document.cookie.length;
   var i = 0;
   while (i < clen) {
     var j = i + alen;
     if (document.cookie.substring(i, j) == arg)
       return getCookieVal (j);
     i = document.cookie.indexOf(" ", i) + 1;
     if (i == 0) break;
   }
   return null;
}


//
//   Function to create or update a cookie.
//      name - String object containing the cookie name
//      value - String object containing the cookie value.  May contain
//        any valid string characters, including whitespace, commas and quotes.
//      expires - Date object containing the expiration data of the cookie,
//        or null to expire the cookie at the end of the current session.
//
function SetCookie (name, value, expires) {
   document.cookie = name + "=" + encode(value) + ((expires == null) ? "" : ⇐
("; expires=" + expires.toGMTString()));
}


//   Function to delete a cookie. (Sets expiration date to current date/time)
//      name - String object containing the cookie name
//
function DeleteCookie (name) {
   var exp = new Date();
   var cval = GetCookie (name);
   document.cookie = name + "=" + cval + "; expires=" + exp.toGMTString();
```

continued on next page

continued from previous page

```
    }


    function intro()
    {
        document.write  ("<CENTER>");

        document.writeln("<BR>");
        document.write  ("<H1>");
        document.write  ("Reminder Calendar");
        document.writeln("</H1>");
        document.writeln("</CENTER>");
        document.writeln("<h2>How to use the Reminder Calendar:</h2>");
        document.writeln("<ul><li>Click on a  date to add a reminder");
        document.writeln("    <li>Click on that date again to see the reminder");
        document.writeln("    <li>Reload the page to see dates with ⇐
    reminders in different colors");
        document.writeln("</ul>");

        document.writeln("<h2>Notes:</h2>");
        document.writeln("<ul><li>Lame user interface");
        document.writeln("    <li>Can't delete a reminder");
        document.writeln("    <li>Reminders disappear in about 24 hours");
        document.writeln("</ul>");

        document.writeln("<h2>This is mostly a programming example of:</h2>");
        document.writeln("<ul><li>Using cookies in JavaScript");
        document.writeln("    <li>Using text links to call a ⇐
    function, not open a URL");
        document.writeln("</ul>");

        document.writeln("<h2>Credits:</h2>");
        document.writeln("<ul><li>Cookie Functions written by:  ⇐
    <A href='mailto:bdortch@netw.com'>Bill Dortch</A>, hIdaho Design");
        document.writeln("<ul>The functions are at:");

        document.writeln("    <li>Code: <A href='http://www.hidaho.com/cookies/ ⇐
    cookie.txt'> http://www.hidaho.com/cookies/cookie.txt</A>");
        document.writeln("    <li>Demo: <A href='http://www.hidaho.com/cookies/ ⇐
    cookie.html'> http://www.hidaho.com/cookies/cookie.html</A>");
        document.writeln("</ul>");
        document.writeln("    <li>Reminder Calendar by ⇐
    James Thiele who can be reached:");
        document.writeln("    <UL><LI>at his home page ");
        document.writeln("         <A href='http://www.eskimo.com/~jet'> ⇐
    http://www.eskimo.com/~jet</A>");
        document.writeln("         <LI> via email at ");
        document.writeln("          <address><A href='mailto:jet@eskimo.com'> ⇐
    jet@eskimo.com</a></address></p>");
        document.writeln("</ul>");
    }



    function arrayOfDaysInMonths(isLeapYear)
```

```
{
    this[0] = 31;
    this[1] = 28;
    if (isLeapYear)
                this[1] = 29;
    this[2] = 31;
    this[3] = 30;
    this[4] = 31;
    this[5] = 30;
    this[6] = 31;
    this[7] = 31;
    this[8] = 30;
    this[9] = 31;
    this[10] = 30;
    this[11] = 31;
}


function daysInMonth(month, year)
{
                                        // do the classic leap year calculation
    var isLeapYear = (((year % 4 == 0) && ⇐
(year % 100 != 0)) || (year % 400 == 0));
    var monthDays  = new arrayOfDaysInMonths(isLeapYear);

    return monthDays[month];
}



function calendar()
{
    var monthNames = "JanFebMarAprMayJunJulAugSepOctNovDec";
    var today       = new Date();
    var day         = today.getDate();
    var month       = today.getMonth();
    var year        = today.getYear() + 1900;

    // figure out how many days this month will have...
var numDays     = daysInMonth(month, year);

    // and go back to the first day of the month...
    var firstDay   = today;
        firstDay.setDate(1);
    // and figure out which day of the week it hits...
    var startDay = firstDay.getDay();

    var column = 0;

    // Start the calendar table
    document.write("<CENTER>");
    document.write("<TABLE BORDER>");
    document.write("<TR><TH COLSPAN=7>");
    document.write(monthNames.substring(3*month, 3*(month + 1)) + " " + year);
```

continued on next page

continued from previous page

```
        document.write("<TR><TH>Sun<TH>Mon<TH>Tue<TH>Wed<TH>Thu<TH>Fri<TH>Sat");

        // put blank table entries for days of week before beginning of the month
        document.write("<TR>");
        for (i=1; i < startDay; i++)
        {
            document.write("<TD>");
            column++;
        }

        for (i=1; i <= numDays; i++)
        {
            // Write the day
            var s = "" + i;
            if ((GetCookie("d"+i) != null))
              // s = s.fontcolor(document.vlinkColor);
              s = s.fontcolor("#FF0000");
            s = s.link("javascript:dayClick(" + i + ")")
                document.write("<TD>" + s);

            // Check for end of week/row
            if (++column == 7)
            {
                document.write("<TR>"); // start a new row
                column = 0;
            }
        }
        document.write("</TABLE>");
        document.writeln("</CENTER>");
}


/////////////////////////////
///////// dayClick //////////
/////////////////////////////
function dayClick(day)
{
        var expdate = new Date ();
            expdate.setTime (expdate.getTime() + (24 * 60 * 60 * 1000)); ⇐
// 24 hrs from now
        var prefix                = "d";
        var theCookieName         = prefix + day;
        var theDayclickedReminder = GetCookie(theCookieName);

    if (theDayclickedReminder != null) {
        alert("The reminder for day " + day + " is:"  + theDayclickedReminder);
    } // end if
```

```
        if (confirm("Do you wish to enter a reminder for day " + ⇐
day + " of this month?"))
        {
                x = prompt("Enter a reminder for day "+ day + ⇐
" of this month", theDayclickedReminder);
        SetCookie (theCookieName, x, expdate);
    } // end if
}


// --> <!-- end hiding contents from old browsers  -->

</SCRIPT>

<TITLE>James Thiele's Calendar reminders
</TITLE>
</HEAD>

<BODY>

<SCRIPT LANGUAGE="JavaScript">


<!--  to hide script contents from old browsers

// Write the intro
// Write the calendar
calendar();
document.write("<HR>");
intro();
// --> <!-- end hiding contents from old browsers  -->

</SCRIPT>

<IMG SRC="../RainbowLine.gif">
<A href="index.html"><IMG SRC="javascriptlogo.gif">To JavaScript stuff</A>
<br><em>Page last modified 24 Jan 96</em>

</BODY>
</HTML>
```

Output　　The results look like Figures L4-1 and L4-2.

Figure L4-1
A reminder
prompt dialog
appears when
users click a date
for the first time.

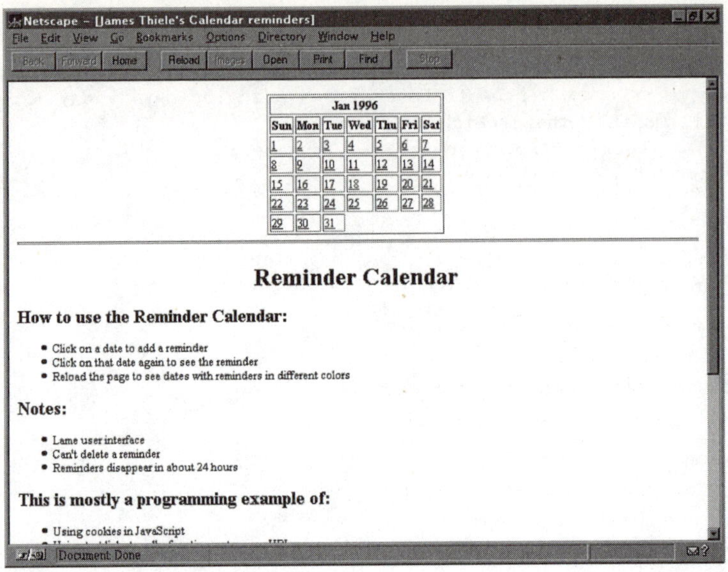

Figure L4-2
In future visits,
the days with
reminders are
displayed in a
different color.

Analysis

The first thing you notice is that Thiele is using an early version of Bill Dortch's cookie function set. This version was written before JavaScript included the **escape()** and **unescape()** functions, which forced Dortch to write his own functions, **encode()** and **decode()**, to perform the encoding of values.

In any case, the newer version of Dortch's functions is backward compatible and could replace the old version in this script without affecting its operation in newer browsers.

Thiele has written five functions to implement his calendar program: **intro()**, **arrayOfDaysInMonth()**, **daysInMonth()**, **calendar()**, and **dayClick()**.

In addition, he builds most of the body of his HTML document using a JavaScript script:

```
<SCRIPT LANGUAGE="JavaScript">


<!--  to hide script contents from old browsers


// Write the intro
// Write the calendar
calendar();
document.write("<HR>");
intro();
// --> <!-- end hiding contents from old browsers  -->


</SCRIPT>
```

This script is quite simple: it calls **calendar()** to display the calendar, it draws a horizontal line, and then it calls **intro()**, which displays most of the rest of the text of the script.

The `intro()` Function

This function needs little discussion. It is just a static collection of `document.write()` statements that output the introductory information about the application.

The `arrayOfDaysInMonth()` Function

The `arrayOfDaysInMonth()` function simply creates a twelve-element array containing the number of days in each calendar month. It accepts one Boolean variable as an argument. This enables it to correctly set the number of days in February based on whether or not it is a leap year.

The `daysInMonth()` Function

This function takes two arguments—the month and year—and uses these to determine if it is a leap year. It then creates an array of days in each month of the particular year and returns the number of days in the specified month.

The `calendar()` Function

The `calendar()` function is where some of the more complex processing occurs.

```
var monthNames = "JanFebMarAprMayJunJulAugSepOctNovDec";
var today       = new Date();
var day         = today.getDate();
var month       = today.getMonth();
var year        = today.getYear() + 1900;

// figure out how many days this month will have...
var numDays     = daysInMonth(month, year);

// and go back to the first day of the month...
var firstDay    = today;
    firstDay.setDate(1);
// and figure out which day of the week it hits...
var startDay = firstDay.getDay();

var column = 0;
```

As you might expect, the function starts by setting up key variables for use throughout the function. These include a string of month names—the same technique you saw in Dave Eisenberg's calendar script.

The `firstDay Date` object is used to get the day of the week of the first day of the month and store it in `startDay`.

```
// Start the calendar table
document.write("<CENTER>");
document.write("<TABLE BORDER>");
document.write("<TR><TH COLSPAN=7>");
document.write(monthNames.substring(3*month, 3*(month + 1)) + " " + year);
document.write("<TR><TH>Sun<TH>Mon<TH>Tue<TH>Wed<TH>Thu<TH>Fri<TH>Sat");
```

continued on next page

continued from previous page

```
// put blank table entries for days of week before beginning of the month
document.write("<TR>");
for (i=1; i < startDay; i++)
{
    document.write("<TD>");
    column++;
}
```

After building the header of the table, which holds the calendar for the month, the `for` loop inserts blank cells for each of the unused days of the week before the first day of the month.

```
for (i=1; i <= numDays; i++)
{
    // Write the day
    var s = "" + i;
    if ((GetCookie("d"+i) != null))
      // s = s.fontcolor(document.vlinkColor);
      s = s.fontcolor("#FF0000");
      s = s.link("javascript:dayClick(" + i + ")")
        document.write("<TD>" + s);

    // Check for end of week/row
    if (++column == 7)
    {
        document.write("<TR>"); // start a new row
        column = 0;
    }
}
```

Next, another `for` loop repeats for each day in the month. For each day, a cell is created and the number is displayed with a hypertext link to the URL `javascript:dayClick(number)`. This is done by using the string's `link` method to add the URL. As you will see in Chapter 10, "Strings, Math, and the History List," if the `link` method is used, then the value of the string is surrounded by an appropriate **<A>** HTML container tag.

Notice the use of the `javascript:` URL. This type of URL can be used to call a function in the current document. When used in the **HREF** attribute of the **<A>** tag, this is often an alternative to using the `onClick` event handler. It can also be used in the open location dialog box of the Navigator browser to test what a line of JavaScript code will evaluate to. In this case, the result of evaluating an expression is displayed in the browser window.

Similarly, the `fontcolor()` method adds the appropriate HTML tags to the value of the string. In this case, the `fontcolor()` method is called only if the cookie for that day has been previously set with a reminder.

The final **if** statement checks whether you have reached the last column, and if so, closes the row, opens a new row in the table, and resets the **column** counter.

The dayClick() Function

This function handles both prompting for a reminder and displaying existing reminders. It is invoked when the user clicks on a date. It accepts the date as an argument.

```
var expdate = new Date ();
        expdate.setTime (expdate.getTime() + (24 * 60 * 60 * 1000)); ⇐
// 24 hrs from now
    var prefix              = "d";
    var theCookieName       = prefix + day;
    var theDayclickedReminder = GetCookie(theCookieName);
```

The function starts by setting up its variables, including an expiry date for cookies and a value of the cookie for the selected date.

```
if (theDayclickedReminder != null) {
    alert("The reminder for day " + day + " is:"  + theDayclickedReminder);
} // end if
```

If the value of the cookie is not **null**, then the reminder is displayed in an alert dialog box.

```
    if (confirm("Do you wish to enter a reminder for day " + ⇐
day + " of this month?"))
        {
            x = prompt("Enter a reminder for day "+ day + ⇐
" of this month", theDayclickedReminder);
        SetCookie (theCookieName, x, expdate);
    } // end if
```

If the value of the cookie is **null**, then users are asked whether they wish to enter a reminder for the current day and, if they do, they are further prompted for the text of the reminder. The reminder is then stored in a cookie. Notice the use of the **confirm()** call as the condition of the **if** statement—**confirm()** returns a value of **true** or **false** based on the user's response.

MICHAL SRAMKA'S MATCHES GAME

Michal Sramka has used JavaScript to produce one of the traditional games used in many programming courses: the matches game. His game is on-line at

`http://www.sanet.sk/~ms/js/matches.html`

The rules of the game are simple: There is a supply of matches—in this case the number is selected by the user. The user and the computer take turns taking one, two, or three matches in an attempt to force the other player to take the last match. If you take the last match, you lose. If the computer is forced to take it, then you win.

In Sramka's example, he has developed a fairly sophisticated table-based interface that makes extensive use of JavaScript.

Input   **Listing L5-1** Source code for Michal Sramka's Matches Game.

```
<html>
<head>
<title>JavaScript</title>
</head>

<body onload="welcome()" onunload="bye()">

<script language="JavaScript">
<!-- Begin
function welcome() {
   document.game.help.value=" Please enter ⇐
number of matches and click Start game.";
document.game.number.focus();
   window.defaultStatus="JavaScript Safety Matches Game"; }

function bye() {
   window.defaultStatus=""; }

function come_on() {
   if(document.game.number.value<5) alert("Must be more than 4");
   else {
     document.game.help.value="           Wow, it's your turn. Click 1, 2 or 3.";
     document.game.count.value=document.game.number.value; } }

function letsgo(yourchoice) {
   var date=new Date(),mychoice;
   if(document.game.count.value-yourchoice<=1) {
     document.game.help.value="                    You win !";
     document.game.count.value=1; }
   else {
     if(document.game.count.value%4==0) {
```

```
    if(yourchoice==1) mychoice=2;
    else {
      if(date.getSeconds()%2==0) mychoice=3;
      else mychoice=1; } }
  else if(document.game.count.value%4==1) mychoice=4-yourchoice;
  else if(document.game.count.value%4==2) {
    if(yourchoice==2) mychoice=3;
    else {
      if(date.getSeconds()%2==0) mychoice=1;
      else mychoice=2; } }
  else {
    if(yourchoice==1) mychoice=1;
    else {
      if(date.getSeconds()%2==0) mychoice=2;
      else mychoice=3; } }
  if(document.game.count.value-yourchoice<4)⇐
 mychoice=document.game.count.value-yourchoice-1;
document.game.count.value-=yourchoice+mychoice;
  document.game.me.value=" "+mychoice;
  if(document.game.count.value==1) document.game.help.value= ⇐
"          I took "+mychoice+" matches and win this game !";
else document.game.help.value= ⇐
"          I took "+mychoice+" matches. It's your turn again."; } }
// End -->
</script>

<center>

<h1>Safety Matches Game</h1>
This is a very easy game. It's available as JavaScript Applet as well as
<a href="/~milan/JAVA/matches.html">Java Applet</a><br>
At first choose the number of matches. Then you have to take 1, 2 or 3
matches by clicking on the appropriate button. The Master will do the
same. Who takes the last match - LOSE !<p>

<form name="game">
<table border="3" cellpadding="0" cellspacing="2">
<tr>
<td align="left">How many matches ?</td>
<td align="right"><input type="text" name="number" size="10"> ⇐
<input type="button" name="start" value=" Start game " ⇐
onclick="if(confirm('Really start new game ?')) come_on()"></td>
</tr>
<tr>
<td align="center" colspan="2"><input type="text" name="help" size="55"></td>
</tr>
<tr>
<td align="left">Counter:</td>
<td align="right"><input type="text" name="count" size="10"></td>
</tr>
<tr>
<td align="left">Your Choice:</td>
```

continued on next page

continued from previous page

```
<td align="right"><input type="button" name="one" ⇐
value=" 1 " onclick="letsgo(1)"><input type="button" ⇐
name="two" value=" 2 " onclick="letsgo(2)"> ⇐
<input type="button" name="three" value=" 3 " onclick="letsgo(3)"></td>
</tr>
<tr>
<td align="left">My Choice:</td>
<td align="right"><input type="text" name="me" size="3"></td>
</tr>
</table>
</form>

<hr><b><i><a href="/~ms/ms.html">Michal Sramka</a>'s ⇐
<a href="/~ms/js/">JavaScript Archive</a></i></b>
</center>
</body>
</html>
```

Output   The script produces results similar to those in Figure L5-1.

Analysis   To understand Sramka's program, you need to start by looking at the table, which is the primary interface for the game.

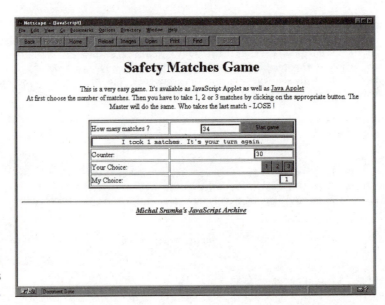

Figure L5-1
Michal Sramka's
Matches Game.

```
<form name="game">
<table border="3" cellpadding="0" cellspacing="2">
<tr>
<td align="left">How many matches ?</td>
<td align="right"><input type="text" name="number" size="10">  ⇐
<input type="button" name="start" value=" Start game "  ⇐
onclick="if(confirm('Really start new game ?')) come_on()"></td>
</tr>
<tr>
<td align="center" colspan="2"><input type="text" name="help" size="55"></td>
</tr>
<tr>
<td align="left">Counter:</td>
<td align="right"><input type="text" name="count" size="10"></td>
</tr>
<tr>
<td align="left">Your Choice:</td>
<td align="right"><input type="button" name="one" value=" 1 "  ⇐
onclick="letsgo(1)"><input type="button" name="two"  ⇐
value=" 2 " onclick="letsgo(2)"><input type="button"  ⇐
name="three" value=" 3 " onclick="letsgo(3)"></td>
</tr>
<tr>
<td align="left">My Choice:</td>
<td align="right"><input type="text" name="me" size="3"></td>
</tr>
</table>
</form>
```

There is a Start button that confirms the user wants to start and then calls come_on(). If a new game starts, it uses the number in the number field to determine the number of matches in the game. The help text field is the primary display point for messages about the status of the game. The count field is used to display the number of matches left in the current game. There are three buttons that the user uses to select the number of matches he wants to take each turn. The me field is used to display the computer's choice each round.

There are four functions in the main script: welcome(), bye(), come_on(), and letsgo(). The welcome() and bye() functions display welcome and farewell messages and are invoked from the BODY tag's onLoad and onUnload event handler.

The come_on() function is called when the user decides to start a new game.

```
function come_on() {
  if(document.game.number.value<5) alert("Must be more than 4");
  else {
    document.game.help.value="                Wow, it's your turn. Click 1, 2 or 3.";
    document.game.count.value=document.game.number.value; } }
```

The function checks that the value in number is valid (greater than or equal to 5). If not, the user is alerted to choose another number. Otherwise, the help field informs the user that it is his turn, and the count field is updated with the starting number of matches.

The real work of the game takes place in `letsgo()`. The function is invoked when the user clicks on one of the three buttons to select a number of matches to take. The function takes one argument: the number of matches selected by the user.

The first step is to declare the global variables and objects: `date` and `mychoice`. The next step is to check whether the user has won, by subtracting the selected number from the value in the `count` field and comparing it to **1**.

```
function letsgo(yourchoice) {
  var date=new Date(),mychoice;
  if(document.game.count.value-yourchoice<=1) {
    document.game.help.value="                            You win !";
    document.game.count.value=1; }
```

If the user has won, the `help` field is updated with an appropriate message, and the single match left is displayed in `count`.

Assuming the user hasn't won, the next step is to decide the computer's next play.

```
else {
  if(document.game.count.value%4==0) {
    if(yourchoice==1) mychoice=2;
    else {
      if(date.getSeconds()%2==0) mychoice=3;
      else mychoice=1; } }
```

To do this, see whether the number of matches left is a multiple of four before the user selected. If it is, and the user chooses one match, then the computer chooses two. Otherwise, the computer makes a random choice between one and three matches.

```
  else if(document.game.count.value%4==1) mychoice=4-yourchoice;
```

If the remainder of dividing the number (before the user's choice) by four is one, then the computer selects the result of subtracting the user's choice from four.

```
  else if(document.game.count.value%4==2) {
    if(yourchoice==2) mychoice=3;
    else {
      if(date.getSeconds()%2==0) mychoice=1;
      else mychoice=2; } }
```

If the remainder is two, and if the user chooses two, the computer chooses three matches. Otherwise, it makes a random choice between one and two.

```
  else {
    if(yourchoice==1) mychoice=1;
    else {
      if(date.getSeconds()%2==0) mychoice=2;
      else mychoice=3; } }
```

If the remainder is three, and the user chooses one match, the computer follows suit and chooses one. Otherwise, a random choice is made between two and three.

```
    if(document.game.count.value-yourchoice<4) ⇐
mychoice=document.game.count.value-yourchoice-1;
document.game.count.value-=yourchoice+mychoice;
    document.game.me.value=" "+mychoice;
    if(document.game.count.value==1) document.game.help.value= ⇐
"         I took "+mychoice+" matches and win this game !";
else document.game.help.value= ⇐

"         I took "+mychoice+" matches. It's your turn again."; } }
```

Finally, if the user's play results in the number of remaining matches being less than four, then the computer chooses the number of remaining matches less one.

The function then updates the value of the **count** field and displays the computer's choice in **me**. Then a check is made to see whether the computer has won. If the number of remaining matches is one, then the computer has won, and a message is displayed in **help** to that effect. Otherwise, a message informing the user of how many matches the computer took is displayed in **help**.

CCAS INDIRECT COST WORKSHEET

CCAS Inc., which produces accounting software for Government Contractors, uses JavaScript to demonstrate one of the formulas included in its CCAS for Government Contractors financial and job cost accounting package.

The Indirect Cost Rate sheet is available at this site:

`http://www.ccas.com/ccasrate.html`

It provides a good example of building a complex worksheet using JavaScript.

The application uses one large form, spanning four separate tables, to guide the user through entering the required information for the form. The worksheet is designed to calculate the Fringe Benefit Rate, Overhead Rate, and G&A Rate based on information in the form. At the bottom of the page, the formulas being used are described. The source code for the CCAS Worksheet appears in Listing L6-1.

Input   **Listing L6-1** Source code for the CCAS Worksheet.

```
<HTML>
<HEAD>
<TITLE>CCAS Indirect Cost Rate Worksheet (JavaScript)</TITLE>

<SCRIPT LANGUAGE="LiveScript">


<!-- hide this script tag's contents from old browsers

function checkNumber(input, min, max, msg)
{
    msg = msg + " field has invalid data: " + input.value;

    var str = input.value;
    for (var i = 0; i < str.length; i++) {
        var ch = str.substring(i, i + 1)
        if ((ch < "0" || "9" < ch) && ch != '.') {
            alert(msg);
            return false;
        }
    }
    var num = 0 + str
    if (num < min || max < num) {
        alert(msg + " not in range [" + min + ".." + max + "]");
        return false;
    }
    input.value = str;
    return true;
}
```

```
function computeField(input)
{
    if (input.value != null && input.value.length != 0)
        input.value = "" + eval(input.value);
      computeForm(input.form);
}

function computeForm(form)
{
    if ((form.DL.value == null || form.DL.value.length == 0) ||
        (form.ODC.value == null || form.ODC.value.length == 0) ||
        (form.TFB.value == null || form.TFB.value.length == 0) ||
        (form.TOH.value == null || form.TOH.value.length == 0) ||
        (form.TGA.value == null || form.TGA.value.length == 0) ||
        (form.TBP.value == null || form.TBP.value.length == 0) ||
        (form.FBR.value == null || form.TBP.value.length == 0) ||
        (form.OHL.value == null || form.OHL.value.length == 0) ||
        (form.GAL.value == null || form.GAL.value.length == 0) ||
        (form.BPL.value == null || form.BPL.value.length == 0)) {
        form.FBR.value = "Incomplete data";
        form.OHR.value = "Incomplete data";
        form.GAR.value = "Incomplete data";
        return;
    }

    if (!checkNumber(form.DL, 1,99999999, "Direct Labor") ||
        !checkNumber(form.ODC,0,99999999, "Other Direct Costs") ||
        !checkNumber(form.TFB,1,99999999, "Total Fringe Benefits") ||
        !checkNumber(form.TOH,1,99999999, "Total Overhead") ||
        !checkNumber(form.TGA,0,99999999, "Total G&A") ||
        !checkNumber(form.TBP,0,99999999, "Total B&P") ||
        !checkNumber(form.TBP,0,99999999, "Total B&P") ||
        !checkNumber(form.DLL,0,99999999, "Total B&P") ||
        !checkNumber(form.OHL,1,99999999, "Total Overhead Labor") ||
        !checkNumber(form.GAL,0,99999999, "Total G&A Labor") ||
        !checkNumber(form.BPL,0,99999999, "Total B&P Labor")) {
        form.FBR.value = "Invalid";
        form.OHR.value = "Invalid";
        form.GAR.value = "Invalid";
        return;
    }

    var i=form.DL.value *1
    var j=form.ODC.value*1
    form.TOTDIR.value=i + j
    form.DLL.value=i

    var k=form.TFB.value *1
    var l=form.TOH.value *1
    var m=form.TGA.value *1
    var n=form.TBP.value *1
```

continued on next page

continued from previous page

```
            form.TOTIND.value=k + l + m + n
            var z=i + j + k + l + m + n
            form.TC.value=z

            var o=form.OHL.value *1
            var p=form.GAL.value *1
            var q=form.BPL.value *1
            var r=i + o + p + q
            form.TOTLAB.value= r

            var s=(k /   r)
            form.FBR.value=s * 100

            var t=(((i + o + q) * s) + l) / (i + q)
            form.OHR.value= t * 100

            var u=(m + n+ (p * s) + (t * q))
            var z=z - u
            var z= u / z
            form.GAR.value=z * 100

            form.DLB.value=i
            var v=i * t
            form.OHRB.value=v
            form.OHRR.value=t * 100
            form.ODCB.value=j
            form.GARR.value=z * 100
            var w=(i + v + j) * z
            form.GARB.value=w
            form.TCB.value=w + i + v + j


}

function clearForm(form)
{
            form.DL.value = "";
            form.ODC.value = "";
            form.TFB.value = "";
}

<!-- done hiding from old browsers -->


</SCRIPT>

<BODY BGCOLOR="#ffffff" TEXT="#020225"></HEAD>
<CENTER>
<FORM method=POST>
<TABLE BORDER=5 CELLSPACING=2 CELLPADDING=5 ALIGN=MIDDLE> <TR><TD><IMG SRC=
"ccaslogoTR.gif" WIDTH="343" HEIGHT="36" NATURALSIZEFLAG="3" ALIGN=bottom ⇐
alt="CCAS accounting solutions for Government Contractors"></TABLE><BR>
```

```
<H1>Indirect Cost Rate Worksheet</H1>
<IMG SRC="javatr.gif" alt="JavaScript(tm)"><BR><BR>
</Center>

<FONT SIZE=3>
In this JavaScript(tm) application, you can determine your indirect cost rates ⇐
based upon a commonly used (and DCAA accepted) rate structure.   ⇐
This rate structure is one of several options that are included in ⇐
<A HREF="ccassw.html">CCAS for Government
Contractors</A><B>, "Internet Edition"</B>. Simply complete Steps 1 and 2, and ⇐
then in Step 3 calculate your indirect cost rates.  Be sure to review ⇐
the proof of the calculation and details of the calculation formulas ⇐
employed.<BR><BR>
Note that if this page (which requires Netscape 2.0b5 or later) is saved using ⇐
the "Save As...Format...Source" command from your browser's "File" menu, ⇐
it can be run locally when loaded into your browser using "Open File"--<B> ⇐
even without an active Internet connection.</B>
<P>


<CENTER>

<H2>Step 1-Enter Your Total Costs</H2>
<TABLE BORDER=6 CELLSPACING=2 CELLPADDING=3 ALIGN=MIDDLE>
<TR>
<TD><DIV ALIGN=CENTER><B>COST CATEGORY<BR>DESCRIPTION</B></DIV></TD>
<TD><DIV ALIGN=CENTER><B><br>AMOUNT</B></DIV></TD>
<TD><DIV ALIGN=CENTER><B>SUBTOTAL<br>(Computed)</B></DIV></TD>
</TR>
<TD><DIV ALIGN=CENTER><B>Total Costs From General Ledger</B></DIV> </TD>
</TR>
<TD><B>Direct Costs:</B></DIV> </TD>
</TR>
<TR>
<TD>A.  <B>Total</B> Direct Labor</TD>
<TD><DIV ALIGN=CENTER><INPUT TYPE=TEXT NAME=DL  SIZE=15 ⇐
onChange=computeField(this)></DIV></TD>
<TD><DIV ALIGN=CENTER> </TD></TR>
<TD>B.  <B>Total</B> Other Direct Costs</TD>
<TD><DIV ALIGN=CENTER><INPUT TYPE=TEXT NAME=ODC SIZE=15 ⇐
onChange=computeField(this)></DIV> </TD>
<TD><DIV ALIGN=CENTER></DIV> </TD></TR>
<TD><DIV ALIGN=RIGHT>Total Direct Costs</DIV></TD>
<TD><DIV ALIGN=CENTER> </DIV></TD>
<TD><DIV ALIGN=CENTER><INPUT TYPE=TEXT NAME=TOTDIR  SIZE=15></DIV> </TD></TR>
<TR>
<TD><B>Indirect Costs:</B> </TD>
</TR>
<TR>
<TD>C.  <B>Total</B> Fringe Benefits</TD>
<TD><DIV ALIGN=CENTER><INPUT TYPE=TEXT NAME=TFB  SIZE=15 ⇐
onChange=computeField(this)> </DIV></TD>
<TD><DIV ALIGN=CENTER></DIV> </TD></TR>
```

continued on next page

continued from previous page

```
<TD>D.  <B>Total</B>  Overhead</TD>
<TD><DIV ALIGN=CENTER><INPUT TYPE=TEXT NAME=TOH  SIZE=15></DIV> </TD>
<TD><DIV ALIGN=CENTER> </DIV></TD></TR>
<TD>E.  <B>Total</B> G&A</TD>
<TD><DIV ALIGN=CENTER><INPUT TYPE=TEXT NAME=TGA SIZE=15></DIV> </TD>
<TD><DIV ALIGN=CENTER></DIV> </TD></TR>
<TD>F.  <B>Total</B> B&P and IR&D</TD>
<TD><DIV ALIGN=CENTER><INPUT TYPE=TEXT NAME=TBP  SIZE=15> </DIV></TD>
<TD><DIV ALIGN=CENTER></DIV> </TD></TR>
<TD><DIV ALIGN=RIGHT>Total Indirect Costs</DIV></TD>
<TD><DIV ALIGN=CENTER> </DIV></TD>
<TD><DIV ALIGN=CENTER><INPUT TYPE=TEXT NAME=TOTIND  SIZE=15></DIV> </TD></TR>
<TD><DIV ALIGN=RIGHT>G.  Total Costs</DIV></TD>
<TD><DIV ALIGN=CENTER> </DIV></TD>
<TD><DIV ALIGN=CENTER><INPUT TYPE=TEXT NAME=TC  SIZE=15></DIV> </TD></TR>
</Table><br><br>

<H2>Step 2-Enter Your Total Labor Costs<BR> (subset of Total Costs)</H2>
<TABLE BORDER=6 CELLSPACING=2 CELLPADDING=3 ALIGN=MIDDLE>
<TR>
<TD><DIV ALIGN=CENTER><B>COST ELEMENT<BR>DESCRIPTION</B></DIV></TD>
<TD><DIV ALIGN=CENTER><B><br>AMOUNT</B></DIV></TD>
<TD><DIV ALIGN=CENTER><B>SUBTOTAL<br>(Computed)</B></DIV></TD></TR>
<TR>
<TD><DIV ALIGN=CENTER><B>Labor Costs from General Ledger</B></DIV> </TD>
</TR>
<TR><TD>A.  <B>Total</B> Direct Labor (from Step 1)</TD>
<TD><DIV ALIGN=CENTER><INPUT TYPE=TEXT NAME=DLL  SIZE=15> </DIV></TD>
<TD><DIV ALIGN=CENTER> </TD></TR>
<TD>H.  <B>Total</B> Overhead Labor</TD>
<TD><DIV ALIGN=CENTER><INPUT TYPE=TEXT NAME=OHL  SIZE=15> </DIV></TD>
<TD><DIV ALIGN=CENTER> </DIV></TD></TR>
<TD>I.  <B>Total</B> G&A Labor</TD>
<TD><DIV ALIGN=CENTER><INPUT TYPE=TEXT NAME=GAL SIZE=15> </DIV></TD>
<TD><DIV ALIGN=CENTER> </DIV></TD></TR>
<TD>J.  <B>Total</B> B&P and IR&D Labor</TD>
<TD><DIV ALIGN=CENTER><INPUT TYPE=TEXT NAME=BPL  SIZE=15> </DIV></TD>
<TD><DIV ALIGN=CENTER> </DIV></TD></TR>
<TD><DIV ALIGN=RIGHT>K.  Total Labor</DIV></TD>
<TD><DIV ALIGN=CENTER></DIV> </TD>
<TD><DIV ALIGN=CENTER><INPUT TYPE=TEXT NAME=TOTLAB  SIZE=15></DIV> </TD></TR>
</Table><br><br>
<A NAME="help">
(If you have difficulty running this worksheet on your Netscape 2.0b6a browser, ⇐
<A HREF="ccasratehelp.html">click here</A>.)
<BR><BR>

<H2>Step 3-Click on Compute for Rate Calculation Results</H2>
<INPUT TYPE="button" VALUE="Compute"    onClick=computeForm(this.form)>
<INPUT TYPE="reset"  VALUE="Reset"      onClick=clearForm(this.form)>
<BR><BR>
<TABLE BORDER=6 CELLSPACING=2 CELLPADDING=3 ALIGN=MIDDLE>
```

```
<TR>
<TD><DIV ALIGN=CENTER>Fringe Benefit Rate</DIV></TD>
<TD><DIV ALIGN=CENTER><INPUT TYPE=TEXT NAME=FBR  SIZE=15> </DIV></TD>
<TD><DIV ALIGN=CENTER>The Fringe Benefit Rate rate is generated to build the ⇐
Overhead and G&A rates and is not separately stated for pricing or ⇐
billing. See formulas, below.</DIV></TD></TR>
<TR>
<TD>Overhead Rate</TD>
<TD></TD>
<TD><DIV ALIGN=CENTER><INPUT TYPE=TEXT NAME=OHR  SIZE=15></DIV> </TD></TR>
<TR>
<TD>G&A Rate</TD>
<TD></TD>
<TD><DIV ALIGN=CENTER><INPUT TYPE=TEXT NAME=GAR  SIZE=15> </DIV></TD></TR>
</TABLE>

<BR><BR>


<H2>The Proof of the Calculated Rates</H2>
<TABLE BORDER=6 CELLSPACING=2 CELLPADDING=3 ALIGN=MIDDLE>
<TR>
<TD><DIV ALIGN=CENTER><B>COST ITEM</B></DIV></TD>
<TD><DIV ALIGN=CENTER><B>RATE%</B></DIV></TD>
<TD><DIV ALIGN=CENTER><B>AMOUNT</B></DIV></TD></TR>
<TR><TD> Direct Labor</TD>
<TD><DIV ALIGN=CENTER> </TD>
<TD><DIV ALIGN=CENTER><INPUT TYPE=TEXT NAME=DLB  SIZE=15> </DIV></TD>
</TR>
<TR>
<TD> Overhead on Direct Labor</TD>
<TD><DIV ALIGN=CENTER><INPUT TYPE=TEXT NAME=OHRR  SIZE=15> </DIV></TD>
<TD><DIV ALIGN=CENTER><INPUT TYPE=TEXT NAME=OHRB  SIZE=15> </DIV></TD>
</TR>
<TR><TD> Other Direct Costs</TD>
<TD><DIV ALIGN=CENTER> </TD>
<TD><DIV ALIGN=CENTER><INPUT TYPE=TEXT NAME=ODCB  SIZE=15> </DIV></TD>
</TR>
<TR>
<TD> G&A on Subtotal of Costs</TD>
<TD><DIV ALIGN=CENTER><INPUT TYPE=TEXT NAME=GARR  SIZE=15> </DIV></TD>
<TD><DIV ALIGN=CENTER><INPUT TYPE=TEXT NAME=GARB  SIZE=15> </DIV></TD>
</TR>
<TR><TD> Total Costs (see Step 1, above)</TD>
<TD><DIV ALIGN=CENTER> </TD>
<TD><DIV ALIGN=CENTER><INPUT TYPE=TEXT NAME=TCB  SIZE=15> </DIV></TD>
</TR>
</Table><br><br>

<H2>The Indirect Cost Rate Calculation Formulas <BR> ⇐
(Keyed to Cost Elements Above)</H2>
</CENTER>
```

continued on next page

continued from previous page

```
<BR>
<B>Fringe Benefit Rate (FBR)</B>= C / K<BR><BR>
<B>Overhead Rate (OHR)</B>= (((A + H + J)  * FBR) + D) / (A + J)<BR><BR>
<B>G&A Rate</B>= ((I * FBR) + E + F + (J *OHR)) / ⇐
(G - ((I * FBR) + E + F + (J *OHR)))

<BR><BR>
</FORM>
<H5>

<img src="back.gif"><A HREF="ccassw.html">Back to CCAS Software</A><BR>
<P>
<CENTER>
<HR SIZE="6">
<A HREF="Default.html">CCAS's home page</A><P>
<A HREF="mailto:info@ccas.com"><IMG SRC="mbox.gif" ⇐
ALIGN=bottom WIDTH="32" HEIGHT=
"32" NATURALSIZEFLAG="3" Border="0"></A><BR>
Forward inquiries to <BR>
<A HREF="mailto:info@ccas.com">info@ccas.com</A> <BR>
<BR>
(c) 1996 CCAS, Inc. All rights reserved.
</H5>
</CENTER>
</BODY>
</HTML>
```

Output   The worksheet looks like Figures L6-1 through L6-4.

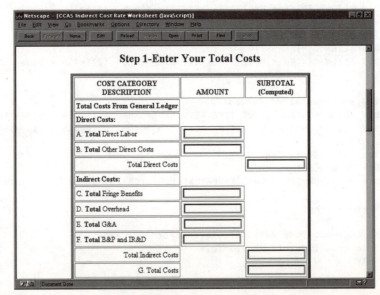

Figure L6-1
The first form
allows users
to enter their
total costs.

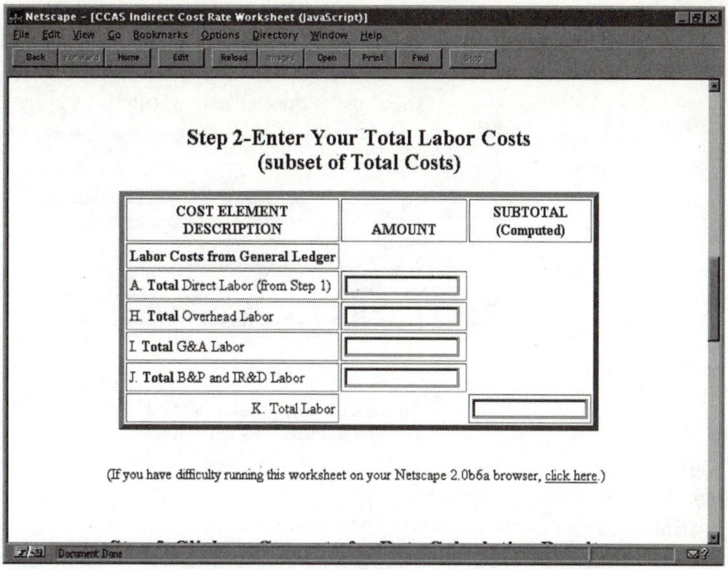

Figure L6-2
Next, users enter their total labor costs.

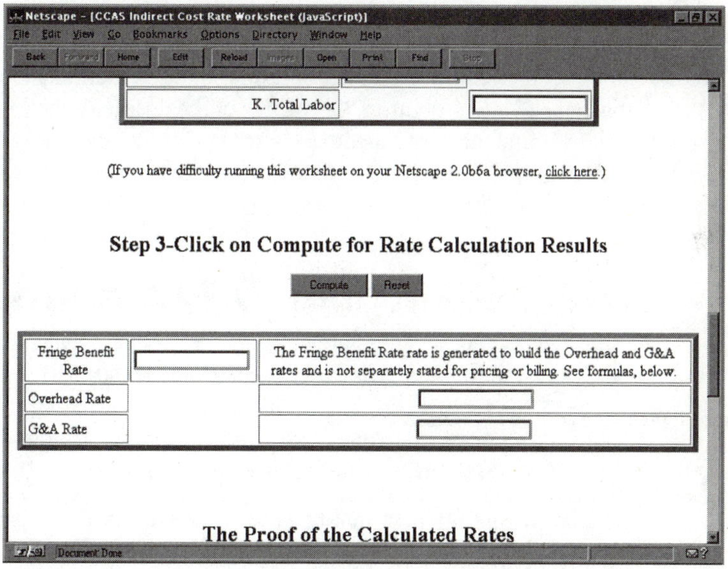

Figure L6-3
The third form allows users to compute the results.

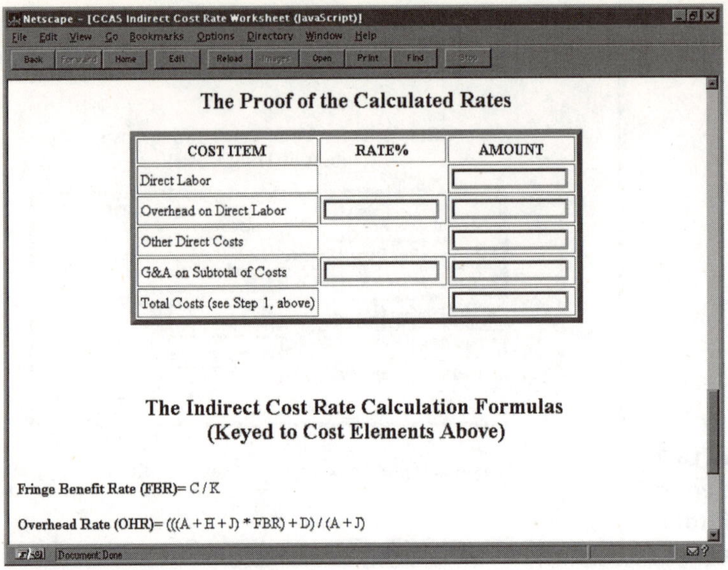

Figure L6-4
The fourth
form provides
breakdown proofs
of the calculations.

Analysis

The Indirect Cost Rate Sheet is built out of four functions. The HTML form itself is rather simple, consisting of a number of text input fields spanning four tables with a Compute button and a Reset button. Only three of the text fields have event handlers, which all call the same function: `computeField()`. This function makes calls to two of the other functions: `checkNumber()` and `computeForm()`. `clearForm()` is invoked when the user clicks on the Reset button.

The `checkNumber()` Function

This function takes four arguments and checks that a given number falls within a specified range. If not, it warns the user that a particular field contains invalid data.

```
function checkNumber(input, min, max, msg)
{
    msg = msg + " field has invalid data: " + input.value;
```

The function starts by building the message that will be displayed if there is an error.

```
    var str = input.value;
    for (var i = 0; i < str.length; i++) {
        var ch = str.substring(i, i + 1)
        if ((ch < "0" || "9" < ch) && ch != '.') {
            alert(msg);
            return false;
        }
    }
```

Next, the function scans each character of the `input` string to make sure it is a numeric value. This program was written before the `parseInt()` function became available in JavaScript, which could also be used with certain limitations, to check whether a value was numeric.

If the value is not numeric, the user is alerted and a `false` value is returned by the function.

```
var num = 0 + str
if (num < min || max < num) {
    alert(msg + " not in range [" + min + ".." + max + "]");
    return false;
}
input.value = str;
return true;
}
```

The final step is to check whether the value falls within the specified range, and if not, to alert the user and return a `false` value.

The `computeField()` Function

This function is called by the event handler in three of the form fields. It ensures that the value stored in a field is a string by adding an empty string to the start of the field and then calling `computeForm()` to evaluate the whole form based on the new value of the field.

The `computeForm()` Function

The `computeForm()`function performs all the work of calculating the results of the three formulas.

```
function computeForm(form)
{
    if ((form.DL.value == null || form.DL.value.length == 0) ||
        (form.ODC.value == null || form.ODC.value.length == 0) ||
        (form.TFB.value == null || form.TFB.value.length == 0) ||
        (form.TOH.value == null || form.TOH.value.length == 0) ||
        (form.TGA.value == null || form.TGA.value.length == 0) ||
        (form.TBP.value == null || form.TBP.value.length == 0) ||
        (form.FBR.value == null || form.TBP.value.length == 0) ||
        (form.OHL.value == null || form.OHL.value.length == 0) ||
        (form.GAL.value == null || form.GAL.value.length == 0) ||
        (form.BPL.value == null || form.BPL.value.length == 0)) {
        form.FBR.value = "Incomplete data";
        form.OHR.value = "Incomplete data";
        form.GAR.value = "Incomplete data";
        return;
    }
```

The function starts by checking that certain critical fields contain valid data. If not, error messages are displayed in selected fields and the function returns.

```
if (!checkNumber(form.DL, 1,99999999, "Direct Labor") ||
    !checkNumber(form.ODC,0,99999999, "Other Direct Costs") ||
    !checkNumber(form.TFB,1,99999999, "Total Fringe Benefits") ||
    !checkNumber(form.TOH,1,99999999, "Total Overhead") ||
    !checkNumber(form.TGA,0,99999999, "Total G&A") ||
    !checkNumber(form.TBP,0,99999999, "Total B&P") ||
    !checkNumber(form.TBP,0,99999999, "Total B&P") ||
    !checkNumber(form.DLL,0,99999999, "Total B&P") ||
    !checkNumber(form.OHL,1,99999999, "Total Overhead Labor") ||
    !checkNumber(form.GAL,0,99999999, "Total G&A Labor") ||
    !checkNumber(form.BPL,0,99999999, "Total B&P Labor")) {
    form.FBR.value = "Invalid";
    form.OHR.value = "Invalid";
    form.GAR.value = "Invalid";
    return;
}
```

Next, the function checks that the values in selected fields fall within the desired range using `checkNumber()`. Again, if there is a problem, a message to that effect is displayed in selected text fields and the function exits.

```
var i=form.DL.value *1
var j=form.ODC.value*1
form.TOTDIR.value=i + j
form.DLL.value=i

var k=form.TFB.value *1
var l=form.TOH.value *1
var m=form.TGA.value *1
var n=form.TBP.value *1
form.TOTIND.value=k + l + m + n
var z=i + j + k + l + m + n
form.TC.value=z

var o=form.OHL.value *1
var p=form.GAL.value *1
var q=form.BPL.value *1
var r=i + o + p + q
form.TOTLAB.value= r

var s=(k /  r)
form.FBR.value=s * 100

var t=(((i + o + q) * s) + l) / (i + q)
form.OHR.value= t * 100

var u=(m + n+ (p * s) + (t * q))
var z=z - u
var z= u / z
form.GAR.value=z * 100
```

```
form.DLB.value=i
var v=i * t
form.OHRB.value=v
form.OHRR.value=t * 100
form.ODCB.value=j
form.GARR.value=z * 100
var w=(i + v + j) * z
form.GARB.value=w
form.TCB.value=w + i + v + j


}
```

Finally, the function makes all the mathematical calculations and stores the results in the relevant fields.

The clearForm() Function

The clearForm() function simply clears three critical fields in the form by assigning empty strings to them.

APPENDIX D

GLOSSARY

Applet: Small program, usually written in Java, that is downloaded as needed to extend the functionality of a Web page or a Web browser.

Array: An ordered, named set of values, indexed by number.

Associative Array: A named set of values in association pairs.

Boolean: A binary literal value which can be either true or false.

CGI (Common Gateway Interface): The standard mechanism for processing data entered in an HTML form on a Web server and returning the results.

Comments: Portions of a JavaScript script or an HTML file that are not interpreted or displayed.

Cookies: A method for saving client-side state information that is sent back to the server along with specific page requests.

Dialog Boxes: Small user interaction boxes which allow the user to react to information presented by an application or a script.

Event Handlers: Event handlers define the program code to execute when an event occurs.

Events: Signals that are triggered when a particular user action occurs or when the browser has completed a specific task.

Expression: A combination of variables, literals, and operators that evaluates to a single value.

Floating Point: A type of literal value that represents a number including a fractional portion (that is, the portion after a decimal place).

Forms: A standard HTML element which offers tools for the user to provide information through textboxes, checkboxes, radio buttons, selection lists, and buttons.

Frames: An extension to HTML developed by Netscape that allows the browser to be divided into discrete rectangular spaces, each of which contains separate files. Links in one frame can target the resulting file to another frame.

Functions: Stand-alone, reusable segments of program code that are not part of an object.

HTML (Hypertext Markup Language): A series of tags included in text files that define the structure of a Web document and its links to other documents. Web browsers interpret these tags to determine how to display a Web page.

Instance: A particular occurrence of an object structure. Objects can have multiple instances that are independent of each other but share a similar structure of properties and methods.

Integer: A literal value expressing a number with no fraction component.

Internet: A globe-spanning network of computer networks linking tens of millions of people worldwide.

Java: A compiled, object-oriented programming language developed by Sun Microsystems. Java is well-suited for developing distributed applications on the World Wide Web using applets.

JavaScript: An interpreted, object-based scripting language developed by Netscape Communications that adds interactivity to Web pages.

Literals: A literal expression of a value, including a number or a text string.

Loop: A programming structure that allows a segment of code to be repeated a specified number of times or to be repeated until a specified condition exists.

Methods: The segments of program code, or functions, tied to an object.

Null: A special literal value that represents the lack of any other value.

Object-oriented: A style of programming that links data to the processes that manipulate it.

Operators: Perform actions on one or more variables, literals, or expressions and evaluate to a single value.

Plug-ins: A technology that allows third-party vendors to develop extensions to Navigator 2.0. These extensions enable Navigator 2.0 to view additional formats or enable it to be used as the interface for complex applications, such as spreadsheets or image editors.

Properties: Refers to the data structures available in an object.

Recursion: A programming technique whereby a function or method calls itself one or more times.

Status Bar: The small bar at the bottom of the Navigator window where messages about the current action are displayed. JavaScript can write text to the status bar.

Strings: A literal value representing text.

Tables: A feature of HTML that allows the creation of structured tables of information with distinct columns and rows.

Variables: Named pieces of different types of data. The value of variables can be changed, and the value can be referred to by the name of the variable.

WWW (World Wide Web): A collection of millions of linked documents on the Internet exchanged using the Hypertext Transfer Protocol (HTTP). These documents include text, images, video, and sound.

APPENDIX E

QUIZ ANSWERS

Chapter 1, Where Does JavaScript Fit In?

Lesson 1   JavaScript and Netscape Navigator

1. c

2. b

3. c

4. a

5. d

Lesson 2   Java and JavaScript

1. b

2. b

3. c

4. a

5. d

Lesson 3   JavaScript Overview

1. d

2. d

3. d

4. b

5. a

Lesson 4   Scripting with Objects

1. a

2. b

3. d

4. a

5. b

Lesson 5   Pros and Cons

1. a

2. c

3. c

4. a

5. d

Chapter 2, Your First Script

Lesson 1   Using the `Script` *Tag*

1. b

2. d

3. a

4. b

5. c, d

Lesson 2   Syntax and Command Blocks

1. b

2. c

3. a

4. d

5. b

Lesson 3   Output

1. c

2. b

3. d

4. a

5. c

Lesson 4   Dialogs and Prompts

1. b, c

2. b

3. a

4. c

5. d

Chapter 3, Working with Data and Information

Lesson 1   Data Types

1. b

2. a

3. c

4. b

5. d

Lesson 2   Variables

1. a

2. b

3. a, d

4. c

5. c

Lesson 3   Expressions

1. d

2. b

3. b

4. a

5. a

Lesson 4   Operators and Comparison Expressions

1. a

2. c

3. a

4. d

5. c

Chapter 4, Functions and Objects—The Building Blocks of Programs

Lesson 1   Functions

1. c

2. a

3. b

4. a

5. d

Lesson 2   Objects

1. a, c
2. a
3. d
4. b
5. d

Lesson 3   Arrays

1. d
2. a
3. c
4. a
5. c

Chapter 5, Events in JavaScript

Lesson 1   Events

1. c
2. a
3. b
4. d
5. b

Lesson 2   Event Handlers and Forms

1. c
2. d
3. c
4. b
5. c

Chapter 6, Creating Interactive Forms

Lesson 1   The Form Object and Its Elements

1. b

2. c

3. b

4. c

5. a

Lesson 2   Form Elements

1. a

2. b

3. c

4. b

5. a

Lesson 3   More Form Elements

1. a

2. c

3. a

4. d

5. c

Lesson 4   Using Tables and Arrays

1. b

2. a

3. d

4. b

5. b

Chapter 7, Loops

Lesson 1   Using Loops

    1. c

    2. d

    3. a

    4. a

    5. c

Lesson 2   The While *Loop and the* Break *and* Continue *Statements*

    1. b

    2. c

    3. a

    4. b

    5. d

Chapter 8, Frames, Documents, and Windows

Lesson 1   Setting Up Frames

    1. a

    2. c

    3. b

    4. b

    5. a

Lesson 2   Nesting, the NOFRAMES TAG, and Naming Forms

1. b

2. d

3. c

4. c

5. b

Lesson 3   Using Frames and Nested Framesets

1. a

2. c

3. b

4. a

5. d

Lesson 4   The Document Object and Its Properties

1. b

2. c

3. a

4. b

5. a

Lesson 5   The Window Object and the Status Bar

1. b

2. c

3. a

4. b

5. c

Chapter 9, Remember Where You've Been with Cookies

Lesson 1 Cookies and How to Use Them

1. c

2. b

3. b

4. d

5. a

Lesson 2 Cookies in JavaScript and Storing User Choices

1. c

2. c

3. b

4. a

5. d

Lesson 3 Encoding Cookies and the Navigator Object

1. b

2. a

3. c

4. b

5. a

Chapter 10, Strings, Math, and the History List

Lesson 1   The Property and Methods of the `String` *Object*

1. d

2. c

3. b

4. c

5. d

Lesson 2   Using the Search, Replace, and Space Functions

1. b

2. d

3. b

4. c

5. d

Lesson 3   The `Math` *Object, the Triangle Function, and the History List*

1. b

2. c

3. d

4. b

5. a

Chapter 11, Having Fun with JavaScript

Lesson 1   Building and Extending Your Application

1. d

2. a

3. b

4. a

5. c

Chapter 12, Creating a Spreadsheet in JavaScript

Lesson 1   Defining and Designing Your Spreadsheet

1. c

2. b

3. a

4. c

5. d

Chapter 13, Navigator Gold — A JavaScript Development Tool

Lesson 1   Navigator Gold and the Browser

1. b

2. a

3. c

4. b

5. c

Lesson 2   HTML and Navigator Gold

1. d

2. a

3. c

4. b

5. d

Lesson 3   JavaScript and Navigator Gold

1. c

2. b

3. c

4. d

5. d

Chapter 14, From JavaScript to Java —Looking into the Future

Lesson 1   Java

1. b

2. c

3. c

4. a

5. b

Lesson 2   Java, JavaScript, and HTML

1. c

2. b

3. d

4. b

5. a

APPENDIX F

EXERCISE ANSWERS

CHAPTER 2

1. The following code uses the **writeln()** method to produce the desired result:

```
<HTML>

<HEAD>
<TITLE>Welcome to Netscape Navigator!</TITLE>
</HEAD>

<BODY>

<SCRIPT LANGUAGE="JavaScript">
<!-- HIDE FROM OTHER BROWSERS

document.write('<IMG SRC="welcome.gif">');
document.writeln("<BR><PRE>Welcome to");
document.write("Netscape Navigator 2.0!</PRE>");

// STOP HIDING FROM OTHER BROWSERS -->
</SCRIPT>

</BODY>

</HTML>
```

2. Using the **\n** special character, it is possible to produce the same results as the previous exercise question using only one call to the **write()** method:

```
<HTML>

<HEAD>
<TITLE>Welcome to Netscape Navigator 2.0!</TITLE>
</HEAD>

<BODY>

<SCRIPT LANGUAGE="JavaScript">
<!-- HIDE FROM OTHER BROWSERS

document.write('<IMG SRC="welcome.gif"><BR><PRE>Welcome to\nNetscape ⇐
Navigator </PRE>');
// STOP HIDING FROM OTHER BROWSERS -->
</SCRIPT>

</BODY>

</HTML>
```

3. The following example customizes the script from Listing 2-5 to include the user's name:

```
<HTML>

<HEAD>
<TITLE>Exercise 2.3</TITLE>
</HEAD>

<BODY>
<SCRIPT LANGUAGE="JavaScript">
<!-- HIDE FROM OTHER BROWSERS

alert("Greetings, " + prompt("Enter Your Name:","Name") + ".\nWelcome to ⇐
Netscape Navigator!");
document.write('<IMG SRC="welcome.gif">');

// STOP HIDING FROM OTHER BROWSERS -->
</SCRIPT>
</BODY>

</HTML>
```

4. You learn several things from the tests in this exercise:

- Clicking on Cancel returns a value of **null**. You learn about the **null** value in Chapter 3.

- HTML tags entered by the user are interpreted by the Web browser before displaying the text on the page.

● Special characters entered in a string returned by the prompt()
method are not evaluated but are just displayed as plain text. In
this way, if the user types \n, it will be displayed as \n rather than
being evaluated to a new line.

CHAPTER 3

1. The expressions evaluate as follows:

   a. 12

   b. "75"

   c. true

   d. true

   e. true

   f. 5

   g. false

   h. true

2. The following code uses the confirm() method and an if statement to
complete the task:

```
if (confirm("Click OK to see a welcome message")) {
   document.write('<IMG SRC="welcome.gif">');
   document.write("<BR><H1>Welcome to Netscape Navigator!</H1>");
}
```

3. In order to add this functionality, use an if-else construct:

```
<HTML>

<HEAD>
<TITLE>Exercise 3.3</TITLE>

<SCRIPT LANGUAGE="JavaScript">
<!-- HIDE FROM OTHER BROWSERS

// DEFINE VARIABLES FOR REST OF SCRIPT
var question="What is 10+10?";
var answer=20;
var correct='<IMG SRC="correct.gif">';
var incorrect='<IMG SRC="incorrect.gif">';

// ASK THE QUESTION
var response = prompt(question,"0");
```

continued on next page

continued from previous page

```
// CHECK THE ANSWER THE FIRST TIME
if (response != answer) {
  // THE ANSWER WAS WRONG: OFFER A SECOND CHANCE
  if (confirm("Wrong! Press OK for a second chance."))
    response = prompt(question,"0");
} else {
  // THE ANSWER WAS RIGHT: OFFER A SECOND QUESTION
  if (confirm("Correct! Press OK for a second question.")) {
    question = "What is 10*10?";
    answer = 100;
    response = prompt (question,"0");
  }
}


// CHECK THE ANSWER
var output = (response == answer) ? correct : incorrect;

// STOP HIDING FROM OTHER BROWSERS -->
</SCRIPT>

</HEAD>

<BODY>

<SCRIPT LANGUAGE="JavaScript">
<!-- HIDE FROM OTHER BROWSERS

// OUTPUT RESULT
document.write(output);

// STOP HIDING FROM OTHER BROWSERS -->
</SCRIPT>

</BODY>

</HTML>
```

CHAPTER 4

1. The object definition would look like this:

```
function car(model, make, year, price) {
  this.model = model;
  this.make = make;
  this.year = year;
  this.price = price;
}
```

2. The values are as follows:

a. `10`

b. `"Mary"`

c. `"10 Maple St."`

3. The `power()` function could be written using recursion:

```
function power(number, exponent) {
  if (exponent > 1) {
    return number * power(number, exponent - 1);
  } else {
    return 1;
  }
}
```

This function makes use of a similar principle as the factorial example earlier in the chapter. This function uses the fact that **x** to the power of **y** equals **x** multiplied by **x** to the power of **y-1**.

While this function works, it is important to note that it isn't perfect. Although negative exponents are mathematically legal, this function will not calculate the result correctly for this type of exponent.

Remembering that **x** to the power of **-y** is the same as **1** divided by **x** to the power of **y**, you could fix the problem with negative exponents by making the following change to the function:

```
function power(number, exponent) {

  // CHECK IF WE HAVE A NEGATIVE EXPONENT
  var negative = (exponent < 0) ? true : false;

  // DECLARE WORKING VARIABLE
  var value=0;

  // CALCULATE number TO THE POWER OF exponent
  if (exponent > 1) {
    value = number * power(number, exponent - 1);
  } else {
    value = 1;
  }

  // IF THE EXPONENT WAS NEGATIVE, TAKE THE RECIPROCAL
  if (negative)
    value = 1 / value;

  return value;
}
```

JavaScript includes a method that performs the same thing as your **power()** function. The **Math.pow()** method is part of the **Math** object and is discussed in Chapter 10, "Strings, Math, and the History List."

CHAPTER 5

1. Lines b, d, and f are valid according to Table 5-2. Choices a, c, and e all use event handlers which are not available for the particular objects in question.

2. The script welcomes the user and asks for a name after the page (and graphic) have loaded. When the user moves on to another URL, a good-bye message is displayed in an alert dialog box. Results would be similar to Figures F-1 and F-2.

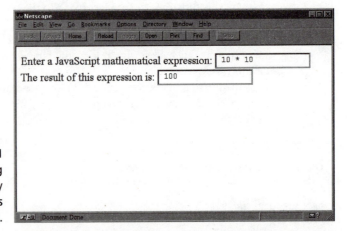

Figure F-1
The prompt dialog box is displayed only after the page has finished loading.

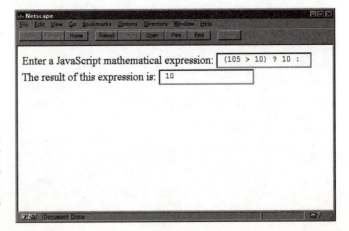

Figure F-2
Loading another Web page triggers the farewell() function and this alert box.

3. The following script would achieve the desired results:

```
<HTML>

<HEAD>
<TITLE>Exercise 5.3</TITLE>

<SCRIPT>
<!-- HIDE FROM OTHER BROWSERS

function calculate(form) {

    form.twice.value = form.entry.value * 2;
    form.square.value = form.entry.value * form.entry.value;

}

// STOP HIDING FROM OTHER BROWSERS -->
</SCRIPT>

</HEAD>

<BODY>

<FORM METHOD=POST>

Value: <INPUT TYPE=text NAME="entry" VALUE=0
                onChange="calculate(this.form);">
<BR>
Double: <INPUT TYPE=text NAME="twice" VALUE=0
                 onChange="this.form.entry.value = this.value / 2; ⇐
calculate(this.form);">
<BR>
Square: <INPUT TYPE=text NAME="square" VALUE=0
                 onChange="this.form.entry.value = Math.sqrt(this.value); ⇐
calculate(this.form);">

</FORM>

</BODY>

</HTML>
```

This script page produces results similar to those in Figure F-3.

Figure F-3
The onChange event
handler calculates
and updates fields.

Notice the use of the `this.form` argument again in the calls to the `calculate()` function. In addition, the `onChange` event handlers for both the `double` and `square` fields have multiline scripts for their event handlers. The semicolons separate the lines of the script, even though the script appears on a single physical line.

The `onChange` event handlers in both the `double` and `square` fields first calculate the value of the `entry` field and then call `calculate()`, which calculates the value of both `double` and `square` based on the value of the `entry` field. While this technique works, it has a couple of problems.

First, you end up replacing the value the user has entered in the `double` or `square` field with a new value calculated when you call `calculate()`. This is an extra, unnecessary step.

Second, due to limitations in floating-point calculations, it is possible that if a user enters a value in the `square` field, for example, the result of calculating the square root and then recalculating the value of the `square` field may produce a result slightly different from the original value the user entered.

This can be remedied with the following script. At first glance, these changes make the script seem more complex, but they stop the script from calculating the value the user has just entered, preventing both these problems.

```
<HTML>

<HEAD>
<TITLE>Exercise 5.3</TITLE>

<SCRIPT>
<!-- HIDE FROM OTHER BROWSERS

function calculate(form,currentField) {

  if (currentField == "square") {
    form.entry.value = Math.sqrt(form.square.value);
    form.twice.value = form.entry.value * 2;
  } else if (currentField == "twice") {
    form.entry.value = form.twice.value / 2;
    form.square.value = form.entry.value * form.entry.value;
  } else {
    form.twice.value = form.entry.value * 2;
    form.square.value = form.entry.value * form.entry.value;
  }

}

// STOP HIDING FROM OTHER BROWSERS -->
</SCRIPT>

</HEAD>
```

```
<BODY>

<FORM METHOD=POST>

Value: <INPUT TYPE=text NAME="entry" VALUE=0
               onChange="calculate(this.form,'entry');">
Double: <INPUT TYPE=text NAME="twice" VALUE=0
               onChange="calculate(this.form,'twice');">
Square: <INPUT TYPE=text NAME="square" VALUE=0
               onChange="calculate(this.form,'square');">

</FORM>

</BODY>

</HTML>
```

Here you see that you have added a second argument passing an indicator of which field's event handler called the `calculate()` function. The function uses this in a complex `if ... else` construct to do only the necessary calculations and not rewrite the values just entered by the users.

The `if ... else` construct used in the `calculate()` function shows how it is possible to have more than one alternative:

```
if (condition1) {
   JavaScript commands
} else if (condition2) {
   JavaScript commands
} else if (condition3) {
   JavaScript commands
} else {
   JavaScript commands
}
```

This example can be extended to any number of conditions.

The script can be made easier to use and more general in purpose by using the `name` property of the `text` field object. For instance, you can pass `this.name` to the function in all three event handlers (because the current object in each case is a text field):

```
<FORM METHOD=POST>

Value: <INPUT TYPE=text NAME="entry" VALUE=0
               onChange="calculate(this.form,this.name);">
Double: <INPUT TYPE=text NAME="twice" VALUE=0
               onChange="calculate(this.form,this.name);">
Square: <INPUT TYPE=text NAME="square" VALUE=0
               onChange="calculate(this.form,this.name);">

</FORM>
```

CHAPTER 6

1. The following are valid: (c) and (e). Example (a) is not valid because onClick is not a valid event handler for the **BODY** tag; (b) is wrong because JavaScript is case sensitive and the correct form is onLoad; (d) is incorrect because checkboxes have the onClick event handler only; and (f) is incorrect because the onClick event handler is not available for text fields.

2. In Listing F-1 you can add three functions to implement the additional features:

 Listing F-1 Adding features to the calculator.

```html
<HTML>

<HEAD>
<TITLE>Exercise 6.2</TITLE>

<SCRIPT>
<!-- HIDE FROM OTHER BROWSERS

var total = 0;
var lastOperation = "+";
var newnumber = true;

function enterNumber(digit) {

  var form = digit.form;

  if (newnumber) {
    clearNumber(form);
    newnumber = false;
  }

  form.display.value = form.display.value + digit.name;

}

function clear(form) {

  total = 0;
  lastOperation = "+";
  form.display.value = 0;

}

function clearNumber(form) {

  form.display.value = 0;

}
```

```
function calculate(operation) {

  var form = operation.form;

  if (checkErrors(form)) {

    var expression = total + lastOperation + form.display.value;

    lastOperation = operation.value;
    total = eval(expression);
    form.display.value = total;
    newnumber = true;
  } else {
    alert("You cannot divide by zero!");
    form.display.value = "";
  }

}

function changeSign(form) {

  var num = eval(form.display.value);
  form.display.value = -num;
  if (newnumber)
    total = -num;

}

function decimalPoint(form) {

  if (Math.floor(form.display.value) == form.display.value) {
    form.display.value += ".";
  }

}

function checkErrors(form) {

  noErrors = true;

  if ((lastOperation == "/") && (form.display.value == 0))
    noErrors = false;

  return noErrors;

}


// STOP HIDING FROM OTHER BROWSERS -->
</SCRIPT>

</HEAD>
```

continued on next page

continued from previous page

```
<BODY>

<FORM>

<TABLE BORDER = 1>

<TR>
<TD COLSPAN=4>
<INPUT TYPE=text NAME=display VALUE="0" >
</TD>
</TR>


<TR>
<TD>
<INPUT TYPE=button NAME="7" VALUE=" 7 " onClick="enterNumber(this);">
</TD>
<TD>
<INPUT TYPE=button NAME="8" VALUE=" 8 " onClick="enterNumber(this);">
</TD>
<TD>
<INPUT TYPE=button NAME="9" VALUE=" 9 " onClick="enterNumber(this);">
</TD>
<TD>
<INPUT TYPE=button NAME="+" VALUE=" + " onClick="calculate(this);">
</TD>
</TR>


<TR>
<TD>
<INPUT TYPE=button NAME="4" VALUE=" 4 " onClick="enterNumber(this);">
</TD>
<TD>
<INPUT TYPE=button NAME="5" VALUE=" 5 " onClick="enterNumber(this);">
</TD>
<TD>
<INPUT TYPE=button NAME="6" VALUE=" 6 " onClick="enterNumber(this);">
</TD>
<TD>
<INPUT TYPE=button NAME="-" VALUE="  -  " onClick="calculate(this);">
</TD>
</TR>


<TR>
<TD>
<INPUT TYPE=button NAME="1" VALUE=" 1 " onClick="enterNumber(this);">
</TD>
<TD>
<INPUT TYPE=button NAME="2" VALUE=" 2 " onClick="enterNumber(this);">
</TD>
<TD>
<INPUT TYPE=button NAME="3" VALUE=" 3 " onClick="enterNumber(this);">
</TD>
```

```
<TD>
<INPUT TYPE=button NAME="*" VALUE=" * " onClick="calculate(this);">
</TD>
</TR>

<TR>
<TD>
<INPUT TYPE=button NAME="0" VALUE=" 0 " onClick="enterNumber(this);">
</TD>
<TD>
<INPUT TYPE=button NAME="C" VALUE=" C " onClick="clear(this.form);">
</TD>
<TD>
<INPUT TYPE=button NAME="CE" VALUE="CE" ⇐
onClick="clearNumber(this.form);">
</TD>
<TD>
<INPUT TYPE=button NAME="/" VALUE="  /  " onClick="calculate(this);">
</TD>
</TR>

<TR>
<TD>
<INPUT TYPE=button NAME="sign" VALUE="+/-" ⇐
onClick="changeSign(this.form);">
</TD>
<TD>
</TD>
<TD>
<INPUT TYPE=button NAME="decimal" VALUE="  .  " ⇐
onClick="decimalPoint(this.form);">
</TD>
<TD>
</TD>
</TR>

</TABLE>

</FORM>

</BODY>

</HTML>
```

This script produces a calculator that looks like the one in Figure F-4.

There are several points worth noting in this new version of the calculator program. First, you make use of the unary negation operation (–) in the `changeSign()` function.

In the `decimalPoint()` function, you check whether the number is currently a floating point value by using the `Math.floor()` method. Only an integer evaluates to itself using `Math.floor()` and only integers lack a decimal point (in this particular case). It is important to note that this method isn't foolproof. A user could still enter two decimal points in a row.

Figure F-4
Two buttons and
three functions
added to the
calculator.

You can handle this by using the **substring()** method of the **string** object to check if the last character of the display field is already a decimal point. The **substring()** method takes two arguments as follows:

```
stringname.substring(firstCharacter,lastCharacter)
```

where **firstCharacter** and **lastCharacter** are the numeric offset of the desired characters from the start of a string. The numeric offset is calculated based on the first character being number zero. So, if you have a variable called **testString** with the value **"JavaScript"**, then **testString.substring(1,4)** returns a value of **"avaS"**.

Of course, in this example, you don't know the numeric offset of the last character in **form.display.value**. You can find this out by using the **string.length** property. Now you can test whether the last character is a decimal point using the expression:

```
(form.display.value.substring(form.display.value.length,
_form.display.value.length) == ".")
```

Then, the **decimalPoint()** function would look like this:

```
function decimalPoint(form) {

  var lastChar = form.display.value.length;
  var display = form.display.value;

  if ((Math.floor(form.display.value) == form.display.value) ||
      (display.substring(lastChar,lastChar) == ".")) {
    form.display.value += ".";
  }

}
```

The last function you added to your script is **checkErrors()**. In this script you simply check whether the last operation is divide and the current value is zero, and then you alert the user and disallow the operation.

3. In order to extend the functionality to include the optional range checking and alert, you need to add an additional function:

```
function checkRange(field,low,high,message) {

  if (field.value != "") {
    if ((field.value < low) || (field.value > high)) {
      alert(message);
      field.value="";
      field.focus();
    }
  } else {
    checkField(field);
  }

}
```

This function first checks whether the user has entered information. If she has, it checks the range; if the information is outside the range, the function alerts the user, clears the field, and returns focus to the field.

If there is no data entered, the function calls **checkField()**, which displays the default value in the field.

CHAPTER 7

1. **while** loops can be used in all three cases:

a.

```
j = 5;
  while (--j > 0) {
    document.writeln(j + "<BR>");
  }
```

b.

```
k = 1;
  while (k <= 99) {
    k = k * 2 / 1.5;
  }
```

c.

```
num = 0;
  while (num <= 10) {
    if (num++ == 8)
    break;
  }
```

2. A factorial function can easily be written using a single **for** loop:

```
function factorial(num) {
   var factorial = 1;
   for (var i=2; i<=num; i++) {
     factorial *= i;
   }
   return factorial;
}
```

3. In order to improve the computer's strategy used at the end of the **play()** function, you need to build some complex **if** statements into a pair of embedded **for** loops. The following is the complete replacement for the **play()** function in Listing 7-4:

```
function play(form,field) {

   var index = eval(field.name);
   var playIndex = 0;
   var winIndex = 0;
   var done = false;
   field.value = playerSymbol;
   board[index] = playerSymbol;

   //CHECK FOR PLAYER WIN
   if (win(index)) {
     // PLAYER WON
     alert("Good Play! You Win!");
     clear(form);
   } else {
     // PLAYER LOST, CHECK FOR WINNING POSITION
     for (row = 1; row <= 3; row++) {
       for (col = 1; col <= 3; col++) {
         index = (row*10) + col;
         if (board[index] == "") {
           board[index] = computerSymbol;
           if(win(index)) {
             playIndex = index;
             done = true;
             break;
           }
           board[index] = "";
         }
       }
       if (done)
         break;
     }
     // CHECK IF COMPUTER CAN WIN
     if (done) {
       board[playIndex] = computerSymbol;
       buildBoard(form);
       alert("Computer Just Won!");
       clear(form);
```

```
    } else {
      // CAN'T WIN, CHECK IF NEED TO STOP A WIN
      for (row = 1; row <=3; row++) {
        for (col = 1; col <= 3; col++) {
          index = (row*10) + col;
          if (board[index] == "") {
            board[index] = playerSymbol;
            if (win(index)) {
              playIndex = index;
              done = true;
              board[index] = "";
              break;
            }
            board[index] = "";
          }
        }
        if (done)
          break;
      }
      // CHECK IF DONE
      if (done) {
        board[playIndex] = computerSymbol;
        buildBoard(form);
      } else {
        // NOT DONE, CHECK FOR FIRST EMPTY SPACE
        for (row = 1; row <= 3; row ++) {
          for (col = 1; col <= 3; col ++) {
            index = (row*10) + col;
            if (board[index] == "") {
              //CHECK ROW
              if (
                  ((board[index] == board[(index < 30)?index+10:index-20]) &&
                  (board[(index>9)?index-10:index+20] == "")) ||    ⇐
              ((board[index] == board[(index>9)?index-10:index+20]) &&
                  (board[(index<30)?index+10:index-20]))
                  ) {
              playIndex = index;
              done = true;
              break;
              }
              // CHECK COLUMNS
              if (
                  ((board[index] == board[(index%10<3)?index+1:index-2]) &&
                  (board[(index%10>1)?index-1:index+2] == "")) ||
                  ((board[index] == board[(index%10>1)?index-1:index+2]) &&
                   (board[(index%10<3)?index+1:index-2]))
                  ) {
              playIndex = index;
              done = true;
              break;
              }
```

continued on next page

continued from previous page

```
                   }
               }
               if (done)
                  break;
           }
           if (done) {
               board[playIndex] = computerSymbol;
               buildBoard(form);
           } else {
               // NOT DONE, CHECK FOR FIRST EMPTY SPACE
               for (row = 1; row <= 3; row ++) {
                  for (col = 1; col <= 3; col ++) {
                      index = (row*10) + col;
                      if (board[index] == "") {
                         playIndex = index;
                         done = true;
                         break;
                      }
                  }
                  if (done)
                      break;
               }
               board[playIndex] = computerSymbol;
               buildBoard(form);
           }
       }
   }
 }

}
```

Note that this function checks only rows and columns for possible good moves before going on the check for any empty space. A good exercise would be to extend this function to also check for diagonal moves before opting for the first available blank space.

CHAPTER 8

1. In order to add random order to the tests, you need to add two things to the program: a function to produce a suitable random number and a method to keep track of which questions have already been asked. All the changes are to **form.htm** and should look like this:

```
<!-- SOURCE CODE OF form.htm -->
<HTML>

<HEAD>
<SCRIPT LANGUAGE="JavaScript">
<!-- HIDE FROM OTHER BROWSERS

var currentLevel=1;
```

```
var currentQuestion=1;
var askedQuestion=0;
var toOutput = "";

// DEFINE LEVEL ONE
q1 = new question("1 + 3",4);
q2 = new question("4 + 5",9);
q3 = new question("5 - 4",1);
q4 = new question("7 + 3",10);
q5 = new question("4 + 4",8);
q6 = new question("3 - 3",0);
q7 = new question("9 - 5",4);
q8 = new question("8 + 1",9);
q9 = new question("5 - 3",2);
q10 = new question("8 - 3",5);
levelOne = new level(q1,q2,q3,q4,q5,q6,q7,q8,q9,q10);

// DEFINE LEVEL TWO
q1 = new question("15 + 23",38);
q2 = new question("65 - 32",33);
q3 = new question("99 + 45",134);
q4 = new question("34 - 57",-23);
q5 = new question("-34 - 57",-91);
q6 = new question("23 + 77",100);
q7 = new question("64 + 32",96);
q8 = new question("64 - 32",32);
q9 = new question("12 + 34",46);
q10 = new question("77 + 77",154);
levelTwo = new level(q1,q2,q3,q4,q5,q6,q7,q8,q9,q10);

// DEFINE LEVEL THREE
q1 = new question("10 * 7",70);
q2 = new question("15 / 3",5);
q3 = new question("34 * 3",102);
q4 = new question("33 / 2",16.5);
q5 = new question("100 / 4",25);
q6 = new question("99 / 6",16.5);
q7 = new question("32 * 3",96);
q8 = new question("48 / 4",12);
q9 = new question("31 * 0",0);
q10 = new question("45 / 1",45);
levelThree = new level(q1,q2,q3,q4,q5,q6,q7,q8,q9,q10);

// DEFINE TEST
test = new newTest(levelOne,levelTwo,levelThree);

function newTest(levelOne,levelTwo,levelThree) {
  this[1] = levelOne;
  this[2] = levelTwo;
  this[3] = levelThree;
}

function level(q1,q2,q3,q4,q5,q6,q7,q8,q9,q10) {
```

continued on next page

continued from previous page

```
      this[1] = q1;
      this[2] = q2;
      this[3] = q3;
      this[4] = q4;
      this[5] = q5;
      this[6] = q6;
      this[7] = q7;
      this[8] = q8;
      this[9] = q9;
      this[10] = q10;
   }

   function question(question,answer) {
     this.question = question;
     this.answer = answer;
   }

   parent.Register(self.name,"startTest");
   function startTest(newLevel) {
     currentLevel=newLevel;
     currentQuestion=1;
     clearArray(asked);
     askedQuestion = chooseQuestion();
     document.forms[0].answer.value="";
     document.forms[0].score.value=0;
     displayQuestion();
   }

   function displayQuestion() {
     ask = test[currentLevel][askedQuestion].question;
     answer = test[currentLevel][askedQuestion].answer;
     toOutput = "" + currentQuestion + ". What is " + ask + "?";
     document.forms[0].answer.value = "";
     window.open("display.htm","output");
   }

   parent.Register(self.name,"output");
   function output() {
     return toOutput;
   }

   function checkAnswer(form) {
     answer = form.answer.value;
     correctAnswer = test[currentLevel][askedQuestion].answer;
     ask = test[currentLevel][askedQuestion].question;
     score = form.score.value;
     if (eval(answer) == correctAnswer) {
       toOutput = "Correct!";
       score ++;
       form.score.value = score;
     } else {
       toOutput = "Sorry! " + ask + " is " + correctAnswer + ".";
```

```
    }
    window.open("display.htm","output");
    if (currentQuestion < 10) {
      currentQuestion ++;
      askedQuestion = chooseQuestion();
      setTimeout("displayQuestion()",3000);
    } else {
      toOutput = "You're Done!<BR>You're score is " + score + " out of 10.";
      setTimeout("window.open('display.htm','output')",3000);
      form.answer.value="";
      form.score.value="0";
    }
}

function welcome() {
  toOutput = "Welcome!";
  window.open("display.htm","output");
}

asked = new createArray(10);

function createArray(num) {
  for (var j=1; j<=num; j++)
    this[j] = false;
  this.length=num;
}

function clearArray(toClear) {
  for (var j=1; j<=toClear.length; j++)
    toClear[j] = false;
}

function chooseQuestion() {
  choice = (getNumber() % 10) + 1;
  while (asked[choice]) {
    choice = (getNumber() % 10) + 1;
  }
  asked[choice] = true;
  return choice;
}

function getNumber() {
  var time = new Date();
  return time.getSeconds();
}

// STOP HIDING FROM OTHER BROWSERS -->
</SCRIPT>

</HEAD>

<BODY BGCOLOR="#FFFFFF" TEXT="#0000FF" onLoad="welcome();">
```

continued on next page

continued from previous page

```
<FORM METHOD=POST>
<CENTER>
<STRONG>Type Your Answer Here:</STRONG><BR>
<INPUT TYPE=text NAME=answer SIZE=30><P>
<INPUT TYPE=button NAME=done VALUE="Check Answer" ⇐
onClick="checkAnswer(this.form);"><P>
Correct Answers So Far:<BR>
<INPUT TYPE=text NAME=score VALUE="0" SIZE=10>
</FORM>

</BODY>

</HTML>
```

You've added four functions to the script, as well as made a few other subtle changes. First, you've added a simple `createArray()` function that enables you to create the `asked` array. You use this array to keep track of questions already asked. Each element is set to `false` until that question is asked.

The `clearArray()` function takes an array as an argument and simply sets each element to `false`.

The `chooseQuestion()` function adds the ability to randomly select a question. The function uses the `getNumber()` function (which returns the seconds from the current time) to create a pseudo-random number. The `while` loop keeps selecting numbers until it finds one that has a `false` entry in the `asked` array.

Once an available question has been found, the appropriate entry in `asked` is set to `true`, and the number of the question is returned.

In addition to these three functions, you have made some other small changes. You have added a global variable called `askedQuestion`. This variable indicates the index of the question you have asked. `currentQuestion` becomes the sequential number of the question to be displayed to the user.

In the `startTest()` function, you add the lines

```
clearArray(asked);
askedQuestion = chooseQuestion();
```

which clear the `asked` array to `false` and then select a question.

In `displayQuestion()`, you have switched to using `askedQuestion` in place of `currentQuestion` as an index to the `test[currentLevel]` object, and in the function `checkAnswer()`, you have made the same change.

In `checkAnswer()`, you have also changed the way the function selects the next question:

```
currentQuestion ++;
askedQuestion = chooseQuestion();
setTimeout("displayQuestion()",3000);
```

This simply chooses a random question and then calls `displayQuestion()`.

2. The following frameset and HTML document produce the desired results, as shown in Figure F-5.

```
<!-- MAIN FRAMESET FILE -->

<HTML>

<HEAD>
<TITLE>Exercise 8.2</TITLE>
</HEAD>

<FRAMESET COLS="25%,*">
  <FRAME SRC="info.htm">
  <FRAME SRC="blank.htm" NAME="display">
</FRAMESET>

</HTML>
```

The HTML document would look like this:

```
<!-- SOURCE CODE FOR info.htm -->

<HTML>

<HEAD>
<SCRIPT LANGUAGE="JavaScript">
<!-- HIDE FROM OTHER BROWSERS

function loadSite(form) {
```

continued on next page

Figure F-5
Testing colors on a document selected by the user.

continued from previous page

```
        var url = form.url.value;
        doc = open(url,"display");
        form.title.value = doc.document.title;
        form.date.value = doc.document.lastModified;
        form.bg.value = doc.document.bgColor;
        form.fg.value = doc.document.fgColor;
        form.link.value = doc.document.linkColor;
        form.alink.value = doc.document.alinkColor;
        form.vlink.value = doc.document.vlinkColor;
    }

    // STOP HIDING FROM OTHER BROWSERS -->
    </SCRIPT>
    </HTML>

    <BODY>

    <FORM METHOD=POST>
    URL: <INPUT TYPE=text NAME="url"><P>
    <INPUT TYPE=button NAME=load VALUE="Load URL" onClick="loadSite(this.form);"><P>  ⇐
    Title: <INPUT TYPE=text NAME="title" onFocus="this.blur();"><P>
    Last Modified: <INPUT TYPE=text NAME="date" onFocus="this.blur();"><P>
    Background Color: <INPUT TYPE=text NAME="bg" onFoucs="this.blur();"><P>
    Text Color: <INPUT TYPE=text NAME="fg" onFocus="this.blur();"><P>
    Link Color: <INPUT TYPE=text NAME="link" onFocus="this.blur();"><P>
    Active Link Color: <INPUT TYPE=text NAME="alink" onFocus="this.blur();"><P>
    Followed Link Color: <INPUT TYPE=text NAME="vlink" onFocus="this.blur();">
    </FORM>

    </BODY>

    </HTML>
```

You use one simple function to achieve the desired result: `loadSite()`. The function loads the specified URL into the display `frame` using `window.open()`.

Once this is done, you can use the properties of the `document` object to display the desired information into fields in the HTML form.

In the form in the body of the HTML document, you use the `onClick` event handler in the button to call the `loadSite()` function. The display fields for the information about the document all have the event handler `onFocus="this.blur();"` to make sure the user can't alter the information.

3. This script partially addresses the problem in Listings 8-12 and 8-13—that the help messages remain displayed even after you remove mouse focus from a link or remove focus from a field. This particular script displays a help message when the user gives focus to a field. When focus is removed, either a warning message is displayed or the status bar is cleared.

4. The following script makes the necessary changes to enable the user to specify a URL to be displayed in the lower frame:

```
<HTML>

<HEAD>

<SCRIPT LANGUAGE="JavaScript">
<!-- HIDE FORM OTHER BROWSERS

function display(form) {
  parent.output.document.bgColor = form.bg.value;
  parent.output.document.fgColor = form.fg.value;
  parent.output.document.linkClor = form.link.value;
  parent.output.document.alinkColor = form.alink.value;
  parent.output.document.vlinkColor = form.vlink.value;
}

function loadPage(url) {
  var toLoad = url.value;
  if (url.value == "")
    toLoad = "sample.htm";
  open (toLoad,"output");
}

// STOP HIDING SCRIPT -->
</SCRIPT>

</HEAD>

<BODY>

<CENTER>

<SCRIPT LANGUAGE="JavaScript">
<!-- HIDE FROM OTHER BROWSERS

document.write('<H1>The Color Picker</H1>');
document.write('<FORM METHOD=POST>');
document.write('Enter Colors:<BR>');

document.write('Background: <INPUT TYPE=text NAME="bg" ⇐
VALUE="' + document.bgColor + '"> ... ');
document.write('Text: <INPUT TYPE=text NAME="fg" ⇐
VALUE="' + document.fgColor + '"><BR>');
document.write('Link: <INPUT TYPE=text NAME="link" ⇐
VALUE ="' + document.linkColor + '"> ...');
document.write('Active Link: <INPUT TYPE=text NAME="alink" ⇐
VALUE="' + document.alinkColor + '"><BR>');
```

continued on next page

continued from previous page

```
document.write('Followed Link: <INPUT TYPE="text" NAME="vlink" ⇐
VALUE ="' + document.vlinkColor + '"><BR>');
document.write('Test URL: <INPUT TYPE="text" SIZE=40 NAME="url" ⇐
VALUE="" onChange="loadPage(this);"><BR>');
document.write('<INPUT TYPE=button VALUE="TEST" ⇐
onClick="display(this.form);">');

document.write('</FORM>');

// STOP HIDING FROM OTHER BROWSERS -->
</SCRIPT>

</CENTER>

</BODY>

</HTML>
```

You have made two simple changes to the script. In addition to the `display()` function, you have added the `loadPage()` function, which loads a URL into the lower frame using `window.open()`. If the user provides no value for the URL, the standard sample file is loaded.

In the form, you have added a text field for the URL with an `onChange` event handler that calls `loadPage()`. You also need to change the frameset to load the appropriate sample page into the lower frame:

```
<HTML>

<HEAD>
<TITLE>Exercise 8.4</TITLE>
</HEAD>

<FRAMESET ROWS="45%,*">
   <FRAME SRC="pick.htm">
   <FRAME SRC="sample.htm" NAME="output">
</FRAMESET>

</HTML>
```

CHAPTER 9

1. The following strings would be displayed:

a. user=joe.

b. There are no cookies—**user** expired at midnight, 12 hours earlier.

c. There are no cookies—The only cookie set for this site is at a lower level path than the user is accessing.

2. All the changes are needed in the **addURL()** function:

```
function addURL(form) {
  var name = form.name.value;
  var url = form.url.value;
  if ((name == "") || (name == null) || (url == "") || (url == null)) {
alert ("Please Enter both a name and URL.");
    form.name.focus();
    return;
  }
  if (number == 10) {
    var delete = prompt("Cannot enter more than 10 items.\n ⇐
Enter the name of an entry to replace or enter nothing ⇐
to stop adding" + name + ".","");
if ((delete == "") || (delete == null)) {
      form.name.focus();
      return;
    }
    var i=1;
    while (i <= number) {
      if (sites[i] == delete) {
        form.name.value = delete;
        deleteURL(form);
        form.name.value = name;
        break;
      }
      if (i == number) {
        delete = prompt("No such entry to delete. Cannot enter more ⇐
than 10 items.\nEnter the name of an entry to replace or ⇐
enter nothing to stop adding" + name + ".","");

i = 0;
      }
      i++;
    }
  }
  SetCookie(name,url,expiryDate,"/");
  sites[++number] = name;
  SetCookie("sites",makeList(),expiryDate,"/");
  SetCookie("number",number,expiryDate,"/");
  window.open("control.htm","control");
}
```

You can add the following elements to the function to perform the necessary error checking and to make sure the user doesn't enter too many elements.

```
if ((name == "") || (name == null) || (url == "") || (url == null)) {
    alert ("Please Enter both a name and URL.");
    form.name.focus();
    return;
  }
```

This **if** statement checks whether either field is the empty string or the **null** value. If the result is **true**, then an alert message is displayed, focus is returned to the form, and the function ends with the **return** statement.

The next **if** statement handles the 10-item limitation on the list. The work that takes place if there are already 10 entries in the list is a bit more complex than the previous **if** statement.

```
    var delete = prompt("Cannot enter more than 10 items.\n⇐
Enter the name of an entry to replace or enter nothing ⇐
to stop adding" + name + ".","");
```

The first step is to ask users what to do because there are too many entries already. They can either provide an item to replace or they can cancel the addition. The user's selection is stored in the **delete** variable.

```
if ((delete == "") || (delete == null)) {
    form.name.focus();
    return;
  }
```

Once the user responds, the script immediately checks whether the user has decided to cancel the addition of the new entry by entering nothing in the prompt dialog box. If the user is canceling, then focus is returned to the form, and the function exits with the **return** statement.

```
var i=1;
    while (i <= number) {
      if (sites[i] == delete) {
        form.name.value = delete;
        deleteURL(form);
        form.name.value = name;
        break;
      }
```

The **while** loop is used to check whether the entry the user wants to replace actually exists. This is done by looping through each entry in the array. The first step, then, is to check whether the current entry matches the user's selection. If it does, then the value of **delete** is temporarily stored in the **name** field of the form, **deleteURL()** is called, and then the **name** field is returned to its previous value. The **break** statement ends the **while** loop.

```
      if (i == number) {
        delete = prompt("No such entry to delete. Cannot enter more ⇐
than 10 items.\nEnter the name of an entry to replace or ⇐
enter nothing to stop adding" + name + ".","");
i = 0;
      }
```

The next step in the loop is to see if you have exhausted all the entries in the list. You check this with the condition **if (i == number)**. If the last entry has been reached without a match in the previous **if** statement, then the user is again prompted to enter an item to replace or to enter an empty string. Then the counter is reset to start checking again.

3. The following script achieves the desired effect. The output looks like Figures F-6 and F-7.

```
<HTML>

<HEAD>
<TITLE>Exercise 9.3</TITLE>

<SCRIPT LANGUAGE="JavaScript">
<!-- HIDE FROM OTHER BROWSERS
//
//   WE NEED TO INCLUDE THE COOKIE FUNCTIONS
//
//
//   Cookie Functions - Second Helping  (21-Jan-96)
//   Written by:  Bill Dortch, hIdaho Design <bdortch@netw.com>
//   The following functions are released to the public domain.
//
// "Internal" function to return the decoded value of a cookie
//
function getCookieVal (offset) {
```

continued on next page

Figure F-6
The script prompts the first-time visitor for the color and food information.

Figure F-7
On subsequent visits, information stored in the cookies automatically formats the page.

Welcome to the favorite food and color page

continued from previous page

```
      var endstr = document.cookie.indexOf (";", offset);
      if (endstr == -1)
        endstr = document.cookie.length;
      return unescape(document.cookie.substring(offset, endstr));
    }


    //
    //   Function to return the value of the cookie specified by "name".
    //
    function GetCookie (name) {
      var arg = name + "=";
      var alen = arg.length;
      var clen = document.cookie.length;
      var i = 0;
      while (i < clen) {
        var j = i + alen;
        if (document.cookie.substring(i, j) == arg)
          return getCookieVal (j);
        i = document.cookie.indexOf(" ", i) + 1;
        if (i == 0) break;
      }
      return null;
    }


    //
    //   Function to create or update a cookie.
    //
    function SetCookie (name, value) {
      var argv = SetCookie.arguments;
      var argc = SetCookie.arguments.length;
      var expires = (argc > 2) ? argv[2] : null;
      var path = (argc > 3) ? argv[3] : null;
      var domain = (argc > 4) ? argv[4] : null;
      var secure = (argc > 5) ? argv[5] : false;
      document.cookie = name + "=" + escape (value) +
        ((expires == null) ? "" : ("; expires=" + expires.toGMTString())) +
((path == null) ? "" : ("; path=" + path)) +
        ((domain == null) ? "" : ("; domain=" + domain)) +
        ((secure == true) ? "; secure" : "");
    }


    //   Function to delete a cookie. (Sets expiration date to current date/time)
    //
    function DeleteCookie (name) {
      var exp = new Date();
      exp.setTime (exp.getTime() - 1);   // This cookie is history
      var cval = GetCookie (name);
      document.cookie = name + "=" + cval + "; expires=" + exp.toGMTString();
    }


    //
```

```
//   END OF THE COOKIE FUNCTIONS. OUR SCRIPT STARTS HERE.
//

var expiryDate = new Date();
expiryDate.setTime(expiryDate.getTime() + (30 * 24 * 60 * 60 * 1000));

var food = new createArray(3);
food[1] = "Beets";
food[2] = "Jello-Pudding";
food[3] = "Cockroaches";

function createArray(num) {
  this.length = num;
  for (var i = 1; i <= num; i++)
    this[i] = "";
}

function listArray(stuff) {
  var result = "";
  for (var i = 1; i <= stuff.length; i++)
    result += i + ". " + stuff[i] + "/";
  return result;
}

var color = "";
var favFood = "";

function initialize() {
  if (GetCookie("color") == null) {
    color = prompt("Enter your favorite Netscape color.","A Color");
    SetCookie("color",color,expiryDate);
    var foodNum = prompt("Food: - " + listArray(food),"0");
    favFood = food[foodNum];
    SetCookie("food",favFood,expiryDate);
  } else {
    color = GetCookie("color");
    SetCookie("color",color,expiryDate);
    favFood = GetCookie("food");
    SetCookie("food",favFood,expiryDate);
  }
}

// STOP HIDING HERE -->
</SCRIPT>

</HEAD>

<SCRIPT LANGUAGE="JavaScript">
<!-- HIDE FROM OTHER BROWSERS

initialize();
```

continued on next page

continued from previous page

```
document.write('<BODY BGCOLOR="' + color + '">');

document.write("<CENTER>")

document.write('<IMG SRC="' + favFood + '.gif">');

// STOP HIDING -->
</SCRIPT>

<H1>Welcome to the favorite food and color page</H1>

</CENTER>

</BODY>

</HTML>
```

The logic behind this script is rather simple, but it provides an example of how to rebuild cookies after they expire and how to keep cookies current when it is relevant to do so.

The `createArray()` and `listArray()` functions should be obvious. `listArray()` returns a string containing all the items in an array numerically listed by their index numbers in the array. This is used to prompt users for their food choices.

The `initialize()` function is where all the work takes place. The function checks for the existence of the `color` cookie. If the cookie doesn't exist, the program prompts users for the food and color information and stores it in the appropriate cookies, as well as setting the `color` and `favFood` global variables for use in the body of the document.

If the cookies exist, the values are loaded into `color` and `favFood` and then the cookies are updated so that their expiry dates get reset to 30 days into the future.

In the body of the document, a script is used to set the `BGCOLOR` attribute of the `BODY` tag and the `SRC` attribute of the `IMG` tag based on the `color` and `favFood` variables.

CHAPTER 10

1. The phrase `"test."` would print in italics. All the other `method()` calls are useless. Remember that these methods return the new value. They do not directly alter the string. So, the results of all the other method calls went unassigned and unused. If we change the code to read

```
var sample = "test.";
sample = sample.big();
sample = sample.blink();
sample = sample.bold();
sample = sample.strike();
sample = sample.fontsize(7);
document.write(sample.italics());
```

then all the attributes will be applied to the displayed text.

2. The new search function would look like this:

```
function search(target,term,caseSens,wordOnly) {

  var ind = 0;
  var ind2 = 0;
  var next = 0;
  var wildcard = -1;
  var firstTerm = "";
  var secondTerm = "";

  if (!caseSens) {
    term = term.toLowerCase();
    target = target.toLowerCase();
  }

  if ((wildcard = term.indexOf("*",0)) >= 0) {

    if (!checkWildCards(term)) {
      alert("Improper use of the wildcard character.");
      return false;
    }

    firstTerm = term.substring(0,wildcard);
    secondTerm = term.substring(wildcard+1,term.length);

    while ((ind = target.indexOf(firstTerm,next)) >= 0) {
      var afterFirst = ind + firstTerm.length;

      ind2 = target.indexOf(secondTerm,afterFirst);
      if (ind2 < 0) { break; }

      if (wordOnly) {
        for (var i = ind+firstTerm.length; i <= ind2 - 1; i++)
          if (space(target.charAt(i))) {
            next = i + 1;
            continue;
          }

        var before = ind - 1;
        var after = ind2 + secondTerm.length;
        if (!(space(target.charAt(before)) && space(target.charAt(after)))) ⇐
{
next = ind2 + secondTerm.length;
          if (next >= target.length) { break; }
          continue;
        }
      }
      return true;
    }

    return false;
```

continued on next page

continued from previous page

```
      }

   while ((ind = target.indexOf(term,next)) >= 0) {
      if (wordOnly) {
         var before = ind - 1;
         var after = ind + term.length;
         if (!(space(target.charAt(before)) && space(target.charAt(after)))) {
next = ind + term.length;
            continue;
         }
      }
      return true;
   }

   return false;
}
```

You would also need to add the **checkWildCards()** function:

```
function checkWildCards(term) {

   if (term.charAt(0) == "*") { return false; }
   if (term.charAt(term.length-1) == "*") { return false; }

   var first = term.indexOf("*",0);
   if (term.indexOf("*",first+1) >= 0) { return false; }

   return true;

}
```

You have not changed the basic functionality of the **search()** function. Rather, you have added a component in the middle which handles the wildcard searches. If there is no wildcard in the search term, the search functions operate in the same way as they did before, simply bypassing the wildcard section.

Assuming you have found a wildcard character, you perform an altered search, which is based on the simple search performed when there is no wildcard.

You start by checking that the use of the wildcard character is valid by calling **checkWildCards()**. If everything is correct, then you split the search term into two terms: the portion before the wildcard and the portion after it.

You then search for the first term in the condition of the **while** loop. If the first term occurs, you look for the second term. If the second term isn't there, you have no match and break out of the loop. Otherwise, you check if you are doing a whole word search. If you are, the function performs a check on the character before the occurrence of the first term and after the occurrence of the second term for word delimiter characters using the **space()** function. You also check that there are no word delimiters between the two terms. If the search fails either of these tests, you jump back to the top of the loop to continue searching the target string.

Otherwise, if you get past the **wordOnly if** statement, you know you have found a match and return a **true** value from the function.

3. The code

```
<FORM METHOD=POST>
<INPUT TYPE=button VALUE="BACK" onClick="history.back();">
<INPUT TYPE=button VALUE="FORWARD" onClick="history.forward();">
</FORM>
```

will implement dynamic forward and back buttons.

CHAPTER 11

1. As you might have expected, the solution lies in cookies. In the file **build.htm**, you need to add a function called **saveFace()**, which saves the three filenames in three separate cookies. Define the path for the cookies to be **"/"** so all the files in your application have access to the cookies. Use Bill Dortch's cookie functions to handle the dirty work of saving and retrieving the cookies.

Next, extend the parent frameset file so that it loads a blank file into each of three frames on the left and then uses an **onLoad** event handler to call a function called **loadFace()** to retrieve the relevant cookies and load the files into the empty frames.

The resulting HTML documents look like Listing F-2 and F-3.

Input   **Listing F-2** The final version of the parent frameset.

```
<!-- SOURCE CODE OF PARENT FRAMESET -->

<HEAD>

<SCRIPT LANGUAGE="JavaScript">
<!-- HIDE FROM OTHER BROWSERS

//
//   Cookie Functions - Second Helping  (21-Jan-96)
//   Written by:  Bill Dortch, hIdaho Design <bdortch@netw.com>
//   The following functions are released to the public domain.
//
// "Internal" function to return the decoded value of a cookie
//
function getCookieVal (offset) {
  var endstr = document.cookie.indexOf (";", offset);
  if (endstr == -1)
    endstr = document.cookie.length;
  return unescape(document.cookie.substring(offset, endstr));
```

continued on next page

continued from previous page

```
}

//
//    Function to return the value of the cookie specified by "name".
//       name - String object containing the cookie name.
//       returns - String object containing the cookie value, or null if
//          the cookie does not exist.
//
function GetCookie (name) {
   var arg = name + "=";
   var alen = arg.length;
   var clen = document.cookie.length;
   var i = 0;
   while (i < clen) {
      var j = i + alen;
      if (document.cookie.substring(i, j) == arg)
         return getCookieVal (j);
      i = document.cookie.indexOf(" ", i) + 1;
      if (i == 0) break;
   }
   return null;
}


//
//    Function to create or update a cookie.
//       name - String object object containing the cookie name.

//       value - String object containing the cookie value.  May contain
//          any valid string characters.
//       [expires] - Date object containing the expiration data of the cookie.
//       If omitted or null, expires the cookie at the end of the current session.
//       [path] - String object indicating the path for which the cookie is valid.
//          If omitted or null, uses the path of the calling document.
//       [domain] - String object indicating the domain for which the cookie
//       is valid.  If omitted or null, uses the domain of the calling document.
//       [secure] - Boolean (true/false) value indicating whether cookie transmission
//          requires a secure channel (HTTPS).
//
//    The first two parameters are required.  The others, if supplied, must
//    be passed in the order listed above.  To omit an unused optional field,
//    use null as a place holder.  For example, to call SetCookie using name,
//    value and path, you would code:
//
//       SetCookie ("myCookieName", "myCookieValue", null, "/");
//
//    Note that trailing omitted parameters do not require a placeholder.
//
//    To set a secure cookie for path "/myPath", that expires after the
//    current session, you might code:
//
//       SetCookie (myCookieVar, cookieValueVar, null, "/myPath", null, true);
//
```

```
function SetCookie (name, value) {
  var argv = SetCookie.arguments;
  var argc = SetCookie.arguments.length;
  var expires = (argc > 2) ? argv[2] : null;
  var path = (argc > 3) ? argv[3] : null;
  var domain = (argc > 4) ? argv[4] : null;
  var secure = (argc > 5) ? argv[5] : false;
  document.cookie = name + "=" + escape (value) +
    ((expires == null) ? "" : ("; expires=" + expires.toGMTString())) +
    ((path == null) ? "" : ("; path=" + path)) +
    ((domain == null) ? "" : ("; domain=" + domain)) +
    ((secure == true) ? "; secure" : "");
}


//   Function to delete a cookie. (Sets expiration date to current date/time)
//      name - String object containing the cookie name
//
function DeleteCookie (name) {
  var exp = new Date();
  exp.setTime (exp.getTime() - 1);   // This cookie is history
  var cval = GetCookie (name);
  document.cookie = name + "=" + cval + "; expires=" + exp.toGMTString();
}

var numEyes = 4;
var numNoses = 4;
var numMouths = 4;

function loadFace() {

      var eye = GetCookie("eye");
      if ((eye == null) || (eye == "")) { eye = "eye1.gif"; }
      parent.eye.location = eye;

      var nose = GetCookie("nose");
      if ((nose == null) || (nose == "")) { nose = "nose1.gif"; }
      parent.nose.location = nose;

      var mouth = GetCookie("mouth");
      if ((mouth == null) || (mouth == "")) { mouth = "mouth1.gif"; }
      parent.mouth.location = mouth;

}

// STOP HIDING -->
</SCRIPT>

</HEAD>

<FRAMESET ROWS="150,150,150,*" onLoad="loadFace();">
```

continued on next page

continued from previous page

```
<FRAMESET COLS="400,*">
  <FRAME SRC="blank.htm" NAME="eye" MARGINHEIGHT=0 MARGINWIDTH=0 SCROLLING="no">
  <FRAME SRC="eyes.htm" MARGINHEIGHT=0 MARGINWIDTH=0 SCROLLING="auto">
</FRAMESET>

<FRAMESET COLS="400,*">
  <FRAME SRC="blank.htm" NAME="nose" MARGINHEIGHT=0 MARGINWIDTH=0 SCROLLING="no">
  <FRAME SRC="noses.htm" MARGINHEIGHT=0 MARGINWIDTH=0 SCROLLING="auto">
</FRAMESET>

<FRAMESET COLS="400,*">
  <FRAME SRC="blank.htm" NAME="mouth" MARGINHEIGHT=0 MARGINWIDTH=0 SCROLLING="no">
  <FRAME SRC="mouths.htm" MARGINHEIGHT=0 MARGINWIDTH=0 SCROLLING="no">
</FRAMESET>

<FRAME SRC="build.htm">

<SCRIPT LANGUAGE="JavaScript">
<!-- HIDE FROM OTHER BROWSERS


// STOP HIDING -->
</SCRIPT>

</FRAMESET>
```

Input   **Listing F-3** Revised version of `build.htm`.

```
<!-- SOURCE CODE FOR build.html -->

<HEAD>

<SCRIPT LANGUAGE="JavaScript">
<!-- HIDE FROM OTHER BROWSERS

//
//   Cookie Functions - Second Helping  (21-Jan-96)
//   Written by:  Bill Dortch, hIdaho Design <bdortch@netw.com>
//   The following functions are released to the public domain.
//
//
// "Internal" function to return the decoded value of a cookie
//
function getCookieVal (offset) {
  var endstr = document.cookie.indexOf (";", offset);
  if (endstr == -1)
    endstr = document.cookie.length;
  return unescape(document.cookie.substring(offset, endstr));
}


//
//   Function to return the value of the cookie specified by "name".
```

```
//     name - String object containing the cookie name.
//     returns - String object containing the cookie value, or null if
//        the cookie does not exist.
//
function GetCookie (name) {
  var arg = name + "=";
  var alen = arg.length;
  var clen = document.cookie.length;
  var i = 0;
  while (i < clen) {
    var j = i + alen;
    if (document.cookie.substring(i, j) == arg)
      return getCookieVal (j);
    i = document.cookie.indexOf(" ", i) + 1;
    if (i == 0) break;
  }
  return null;
}


//
//   Function to create or update a cookie.
//     name - String object object containing the cookie name.

//     value - String object containing the cookie value.  May contain
//        any valid string characters.
//     [expires] - Date object containing the expiration data of the cookie.
//        If omitted or null, expires the cookie at the end of the current session.
//     [path] - String object indicating the path for which the cookie is valid.
//        If omitted or null, uses the path of the calling document.
//     [domain] - String object indicating the domain for which the cookie ⇐
//        is valid.  If omitted or null, uses the domain of the calling document.
//     [secure] - Boolean (true/false) value indicating whether cookie transmission
//        requires a secure channel (HTTPS).
//
//   The first two parameters are required.  The others, if supplied, must
//   be passed in the order listed above.  To omit an unused optional field,
//   use null as a place holder.  For example, to call SetCookie using name,
//   value and path, you would code:
//
//       SetCookie ("myCookieName", "myCookieValue", null, "/");
//
//   Note that trailing omitted parameters do not require a placeholder.
//
//   To set a secure cookie for path "/myPath", that expires after the
//   current session, you might code:
//
//       SetCookie (myCookieVar, cookieValueVar, null, "/myPath", null, true);
//
function SetCookie (name, value) {
  var argv = SetCookie.arguments;
  var argc = SetCookie.arguments.length;
  var expires = (argc > 2) ? argv[2] : null;
```

continued on next page

continued from previous page

```
      var path = (argc > 3) ? argv[3] : null;
      var domain = (argc > 4) ? argv[4] : null;
      var secure = (argc > 5) ? argv[5] : false;
      document.cookie = name + "=" + escape (value) +
        ((expires == null) ? "" : ("; expires=" + expires.toGMTString())) +
        ((path == null) ? "" : ("; path=" + path)) +
        ((domain == null) ? "" : ("; domain=" + domain)) +
        ((secure == true) ? "; secure" : "");
   }


   //  Function to delete a cookie. (Sets expiration date to current date/time)
   //     name - String object containing the cookie name
   //
   function DeleteCookie (name) {
      var exp = new Date();
      exp.setTime (exp.getTime() - 1);  // This cookie is history
      var cval = GetCookie (name);
      document.cookie = name + "=" + cval + "; expires=" + exp.toGMTString();
   }


   var windowNumber = 1;


   function buildFace() {

      var eye = parent.eye.location;
      var nose = parent.nose.location;
      var mouth = parent.mouth.location;

      var face = window.open("","builtFace" + windowNumber ++,"width=400,height=450");
      face.document.open("text/html");
      face.document.write('<IMG SRC="' + eye + '">');
      face.document.write('<IMG SRC="' + nose + '">');
      face.document.write('<IMG SRC="' + mouth + '">');
      face.document.close();

   }


   function randomFace() {

      var eye = "eye" + getRandom(parent.numEyes) + ".gif";
      var nose = "nose" + getRandom(parent.numNoses) + ".gif";
      var mouth = "mouth" + getRandom(parent.numMouths) + ".gif";

   parent.eye.location = eye;
   parent.nose.location = nose;
   parent.mouth.location = mouth;
```

```
}

function getRandom(num) {

  today = new Date();
  var bigNumber = today.getSeconds() * today.getTime() * ⇐
Math.sqrt(today.getMinutes());
  var randomNum = Math.floor(bigNumber % num);

  return randomNum + 1;

}

function saveFace() {

  var eye = parent["eye"].location;
  var nose = parent["nose"].location;
  var mouth = parent["mouth"].location;

  var expiry = new Date;
  expiry.setTime(expiry.getTime() + 365*24*60*60*1000);

  SetCookie("eye",eye,expiry,"/");
  SetCookie("nose",nose,expiry,"/");
  SetCookie("mouth",mouth,expiry,"/");

}

// STOP HIDING -->
</SCRIPT>

</HEAD>

<BODY BGCOLOR="#000000" TEXT="iceblue">
<FORM METHOD=POST>
<CENTER>
<INPUT TYPE="button" VALUE="Build This Face" onClick="buildFace();">
<INPUT TYPE="button" VALUE="Make A Random Face" onClick="randomFace();">
<INPUT TYPE="button" VALUE="Save This Face" onClick="saveFace();">
</CENTER>
</FORM>
</BODY>
```

You may also want to extend the form in `build.htm` to add a button to load a saved face:

```
<INPUT TYPE="button" VALUE="Load Saved Face" onClick="parent.loadFace();">
```

CHAPTER 12

1. To add the clear function, add a single button to the second HTML form:

```
<FORM METHOD=POST>
<TABLE BORDER=1>

<TR>
<TD><DIV ALIGN=CENTER>Field Name</DIV></TD>
<TD><DIV ALIGN=CENTER>Expression</DIV></TD>
</TR>

<TR>
<TD><DIV ALIGN=CENTER><INPUT TYPE=text SIZE=10 NAME="expField"
   onChange="var exp = GetCookie(this.value); this.form.expression.value = ⇐
(exp == null) ? ''
: exp;"></DIV></TD>
<TD><DIV ALIGN=CENTER><INPUT TYPE=text SIZE=50 NAME="expression"></DIV></TD>
<TD><DIV ALIGN=CENTER><INPUT TYPE=button VALUE="Apply"
onClick="saveExp(this.form);"></DIV></TD>
<TD><DIV ALIGN=CENTER><INPUT TYPE=button VALUE="Delete"
onClick="deleteExp(this.form);"></DIV></TD>
<TD><DIV ALIGN=CENTER><INPUT TYPE=button VALUE="Clear"
onClick="clearSpreadSheet();"></DIV></TD>
</TR>

</TABLE>
</FORM>
```

You then need to add a `clearSpreadSheet()` function:

```
function clearSpreadSheet() {

  var form = document.spreadsheet;

  var index = 0;
  var next = 0;
  var expField = "";
  var field = "";
  var fieldList = GetCookie("fieldList");

  // Clear Expression Cookies
  if (fieldList != null) {
    while (index != fieldList.length) {
      next = fieldList.indexOf(";",index);
      expField = fieldList.substring(index,next);
      SetCookie(expField,"",deleteExpiry);
      index = next + 1;
    }
  }

  SetCookie("fieldList","",deleteExpiry);
  SetCookie("numExpressions",0,expiryDate);
```

```
// Clear form fields

for (var x = 0; x < width; x++) {
  for (var y = 1; y <= height; y++) {
    field = letters.charAt(x) + y;
    form[field].value = "";
  }
}

}
```

There are two main steps in this function. First, you extract the field list from its cookie and loop through each of the expressions in the list the same way you did in the revised `calculate()` function. For each expression, you delete its cookie. Then you delete the field list cookie and set the number of expressions to zero.

Next, you use a set of nested **for** loops to place an empty string in each form text entry field in the spreadsheet.

2. In this solution, use a simple syntax for defining ranges: **<fieldNameOne;fieldNametwo;>**. If you want to define the sum of all fields from A1 to A6, you could use **<A1;A6;>**. Similarly, all fields from A1 to C1 would be **<A1;C1;>**. All ranges must be on the same row or column and must be indicated from lowest field to highest (that is, **<C1;A1;>** is invalid).

You add support for this range feature by adding a section to the **evaluateExp()** function:

```
function evaluateExp(form,expression) {

  var column = "";
  var index = 0;
  var nextExpField;
  var nextExpression = "";
  var nextResult = "";
  var next = 0;
  var firstField = "";
  var lastField = "";
  var rangeExp = ""

  if (expression.charAt(0) == '"') {
    return(expression.substring(1,expression.length));
  }

  // Check for ranges
  index = expression.indexOf("<",index);
  while (index >= 0) {
    next = expression.indexOf(">",index+1);
    nextExpField = expression.substring(index,next+1);
    firstField = expression.substring(index+1,expression.indexOf(";",index+1));
    lastField = expression.substring (expression.indexOf(";",index+1) + 1,next - 1);
```

continued on next page

continued from previous page

```
        if (firstField.charAt(0) == lastField.charAt(0)) {
          var start = parseInt(firstField.substring(1,firstField.length));
          var end = parseInt(lastField.substring(1,lastField.length));
          nextResult = firstField.charAt(0) + start + ";";
          for (var i = start + 1; i <= end; i++)
            nextResult += " + " + firstField.charAt(0) + i + ";";
        } else {
          var tempChar = firstField.charAt(0);
          var start = letters.indexOf(tempChar,0);
          tempChar = lastField.charAt(0);
          var end = letters.indexOf(tempChar,0);
          nextResult = letters.charAt(start) + ⇐
firstField.substring(1,firstField.length) + ";";
for (var i = start + 1; i <= end; i++)
          nextResult += " + " + letters.charAt(i) + ⇐
firstField.substring(1,firstField.length) + ";";
}

      rangeExp = "<" + firstField + ";" + lastField + ";>";
      nextResult = "(" + nextResult + ")";
      expression =
replace(expression,rangeExp,nextResult,notCaseSensitive,anySubstring);
index += nextResult.length;
      if (index >= expression.length - 1) { break; }
      index = expression.indexOf("<",index);

    }

  // Scan the expression for field names
  for (var x = 0; x < width; x ++) {
    column = letters.charAt(x);
    index = 0;
    index = expression.indexOf(column,index);

    // If we find a field name, evaluate it
    while(index >= 0) {

      // Check if the field has an expression associated with it
      nextExpField = expression.substring(index,expression.indexOf(";",index));

      // If there is an expression, evaluate--otherwise grab the value of the field
if ((nextExpression = GetCookie(nextExpField)) != null) {
        nextResult = evaluateExp(form,nextExpression);
        if ("" + nextResult == "error") {
          return "error";
        }
      } else {
        nextResult = form[nextExpField].value;

        if ((nextResult == "") || (nextResult == null)) {
          nextResult = "0";
        } else {
```

```
      // Check if this is a numeric expression
      var checkNum = parseInt(nextResult);
      if ((checkNum == 0) && (nextResult.charAt(0) != "0")) {
        return "error";
      }
    }

  }

  // Replace the field name with the result
  nextExpField = nextExpField + ";";
  nextResult = "(" + nextResult + ")";
  expression = replace(expression,nextExpField,nextResult,⇐
notCaseSensitive,anySubstring);

  // Check if we have reached the end of the expression
  index = index + nextResult.length;
  if (index >= expression.length - 1) { break; }

  // If not, search for another field name
  index = expression.indexOf(column,index);
  }
}

// Evaluate the expression
with (Math) {
  var result = eval(expression);
}

// Return the result
return result;

}
```

What you have done is add a section that replaces ranges with a mathematical expression. For instance, `<A1;A4;>` is replaced by `(A1; + A2; + A3;)`. Once this is done, you can evaluate the expression in the same way you did before.

You check for ranges by scanning the string for the `<` character using `indexOf()`. All the processing takes place inside a `while` loop:

```
index = expression.indexOf("<",index);
while (index >= 0) {
  next = expression.indexOf(">",index+1);
  firstField = expression.substring(index+1,expression.indexOf(";",index+1));
  lastField = expression.substring(expression.indexOf(";",index+1) + 1,next - 1);
```

You start by finding the end of the range by looking for `>`. Then you are able to extract the first field name and the last field name.

```
if (firstField.charAt(0) == lastField.charAt(0)) {
  var start = parseInt(firstField.substring(1,firstField.length));
  var end = parseInt(lastField.substring(1,lastField.length));
```

continued on next page

continued from previous page

```
      nextResult = firstField.charAt(0) + start + ";";
      for (var i = start + 1; i <= end; i++)
        nextResult += " + " + firstField.charAt(0) + i + ";";
   } else {
```

If you have a range on the same row (the first character of both `lastField` and `firstField` are the same), then you loop through each field in the range and build a mathematical expression that adds the fields.

```
   var tempChar = firstField.charAt(0);
   var start = letters.indexOf(tempChar,0);
   tempChar = lastField.charAt(0);
   var end = letters.indexOf(tempChar,0);
   nextResult = letters.charAt(start) + ⇐
firstField.substring(1,firstField.length) + ";";
for (var i = start + 1; i <= end; i++)
     nextResult += " + " + letters.charAt(i) + ⇐
firstField.substring(1,firstField.length) + ";";
}
```

If you don't have a range on the same row, then it must run down a single column. If it does, you build an expression appropriately.

```
   rangeExp = "<" + firstField + ";" + lastField + ";>";
   nextResult = "(" + nextResult + ")";
   expression = replace(expression,rangeExp,nextResult,⇐
notCaseSensitive,anySubstring);
index += nextResult.length;
   if (index >= expression.length - 1) { break; }
   index = expression.indexOf("<",index);


}
```

Finally, you use `replace()` to replace the range syntax with its mathematical equivalent. Then you see if you are at the end of the expression; if not, you scan for another range.

The range syntax you are using still enables `checkExp()` to accurately perform the checks it is making. However, you are not checking that the format of the range syntax is correct. For instance, you don't know that each open symbol `<` is matched with its partner `>`, and you don't know if extra characters have been introduced into the middle of the range structure.

You can add support for this in the `checkExp()` function. After you complete all of the checks, before you would return `true`, you can add a `while` loop that checks the range syntax:

```
index = expression.indexOf("<",0);
while (index >= 0) {
  next = index + 1;

  for (i = 1; i <= 2; i++) {
    thisLetter = expression.charAt(next);
```

```
    if (letters.indexOf(thisLetter,0) < 0) {
      alert("Incorrect Range format.");
      return false;
    }

    while(expression.charAt(++next) != ";") {
      checkNum = parseInt(expression.charAt(next));
      if ((checkNum == 0) && (expression.charAt(next) != "0")) {
        alert("Incorrect Range format.");
        return false;
      }
    }

    next ++;

  }

  if (expression.charAt(next) != ">") {
    alert("Incorrect Range format.");
    return false;
  }

  if (next + 1 == expression.length) { break; }
  index = expression.indexOf("<",next);

}
```

The process of checking for errors is fairly simple. When you find occurrences of <, you first check the next letter to make sure it is a legitimate column name. If it is, you check that you have only numbers until a semicolon. Then you check if you have a valid letter again, and then check numbers again until another semicolon. Finally, you check for the closing >.

APPENDIX G

INTERNET EXPLORER 3.0: A FIELD GUIDE

A new day dawned. The sun reached its fingers over the digital outback. The mighty Navigators (*Netscapus navigatorus*)—a species that reproduced like rabbits and ran nearly as fast—covered the landscape. Yonder, on a cliff that seemed to be beyond the horizon, a trembling new creature looked out over the Internet jungle. This strange new creature, calling itself the Explorer (*Microsoftus interneticus explorus*), sniffed around, considering whether it should enter the fragile ecosystem. Netscape gators gnashed their teeth, but the Explorers were not daunted. Explorer was a formidable beast. It became a part of the jungle and thrived. And even though it began as a mere pup, it evolved, and it evolved and it evolved.

Now the jungle is rife with two intelligent species.

What follows is a guide to domesticating Internet Explorer. You will learn how to care for your Explorer and even how to teach it tricks. Before long, you shall find truth behind the old axiom that the Explorer is man's (and woman's) best friend.

INTRODUCING EXPLORER TO YOUR ECOSYSTEM

Whether you're running Windows NT or Windows 95, installing Explorer is easy. Explorer's own installation program makes setup a breeze, and you need only to select the appropriate file on the CD-ROM to launch this installer. Make sure the CD-ROM included with this book is in the CD-ROM drive; then, depending upon your system, follow the directions below for either Windows 95 or Windows NT.

Windows 95 Installation

1. Click the Start button in the lower left corner of your screen.

2. Click on the Run... option in the Start menu. A dialog box similar to the one shown in Figure G-1 appears.

3. Using the Run dialog box, type in a pathname and specify the location of the Explorer installation program. IE301M95.EXE is in the CD's \Explorer directory, so if your CD-ROM drive is designated as D:, you'd type

   ```
   d:\explorer\ie301m95.exe
   ```

   If your CD-ROM drive has a different designation letter, type in the appropriate drive designation letter in place of d:.

4. After typing the proper pathname, click the OK button to start the Explorer's installation program. Depending upon your system, it may take a moment to load.

5. Once the installation program loads, follow the on-screen prompts to set up Explorer on your computer.

Windows NT 4 Installation

1. Click the Start button in the lower left corner of your screen.

2. Click on the Run... option in the Start menu. A dialog box similar to the one shown in Figure G-2 appears.

Figure G-1
The Windows 95
Run dialog box.

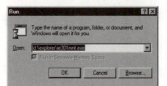

Figure G-2
The Windows NT
Run dialog box.

3. Using the Run dialog box, type in a pathname and specify the location of the Explorer installation program. MSIE30M.EXE is in the CD's \Explorer directory, so if your CD-ROM drive is designated as D:, you'd type:

```
d:\explorer\ie301mnt.exe
```

If your CD-ROM drive has a different designation letter, type in the appropriate drive designation letter in place of d:.

4. After typing the proper pathname, click the OK button to start the Explorer's installation program. Depending upon your system, it may take a moment to load.

5. Once the installation program loads, follow the on-screen prompts to set up Explorer on your computer.

Once you've run the installation, you'll need to restart your system. You can then click on the Internet icon on your desktop. If you've already selected an Internet provider with Windows dial-up networking, you'll be connected. If not, you'll be walked through the dial-in process. You'll need to enter the phone number of your Internet provider, your modem type, and other related information. Ultimately, you'll be taken to Microsoft's home page, where you can register your Explorer and find out about its latest features.

 The Explorer is a constantly evolving animal. For the latest updates, plug-ins, and versions, be sure to regularly check out Microsoft's neck of the woods at `http://www.microsoft.com/ie/`.

Explorer Components

Explorer is more than a plain-Jane Web browser. As you work through the installation, you'll be able to choose a variety of components. You can select the following add-ons:

● Internet Mail—This is a comprehensive e-mail package. Using simple icons, you can write and read your mail off-line and then log on quickly to send and receive your latest batch of correspondence. See Figure G-3.

● Internet News—This is a window that lets you browse through thousands of newsgroups, read through the threads, and post your own messages. The News system is very easy to use. You can easily keep track of your favorite topics and automatically update with the latest news.

● ActiveMovie—This feature of Explorer lets you watch all sorts of video clips—MPEG, AVI, and QuickTime formats. It even supports a special streaming version of video that downloads movies as you watch them, letting you view video with little delay. The ActiveMovie system also lets you listen to all popular formats of audio files—AU, WAV, MIDI, MPEG, and AIFF. This makes it easy to add background sound to Web pages.

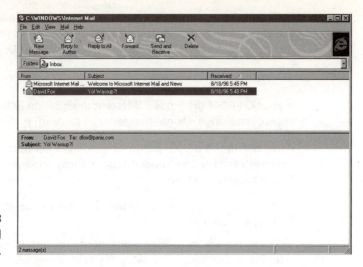

Figure G-3
The Internet Mail
main window.

● VRML Support—This feature is a separate module that lets you download and coast through Virtual Reality Modeling Language worlds. This allows you to explore true 3D landscapes and objects.

● NetMeeting—This is a full-featured package that lets you hold entire meetings over the Internet. You can chat with one person or with dozens. If you have a microphone, you can use the Internet phone feature to hold voice conversations with other people. You can share applications. For example, you and a client can edit the same word processing document together. A whiteboard feature lets you draw on a "digital blackboard" that can be updated live across the Internet.

● HTML Layout Control—This tool lets Web page publishers create spiffy versions of HTML pages, the way professional designers would lay out a magazine page or a newspaper. Designers can choose exactly where to place elements within a Web page. You can make objects transparent and layer objects over each other, which helps make a Web page eye-catching yet uncluttered.

THE NATURE OF THE BEAST

Internet Explorer features very up-to-date HTML. It supports HTML 3.2, including the following:

● Frames—These break up the Web page window into several areas. For example, you can keep an unchanging row of navigation controls along the top of the page while constantly updating the bottom. You can use *borderless frames*, which split up the page without making it seem split.

A special type of frame known as the *floating frame* lets you view one Web page within another.

- Cascading Style Sheets—This allows all your Web sites to have the same general look and feel.

- Tables—You can create or view all sorts of fancy tables, with or without graphics, borders, and columns.

- Embedded Objects—Internet Explorer can handle Java applets, ActiveX controls, and even Netscape plug-ins. These objects are discussed later, in the Symbiotic Partners section of this appendix.

- Fonts—Explorer supports many fonts, allowing Web pages to have a variety of exciting designs.

From the get-go, Internet Explorer has included a few special bells and whistles. For example, it's easy to create and view marquees across Web pages. This lets you scroll a long, attention-drawing message, similar to a tickertape, that puts a great deal of information in a very small space.

TRAINING THE EXPLORER

By its very nature, the Explorer is a friendly beast. You can access the full range of the Explorer's talents by pushing its buttons. These buttons, which appear in the toolbar at the top of the screen as depicted in Figure G-4, are as follows:

- Back—Use this to return to the Web page you've just come from. This will help you retrace your steps as you take Explorer through the Internet maze.

- Forward—Use this after you've used the Back button, to jump forward again to the page from which you began.

- Stop—If a Web page is taking too long to load, press this button. Any text and graphics will immediately stop downloading.

- Refresh—If your Web page is missing some graphics, or if you've previously stopped its loading using the Stop button, you can reload it using Refresh.

- Home—This takes you to your pre-set home page. By default, this is Microsoft's main Web page, but you can set your home to any you'd like. See the Taming the Beast section.

- Search—This takes you to a special page that allows you to search for a Web page, using a number of cool search engines. See the Hunting Skills section.

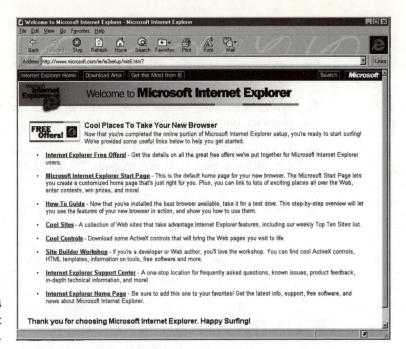

Figure G-4
A cosmetic look at Explorer.

- Favorites—This button lets you access a list of your favorite Web sites. See the Favorite Haunts section.

- Print—This allows you to print out the current Web page, allowing you to keep a perfect hard copy of it.

- Font—Find yourself squinting at a Web page? Just click here to zoom in. The font size will grow several degrees. Too big now? Click a few more times and the size will shrink once again.

- Mail—This will launch the Internet Mail program, which allows you to send and receive e-mail and to access newsgroups.

PLAYING FETCH

Your Explorer is a devoted friend. It can scamper anywhere within the Internet, bringing back exactly what you desire.

If you know where you want to go, just type the URL into Explorer's Address box at the top of the screen. If you like, you can omit the `http://` prefix. The Web page will be loaded up. You can also search for a page or load up a previously saved page.

You can now click on any *hyperlink*—an underlined or colored word or picture—to zoom to that associated Web page or Internet resource. Some hyperlinked graphics may not be obvious. Explorer will tell you when you are positioned over a valid hyperlink, because the cursor will change into a pointing finger. Continue following these links as long as you like. It's not uncommon to start researching knitting needles and end up reading about porcupines.

If you're an aspiring Web page writer, you might want to take a peek at the HTML source code to see how that page was created. Just select View, Source.

HUNTING SKILLS

If you want to find Web pages dealing with a specific category, the Explorer makes it easy to find them. Click the Search button. The Search screen will appear, as in Figure G-5. You can search for more than Web pages. With Explorer, it's easy to find

● Phone numbers, ZIP codes, and addresses

● Information on a number of topics—health, home, education, consumer affairs, finance, weather, sports, travel, and so on

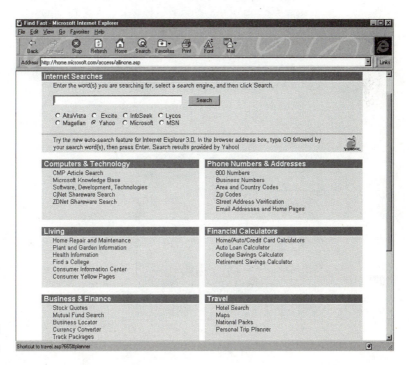

Figure G-5
The Search screen.

● References—maps, a dictionary, a thesaurus, quotations, and an encyclopedia

● On-line books, newspapers, and magazines

You can also quickly hunt for any idea, word, or category. Simply type GO in the Address box at the top of the screen, followed by the word or phrase you want to search for.

FAVORITE HAUNTS

It's easy to keep track of the Web pages you visit most. When you want to save a page for future reference, simply click the Favorites button or choose the Favorites menu item. Select the Add To Favorites option. The current Web page will now be added to the list of favorites, which appears each time you click on the Favorites button or menu.

After a while, your list of favorites will get long and cluttered. It's simple to keep track of huge lists of favorites—just put them into separate folders. Organize your favorites, as shown in Figure G-6, by selecting Favorites, Organize Favorites.

To create a new folder, click on the New Folder icon (the folder with the little glint on it) at the top of the window. Now drag and drop your Web page bookmarks into the appropriate folders. You can also move, rename, or delete a folder by selecting it and using the corresponding buttons at the bottom of the screen.

You can even include or attach a favorite Web document within an e-mail message, the way you would attach any other file.

Figure G-6
Organizing the
Favorites list

On Windows systems, the Favorites list is actually a folder within your Windows directory. This reflects a Microsoft trend—treating the entire World Wide Web as just another folder to explore on your desktop. Eventually, you'll be able to drag and drop documents across the Internet as easily as you would within your own hard drive.

MEMORY

Internet Explorer keeps track of every Web page you visit. This is kept in a vast History list. You can view the entire History list, in chronological order, by clicking the View History button. Just click on any page you'd like to revisit.

The History list is cleared every 20 days—you can set this value within the Navigation properties sheets.

TAMING THE BEAST

Now that you and your Explorer are getting acquainted, why not tame it so that it acts and looks exactly like you want? Select View, Options and pick a tab at the top of the window to customize the following properties:

- General—The general properties sheet is illustrated in Figure G-7. Since multimedia content (such as sounds, movies, and graphics) takes longer to load in Web pages, you can choose to not load certain media types. You can also easily customize the color of the text and hyperlinks. Finally, you can decide how little or how much information appears in your toolbar.

Figure G-7
The general
properties sheet

Note You can change the size and position of your toolbar simply by clicking on its borders and dragging it to a desired location.

- **Connection**—You can adjust your connections settings, as shown in Figure G-8, by clicking on this tab. This lets you choose your Internet provider. If you're connecting to the Internet through a network firewall, you can also set your proxy server information here.

- **Navigation**—You can customize which page you'd like to use as your starting home page. Just enter its URL in the Address box here.

- **Programs**—This allows you to set which programs you'd like to use for e-mail and for Usenet news. By default, you can use Microsoft's Internet Mail and Internet News, which are included with Explorer. You can also tell Explorer how to handle various types of files by selecting the File Types button. It allows you to designate which program or plug-in should be launched whenever Explorer comes across various unfamiliar file formats.

- **Security**—You are able to customize how securely documents will be handled by Explorer. If you want to keep your computer extremely safe, you may tell Explorer not to download possible security risks such as ActiveX controls, Java applets, or other plug-ins. Another nice feature is a Content Advisor. Click on Settings; the Content Advisor window will appear as in Figure G-9. You may now decide which Web pages to skip based on Adult Language, Nudity, Sex, or Violence. Many questionable Web pages are written with certain tags so that the pages can be weeded out by people who don't want to see them. This is a great option to use if your kids surf the Internet, or if your sensibilities are easily offended. To turn ratings on, click on the Enable Ratings button. You can also lock this window with a password.

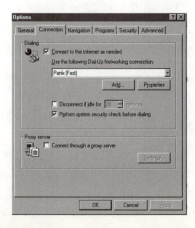

Figure G-8
The connection property sheet.

Figure G-9
The Content
Advisor window.

● Advanced—This properties sheet lets you customize when Internet Explorer will issue warnings. This is useful if you deal with sensitive information and want to know which Web pages are secure and which are not. You can also set a number of other advanced Java and Security options here.

SYMBIOTIC PARTNERS

Explorer includes many of the latest Web technologies. These make your Web pages sing, dance, and even act as entire applications. The line between what a computer can do in general and what a computer can do over the Internet is thinning.

ACTIVEX

Microsoft's proprietary ActiveX technology lets you drop controls into your Web pages. Controls are software components such as specialized buttons, input forms, graphics viewers, sound players, and so forth.

When you load a page with an ActiveX control, Explorer will check if you already have that control on your system. If not, you'll be asked whether you'd like to download it. You'll be told whether the control has been authenticated by Microsoft. If the control is secure, it'll automatically be downloaded and installed for you. The resulting Web page may look more like a software program than a Web page. Don't be surprised to find all new types of buttons, such as the up and down arrow controls in Figure G-10.

SCRIPTS

Internet Explorer allows Web page writers to add different types of scripts right into the source code of the Web page itself. This means you can get instantaneous feedback and control of the Web browser, ActiveX controls, Java applets, and other plug-ins. This

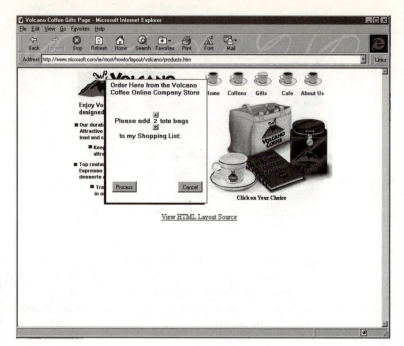

Figure G-10
Loading a page
with an ActiveX
control.

makes interactivity fast and easy. Internet Explorer supports Visual Basic, Scripting Edition and JavaScript languages.

JAVA

Finally, Explorer fully supports the popular Java language. Java is a programming language that lets you write full applications that run directly within your Web browser. Java is great for writing games, graphics demonstrations, databases, spreadsheets, and much more.

TOTAL MASTERY

Now that you are fully in control of Explorer, you can learn, work, and have fun using it with the greatest of ease. Wandering through the Internet faster than ever, you are ready to investigate new paths of adventure with your trusty, obedient Explorer guiding you every step of the way.

INDEX

W-X-Y-Z

ENVIRONMENTAL AWARENESS

Books have a substantial influence on the destruction of the forests of the Earth. For example, it takes 17 trees to produce one ton of paper. A first printing of 30,000 copies of a typical 480-page book consumes 108,000 pounds of paper, which will require 918 trees!

Waite Group Press™ is against the clear-cutting of forests and supports reforestation of the Pacific Northwest of the United States and Canada, where most of this paper comes from. As a publisher with several hundred thousand books sold each year, we feel an obligation to give back to the planet. We will therefore support organizations that seek to preserve the forests of planet Earth.

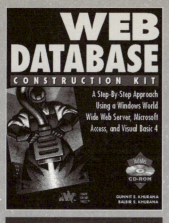
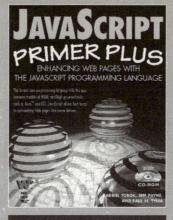
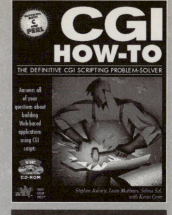

FREE SUBSCRIPTION

Don't Miss a Single Issue!

- **Interactive Java**
- **Applet Development**
- **CORBACorner**
- **Java Class Libraries**
- **Interviews with Java Gurus**
- **Product Reviews with the JDJ World Class Award**

JAVA DEVELOPER'S JOURNAL
JDJ WORLD CLASS AWARD

- **Tips & Techniques • Infinite Java • Book Reviews**
- **Java Animation • Games & Graphics... and Much More**

DEVELOPER'S JAVA JOURNAL

FREE SUBSCRIPTION CERTIFICATE

Message from the
Publisher

WELCOME TO OUR NERVOUS SYSTEM

Some people say that the World Wide Web is a graphical extension of the information superhighway, just a network of humans and machines sending each other long lists of the equivalent of digital junk mail.

I think it is much more than that. To me, the Web is nothing less than the nervous system of the entire planet—not just a collection of computer brains connected together, but more like a billion silicon neurons entangled and recirculating electro-chemical signals of information and data, each contributing to the birth of another CPU and another Web site.

Think of each person's hard disk connected at once to every other hard disk on earth, driven by human navigators searching like Columbus for the New World. Seen this way, the Web is more of a super entity, a growing, living thing, controlled by the universal human will to expand, to be more. Yet, unlike a purposeful business plan with rigid rules, the Web expands in a nonlinear, unpredictable, creative way that echoes natural evolution.

We created our Web site not just to extend the reach of our computer book products but to be part of this synaptic neural network, to experience, like a nerve in the body, the flow of ideas and then to pass those ideas up the food chain of the mind. Your mind. Even more, we wanted to pump some of our own creative juices into this rich wine of technology.

TASTE OUR DIGITAL WINE

And so we ask you to taste our wine by visiting the body of our business. Begin by understanding the metaphor we have created for our Web site—a universal learning center, situated in outer space in the form of a space station. A place where you can journey to study any topic from the convenience of your own screen. Right now we are focusing on computer topics, but the stars are the limit on the Web.

If you are interested in discussing this Web site or finding out more about the Waite Group, please send me e-mail with your comments, and I will be happy to respond. Being a programmer myself, I love to talk about technology and find out what our readers are looking for.

Sincerely,

Mitchell Waite

Mitchell Waite, C.E.O. and Publisher

200 Tamal Plaza
Corte Madera, CA 94925
415-924-2575
415-924-2576 fax

Website:
http://www.waite.com/wa
ite

CREATING THE HIGHEST QUALITY COMPUTER BOOKS IN THE INDUSTRY

Waite Group Press

Come Visit
WAITE.COM
Waite Group Press
World Wide Web Site

Now find all the latest information on Waite Group books at our new Web site, **http://www.waite.com/waite.** You'll find an online catalog where you can examine and order any title, review upcoming books, and send e-mail to our authors and editors. Our FTP site has all you need to update your book: the latest program listings, errata sheets, most recent versions of Fractint, POV Ray, Polyray, DMorph, and all the programs featured in our books. So download, talk to us, ask questions, on **http://www.waite.com/waite.**

The New Arrivals Room has all our new books listed by month. Just click for a description, Index, Table of Contents, and links to authors.

The Backlist Room has all our books listed alphabetically.

The People Room is where you'll interact with Waite Group employees.

Links to Cyberspace get you in touch with other computer book publishers and other interesting Web sites.

The FTP site contains all program listings, errata sheets, etc.

The Order Room is where you can order any of our books online.

The Subject Room contains typical book pages that show description, Index, Table of Contents, and links to authors.

World Wide Web:

COME SURF OUR TURF—THE WAITE GROUP WEB

http://www.waite.com/waite
Gopher: gopher.waite.com
FTP: ftp.waite.com

LIMITED WARRANTY

The following warranties shall be effective for 90 days from the date of purchase: (i) The Waite Group, Inc. warrants the enclosed disk to be free of defects in materials and workmanship under normal use; and (ii) The Waite Group, Inc. warrants that the programs, unless modified by the purchaser, will substantially perform the functions described in the documentation provided by The Waite Group, Inc. when operated on the designated hardware and operating system. The Waite Group, Inc. does not warrant that the programs will meet purchaser's requirements or that operation of a program will be uninterrupted or error-free. The program warranty does not cover any program that has been altered or changed in any way by anyone other than The Waite Group, Inc. The Waite Group, Inc. is not responsible for problems caused by changes in the operating characteristics of computer hardware or computer operating systems that are made after the release of the programs, nor for problems in the interaction of the programs with each other or other software.

THESE WARRANTIES ARE EXCLUSIVE AND IN LIEU OF ALL OTHER WARRANTIES OF MERCHANTABILITY OR FITNESS FOR A PARTICULAR PURPOSE OR OF ANY OTHER WARRANTY, WHETHER EXPRESS OR IMPLIED.

EXCLUSIVE REMEDY

The Waite Group, Inc. will replace any defective disk without charge if the defective disk is returned to The Waite Group, Inc. within 90 days from date of purchase.

This is Purchaser's sole and exclusive remedy for any breach of warranty or claim for contract, tort, or damages.

LIMITATION OF LIABILITY

THE WAITE GROUP, INC. AND THE AUTHORS OF THE PROGRAMS SHALL NOT IN ANY CASE BE LIABLE FOR SPECIAL, INCIDENTAL, CONSEQUENTIAL, INDIRECT, OR OTHER SIMILAR DAMAGES ARISING FROM ANY BREACH OF THESE WARRANTIES EVEN IF THE WAITE GROUP, INC. OR ITS AGENT HAS BEEN ADVISED OF THE POSSIBILITY OF SUCH DAMAGES.

THE LIABILITY FOR DAMAGES OF THE WAITE GROUP, INC. AND THE AUTHORS OF THE PROGRAMS UNDER THIS AGREEMENT SHALL IN NO EVENT EXCEED THE PURCHASE PRICE PAID.

COMPLETE AGREEMENT

This Agreement constitutes the complete agreement between The Waite Group, Inc. and the authors of the programs, and you, the purchaser.

Some states do not allow the exclusion or limitation of implied warranties or liability for incidental or consequential damages, so the above exclusions or limitations may not apply to you. This limited warranty gives you specific legal rights; you may have others, which vary from state to state.

SATISFACTION REPORT CARD

Please fill out this card if you wish to know of future updates to
***JavaScript Interactive Course,* or to receive our catalog.**

First Name: _____ **Last Name:** _____

Street Address: _____

City: _____ **State:** _____ **Zip:** _____

E-Mail Address _____

Daytime Telephone: (_____)_____

Date product was acquired: Month _____ **Day** _____ **Year** _____ **Your Occupation:** _____

Overall, how would you rate *JavaScript Interactive Course?*

☐ Excellent ☐ Very Good ☐ Good
☐ Fair ☐ Below Average ☐ Poor

What did you like MOST about this book? _____
_____
_____

What did you like LEAST about this book? _____
_____
_____

Please describe any problems you may have encountered with installing or using the disk: _____
_____

How did you use this book (problem-solver, tutorial, reference...)?
_____

What is your level of computer expertise?

☐ New ☐ Dabbler ☐ Hacker
☐ Power User ☐ Programmer ☐ Experienced Professional

What computer languages are you familiar with?_____
_____

Please describe your computer hardware:

Computer _____ Hard disk _____
5.25" disk drives _____ 3.5" disk drives_____
Video card _____ Monitor _____
Printer _____ Peripherals _____
Sound Board _____ CD ROM_____

Where did you buy this book?

☐ Bookstore (name):_____
☐ Discount store (name):_____
☐ Computer store (name):_____
☐ Catalog (name):_____
☐ Direct from WGP ☐ Other _____

What price did you pay for this book? _____

What influenced your purchase of this book?

☐ Recommendation ☐ Advertisement
☐ Magazine review ☐ Store display
☐ Mailing ☐ Book's format
☐ Reputation of Waite Group Press ☐ Other

How many computer books do you buy each year?_____

How many other Waite Group books do you own?_____

What is your favorite Waite Group book?_____
_____

Is there any program or subject you would like to see Waite Group Press cover in a similar approach?_____
_____

Additional comments?_____
_____
_____

Please send to: **Waite Group Press**
                     200 Tamal Plaza
                     Corte Madera, CA 94925

☐ **Check here for a free Waite Group catalog**

STOP!

BEFORE YOU OPEN THE DISK OR CD-ROM PACKAGE ON THE FACING PAGE, CAREFULLY READ THE LICENSE AGREEMENT.

Opening this package indicates that you agree to abide by the license agreement found in the back of this book. If you do not agree with it, promptly return the unopened disk package (including the related book) to the place you obtained them for a refund.